Charity in Rabbinic Juda

Studying the many ideas about how giving charity atones for sin and other rewards in late antique rabbinic literature, this volume contains many, varied, and even conflicting ideas, as the multiplicity must be recognized and allowed expression.

Topics include the significance of the rabbis' use of the biblical word "tzedaqah" as charity, the coexistence of the idea that God is the ultimate recipient of *tzedaqah* along with rabbinic ambivalence about that idea, redemptive almsgiving, and the reward for charity of retention or increase in wealth. Rabbinic literature's preference for "*teshuvah*" (repentance) over *tzedeqah* to atone for sin is also closely examined. Throughout, close attention is paid to chronological differences in these ideas, and to differences between the rabbinic compilations of the land of Israel and the Babylonian Talmud. The book extensively analyzes the various ways the Babylonian Talmud especially tends to put limits on the divine element in charity while privileging its human, this-worldly dimensions. This tendency also characterizes the Babylonian Talmud's treatment of other topics. The book briefly surveys some post-Talmudic developments.

As the study fills a gap in existing scholarship on charity and the rabbis, it is an invaluable resource for scholars and clergy interested in charity within comparative religion, history, and religion.

Alyssa M. Gray is the Emily S. and Rabbi Bernard H. Mehlman Chair in Rabbinics and Professor of Codes and Responsa Literature at HUC-JIR in New York. She is the author of *A Talmud in Exile: The Influence of Yerushalmi Avodah Zarah on the Formation of Bavli Avodah Zarah* (2005) nerous shorter studies on wealth, poverty, an on the formation of the Babylonian Talmud.

Routledge Jewish Studies Series

Series Editor: Oliver Leaman

University of Kentucky

Jewish Studies, which are interpreted to cover the disciplines of history, sociology, anthropology, culture, politics, philosophy, theology, religion, as they relate to Jewish affairs. The remit includes texts which have as their primary focus issues, ideas, personalities and events of relevance to Jews, Jewish life and the concepts which have characterised Jewish culture both in the past and today. The series is interested in receiving appropriate scripts or proposals.

For more information about this series, please visit:
www.routledge.com/middleeaststudies/series/JEWISH

Charity in Rabbinic Judaism
Atonement, Rewards, and Righteousness

Alyssa M. Gray

Routledge
Taylor & Francis Group

LONDON AND NEW YORK

First published 2019 by Routledge

2 Park Square, Milton Park, Abingdon, Oxon, OX14 4RN
605 Third Avenue, New York, NY 10017

Routledge is an imprint of the Taylor & Francis Group, an informa business

First issued in paperback 2020

British Library Cataloguing-in-Publication Data
A catalogue record for this book is available from the British Library

Library of Congress Cataloging-in-Publication Data
Names: Gray, Alyssa M., author.
Title: Charity in rabbinic Judaism: atonement, rewards, and righteousness / Alyssa M. Gray.
Description: First edition. | New York, NY: Routledge, July 2019. | Series: Routledge Jewish studies series | Includes bibliographical references and index.
Identifiers: LCCN 2019009029| ISBN 9781138599963 (hardback) | ISBN 9780429471162 (ebook) | ISBN 9780429895906 (epub) | ISBN 9780429895890 (mobipocket)
Subjects: LCSH: Charity–Religious aspects–Judaism. | Rabbinical literature–History and criticism.
Classification: LCC BJ1286.C5 G73 2019 | DDC 296.3/677–dc23
LC record available at https://lccn.loc.gov/2019009029

ISBN: 978-1-138-59996-3 (hbk)
ISBN: 978-0-367-72864-9 (pbk)

Typeset in Times New Roman
by Wearset Ltd, Boldon, Tyne and Wear

For Robin, who knew it would happen

Contents

Acknowledgments and credit

It is my pleasant duty to acknowledge the many colleagues, friends, and students who have helped me refine my thinking and hone my arguments and perspectives during the years this book has been in the making. I gratefully acknowledge Professors Yaacov Lev and Miriam Frenkel, who invited me in 2009 to present "Certainty and Skepticism: Approaches to Redemptive Almsgiving in Rabbinic Literature of Late Antiquity" at the "Reunion of the Charity and Piety Group" of the Institute for Advanced Studies at the Hebrew University of Jerusalem. A revised version of that paper became the presentation "Redemptive Almsgiving and the Rabbis of Late Antiquity" at that year's Society for Biblical Literature Annual Meeting, and an article of that title two years later in the *Jewish Studies Quarterly*. Subsequent invitations and colleagues who have broadened my horizons and enriched my thinking about the topic of this book include the conference "A History of Jewish Giving" at the Center for Jewish History in New York City (2012); an invitation from Professor Leonard J. Greenspoon to present on wealth and the rabbis at the 2013 Klutznick-Harris Symposium on "Wealth and Poverty in Jewish Tradition"; an invitation from Professor Gary A. Anderson to be a panelist discussing his book *Charity: The Place of the Poor in the Biblical Tradition* at the 2013 Society for Biblical Literature Annual Meeting; and an invitation from Professor Michael L. Satlow in 2015 to participate in a lively two-day workshop entitled "Jewish Attitudes Toward Wealth and Poverty" at Brown University. Special thanks are due to Professor Krista N. Dalton, who in 2016 organized and invited me to contribute to a superb "Charity Forum" in the on-line publication www.ancientjewreview.com, of which she is a co-editor. An invitation to present at a 2017 regional conference of the Jewish Law Association in New York City prompted me to think more clearly about the Talmud *Bavli*'s distinct perspectives on the working and non-working poor. I'm also indebted to Professor Aaron Amit, whose invitation to me to present at a Bar-Ilan University conference in 2018 caused me to think more carefully about the different perspectives on charity in the *Bavli*'s literary layers. I am especially pleased that in 2009 I made the acquaintance of Professor Judah Galinsky, with whom I have interacted in scholarly venues and over email in the years since, and who is a rigorous, fair, generous, and learned interlocutor.

I am also pleased to thank the many students with whom I have wrestled with this material: those enrolled in a 2011 summer session and later in a spring 2013 course with me at the Jewish Theological Seminary, and too many students to count at my home institution, Hebrew Union College-Jewish Institute of Religion. Apropos of my home institution, I'm delighted to offer my deep thanks to the indefatigable librarians of the Klau Library on the New York campus of HUC-JIR: Yoram Bitton, Tina Weiss, and Eli Lieberman. Each of you has helped me in many ways with the research for this book. And, as always, my teachers at the Hebrew University of Jerusalem and the Jewish Theological Seminary of America: whether or not you agree fully with what you read in these pages, know that I always feel my debt to you and remain deeply honored to be your student. Your influence is threaded throughout this book.

I owe a very special thanks to my close friend of many years, Professor Gwynn Kessler. She is a model friend and colleague, and exemplar of rigorous and careful scholarship. Her encouragement at key points in the writing of this book was vital and is deeply and warmly appreciated.

One final, personal debt: in my first book I mentioned my nieces Erica and Skylar Gray. I'm now pleased to add an acknowledgment of their brothers, my nephews Derrick and Jake Gray. As before, my hope is that they will one day pick up this book and see what their aunt is up to. I deeply regret that my uncle, Professor Joel L. Kraemer (1933–2018) did not live to see this book's completion. Apropos, the support and love of my entire family has played a role in the genesis of this book: my brother and sister-in-law Michael and Stephanie Gray, my sister Ann Gray, my parents Robert and Miriam Gray, and Robin, to whom this book is dedicated.

Abbreviations and a note about editions

Hebrew transliteration is phonetic. "B." stands for "Babylonian Talmud" ("*Bavli*"), "Y." for the Jerusalem Talmud ("*Yerushalmi*"), "M." for "*Mishnah*," and "T." for "*Tosefta*." Unless otherwise noted, citations to the late antique rabbinic compilations are to the critical or other editions commonly cited in scholarly writing: *Mishnah* (ed. Albeck), *Tosefta* (ed. Lieberman or, if this is lacking, ed. Zuckermandel), *Mekhilta deRabbi Ishmael* (ed. Horovitz-Rabin), *Sifre Numbers* (ed. Horovitz), *Sifre Deuteronomy* (ed. Finkelstein), Jerusalem Talmud (ed. Academy for the Hebrew Language), *Genesis Rabbah* (ed. Theodor-Albeck), *Leviticus Rabbah* (ed. Margulies), *Pesiqta deRav Kahana* (ed. Mandelbaum), Babylonian Talmud (standard reprinting of ed. Vilna-Romm with standard commentaries).

Manuscript citations are principally drawn from the Saul and Evelyn Henkind Talmud Text Databank of the Saul Lieberman Institute of Talmudic Research at the Jewish Theological Seminary of America.

1   Introduction

Rabbis, charity, *tzedaqah*

Overview and methodology

In classical rabbinic and medieval Judaism (and the modern varieties of Judaism that have evolved from them), charity, frequently referred to as "*tzedaqah*," is not simply the "right" thing to do, as many moderns would have it; it is a divine commandment (*mitzvah*) with clear biblical roots, the performance of which is divinely rewarded.[1] Deuteronomy 15:7–8 expresses the commandment in language that has an extensive interpretive afterlife in rabbinic literature: *do not harden your heart and shut your hand against your needy kinsman ... open your hand and lend him sufficient for whatever he needs.* Another aspect of a divine element in charity is vocally and robustly on display to this day three days a year, on *Rosh Hashanah* and *Yom Kippur*, in the synagogue services of all contemporary varieties of Judaism: the climax of the stirring medieval *Unetaneh Tokef* liturgical poem that "*teshuvah* (repentance), *tefillah* (prayer), and *tzedaqah* (recently rendered 'righteous giving') *ma'avirin et ro'a ha-gezerah* (cause the "evil decree" to pass away)."[2] On the other 362 days of the year, however, charity's rewards and its role in nullifying an "evil decree" are at best interesting, albeit mostly irrelevant features of most contemporary practicing (individual) Jews' charity. This is not to say that there is no contemporary Jewish interest in the linkage of caring for the needy and the divine. A growing number of rabbis, scholars, activists, and Jewish religious and communal organizations emphasize a religious imperative to engage in the work of caring for the needy and/or "repairing the world" ("*tikkun olam*"), some drawing learnedly and with sophistication on the literary sources of Judaism.[3] But there is a clear difference between ancient and medieval notions of *tzedaqah* and the contemporary emphasis on a divine imperative to engage in acts that improve the lives of the impoverished (and the world). The ancient and medieval notions—that charity to the poor is a "gift" to God, redemptive almsgiving,[4] charity as stocking a donor's heavenly treasury of merits, and rescue from death and grant of long life as charity's reward—describe an intricate and intimate divine–human encounter triangulating God, the donor, and the recipient. The contemporary activist emphasis on a divine imperative is much less (if at all) about such a triangulated divine–human encounter and more about a divine expectation that we human beings ourselves set about the business of righting our own fractured and frequently unjust relationships and social and political frameworks.

Scholarly interest in ancient and medieval ideas about charity's role in atoning for sin and its rewards is on the upswing, catalyzed in large part by the important studies of Peter Brown and Gary A. Anderson. Anderson identifies the origins and outlines of a biblical theology of charity in the Hebrew Bible and Apocrypha, while Brown details the elaboration, spread, and institutionalization of religious ideas about charity within late antique Christian circles. Among scholars of Judaism, Judah Galinsky and Elisheva Baumgarten describe the imbrication of Jewish religious ideas about charity and charitable praxis in medieval Spain, northern France, Germany, and central Europe, while Madeline Kochen comprehensively explores the legal implications of the notion of charity as a gift to God in late antique and medieval legal sources. Eliezer Segal and Moshe Hallamish examine the influence of mystical, notably Zoharic, influences on medieval Jewish charitable praxis.[5]

Scholars of charity in late antique rabbinic literature have touched on charity's rewards and role in atonement, but these and related notions have not yet received a comprehensive treatment, which is the goal of this book.[6] This seminal period in the development of Judaism deserves close attention; it follows the Hebrew Bible and Second Temple period and coexists in part with the growth of varieties of late antique Christianity. Specifically, this book will concentrate on religious ideas about charity's rewards and role in atoning for sin found in the literatures of the third–sixth century CE *amoraim* in the land of Israel and Babylonia: *Genesis Rabbah*, *Leviticus Rabbah*, *Pesiqta deRav Kahana*, *Lamentations Rabbah*, and the Jerusalem ("*Yerushalmi*") and Babylonian ("*Bavli*") Talmuds. These late antique religious ideas about charity's role in atoning for sin, its rewards, and how it functions as a concrete expression of a donor's righteousness form the literary, spiritual, and intellectual core of many medieval Jewish developments in charitable theory and praxis and leave threads and traces in Jewish liturgy and practice to this day.

My identification of the various threads of charity ideas in these compilations and my study of the relevant texts in their literary contexts led me in an unanticipated direction. I came to realize that the various threads cannot really be disentangled; I had to follow their intertwining, noting where one thread breaks off and (sometimes) suddenly reappears, how ideas that initially appear distinct sometimes come together in unexpected ways. As an example, the early rabbis of the *Mishnah*, *Tosefta*, and so-called "tannaitic *midrashim*," known as the "*tannaim*" (second–third centuries CE, Palestine) understand "redemptive almsgiving" to mean that charity redeems one from the burden of one's sins; that is, charity atones for sin. In an entirely separate context they teach that, in general, sin is punished by a loss of wealth. The later Palestinian "*amoraim*" (third–fourth centuries CE) do not perpetuate as robustly the notion that charity atones for sin, but they do teach a form of pre-emptive charity that can be religiously efficacious for a donor fated to lose his money anyway on account of sin. That unavoidable, fated loss can be "redeemed" (as it were) by the donor's pre-emptive giving of the money as *tzedaqah*. The *amoraim* thus bring together two theological threads that the *tannaim* had left separate, thereby creating something new. *Tannaim* also teach the atoning power of "*teshuvah*," but keep this particular thread separate from charity, notwithstanding that redemptive almsgiving would seem naturally to be a notion that brings them together. Later, Palestinian *amoraim* do indeed bring *teshuvah* and charity closer together to some extent, as does the later *Bavli* (seventh century CE), which for the first time clearly brings *teshuvah, tzedaqah,* and *tefillah* ("prayer") together with *Rosh Hashanah*, considered by the rabbis to be the "day of judgment."

This book's study of these late antique rabbinic charity ideas is also informed methodologically by the view that the literary contexts in which they are now found and the twists and turns in how they are represented and reworked must not be ignored. For example, we can discern the presence in classical rabbinic literature of the notion that charity is a gift made by the donor to God. But the fact that this notion is found in the literature does not necessarily mean that it was widespread and uncontested in late antique Jewish societies (or even only among the circles of rabbis and their disciples in Palestine and Babylonia). The presence of a given religious idea within a rabbinic compilation can mean one or more of a few things: the idea is present in the compilation because it was widely held among rabbis within the rabbinic culture that produced the compilation; the idea had some currency and so is mentioned, but was not widely held by the rabbis; or the idea was widely held both within and without rabbinic circles. The path from "text" to "context" in assessing the widespread appeal of a given charity idea is a difficult one to traverse, perhaps in some cases even impossible. At the end of the day what we have are the rabbinic compilations themselves; careful attention must therefore be paid to which ideas are present in which compilations and how these ideas are presented, reworked, criticized, and changed. Naturally account must be taken of the textual, intellectual, and dialectical differences between the rabbinic cultures of the land of Israel and Babylonia, and of patterns of difference between generations of *amoraim*.[7] In sum, this book's interest is not simply in the *presence* of religious ideas about charity in the late antique rabbinic compilations, but in discerning the dynamic *changes*, the *discontinuities*, we see in the presentation and transmission of those ideas. The complexity, changes, and discontinuities visible in these compilations rule out the possibility of charting chronological developments of charity ideas with precision. In seeking to chart these changes and discontinuities, Michel Foucault's notion of "problematizations" will be of some assistance: the point is not simply to note the presence in a corpus of a given theme, but to note when it is treated as a "problem" requiring resolution.[8] "Problematizing" late antique rabbinic charity ideas requires that we study the literary evidence of questions and doubts raised about these ideas, the supersession of some of these ideas by others, and new interpretations or applications given later to older ideas found in earlier compilations.

This book's methodology in reading the Talmud Bavli

The *Bavli* itself is an enduringly mysterious body of literature that famously poses particular challenges to the researcher, especially, but not exclusively, the social historian. While discrete amoraic generations can be demonstrated to display commonalities that distinguish them from others, scholars debate whether these commonalities reflect historical reality or are the inventions of the *Bavli* redactors.[9] At times, these redactors intervene in earlier sources in ways that complicate a facile assumption that these relatively "earlier" sources are in fact authentically "early."[10] Apropos, Shamma Friedman and David Halivni have devoted decades to the study of the *Bavli*'s elusive anonymous voice ("*stam*"). Their important studies and those of other scholars are divided as to how much of the *Bavli*'s *stam* layer should be presumed post-amoraic.[11] Moreover, scholarly debate about the *Bavli* redactors has recently entered a new phase, with a suggestive observation that perhaps the Bavli *stam* should not be assigned agency and viewed as the work of an anonymous scholarly cadre, but should be understood instead as a literary function.[12] This suggestion is bound to catalyze new research that will undoubtedly complicate the ongoing debate about the *Bavli stam* even further.

I rehearse these well-known issues as a background to the somewhat unorthodox approach I take in this book to classifying and studying charity sources found in the *Bavli*. Heuristically, I sort these sources into the following categories:

1   sources the *Bavli* identifies as Palestinian that are found in Palestinian compilations with the attributions and content the *Bavli* ascribes to them;
2   content the *Bavli* attributes to particular Palestinian sages that is found in Palestinian compilations, but not attributed to those sages;
3   *Bavli* reworkings of categories (1) and (2);
4   statements the *Bavli* attributes to Babylonian *amoraim*; and
5   sources of uncertain authorship and provenance (such as stories about rabbis), as well as anonymous interpolations into amoraic statements and other anonymous source-material conventionally classified as "*Bavli stam.*"

These categories are deceptively neat, and their boundaries inevitably blurred. The *Bavli*'s nearly verbatim re-presentation of the Toseftan story of King Monbaz's "scattering" of his treasuries (B. *Baba Batra* 11a) is a clear example of category (1). Category (2) may be illustrated by B. *Baba Batra* 10a's attribution to R. Yohanan of the view that *righteousness saves from death* (Proverbs 10:2, 11:4); this view is found in the *Yerushalmi*, but not attributed to R. Yohanan.[13] Examples of category (3) can be more complex, and we will begin with a straightforward one. B. *Baba Batra* 10a reworks a story found in *Leviticus Rabbah* 34:12.[14] Its reworking includes a change in the protagonist's identity and significant alteration of the story's religious message.[15] Another, more intricate example: in the *Yerushalmi* R. Eleazar says that "*tefillah, tzedaqah, teshuvah*" nullify the "difficult decree," and he quotes Psalm 17:15 (*Then I, justified, will behold Your face; awake, I am filled with the vision of You*) as one prooftext for "*tzedaqah.*"[16] *Justified* is the translation of "*b'tzedeq,*" which is understood as a *tzedaqah* reference; the *Yerushalmi*'s meaning therefore is that a person will behold God's face by means of his *tzedaqah,* but what "behold God's face" means is unclear. The *Bavli* represents R. Eleazar as relying on Psalm 17:15 to teach that one should give a coin to the poor before prayer (B. *Baba Batra* 10a). To the *Bavli,* then, the verse's meaning is "Then I, with *tzedaqah,* will behold your face [in prayer]." The specific prayer praxis the *Bavli* attributes to R. Eleazar is unattested in the *Yerushalmi,* although it is clearly based upon (and a reworking of) what he teaches there. Category (4) is deceptively neat; attention must be given to separating out amoraic statements from what may be anonymous interpolations into them, such as the Aramaic question and answer appended to Rava's statement about the need to fulfill a charity vow right away (B. *Rosh Hashanah* 6a). An example of category (5) is the *Bavli*'s creation of a fictitious dialogue between the *tanna* R. Aqiva and the Roman Tineius Rufus (B. *Baba Batra* 10a). The dialogue is unattested in Palestinian compilations. In Chapter 4 an argument will be made for the story's entirely Babylonian origin; for now, we simply note that the position attributed to R. Aqiva at the beginning of the story is an authentic Palestinian position, albeit not one attributed to him in Palestinian compilations. This example therefore fits into category (2) as well as (5).

This lengthy methodological discussion leads to this important point: in this book material falling into categories (3) and (5) will be "attributed" to the "*Bavli* narrator." The terminological shift is meant to mute a distracting conversation about whether a given example of *Bavli* "*stam*" is "early" or "late" and move the conversation more toward a focus on the substance of what this unattributed, narratival voice is actually saying. That said, where there is a clear and compelling argument that the *Bavli* narrator's contribution is indeed "late" (i.e., post-amoraic), that argument will be made and its implications spelled out. But questions about the dating and provenance of the "*Bavli stam*" are secondary to this book's primary goal: exploring charity's rewards and role in atonement in late antique rabbinic literature.

Ideas about the divine role in rewarding charity and/or in forgiving the sins of the charitable donor are not only about vertical relationships between the divine and humans but may have social implications as well. Source- and redaction-critical analysis of the late antique rabbinic compilations may at times reveal how the rabbinic authors portray the various tensions—including social tensions—they see as linked with certain religious ideas. The cultural fault lines disclosed by careful attention to the literary presentations of these ideas can reveal something of how the rabbis saw the relationships between and among the groups making up Jewish society and their own roles within it. Our examination of these religious ideas in their literary contexts will thus sharpen our awareness of the complex interaction between religious ideology and social context. Ideas have consequences; there are social groups that may benefit from one or other charity idea that they may wield like a weapon to their own benefit, while other groups may seek to parry that ideational thrust in various ways, including by wielding other ideas in response. The not-always irenic interplay between different religious ideas and between religious ideas and ideologies and social context is not confined to late antique rabbinic Judaism; it has and continues to be a flashpoint of social conflict in the contemporary United States and beyond. While there is no expectation that this book will solve any contemporary social ills, it is hoped that it will shed light on a lesser-known part of the (rabbinic) Jewish past and illustrate the ancient rabbis' awareness—one that we twenty-first century people are relearning—that religious ideas can and do indeed have consequences.

Following this introduction, Chapter 2 ("God as the true recipient of *tzedaqah*") will examine the rabbinic reception, reworking, and particularly Babylonian amoraic skepticism about a notion inherited from pre-rabbinic varieties of Judaism: giving *tzedaqah* to the poor is actually the giving of a gift to God. Chapter 3 ("Redemptive almsgiving and charity's rewards in the land of Israel") examines the complex interrelationship of a number of themes in tannaitic and amoraic literature: redemptive almsgiving, charity as the accumulation of heavenly merits, loss of wealth due to sin, and the reward for charity of rescue from death or from a bad afterlife or the grant of a long earthly life. This examination will continue with the Talmud *Bavli* in Chapter 4 ("Redemptive almsgiving and charity's rewards in the Talmud *Bavli*"). Chapter 4 will highlight, *inter alia*, the Bavli's skepticism about redemptive almsgiving and how it tends to confine redemptive almsgiving to communal, rather than individual, *tzedaqah*. This book's analysis from Chapters 1–4 will enable us to identify a thread of Babylonian ambiguity and even ambivalence about too close a linkage between the doing of *tzedaqah* and the forging of connections between the donor and the divine; this ambiguity and ambivalence appears in both amoraic and *Bavli* narrator material. We will discern a heightened Babylonian tendency to accentuate the human elements and role in charity, and to minimize the divine. Chapter 5 ("*Tzedaqah* and *teshuvah*: partially overlapping magisteria") will explore the curious, uneasy coexistence of *tzedaqah* and *teshuvah* as modes of atonement in both Palestinian rabbinic literature and the *Bavli*. This chapter will argue that both rabbinic cultures implicitly but demonstrably privilege *teshuvah* over *tzedaqah*. Chapter 6 ("Charity and beyond: the Talmud *Bavli*'s limitations on a divine role in human affairs") argues that Chapter 4's findings about the *Bavli*'s ambiguity and ambivalence about certain religious ideas about charity should be viewed within the broader theological context of its emphasis in various places on the centrality of human, rather than divine, action. The *Bavli*'s tendency to limit divine providence in charity is entirely consistent with its limitations on divine providence in other areas. Chapter 7 ("Select post-Talmudic developments") will briefly survey some post-Talmudic developments including the "competition" between *tzedaqah* and *teshuvah*, the post-Talmudic emergence of the idea that *tzedaqah* atones for the dead, and how Maimonides' magisterial codification of *tzedaqah* law in his *Mishneh Torah* (twelfth century) reflects his uniquely deep understanding and legal application of the *Bavli*'s ambivalence about the imbrication of the human and the divine in *tzedaqah*. Chapter 8 ("Conclusion: righteous before God") will draw together this book's major conclusions in light of some contemporary reflections.

We will round out this methodological overview with a couple of terminological clarifications. Finding an appropriate English language equivalent to "*tzedaqah*" in the sense of "giving money or aid to the poor" is difficult. "Alms" and "almsgiving" stem from the Greek "*eleemosyne*" (compassion, pity, or mercy), which, as Gary Anderson has pointed out, was Latinized into "*elemosina*," then rendered into Old English as "*aelmysse*," and ultimately shortened to "*almes*" and then "*alms*."[17] "Charity" stems from the Latin "*caritas*," which connotes a Christian love for others, expressed as the free giving to those in need. Despite the strong Christian connotations of both terms this book will opt throughout for "charity," which has greater linguistic economy than longer, admittedly more precise formulations like "giving money or aid to the poor." Nevertheless, this book will retain the ubiquitous scholarly term "redemptive almsgiving" for the notion that, as David J. Downs has put it, charity may be a "means of canceling, cleansing, covering, extinguishing, lightening, or ... atoning for human sin and/or its consequences."[18] Unlike the more precise "atoning charity," "redemptive almsgiving" is broader and makes space for related rabbinic notions such as the manifestation of charity's atoning power through the donor's rescue ("redemption") from unnatural death or from an unpleasant afterlife.

"*Tzedaqah*": its ubiquity and multivalence in rabbinic literature

Why do the rabbis settle on "*tzedaqah*" as their principal term for charity? What are its various shades of meaning in their compilations?[19] What religious significance does the term "*tzedaqah*" have for the rabbis? The rabbis certainly understand "*tzedaqah*" as "charity," but they also understand it more literally as "justice," "righteousness," and "justification" in certain biblical and other contexts. We can enrich our understanding of the religious significance to the rabbis of *tzedaqah* as charity by mapping onto it these other understandings of *tzedaqah*. Moreover, even in contexts in which such mapping is not possible, we may be able to detect nuances in the rabbis' use of "*tzedaqah*" that deepen our understanding of just why it is religiously significant to them that charity be designated as such.

A nuanced analysis of the meanings of "*tzedaqah*" in rabbinic literature is clouded by a modern and contemporary Jewish polemic about the term (not always explicit) about the superiority of the Jewish notion of "*tzedaqah*" to Christian "charity" or "alms." This polemic is based on the recognition that the trilateral Hebrew root of "*tzedaqah*" is well known to be "*tz-d-q*," also the root of "*tzedeq*" ("justice") and "*tzaddiq*" ("righteous person").[20] "Justice," or "being righteous," is thus held to be superior to "charity" ("*caritas*"). The nineteenth–twentieth century American Reform rabbi–scholar Kaufmann Kohler was an early advocate of this polemic. In his 1906 entry "Alms" in the *Jewish Encyclopedia*, Kohler emphasizes the distinction between "alms" (*eleemosyne*) and "*tzedaqah*."[21] Kohler stresses that *eleemosyne* is not truly equivalent to "*tzedaqah*," which is "charity in the spirit of uprightness or justice." The

"Mosaic conception" is that "the poor have a certain claim on the possessions of the rich" while "the rich are positively enjoined to share God's bounties with the poor." To Kohler "*tzedaqah*" is a matter of legalities, social class, and entitlements, and "alms" is a devotional matter between the donor and God. Kohler's distinction between "alms" and "*tzedaqah*" thus accounts for the direction he takes in his *Jewish Encyclopedia* entry—entitled "Alms"—which is essentially an exploration of theological ideas about charity. While Kohler believes that God certainly commands *tzedaqah*, *tzedaqah* has a this-worldly, social justice aspect not necessarily present in "charity."[22]

The polemic persists to the present. Source materials published on the Internet by Amplifier: The Jewish Giving Circle Movement, make the point that "charity" and "philanthropy" stem from Latin words meaning "love" while *tzedaqah* means "righteousness, fairness, justice." This being so, "[t]he poor have a right to *tzedakah* and the donor has an obligation to give it," unlike "charity," which is not obligatory.[23] Note that what makes *tzedaqah* superior to "charity" and "philanthropy" is the former's implicit linkage to Judaism's system of religious law and divinely commanded behaviors. There is a softer version of this polemic in a pamphlet entitled "Tzedaka: A Coin a Day Keeps the World Spinnin' Round," published for outreach purposes by an arm of Chabad (the worldwide Hasidic Jewish movement also known as "Lubavitch"):

> Charity, everyone knows, means being a nice guy
> and giving your money to someone with less. That's
> why, in Jewish tradition, we never give charity. It's
> unheard of.
>
> Because everyone knows that whatever we have doesn't really
> belong to us....We are no more than treasurers, our sages
> taught, and everything that comes through our hands is given
> to us to use for good things ...
>
> That's why, in Jewish tradition, we call it "giving tzedaka."
> Tzedaka means "doing the right thing" ...[24]

In some other contemporary writing, the Jewish religious obligation of *tzedaqah* is seen as a task that blurs into the contemporary call for "social justice."[25] The reasons for the emergence and persistence of this polemic deserve greater attention than can be provided here. We may hypothesize *pro tempore* that the polemic is at least in part an assertive response to a perceived Christian view that Jewish *tzedaqah* (which is both commanded and explicitly acknowledged to be rewarded by God) is inferior to Christian charity, which is (to be) done voluntarily, out of a disinterested love of humanity.

But what were the meanings of *tzedaqah* for the rabbis, and even earlier? When did "*tzedaqah*" take on the meaning of "charity"? It is to this question that we now turn.

Tzedaqah *in the Hebrew Bible and Second Temple literature*

Moshe Weinfeld points out that in the Hebrew Bible "*tzedeq*" ("justice") means "the abstract principle of righteousness" while "*tzedaqah*" refers "to the concrete act." "*Tzedeq*" is thus connected at times to the heavens (e.g., Psalm 85:12; 89:15) while "*tzedaqah*" is connected to actions, including giving charity to the poor (Daniel 4:24).[26] Weinfeld also discerns a link between "*tzedaqah*" and succoring the poor in Ezekiel 18.[27] In verse 5 the prophet declares that *Thus, if a man is righteous* ("*tzadiq*") *and does what is just and right* ("*tzedaqah*") he will perform a number of righteous acts, including giving *bread to the hungry and cloth*[ing] *the naked* (v. 7). *Wrong[ing] the poor and the needy* (v. 12) is taken to be the opposite of such righteous behavior. Isaiah 58:2 describes Israel as a nation acting *like a nation that does what is right* ("*tzedaqah*"), later specified as *to share your bread with the hungry, and to take the wretched poor into your home; when you see the naked to cover him ...* (v. 7).[28]

The Hebrew Bible's linkage of "*tzedaqah*" with providing for the poor raises the question of how far back before the rabbis the equation of "*tzedaqah*" and charity goes. Contemporary scholars' conclusions differ, although a core of agreement is discernible. In his seminal study of the term, Franz Rosenthal posits that "*tzedaqah*" came to mean "charity" in roughly the first or second century BCE, although he opines that one biblical appearance of the Aramaic "*tzidqah*" ("*tzedaqah*"; Daniel 4:24) means "charity" even earlier.[29] Roman Garrison and, more recently, Gary A. Anderson, have also devoted considerable attention to this issue.[30] We will confine our attention at this point to three "*tzedaqah*" verses in the Hebrew Bible that are particularly important in the evolution of rabbinic ideas about charity: Proverbs 10:2 (and 11:4), and the aforementioned Daniel 4:24.

Ill-gotten wealth is of no avail,
But righteousness saves from death.

(Proverbs 10:2)

Wealth is of no avail on the day of wrath,
But righteousness saves from death.

(Proverbs 11:4)

The Jewish Publication Society (JPS) translation renders *tzedaqah* in these verses as "righteousness." Roman Garrison accepts Franz Rosenthal's earlier conclusion that the original meaning of the Hebrew "*tzedaqah*" in these verses is not "charity." Indeed, there is no clear indication in the Masoretic text that these verses' "*tzedaqah*" means "charity."[31] The equation of "*tzedaqah*" and "charity" is the result of a linguistic development stemming from possibly as early as the second century BCE and adopted by the rabbis, for whom these verses became "two of the most significant ... prooftexts for redemptive almsgiving."[32] Gary Anderson, on the other hand, forthrightly renders "*tzedaqah*" as "charity" in his translation and discussion of these verses, relying in large part on the rendering of "*tzedaqah*" as "charity" in Second Temple Jewish literature, as well as on recent linguistic scholarship according to which "charity" might even be the more accurate understanding of "*tzedaqah*" in the Hebrew Bible.[33]

While Rosenthal and Garrison differ with Anderson as to Proverbs 10:2 and 11:4, all three scholars agree (as does Moshe Weinfeld) that the Aramaic "*tzidqah*" (= *tzedaqah*) in Daniel 4:24 means "charity." In its entirety, the verse reads as follows: *Therefore, O king, may my advice be acceptable to you: Redeem your sins by beneficence* (*tzidqah*) *and your iniquities by generosity to the poor; then your serenity may be extended.* Daniel 4:24 seems to be a clear-cut case of the root "*tz-d-q*" meaning "charity" in the Hebrew Bible, in a text dating to the second century BCE.[34] Anderson devotes considerable attention to this verse, highlighting—as Garrison had previously—Rosenthal's observation that the meaning of "*tzidqah*" in Daniel 4:24 should be gleaned through attention to the parallelism in the verse. *Redeem your sins by* "*tzidqah*" is balanced by *generosity to the poor*, and the Aramaic for *generosity* ("*mihan*") is formed of the trilateral root *h-n-n*, which, in the Hebrew of Psalms 37:21 (*honen v'noten*) means *is generous and keeps giving.*[35] Anderson collects other examples of this use of the verb root: Proverbs 14:21 (*mehonen aniyyim*), 14:31 (*honen*), 19:17 (*honen dal*), and 28:8 (*honen dalim*), all of which also establish that the root *h-n-n* refers to giving generously to the poor. In sum, Daniel 4:24's "*tzidqah*" most likely means "charity" rather than a generic "righteousness."[36] Garrison points out the Septuagint's (Daniel 4:27) later rendering of the Aramaic "*tzidqah*" as the Greek *eleemosyne*, or "mercy" in the sense of "charity."

At bottom, then, these scholars agree that Daniel 4:24's "*tzidqah*" likely means "charity" even in the original Aramaic, and that "*tzedaqah*" in Proverbs 10:2 and 11:4 also came to mean "charity" early in the Second Temple period. Anderson, unlike Garrison, understands Proverbs 10:2 and 11:4's "*tzedaqah*" to mean "charity" even earlier. Yael Wilfand, in her own survey of the evolving meaning of "*tzedaqah*" in the Hebrew Bible and Second Temple literature, is also careful to point out the numerous verses in the Hebrew Bible in which "*tzedaqah*" means "justice" and/or "righteousness," and the merit gained by the performance of righteous acts (in general).[37] Putting all this together, we may say that the Hebrew Bible does not view "charity" as the primary meaning of "*tzedaqah*," although it links the two in Ezekiel 18 and Isaiah 58 and does use the Aramaic equivalent "*tzidqah*" to mean "charity" in Daniel 4:24. "*Tzedaqah*" in the Hebrew Bible refers to righteousness, justice, the earning of merits before God, and the doing of righteous acts; despite the hints of a link to the concrete act of charity, the Hebrew Bible does not yet see charity as the primary, let alone exclusive meaning of "*tzedaqah*." This has two related consequences for later developments in the meaning of the term: (1) when *tzedaqah* comes to be associated closely with charity in the Second Temple and rabbinic periods there will be a well-stocked repository of verses on which to draw in buttressing that association;[38] and (2) rabbinic interpretations of verses in which *tzedaqah* refers to righteousness, merits, and/or justice should be probed to see what, if any, connections are made between those interpretations and the rabbis' understanding of *tzedaqah* as charity.

"Tzedaqah" and "mitzvah" as "competing" terms for charity in Palestinian literature and in the Bavli

"*Tzedaqah*" is the rabbinic term of choice for charity in tannaitic literature.[39] "*Tzedaqah*" is also the rabbinic term of choice in Palestinian amoraic literature and the *Bavli*, notwithstanding scholars' recognition that "*mitzvah*" is also used to mean "charity" in pre-rabbinic Jewish and Palestinian rabbinic literature.[40] Gary Anderson accepts Saul Lieberman's decades-old observation that this usage of "*mitzvah*" may go back to the Second Temple period. Noam Zion has pointed out that "*mitzvah*" as "charity" is also found in the Aramaic dedication of a fourth-century synagogue in Hammath-Tiberias, where the donors who "gave *mitzvata*" are blessed.[41] Michael Satlow, following Theodor Nöldeke, has pointed out that the use of "*mitzvah*" to mean "charity" is even found in Christian texts written in Amharic, the Ethiopian Christian Semitic language.[42]

The word "*mitzvah*" is also used generally in Palestinian rabbinic literature to refer to other commandments as well to items used in the *performance* of commandments. For example, in *Yerushalmi Peah*, R. Haviva teaches in the name of the Babylonian rabbis that if a man buys a "*mitzvah*" and then finds a nicer one, he should spend an additional amount up to 33.3 percent of the price of the original to buy the superior one.[43] Examples of such *mitzvah*-items follow later in the passage: *lulav, sukkah, shofar,* and *tefillin* (phylacteries). This brief discussion of the purchase of a "*mitzvah*" is located within a larger context of a discussion about charity: the legal limitation on charitable outlays, the notion that giving *tzedaqah* "from your pocket" will save one from taxes, and the story of King Monbaz of Adiabene and his description of (and confidence in) the role of *tzedaqah* in funding his heavenly treasury of merits. This overall context is important. We see the term "*mitzvah*" used here to describe *any* item used in the performance of a commandment—*implicitly* including charity for the poor. But the *Yerushalmi* refers *explicitly* to the giving of monies to the poor as "*tzedaqah*," *not* as "*mitzvah*."[44]

There is no obvious reason for the prevalence of "*tzedaqah*" over "*mitzvah*" as the preferred term for charity in Palestinian amoraic literature, but two suggestive observations may be made. First, we see that the rabbis deploy "*mitzvah*" to refer to commandments in general, while "*tzedaqah*" is unique, referring explicitly and unmistakably to one only commandment—charity. Second, while both "*tzedaqah*" and "*mitzvah*" are biblical terms, the equation of "*tzedaqah*" with charity is arguably more ancient and more religiously efficacious for the donor than the association of "*mitzvah*" with charity. Daniel 4:24's *tzidqah* is proclaimed to be the means through which the king can expiate his sins. Psalm 112 is also instructive. The psalmist opens with praise of the man who "fears God," *who is ardently devoted to His commandments* (Psalms 112:1). The God-fearing man is described in verses 4, 5, and 9 as engaged in grace and mercy, and distribution of possessions to the poor; the psalmist thereby implicitly equates verse 1's *commandments* (*mitzvoth*) with mercy and gifts to the poor. Yet verse 9 quite explicitly equates distributing possessions to the poor with *his* (the giver's) *beneficence* (*tzidqato*) that will stand forever.[45] Psalm 112 thus draws a loose connection between "*mitzvoth*" and charity and a stronger connection between *tzedaqah* (understood as the protagonist's enduring righteousness before God) and charity. The Palestinian rabbinic preference for "*tzedaqah*" over "*mitzvah*" may therefore have been their adoption of what they perceived to be an earlier biblical weighting of "*tzedaqah*" as greater than "*mitzvah*."

Given that both "*mitzvah*" and "*tzedaqah*" refer to charity in Palestinian rabbinic literature, one may be tempted to search for patterns in the usages of the terms. While "pattern" may be too strong a word for the results of such an inquiry, there is a discernible tendency. "*Mitzvah*" tends to refer to monies that have already been collected and set aside for the poor. Thus R. Hananya bar Papa is described in *Yerushalmi Peah* as "distributing the *mitzvah*" at night, and a poor person is described in *Leviticus Rabbah* as saying, "Give me a *mitzvah*."[46] "*Tzedaqah*" appears to refer to the idea of charity generally (such as in comparison and contrast to *gemilut hasadim*, "reciprocal acts of kindness"), as well as to charity that has not yet been separated or collected (as in R. Abba's general statement on Y. *Peah* 1:1, 15b about "giving *tzedaqah* from your pocket"). Until the charity is collected, requested by, or given to, a poor person, or distributed through a communal social welfare apparatus, it is not "*mitzvah*," perhaps for the simple reason that no religious commandment has yet been performed with it or no discrete monies have as yet been designated for distribution to the poor.

There is also a linkage of "*mitzvah*" and "charity" in the *Bavli*, although the monies are not themselves called "*mitzvah*." In a short narrative on B. *Baba Batra* 10a Rabban Yohanan ben Zakkai refers to his nephews' possibly not doing "the *mitzvah* for its own sake." "*Mitzvah*" here refers to the *act* of giving charity, not the charity monies themselves. This is a change from the Palestinian parallel to this story (*Leviticus Rabbah* 34:12), where the charity monies are themselves called "*mitzvata*."[47] On Y. *Peah* 1:1, 15b, Rabban Gamliel reacts to R. Yeshebab's excessive charitable generosity by noting that one must not give more than one-fifth of one's possessions for "*mitzvoth*." In the *Bavli* parallels to this account (B. *Ketubot* 50a, 67b; B. *Arachin* 28a) the word "*mitzvoth*" is missing—the directive is simply that one must not part with more than one-fifth of one's possessions. Similarly, on B. *Shabbat* 156b, both the *amora* Shmuel and the *tanna* R. Aqiva (in two separate stories) exclaim "you have done a *mitzvah*!" on learning of the charitable act that saved the protagonist from an unnatural and untimely death. Again, "*mitzvah*" in these accounts refers to the charitable *act*, not to the monies themselves. On B. *Baba Batra* 8a the Sasanian King Mother Ifra Hormiz gives a large sum of money to Rav Yosef with the instruction that "let it be [used for] a *mitzvah rabbah*," and the ensuing story gives no indication that the monies are themselves called "*mitzvah*." These sources demonstrate that the *Bavli* is aware of the linkage of "*mitzvah*" and "charity," but does not use "*mitzvah*" to denote the "charity" money itself. Like Palestinian rabbinic literature, the *Bavli* favors "*tzedaqah*" as the term denoting "charity."

Tzedaqah's *multivalence in Palestinian rabbinic literature*

I argue that another reason for the rabbinic preference for "*tzedaqah*" over "*mitzvah*" as the term by which to refer to charity is its multivalence, which goes back to the ubiquity of the trilateral root "*tz-d-q*" in the Hebrew Bible. Palestinian rabbis persist in using "*tzedaqah*" to mean "righteousness," "justice," or "justification" as appropriate in context, and this multivalence informs the contexts in which it means "charity" with three ideationally complex and interesting results. First, *tzedaqah* refers to someone's giving something to others to which the latter are not morally, or perhaps even legally, entitled. Relatedly, *tzedaqah* refers to one person's not maximizing his own legal allowances and entitlements vis-à-vis another, not insisting upon what he is due from another, but acting toward that other with forbearance instead. Second, *tzedaqah* refers to an act by which one demonstrates one's righteousness. Third, *tzedaqah* refers to the "merit" one earns (and that is stored in the heavens) through the performance of righteous acts. Once again, these three meanings of *tzedaqah* include, but are not limited to, the charity context.

Tzedaqah *as giving someone something to which they have no entitlement*

We begin with *Genesis Rabbah* 49:4, in which *tzedaqah* refers clearly to providing sustenance to the needy (in this case, travelers).[48] The verse under discussion is Genesis 18:19, pertaining to the patriarch Abraham (*For I have singled him out, that he may instruct his children and his posterity to keep the way of the Lord by doing what is just* [*tzedaqah*] *and right* [*mishpat*] ...). Genesis 18:19's "*tzedaqah*" most certainly does not mean "charity." It is joined with *mishpat* and is therefore synonymous, or at least related to it. *Mishpat* having the meaning of "law" or the "right" (as JPS renders it), *tzedaqah* therefore has a meaning close to the core meaning of its trilateral root: "just." But there is also an interesting and creative slippage in *Genesis Rabbah* 49:4 between *tzedaqah* as "just" and *tzedaqah* as "charity."

1   R. Azaryah in the name of R. Yehudah: "At the beginning [Abraham would do] *tzedaqah*, and at the end, *mishpat*. How? Abraham would receive wayfarers. When they had eaten and drunk, he would say to them, 'Bless.' They would say to him, 'What should we say?' He would say, 'Blessed be the God of the world of whose bounty we have eaten.' If [the traveler] took it upon himself to bless, he would eat and drink and be on his way. But if he didn't agree [to bless], [Abraham] would say to him, 'Pay what you owe.' And [the traveler] would say to him: 'What do I owe?' ... when he saw, he would cry out: 'Blessed is the God of the world of whose bounty we have eaten.'

2   This is what is written: In the beginning '*tzedaqah*' and in the end '*mishpat*.'"

R. Azaryah quotes R. Yehudah as saying that Abraham would do "*tzedaqah*" at the beginning and "*mishpat*" at the end. His gift of a meal to his guests is initially and provisionally described as "*tzedaqah*," and being a free gift to wayfarers, the gift can be seen as functionally equivalent to *tzedaqah* in the sense of "charity." But this free gift of a meal is only provisionally described as *tzedaqah. Genesis Rabbah* 49:4 contrasts this initial, provisionally free gift to "*mishpat*," understood as Abraham's legally justifiable right to charge for the meal—a legal right upon which he did not insist so long as his guests agreed to bless God using his liturgical formula. So, *Genesis Rabbah* 49:4 understands that Abraham's *tzedaqah*, his free gift to the travelers, was in effect his renunciation of his legal entitlement (*mishpat*) to charge for the meal.

Three other interpretations of "*tzedaqah*" in *Genesis Rabbah*—having no reference to supporting the needy—support this reading. In *Genesis Rabbah* 6:5, R. Yehoshua b. R. Bun interprets Psalm 50:6 (*Then the heavens proclaimed His righteousness*, ["*tzidqo*"]) to mean that God did a "*tzedaqah*" ("righteousness") with the world by not putting the heavens in the first firmament, which would have resulted in an excessively hot world in which no creature could live.[49] As odd as it may seem to put matters this way, the point seems to be that God does not owe the world its existence; God's placing the heavens above the first firmament is an unearned act of kindness on God's part to which the world and its inhabitants have no automatic entitlement. In *Genesis Rabbah* 33:1, R. Yishmael interprets Psalm 36:7 (*Your beneficence* [*tzidqatcha*] *is like the high mountains; Your justice like the great deep*) as referring, respectively, to the righteous who accept the Torah and the wicked who do not. With the righteous God does *tzedaqah* (presumably by not counting every single fault against them), while God is extremely exacting in judging the wicked's conduct.[50] Once again, God's gracious posture toward the righteous is an unearned act of kindness toward them on his part; God presumably is entitled to be as exacting in judging their conduct as he is of the wicked, but he chooses not to. Finally, in *Genesis Rabbah* 82:4, R. Yohanan comments on the prophet Elijah's gathering of Israel on Mount Carmel for the sacrificial contest with the prophets of Baal.[51] From the rabbinic perspective Elijah was forbidden to sacrifice outside of the Jerusalem Temple. Nevertheless, R. Yohanan claims that Deuteronomy 33:19 anticipates Elijah's future sacrifices, calling them "*zivhei tzedeq*"—"righteous" sacrifices. R. Yohanan imagines God's thought process as follows: "I (God) will do *tzedaqah* with them and accept their sacrifice." R. Yohanan's "*tzedaqah*" here seems to mean that, notwithstanding the illegality of Elijah's actions, God undertook not to act on his entitlement to reject the sacrifices. Rather, God resolved to accept the sacrifices, an acceptance to which Elijah (and, presumably, Israel) was not inherently entitled.

Mapping *Genesis Rabbah* 6:5 and 33:1 onto 49:4, Abraham's provision of meals to travelers who agreed to bless God was *tzedaqah*—not merely "charity," but an act of grace and kindness on his part to which the needy travelers had no entitlement. Abraham himself would have been legally entitled to charge them for the meal, but he freely chose not to do so. God's own *tzedaqah* toward the world (*Genesis Rabbah* 6:5) and toward righteous individuals (*Genesis Rabbah* 33:1) illuminates Abraham's *tzedaqah*: giving money, food, or property to others can mean doing to and for them a righteous act of grace to which they are not entitled.

Leviticus Rabbah 26:8 similarly employs "*tzedaqah*" in the sense of "do me a favor."[52] The verse under discussion is Ezekiel 10:2: *He said to the man clothed in linen, and* [he] *said, "Step inside the wheelwork ... and fill your hands with glowing coals from among the cherubs ..."*[53] *Leviticus Rabbah* is exercised by the redundant "*va-yomer*" ("and he said"). The first "and he said" is understood to be God's speaking to the angel, and the second is the angel's speaking to the cherub. The angel is in a bind: God commanded him to take two coals, but the angel lacks authorization to enter into the cherub's domain. Therefore the angel addresses the cherub as if to say "Do *tzedaqah* with me and give me two coals from the altar." Mapping this request onto an ordinary charity transaction between a donor and a recipient, the cherub is clearly the donor, the angel the recipient. The angel is asking the cherub to do "*tzedaqah*" with him because the angel is not permitted to enter the cherub's domain. That is, the angel is asking the cherub not to act on his entitlement to keep his domain angel-free, but to please do something for the angel that the latter is not otherwise entitled to do. Juxtaposed to this teaching is R. Abba bar Kahana's interpretation of Psalm 71:19 (*Your beneficence* [*tzidqatekha*], *high as the heavens, O God*) to mean that just as those "down below" need *tzedaqah* from each other, so do those above—a clear linkage of *tzedaqah* as "charity" with *tzedaqah* as "doing a righteous act of grace for another to which they are not inherently entitled." In *Leviticus Rabbah* 31:1 R. Abba bar Kahana's teaching is found in the mouth of R. Shmuel bar Nahman, who links it to Ezekiel 10:2, thereby closing the conceptual circle: earthly *tzedaqah* as "charity" is linked to the heavenly *tzedaqah* of supernal beings' acting toward each other in benevolent, even undeserved, ways.[54]

Lamentations Rabbah 1:43 draws the connection even more closely between the angelic interaction described on the basis of Ezekiel 10:2 and the *tzedaqah* practiced by human beings toward each other down "below": Psalm 71:19 is there said to teach that the heavens themselves are upheld by the *tzedaqah* that Israel practices below. Again, what is telling is the mapping of the angelic *tzedaqah* interaction onto the human *tzedaqah* transaction: just as the angel was asking the cherub not to insist upon his entitlement to an angel-free domain but to do something for the angel to which the latter was not entitled, so is the giving of *tzedaqah* by one human being to another the gift of something to which the recipient is not inherently entitled, a gift that is a righteous act of grace on the part of the giver.

Pesiqta deRav Kahana 7 includes a series of interpretations of Psalm 119:62 (*At midnight I will rise to praise you for your righteous judgments*).[55] *Pesiqta deRav Kahana* 7:4 applies Psalm 119:62's *your righteous judgments* to Ezekiel 16:6's *in your bloods—live*.[56] Here God was said to have done *tzedaqah* for Israel at the time of the exodus from Egypt. Israel only had the merit of two *mitzvoth* at the time of the exodus: the blood of circumcision and the blood of the Passover offering. God redeemed them despite their *mitzvah* deficit. God is described as having acted on the basis of grace (as it were), in a manner other than he would be required to act on the basis of a careful accounting of commandments fulfilled and merits earned. Israel did not have sufficient merits to be redeemed, and yet God redeemed Israel anyway; God did a *tzedaqah* with Israel.

Pesiqta deRav Kahana 10:8 is an illuminating series of interpretations of Daniel 9:7 (*Yours, o Lord, is the* tzedaqah *and ours is the embarrassment as on this day*).[57] R. Yehudah b. R. Ila'i states that Judges 1:22 shows that God was with Israel even when they went to worship idols. He asks rhetorically: Is there a greater *tzedaqah* than this? (citing Daniel 9:7). Once again, "*tzedaqah*" means God's behaving toward Israel in a gracious manner to which Israel is not inherently entitled. God was not obligated to be by Israel's side when they worshipped idols, yet he was. Finally, R. Shmuel bar Nahman points out that even though Israel took some of the *manna* when it initially fell and offered it to idols (Ezekiel 16:19), God nevertheless did the *tzedaqah* with them of continuing to feed them *manna*. Once again, *tzedaqah* is something Israel received even when they did not deserve it.

We will round out this part of the discussion of *tzedakah*'s multivalence in Palestinian rabbinic literature with appendix 4 to *Pesiqta deRav Kahana*.[58] There Moses asks God to "do a *tzedaqah* with us," quoting Psalm 80:2 (*Give ear, O shepherd of Israel who leads Joseph like a flock!*). Moses is said to appeal to Joseph because the latter fed and sustained his brothers and their families (Genesis 50:21) despite the cruelties they had visited upon him; similarly, Moses wished God to act in such a righteously gracious manner with Israel, presumably despite Israel's many contumacious acts toward God. This text clearly connects the *tzedaqah* given by one human being to another as charity with the richer meaning of "*tzedaqah*" as "righteously giving something to someone to which he is not otherwise entitled."

The Talmud *Bavli* also presents this multivalent understanding of *tzedaqah* as Palestinian in origin. On B. *Avodah Zarah* 4b R. Eleazar interprets Micah 6:5 (*And you will recognize the gracious acts of the Lord*). The word rendered as *gracious acts* is "*tzedaqot.*" R. Eleazar has God saying: "See, my people, how many *tzedaqot* I did with you, not getting angry with you all of those days. For had I become angry with you, nothing of Israel would have remained." To paraphrase R. Eleazar, God was entitled to become angry with and punish Israel, but he chose not to do either. He chose not to act on his legal entitlement to punish Israel, which was a *tzedaqah* to Israel (in fact, many *tzedaqot*). On B. *Qiddushin* 71a R. Yitzhaq interprets Malachi 3:3 (*he shall purify ... and refine them ... so that they shall present offerings in righteousness*). "*Offerings in righteousness*" is the translation of "*minchah b'tzedaqah,*" literally, "gifts with *tzedaqah.*" R. Yitzhaq says: "[God] did a *tzedaqah* for Israel, [in that] a family that was mixed up (with a disqualifying genealogical element) remained mixed up (and the disqualification would simply be ignored)." In other words, these particular Levitical families would present *offerings* to God *in righteousness* because without God's "righteousness," his *tzedaqah*, his gracious willingness to overlook their genealogical unfitness for Temple service, they would not be able to serve. Once again, God's *tzedaqah* in this case is his gracious and legally uncompelled willingness not to act on his legal entitlement to exclude objectively unqualified Levitical families from Temple service.[59]

In sum, these rabbinic sources represent *tzedaqah*, understood as charity, to be a gift by a donor to a person who is not inherently entitled to that gift. That gift is literally "*tzedaqah*," an act of righteousness performed by the donor for the recipient. The donor demonstrates her righteousness by giving a gift to another person who is not inherently or even legally entitled to it. Both God and human beings are described as performing such *tzedaqah*. To the extent that human beings perform such *tzedaqah* they demonstrate righteousness not only toward other human beings, but also before God. The donor's giving of a gift to which the recipient has no entitlement is the concrete manifestation of the donor's righteousness before God.

The informed reader might instantly object that this understanding of *tzedaqah* seems to be contradicted by the Pentateuch's—and the rabbis'—commands of such obligatory acts of giving to the poor as leaving the corners of the fields, the forgotten sheaves, that which falls during the harvest, and the poor man's tithe.[60] How can these commanded gifts be indubitably *obligatory*, while the related act of charity described as *tzedaqah* is an act of undeserved righteousness to which the poor recipient is *not* entitled? The answer is that these agricultural provisions for the poor are indeed commanded, but they are not "*tzedaqah*." The rabbis describe *tzedaqah* as money charity (Y. *Peah* 1:1, 15b–15c; B. *Sukkah* 49b). While the poor are entitled to the various agricultural gifts the Torah sets out, nothing in the Torah entitles to the poor to a specific donor's *money*. Deuteronomy 15:8 commands that Israelites open their hands to their needy kinsmen, but that verse does not entitle any particular "needy kinsman" to what is found in any particular donor's "hand." This being so, when one gives *tzedaqah* to the poor, one is giving the poor something to which they have no specific entitlement at that particular moment. One may be commanded to give, but one is not commanded to give money to that particular person at that particular time.[61] That giving is an act of *tzedaqah*, righteousness, toward the recipient. And, again, this giving is also *tzedaqah* for the donor, who through this gift demonstrates his own righteousness before God.[62]

Tzedaqah *as "a demonstration of one's righteousness" and heavenly merit in Palestinian rabbinic literature*

Palestinian rabbinic literature's portrayal of *tzedaqah* as a demonstration of one's righteousness is multivalent in its own right, applying both to God and to human beings. We will begin with an example that intersects with charity in a small way, and then move on to more straightforward charity examples.

T. *Sanhedrin* 1:4:

> If one adjudicated a judgment, acquitting the
> one in the right, and rendering liable the one
> who was liable: if one rendered a poor man

> liable, one takes [the amount he owes] from
> him and then gives him from his [the judge's]
> own [pocket]. It then turns out that [the judge]
> does *tzedaqah* with this one and adjudication with that
> one.[63]

According to the *Tosefta* a poor man who turns out to be liable to another party is obligated to pay what he owes, after which the judge returns that amount to him out of the judge's own pocket. The *Tosefta*'s concluding sentence would then seem to mean that the judge does "*tzedaqah*" in the sense of "charity" with the poor man by quietly reimbursing him, while the judge "adjudicates" the party whom the poor man had to pay by awarding that party the compensation to which he was legally entitled. The *Yerushalmi* applies this understanding of the passage in its account of the biblical King David's conduct as a judge: "It turns out that [David] would execute judgment for the one and *tzedaqah* (= charity) for the one (= the impoverished litigant)."[64] T. *Sanhedrin* 1:5, however, suggests the possibility of another interpretation:

> Rabbi says: If one adjudicated a judgment,
> acquitting the one in the right, and rendering
> liable the one who was liable: it turns out that
> one does "*tzedaqah*" with the liable—in that he
> removes theft from his hand, and [he does]
> "judgment" with the one in the right, in that he
> returns his [money] to him.[65]

Here, the "*tzedaqah*" that the judge does with the liable party—not described here as "poor"—is that he removes theft from his possession by compelling him to repay the party whom he had wronged. "*Tzedaqah*" seems here to mean "righteousness" or "justice." By causing the liable party to disgorge his ill-gotten gains and compensate the injured party, the judge is activating the liable party's own demonstration of his righteousness. Mapping Rabbi's understanding of *tzedaqah* back onto T. *Sanhedrin* 1:4, the "*tzedaqah*" done by the judge to the poor man is not (only) quiet reimbursement akin to charity; it is also the *tzedaqah*—the act of righteousness—of compelling the poor man to disgorge money he never should have held. The judge's *tzedaqah* with the poor man is his compulsion of the poor man to demonstrate his own righteousness. This understanding of "*tzedaqah*" is also found in another version of this *baraita* on Y. *Sanhedrin* 1:1, 18b:

> If one adjudicated a judgment: acquitting the one
> who is in the right and rendering liable the one
> who was liable, scripture accounts it to him as
> though he did *tzedaqah* with the one in the right
> and as if he did *tzedaqah* with the liable. [He did]

tzedaqah with the one in the right in that he
returned his money to him. [And he did *tzedaqah*]
with the liable one in that he brought out his theft
from his hand.[66]

In this version of the *baraita* the judge is said to do *tzedaqah* with *both* parties. The judge does "*tzedaqah*" (justice) to the party that is owed damages, and "*tzedaqah*" (enabling the demonstration of righteousness) to the party who owed them. By paying the damages she owes, the liable party demonstrates righteousness, *tzedaqah*.

King Monbaz of Adiabene's scriptural defense of his liberality to the poor (T. *Peah* 4:18) also demonstrates how *tzedaqah* means the demonstration of one's righteousness to God—in his case, strictly through charity.[67] A detailed examination of this Toseftan passage will be taken up in Chapter 3. What is of interest here are the Toseftan Monbaz's last two prooftexts, which illustrate the superiority of his "investment strategy" of preserving his wealth by giving it away to his relatives' preferred investment strategy of uninterrupted accumulation. Monbaz quotes Deuteronomy 24:13 (*and it will be to your merit [tzedaqah] before the Lord your God*) and Isaiah 58:8 (*Your Vindicator [tzidqecha] shall march before you*). Monbaz clearly intends Deuteronomy 24:13's *tzedaqah* to refer to his own charity. In context, verses 12 and 13 command that a creditor must not *go to sleep* in a poor man's pledge; the pledge (presumably clothing of some kind) must be returned to him at sunset, so that *he may sleep in his cloth and bless you; and it will be to your merit (tzedaqah) before the Lord your God.* In other words, by returning the pledge at sunset, the creditor is demonstrating his righteousness, his entitlement to "merit," before God. Mapping the scriptural context onto Monbaz's charity, his charity is his demonstration of his "merit," his *tzedaqah*, before God. This point flows smoothly into Isaiah 58:8, his final prooftext, which teaches that Monbaz's *tzedaqah* marches before him—his charity is what will vindicate, or "justify" him, before God.

Tzedaqah in the Palestinian compilations is therefore a theological force field bringing "charity," "justice," and "righteousness" together in subtle ways. *Tzedaqah* is not "merely" charity; it is a gift by a donor to a recipient who is not morally or perhaps even legally entitled to it, a gift by which the donor demonstrates his righteousness, to the recipient certainly, but also to God.

"Tzedaqah" and the Babylonian amoraim

In examining the deployment and multivalence of "*tzedaqah*" in the *Bavli* we must be mindful of the methodological issues raised earlier. Our goal is to identify a distinctly Babylonian voice and doing so requires that we identify the sources most likely to reveal that voice. Consequently, we will focus on *Bavli* sources heuristically sorted into categories (3), (4), and (5) in our earlier methodological discussion.

*Babylonian amoraic usages of "*tzedaqah*" (category [4])*

We may distinguish between two categories of Babylonian amoraic usage of "*tzedaqah*" as "charity": (1) "independent" Babylonian amoraic usages, so called because *amoraim* use the term without reference to a context of interpreting an authentic Palestinian source; and (2) Babylonian amoraic usages of the term in the context of interpreting an authentic Palestinian source. Independent Babylonian usages include those of Rav Yosef and Rehavah (third generation),[68] Rava (fourth generation),[69] and Mar Zutra (sixth generation).[70]

Bavli usages of *tzedaqah* in the context of interpreting Palestinian sources are of greater interest. Rav (first generation), Rav Kahana and Rabbah bar Avuha (second generation), Rav Nahman (third generation), Rava, and Rav Zevid (fifth generation) all use *tzedaqah* to mean "charity" in the context of interpreting T. *Megillah* 2:15 (B. *Arachin* 6a). Rava also uses *tzedaqah* to mean "charity" in the context of interpreting *Sifre Deuteronomy* 265 (B. *Rosh Hashanah* 6a), and M. *Peah* 1:1 (B. *Qiddushin* 40a). Abaye (fourth generation) does so in the context of interpreting *Sifre Deuteronomy* 277 (B. *Baba Metzia* 113b–114a), and an amoraic *baraita* (B. *Baba Batra* 8a). Finally, Rabbah Tosfa'ah (seventh generation) uses *tzedaqah* to mean "charity" in the context of interpreting T. *Baba Qama* 11:5–6 (B. *Baba Qama* 119b).

While second- and third-generation Babylonian *amoraim* are associated with the exegesis of T. *Megillah* 2:15, only *amoraim* of the fourth and seventh generations are associated with the exegesis of Palestinian compilations or sources *other* than T. *Megillah* 2:15. At the most basic level, these data provide concrete support for what would otherwise be a commonsense conclusion: Babylonian *amoraim* derived their understanding of *tzedaqah* as "charity" from Palestine. But these data further suggest that in the third and mid- to late fourth centuries Babylonian *amoraim* were introduced to a wider array of edited Palestinian learning on the topic of *tzedaqah*, which they in turn transmitted and interpreted in Babylonia.[71]

Reworkings of Palestinian sources by Babylonian amoraim *and the* Bavli *narrator (categories [3] and [5])*

On B. *Gittin* 88a Mari bar Mar[72] interprets Daniel 9:14 (*Hence the Lord was intent upon bringing calamity upon us, for the Lord our God is in the right* [tzadiq] *in all that He has done …*) The biblical context is Daniel's supplication to God while he is in exile in Babylon in the first year of Darius's reign (Daniel 9:1). *The Lord our God is in the right* is the translation of "*ki tzadiq Adonai Eloheinu*," literally, God is "righteous," a *tzadiq*. Mari bar Mar's question is: can God be "righteous" in bringing evil upon Israel? The implicit answer being "No," Mari bar Mar's answer is that God "did a '*tzedaqah*' with Israel" by bringing a small number of Israelites to Babylon prior to 587 BCE (II Kings 24:16) in order that these individuals could set up an infrastructure for Jewish life in exile. Upon arriving in Babylon, then, the exiles of 587 BCE were not left religiously and socially adrift; a communal structure was in place, ensuring a rich diasporic existence. To Mari bar Mar, God's arrangement of this pre-587 BCE exile was a *tzedaqah,* an act of kindness and grace to which Israel was not entitled and which he was not bound to do.

Mari bar Mar's exposition is reminiscent of the series of interpretations of verses from Daniel 9 found at *Pesiqta deRav Kahana* 10:8.[73] Reminiscent, but admittedly not quite a reworking, since *Pesiqta deRav Kahana* says nothing about the early exile of II Kings 24:16. Mari bar Mar's exposition is a Babylonian adaptation and reworking of this Palestinian series of interpretations that gives expression to a Babylonian amoraic view that they, the *amoraim,* are structurally equivalent to the individuals exiled to Babylon prior to 587 BCE. The bold Babylonian amoraic point is that their very existence and religious activity in Jewish Babylonia is evidence of God's "*tzedaqah*"; the *amoraim* themselves are a "*tzedaqah,*" a mark of undeserved merit for the Jewish people.

The example of Mari bar Mar has a significance that points beyond itself. The bold Babylonian amoraic self-identification as a "*tzedaqah*" suggests that their approach to *tzedaqah* as charity may be equally innovative, and indeed it is. A famous short *Bavli* narrative presents and answers affirmatively an implicit question of whether an act of "*tzedaqah*" can be legally compelled in the same way that an indisputable legal duty (*din*) one party owes to another can be compelled. We begin with the *Yerushalmi:*[74]

> R. Nehemiah taught: A certain potmaker conveyed his pots
> to a certain man [for transport]. They broke; he took [the
> man's] cloak. The man came before R. Yose b. R. Haninah.
> [R. Yose b. R. Haninah] said to him: "Go and say to him:
> *In order that you might follow the path of the good*
> (Proverbs 2:20)." He went, told him, and he returned his
> cloak. [R. Yose b. R. Haninah] said to him: "Did he pay
> you your wage?" He said to him: "No." He said to him:
> "Go and say to him: *And guard the ways of the righteous*
> [*tzaddiqim*]."[75] He went and told him, and he paid him his
> wage.

And now, the *Bavli* parallel (B. *Baba Metzia* 83a):

> Certain porters broke a barrel of wine belonging to
> Rabbah b. Rav Hanan. He took their cloaks. They
> came and told Rav; he said to him: "Give them their
> cloaks." He said to him: "Is this the law (*dina hachi*)?"
> He said to him: "Yes. *In order that you might follow
> the path of the good* (Proverbs 2:20)." He gave them
> back their cloaks. They said to [Rav]: "We are poor,
> we have worked hard all day and are hungry, and
> we have nothing." [Rav] said to [Rabbah b. Rav Hanan]:
> "Pay them their wage." He said to him: "Is this the law
> (*dina hachi*)?" He said to him: "Yes. *And guard the ways
> of the righteous* (*tzaddiqim*) (Proverbs 2:20)."

In the *Yerushalmi* only one person breaks the pots, and he is conspicuously not described as poor. The *Bavli* turns this narrative into one about the poor; in the *Bavli* the pot-breaker's role is filled by a group of people, who movingly describe the life of a poor day laborer: "We are poor, we have worked hard all day and are hungry, and we have nothing." Apropos, the *Yerushalmi* puts the issue of the wage into the mouth of R. Yose b. R. Haninah, while the *Bavli* puts this concern into the mouths of the poor laborers. The *Yerushalmi*'s R. Yose b. R. Haninah quotes the two parts of Proverbs 2:20 separately to the potmaker, who obeys the instruction based on the verse without inquiring into the legal status of the behavior the verse allegedly requires. In the *Bavli*, the narrative's structural equivalent to the potmaker is another rabbi; he raises the question of the legal status of the behavior and is told that the verse imposes on him a legal obligation to return the men's cloaks and then pay their wage.

The *Bavli*'s quotation of Proverbs 2:20 in this narrative takes on another meaning in light of this chapter's analysis of the multivalence of "*tzedaqah*." "*And guard the ways of the righteous (tzaddiqim)*" means that one must keep the way of *tzedaqah*, the righteous path of not maximizing one's allowances, of demonstrating one's righteousness before God by behaving with forbearance and mercy. "*Tzaddiqim*" and "*tzedaqah*" are not only built of the same trilateral Hebrew root; the *Bavli* elsewhere refers to a certain communal *tzedaqah* collector as "Benjamin the *tzaddiq*," thereby conflating the "righteous" *tzaddiq* and "*tzedaqah*" (B. *Baba Batra* 11a). The *Bavli*'s reworking of the *Yerushalmi* narrative forefronts a practical legal question about *tzedaqah*: is it a legal or a supererogatory requirement? To Rabbah bar Rav Hanan *tzedaqah* cannot be compelled: it is an act of righteousness toward another human being by means of which one demonstrates righteousness before God. The vertical, divine–human aspect of *tzedaqah* predominates; therefore, no human court can compel the horizontal, human–human aspect of the transaction. Rav sees the matter differently: the horizontal, human–human aspect of the transaction removes *tzedaqah* (to some extent) from the vertical, divine–human realm; consequently, the realm of human law applies and a human court *can* legally compel *tzedaqah*. Rav's position here is consistent with his position elsewhere in the *Bavli* that *tzedaqah* collectors can exert pressure on the wealthy to give (B. *Baba Batra* 8b). *Tzedaqah* may be a means through which a donor to the poor demonstrates his righteousness before God, but to Rav, *tzedaqah* is a demonstration of righteousness that the rabbis can *compel* for an earthly, quotidian purpose—in this case, ensuring that impoverished day laborers receive their wages. Rav's privileging of the horizontal, human–human aspect of *tzedaqah* is an important early harbinger of a Babylonian tendency we will examine later in greater depth: a tendency to emphasize the human aspect of the *tzedaqah* interaction and de-emphasize, even delimit, the divine aspect.

To summarize: Babylonian *amoraim* of the first two generations (Rav, Rav Kahana, Rabbah bar Avuha) use "*tzedaqah*" to mean "charity" in the context of interpreting T. *Megillah* 2:15. The *Bavli* also represents Rav as breaking new ground (vis-à-vis Palestinian tradition) in teaching that a rabbi may compel the doing of *tzedaqah*. *Amoraim* of the third (Mari bar Mar), fourth (Rava, Abaye), and seventh (Rabbah Tosfa'ah) generations are associated with the reception and exegesis of a wider array of Palestinian "*tzedaqah*" literary sources. Mari bar Mar is also represented as breaking new ground in his interpretation of Daniel 9:14 to make the case that Babylonian *amoraim* are themselves God's "*tzedaqah*" for the Jewish people. Rabbah also makes a new claim that only *tzedaqah* to "worthy" recipients (whatever that means) earns the donor the divine reward (B. *Baba Qama* 16b). *Tzedaqah* must be a donor's act of righteous giving to someone *worthy of it*, which is critically different from the inherited, implicit Palestinian understanding that the identity and character of the recipient is irrelevant to the donor's demonstration through charity of her righteousness before God. In Chapters 2 and 4 we will examine the implications for charitable praxis of these *Bavli* shifts.

"Doing" *tzedaqah* in late antique rabbinic literature

As *tzedaqah* comes to be used as a noun referring to charity, it is naturally described as being "given," "taken," or "requested." Many such examples can be adduced in both Talmuds: examples from the *Yerushalmi* include R. Abba's teaching about "if you give *tzedaqah* from your pocket" (Y. *Peah* 1:1, 15b); a reference to a person's "demanding" *tzedaqah* (Y. *Peah* 8:9, 21b); and the story of Elisha ben Abuyah's daughters seeking to "take" *tzedaqah* (Y. *Hagigah* 2:1, 77c).[76] In the *Bavli tzedaqah* is described as being "given" (B. *Hagigah* 5a), or "received" (B. *Ketubot* 68a).

But oft-noted yet barely analyzed is the persistence in rabbinic literature of the biblical phrase "to do *tzedaqah*"—or other similar phrases denoting the "doing," as opposed to the "giving" of *tzedaqah* (e.g., Genesis 18:19; I Kings 10:19; Psalm 106:3; Proverbs 21:3; II Chronicles 9:8). References to "doing *tzedaqah*" blur the boundary between *tzedaqah* as charity and *tzedaqah* as a demonstration of righteousness. By describing charitable behavior as "doing" *tzedaqah*, the speaker is clearly indicating that by giving charity, the donor is acting out—*doing*—his righteousness before God. "Doing" *tzedaqah* puts the focus on the donor. This usage is attested in R. Shimon ben Laqish's teaching that "the lender is greater than the one who does *tzedaqah*" (B. *Shabbat* 63a), and in the narrative about Naqdimon ben Gurion's "doing" of *tzedaqah* (B. *Ketubot* 66b–67a). R. Yohanan refers to "doing" *tzedaqah* in secret (B. *Sotah* 5a). In a lovely wordplay, R. Eleazar says that one who compels (*m'aseh*) someone else to do *tzedaqah* is superior to the one who "does" (*oseh*) *tzedaqah* (B. *Baba Batra* 9a).

Not only is *tzedaqah* a donor's "doing" righteousness before God; the rabbis also perpetuate an inherited, pre-rabbinic understanding that charity is a gift made *to* God. The impoverished recipients of these unearned and undeserved demonstrations of righteousness also in some way stand in for God, the true recipient of the gifts. Such a notion, part of the legacy of pre-rabbinic Jewish piety, becomes a problematized part of the rabbinic set of religious ideas about *tzedaqah*. It is to this idea and its potentially problematic social implications as the rabbis present them that we now turn.

Notes

1 A survey of the genealogy of the term *"tzedaqah"* will be undertaken later in this chapter. For a scriptural indication of reward, see, e.g., Deuteronomy 15:10: *Give to him readily ... for in return the Lord your God will bless you in all your efforts and in all your undertakings.*

2 Examining the renderings of *Unetaneh Tokef*'s *"tzedaqah"* in different prayerbooks over the course of the twentieth century and into the twenty-first yields a range of results: *tzedaqah* is variously rendered as a generic "righteousness," at times more straightforwardly as "charity," and even as "good deeds." For "righteous giving," which incorporates the trilateral root *tz-d-q* in its dual sense of "righteousness" and "charity," see most recently, e.g., *Mishkan Hanefesh: Mahzor for the Days of Awe; Yom Kippur* (New York: CCAR Press, 2015), 214. Rivka Ulmer and Moshe Ulmer have also rendered *"tzedaqah"* as "righteous giving" in ibid., *Righteous Giving to the Poor:* Tzedakah *("Charity") in Classical Rabbinic Judaism; Including a Brief Introduction to Rabbinic Literature* (Piscataway: Gorgias, 2014).

3 See, e.g., Aryeh Cohen, *Justice in the City: An Argument from the Sources of Rabbinic Judaism* (Boston: Academic Studies Press, 2013); Jill Jacobs, *There Shall Be No Needy: Pursuing Social Justice through Jewish Law and Tradition* (Woodstock: Jewish Lights, 2008); Shmuly Yanklowitz, *The Soul of Jewish Social Justice* (Jerusalem: Urim, 2014). Apropos, many scholars and other observers have studied and remarked upon the twentieth-century transformation of *"tikkun olam"* from its fairly modest beginning in M. *Gittin* 4:2–3 to the broad, wide-ranging call for "social justice" it has now become. This transformation has been studied by many, applauded by some, and roundly criticized by others. See, e.g., Jane L. Kanarek, "What Does *Tikkun Olam* Actually Mean?," in Rabbi Or N. Rose et al., editors, *Righteous Indignation: A Jewish Call for Justice* (Woodstock: Jewish Lights, 2007), 15–22; Hillel Halkin, "How Not to Repair the World," *Commentary* 126:1 (July/August 2008): 22–23; Joel Fishman, editor, *Jewish Political Studies Review* 25:3–4 (Fall 2013), Special Issue: Tikkun Olam; and David Birnbaum and Martin S. Cohen, *Tikkun Olam: Judaism, Humanism & Transcendence* (New York: New Paradigm Matrix Foundation, 2015).

4 We will discuss the term "redemptive almsgiving" more below; detailed treatments of this idea in Palestinian rabbinic literature and the *Bavli* are the subjects of Chapters 3 and 4 respectively.

5 See, e.g., Judah Galinsky, " 'And It Is for the Glory of the Great That Their Name Be Remembered': Commemorating the Dead and the Practice of Establishing a *Hekdesh* in Christian Spain," *Masechet* 2 (2004): 113–131 (in Hebrew); ibid., "Commemoration and Heqdesh in the Jewish Communities of Germany and Spain in the 13th Century," in Michael Borgolte, editor, *Stiftungen in Christentum, Judentum und Islam vor der Moderne* (Berlin: Akademie, 2005), 191–204; ibid., "Jewish Charitable Trusts and the Hekdesh Trust in Thirteenth-Century Spain," *Journal of Interdisciplinary History* 33 (2004): 423–440; Elisheva Baumgarten, *Practicing Piety in Medieval Ashkenaz: Men, Women, and Everyday Religious Observance* (Philadelphia: University of Pennsylvania Press, 2014), 103–137 and *passim*; Madeline Kochen, *Organ Donation and the Divine Lien in Talmudic Law* (New York: Cambridge University Press, 2014); Eliezer Segal, "Rabbi Eleazar's *Perutah*," *The Journal of Religion* 85:1 (2005): 25–42; Moshe Hallamish, *Kabbalah: In Liturgy, Halakhah and Customs* (Ramat-Gan: Bar-Ilan University, 2000), 383–400.

6 See, e.g., Gregg E. Gardner, *The Origins of Organized Charity in Rabbinic Judaism* (New York and Cambridge: Cambridge University Press, 2015), 1 (in the tannaitic period charity "replaces sacrifices, brings one closer to the divine, and averts the evil decree on the day of judgment"); Rivka Ulmer and Moshe Ulmer, *Righteous Giving to the Poor*, 45–56 and *passim*.

7 There were five generations of *amoraim* in the land of Israel (ranging chronologically from the first third of the third century through the end of the fourth century) and seven generations of *amoraim* in Babylonia (ranging chronologically from the first third of the third century through the early- to mid-sixth century). For a brief overview, see Alyssa M. Gray, "Amoraim," *Encyclopedia Judaica*, 2nd ed. (2007), 2:89–95. Richard Kalmin models the study of intellectual and other patterns of difference between amoraic generations; see, e.g., his *Sages, Stories, Authors, and Editors in Rabbinic Babylonia* (Atlanta: Scholars Press, 1994).

8 Ishay Rosen-Zvi puts Foucault's notion to good use in his "Pauline Traditions and the Rabbis: Three Case Studies," *Harvard Theological Review* 110 (2017): 169–194.

9 The literature on this subject is vast. Richard Kalmin has devoted many studies to demonstrating that the *Bavli*'s component sources may be identified and that amoraic generations may display consistent, identifiable, and distinguishing characteristics. See Richard Kalmin, *Sages, Stories, Authors, and Editors in Rabbinic Babylonia*; ibid., *Jewish Babylonia between Persia and Roman Palestine* (New York and Oxford: Oxford University Press, 2006), 10–13 and *passim*; and ibid., *Migrating Tales: The Talmud's Narratives and Their Historical Context* (Oakland: University of California Press, 2014), ix–xiii, 11–12 and *passim*. Jacob Neusner was a major proponent of the view that the *Bavli* as a whole must be seen as the work of its final redactors; see, e.g., Jacob Neusner, *Making the Classics in Judaism* (Atlanta: Scholars Press, 1989). Kalmin explicitly takes issue with the view that the *Bavli*'s portrayals of interactions between rabbis and non-rabbis are (merely) "internal rabbinic discourse" on the basis of which historical conclusions are difficult if not impossible to draw. See Kalmin, *Jewish Babylonia between Persia and Roman Palestine*, 12–13.

10 See the crucial acknowledgment of this point in Yaacov Sussmann, "V'Shuv le-Yerushalmi Nezikin," in Yaacov Sussmann and David Rosenthal, editors, *Mehkerei Talmud: Talmudic Studies I* (Jerusalem: Magnes, 1990), 55–133.

11 David Halivni's view, which he has developed and refined over the many decades and volumes of his Talmud commentary *Mekorot U-Mesorot* (*Sources and Traditions*) is that the *Bavli*'s *stam* layer is "late," i.e., post-amoraic. Moreover, he has identified a scholarly cadre called "*Stammaim*" as the "authors" of this layer. Halivni has refined this theory of the *Stammaim* and their authorship to account for anonymous materials that can or should reasonably be seen as contemporaneous with the *amoraim*; he has also pushed back the date of the *Bavli*'s redaction to the eighth century (the Geonic period). See the collected introductions to his volumes of commentary in David Halivni, *Introduction to "Sources and Traditions": Studies in the Formation of the Talmud* (Jerusalem: Magnes, 2009) (in Hebrew); and the recent publication of these introductions as *The Formation of the Babylonian Talmud: Introduced, Translated, and Annotated by Jeffrey L. Rubenstein* (New York and Oxford: Oxford University Press, 2013). Of Shamma Friedman's vast *oeuvre*, see especially his "'Al Derekh Heker Hasugya," in H.Z. Dimitrovsky, editor, *Mehkarim U-mekorot I* (New York: Jewish Theological Seminary of America, 1978), 283–321. Other contemporary scholars are more willing forthrightly to acknowledge that some *stam* material may be "early" (i.e., datable to the amoraic period) or at least difficult to date precisely to the post-amoraic period. See, e.g., Richard Kalmin, *Migrating Tales*, xi (who states that he will "make every effort to avoid taking a stand [on the issue of dating] … in the absence of concrete proof"); Alyssa M. Gray, *A Talmud in Exile: The Influence of Yerushalmi Avodah Zarah on the Formation of Bavli Avodah Zarah* (Providence: Brown Judaic Studies, 2005), 178–188; Robert Brody, "Stam Ha-Talmud v'Divrei Ha-Amoraim," in Baruch Schwartz et al., editors, *Ha-Mikra V'olamo: Sifrut Hazal U-Mishpat Ivri U-Mahshevet Yisrael* (Jerusalem: Ha-iggud Ha-olami Le'mada'ei Ha-yahadut, 2008), 213–232.

12 See Moulie Vidas, *Tradition and the Formation of the Talmud* (Princeton: Princeton University Press, 2014).

13 See Y. *Peah* 1:1, 15b (ed. Academy, 79). I have rendered the verse here as it appears in the JPS translation; throughout this book I will render this verse as either *charity saves from death* or more frequently as *tzedaqah saves from death.*

14 *Leviticus Rabbah* 34:12 (ed. Margulies, 796–799).

15 We will explore this particular example in depth in Chapter 4.

16 Y. *Ta'anit* 2:1, 65b (ed. Academy, 712).

17 Gary A. Anderson, *Charity: The Place of the Poor in the Biblical Tradition* (New Haven: Yale University Press, 2013), 42–43.

18 David J. Downs, *Alms: Charity, Reward, and Atonement in Early Christianity* (Waco: Baylor University Press, 2016), 7.

19 The most notable recent treatments are those of Susan Sorek, *Remembered for Good: A Jewish Benefaction System in Ancient Palestine* (Sheffield: Sheffield Phoenix Press, 2010), 230–231; Yael Wilfand, *Poverty, Charity and the Image of the Poor in Rabbinic Texts from the Land of Israel* (Sheffield: Sheffield Phoenix Press, 2014), 44–60; Yael Wilfand Ben-Shalom, *The Wheel that Overtakes Everyone: Poverty and Charity in the Eyes of the Sages of the Land of Israel* (Tel Aviv: Hakibbutz Hameuchad, 2017), 52–59 (in Hebrew); Rivka Ulmer and Moshe Ulmer, *Righteous Giving to the Poor*, 39–43 and *passim*; and Gregg E. Gardner, *Origins of Organized Charity*, 27–32 and *passim*.

20 The shared trilateral root and the consequent identification of *tzedaqah* as charity with justice is not only a matter of polemic. See Jean Juster, *Les Juifs Dans L'Empire Romain: Leur Condition Juridique, Économique et Sociale*, vol. 1 (Paris: Librairie Paul Geuthner, 1914), 427 n. 2 ("Remarquer que charité s'appelle en hébreu *Zedakah* … mot qui signifie aussi justice …").

21 Kaufmann Kohler, "Alms," *Jewish Encyclopedia* vol. 1 (1906), 435–436.

22 Kohler's distinction between "alms" and "*tzedaqah*" draws out an aspect of the ethical monotheism on display in the Central Conference of American Rabbis' 1885 Pittsburgh Platform. Paragraph 8 provides

> In full accordance with the spirit of the Mosaic legislation, which strives to regulate the relations between rich and poor, we deem it our duty to participate in the great task of modern times, to solve, on the basis of justice and righteousness, the problems presented by the contrasts and evils of the present organization of society.

"Justice and righteousness" alludes to the trilateral Hebrew root of "*tzedaqah.*"

23 "Amplifier: The Jewish Giving Circle Movement; https://amplifiergiving.org/media/resources/Select_Jewish_Texts_on_Giving.pdf. Last accessed December 5, 2018.

24 "Tzedaka: A Coin a Day Keeps the World Spinnin' Round," The Shluchim Office (2004), 5.

25 See, e.g., Albert Vorspan and David Saperstein, *Jewish Dimensions of Social Justice: Tough Moral Choices of Our Time* (New York: UAHC Press, 1998), 93 ("*tzedaqah*" means "righteousness"). This discussion contextualizes a discussion of "*tzedaqah*" in a chapter entitled "The Elusive Search for Economic Justice." See also Frank M. Loewenberg, *From Charity to Social Justice: The Emergence of Communal Institutions for the Support of the Poor in Ancient Judaism* (New Brunswick and London: Transaction Publishers, 2001); Bernardo Kliksberg, *Social Justice: A Jewish Perspective* (New York and Jerusalem: Gefen, 2003); and Shmuly Yanklowitz, *The Soul of Jewish Social Justice*, 452–454.

26 Moshe Weinfeld, *Social Justice in Ancient Israel and in the Ancient Near East* (Jerusalem and Minneapolis: Magnes Press and Fortress Press, 1995), 34 and nn. 31–32.

27 Moshe Weinfeld, *Social Justice in Ancient Israel*, 18, 219–220 and *passim*.

28 Ibid. I have rendered Isaiah 58:7 here in accordance with Weinfeld.

29 See Franz Rosenthal, "Sedaka, Charity," *Hebrew Union College Annual* 23 (Part I, 1950–1951): 411–430. See also Moshe Weinfeld, *Social Justice in Ancient Israel*, 34.

30 See Roman Garrison, *Redemptive Almsgiving in Early Christianity* (Sheffield: Sheffield Academic Press, 1993), 46–55; Gary A. Anderson, *Charity,* 53–82 and *passim.*

31 Roman Garrison, *Redemptive Almsgiving in Early Christianity,* 51.

32 Ibid., 50.

33 Gary Anderson, *Charity,* 54 and 197 n. 1, citing Avi Hurvitz, "Reshitam Ha-Miqra'it shel Munahim Talmudiyyim—Le-Toldot Tzemichato shel Musag Ha-Tzedakah," *Mehkarim be-Lashon* 2–3 (1987): 155–160.

34 Roman Garrison, *Redemptive Almsgiving in Early Christianity,* 51. David J. Downs has very recently registered his disagreement with this; see his *Alms,* 50–52 and *passim.*

35 See also Psalm 112:4–5: *he is gracious, compassionate, and beneficent ... he lends generously (hanun v'rahum ... honen u-malveh).*

36 See Roman Garrison, *Redemptive Almsgiving in Early Christianity,* 51, and Gary A. Anderson, *Sin: A History* (New Haven: Yale University Press, 2009), 139–141. But see Gregg Gardner, *Origins of Organized Charity,* 27 who avers that "[n]owhere in the Hebrew Bible does the Hebrew *tsedaqah* mean charity or almsgiving"; but also see his n. 94.

37 See Yael Wilfand, *Poverty, Charity,* 44–45 and *passim.*

38 A point made earlier in Yael Wilfand, ibid., 52 and *passim.*

39 See, e.g., M. *Avot* 2:7, 5:13; M. *Baba Qama* 10:1; M. *Demai* 3:1; M. *Qiddushin* 4:5; T. *Baba Metzia* 3:9 (ed. Lieberman, 74); T. *Baba Qama* 10:22 (ed. Lieberman, 55); T. *Demai* 3:17 (ed. Lieberman, 77); T. *Megillah* 1:5 (ed. Lieberman, 344); T. *Megillah* 2:15 (ed. Lieberman, 352); T. *Peah* 4:15, 18, 19, 21 (ed. Lieberman, 59–61); *Mekhilta de-Rabbi Ishmael* on Exodus (ed. Horovitz-Rabin, 201–202); *Sifre Numbers* 42 (ed. Horovitz, 47). See also Gregg Gardner, *Origins of Organized Charity,* 27 (citing Benno Przybylski's "thorough study of *tsedaqah* in Tannaitic compilations") proving the same point. The reference is to Benno Przybylski, *Righteousness in Matthew and his World of Thought* (Cambridge: Cambridge University Press, 1980).

40 Examples of this usage in Palestinian rabbinic literature include *Leviticus Rabbah* 34:4 (ed. Margulies, 780) ("*tein li mitzvah*"—"give me charity"); Y. *Sheqalim* 5:6, 49b (ed. Academy, 622) (R. Hinena bar Papa would "distribute the *mitzvah*"—charity—at night). See also the discussions in Michael L. Satlow, "'Fruit and the Fruit of Fruit': Charity and Piety among Jews in Late Antique Palestine," *Jewish Quarterly Review* 100:2 (2010): 244–277; Gary Anderson, *Sin: A History,* 174; ibid., *Charity,* 16–17; Saul Lieberman, "Two Lexical Notes," *Journal of Biblical Literature* 65 (1946): 67–72.

41 See Noam Zion, *From Each According to One's Ability: Duties to Poor People from the Bible to the Welfare State and Tikkun Olam* (Cleveland: Zion Holiday Publications, 2012), 45.

42 Michael Satlow, "'Fruit and the Fruit of Fruit'": 256.

43 Y. *Peah* 1:1, 15b (ed. Academy, 79).

44 See also Yael Wilfand, *Poverty, Charity,* 57–59.

45 I have altered JPS's *beneficence* to "righteousness."

46 Y. *Peah* 8:9, 21b (ed. Academy, 112). The word reads "מניה" but should be read as "מצוה" as in Y. *Sheqalim* 5:6, 49b (ed. Academy, 622). See also *Leviticus Rabbah* 34:4 (ed. Margulies, 780).

47 See *Leviticus Rabbah* 34:12 (ed. Margulies, 796–799).

48 *Genesis Rabbah* 49:4 (ed. Theodor-Albeck, 502–503).

49 *Genesis Rabbah* 6:5 (ed. Theodor-Albeck, 47).

50 *Genesis Rabbah* 33:1 (ed. Theodor-Albeck, 298–299). See also *Pesiqta deRav Kahana* 9 (ed. Mandelbaum, 146).

51 *Genesis Rabbah* 82:4 (ed. Theodor-Albeck, 982).

52 *Leviticus Rabbah* 26:8 (ed. Margulies, 608–609).

53 I have altered the JPS translation's "*he spoke*" to "*he said*" in the interest of the unfolding analysis.

54 *Leviticus Rabbah* 31:1 (ed. Margulies, 714–715).

55 *Pesiqta deRav Kahana* 7 (ed. Mandelbaum, 124–125). The translation of the verse is my own.

56 This rendering of the verse is my own.

57 *Pesiqta deRav Kahana* 10 (ed. Mandelbaum, 169–171). The translation of the verse is my own.

58 *Pesiqta deRav Kahana,* appendix 4 (ed. Mandelbaum, 462). Although not completely uncontested, there are scholarly grounds for considering this appendix to be an authentic part of the late antique *Pesiqta deRav Kahana.* See, e.g., H.L. Strack and Günter Stemberger, *Introduction to the Talmud and Midrash* (Minneapolis: Fortress, 1996), 294.

59 See the parallel at Y. *Yebamot* 8:3, 9d (ed. Academy, 871). There R. Haninah the son of R. Abbahu is earlier represented as interpreting Malachi 3:3's "*tzedaqah*" to mean God's doing a kindness which the recipients did not deserve.

60 There are several relevant verses pertaining to "corners of the field," "that which falls during the harvest," and "forgotten sheaf." Leviticus 19:9–10:

> *When you reap the harvest of your land, you shall not reap all the way to the edges of your field, or gather the gleanings of your harvest. You shall not pick your vineyard bare, or gather the fallen fruit of your vineyard; you shall leave them for the poor and the stranger: I the Lord am your God.*

Deuteronomy 24:19: *When you reap the harvest in your field and overlook a sheaf in the field, do not turn back to get it; it shall go to the stranger, the fatherless, and the widow…. Mishnah, Tosefta,* and *Yerushalmi Peah* are *loci classici* for discussions of these laws; relevant material is also found in *Sifra Leviticus* and *Sifre Deuteronomy.* For the poor man's tithe, see Deuteronomy 26:12:

> *When you have set aside in full the tenth part of your yield—in the third year, the year of the tithe—and have given it to the Levite, the stranger, the fatherless, and the widow, that they may eat their fill in your settlements….*

On the poor man's tithe, see Yael Wilfand, "From the School of Shammai to Rabbi Yehuda the Patriarch's Student: The Evolution of the Poor Man's Tithe," *Jewish Studies Quarterly* 22 (2015): 36–61.

61 The Talmud *Bavli* works with a similar legal principle: "money that has no claimants" (B. *Baba Qama* 38b–39a; B. *Hullin* 130b). In *Baba Qama* the principle is deployed to explain why a man is not obligated to pay a fine to a seduced girl who is a *mamzer* or Gentile although he really should have to pay it. While the entirety of the discussion does not concern us, we should note that the suggestion that he pay the amount of the fine to the poor (rather than the girl) is rejected. One ground for rejection is that this money "has no claimants"; a man may put off any poor person who tries to claim it on the grounds that he intended to give it to a different poor person. In other words, no one particular impoverished individual has a claim on the monies.

62 For a related idea, see Gregg Gardner, *Origins of Organized Charity,* 29–32. This said, we will see in Chapter 2 that *Sifre Deuteronomy* 264–265 does in fact link *tzedaqah* to these agricultural gifts.

63 T. *Sanhedrin* 1:4 (ed. Zuckermandel, 415).

64 Y. *Sanhedrin* 2:2, 20a (ed. Academy, 1275–1276). On this see Yael Wilfand, *Poverty, Charity,* 47–48.

65 T. *Sanhedrin* 1:5 (ed. Zuckermandel, 415).

66 Y. *Sanhedrin* 1:1, 18b (ed. Academy, 1264).

67 T. *Peah* 4:18 (ed. Lieberman, 60).

68 B. *Ketubot* 48a, 107a; B. *Baba Qama* 109a; B. *Ketubot* 67a.

69 B. *Baba Qama* 16b.
70 B. *Gittin* 7b.
71 For a recent examination of the transmission of Palestinian learning to Babylonia in the fourth century, see Marcus Mordecai Schwartz, *Rewriting the Talmud: The Fourth-Century Origins of Bavli Rosh Hashanah*, Ph.D. diss., Jewish Theological Seminary of America, 2011; and ibid., "As They Journeyed from the East: the Nahotei of the Fourth Century and the Construction of the Rabbinic Diaspora," *Hebrew Union College Annual* 86 (2015): 63–99.
72 B. *Gittin* 88a identifies this *amora* as Maremar, which is chronologically impossible. B. *Sanhedrin* 38a more sensibly identifies him as "Mari bar Mar," a third-generation Babylonian *amora*.
73 *Pesiqta deRav Kahana* 10:8 (ed. Mandelbaum, 169–171).
74 Y. *Baba Metzia* 6:8, 11a (ed. Academy, 1232).
75 The translation of the verse is my own.
76 Y. *Peah* 1:1, 15b (ed. Academy. 79); y. *Peah* 8:9, 21b (ed. Academy, 112); Y. *Hagigah* 2:1, 77c (ed. Academy, 785).

Bibliography

Primary sources and critical editions

Albeck, Chanoch. 1978. *Shishah Sidre Mishnah: With New Commentary, Introductions, Additions, and Completions.* Tel-Aviv: Dvir

Babylonian Talmud. 1975 (repr.). Vilna-Romm edition with standard commentaries. Jerusalem: n.p.

Finkelstein, Louis. 1969. *Sifre on Deuteronomy.* New York: The Jewish Theological Seminary of America

Horovitz, H.S. 1966. *Siphre D'Be Rab.* Jerusalem: Wahrmann Books

Horovitz, H.S. and I.A. Rabin. 1970. *Mechilta D'Rabbi Ismael.* Jerusalem: Wahrmann Books

Lieberman, Saul. 1955. *The Tosefta: According to Codex Vienna, with Variants from Codex Erfurt, Genizah Mss. And Editio Princeps (Venice 1521). The Order of Zera'im.* New York: The Jewish Theological Seminary of America

Lieberman, Saul. 1962. *The Tosefta: According to Codex Vienna, with Variants from Codex Erfurt, Genizah Mss. And Editio Princeps (Venice 1521). The Order of Mo'ed.* New York: The Jewish Theological Seminary of America

Lieberman, Saul. 1988. *The Tosefta: According to Codex Vienna, with Variants from Codex Erfurt, Ms. Schocken and Editio Princeps (Venice 1521). The Order of Nezikin.* New York: The Jewish Theological Seminary of America

Mandelbaum, Bernard. 1962. *Pesikta de Rav Kahana: According to an Oxford Manuscript; With Variants.* New York: The Jewish Theological Seminary of America

Margulies, Mordecai. 1993. *Midrash Wayyikra Rabbah: A Critical Edition Based on Manuscripts and Genizah Fragments with Variants and Notes.* New York and Jerusalem: The Jewish Theological Seminary of America

Talmud Yerushalmi: According to Ms. Or. 4720 (Scal. 3) of the Leiden University Library With Restorations and Corrections. 2005. Introduction by Yaacov Sussman. Jerusalem: The Academy of the Hebrew Language

Tanakh: *A New Translation of the Holy Scriptures According to the Traditional Hebrew Text.* 1985. Philadelphia, New York, Jerusalem. The Jewish Publication Society

Theodor, Judah and Chanoch Albeck. 1996 (repr.). *Midrash Bereschit Rabbah.* Berlin and Jerusalem: Akademie für die Wissenschaft des Judentums

Zuckermandel, M.S. 1970. *Tosephta: Based on the Erfurt and Vienna Codices.* Jerusalem: Wahrmann Books

Scholarly studies and other contemporary works

Amplifier: The Jewish Giving Circle Movement. Available at: https://amplifiergiving.org/media/resources/Select_Jewish_Texts_on_Giving.pdf

Anderson, Gary A. 2009. *Sin: A History.* New Haven: Yale University Press

Anderson, Gary A. 2013. *Charity: The Place of the Poor in the Biblical Tradition.* New Haven: Yale University Press

Baumgarten, Elisheva. 2014. *Practicing Piety in Medieval Ashkenaz: Men, Women, and Everyday Religious Observance.* Philadelphia: University of Pennsylvania Press

Birnbaum, David and Martin S. Cohen. 2015. *Tikkun Olam: Judaism, Humanism & Transcendence.* New York: New Paradigm Matrix Foundation

Brody, Robert. 2008. "Stam Ha-Talmud v'Divrei Ha-Amoraim." In: Baruch Schwartz, Abraham Melamed and Aharon Shemesh, eds. *Ha-Mikra V'olamo: Sifrut Hazal U-Mishpat Ivri U-Mahshevet Yisrael.* Jerusalem: Ha-iggud Ha-olami Le'mada'ei Hayahadut, pp. 213–232

Cohen, Aryeh. 2013. *Justice in the City: An Argument from the Sources of Rabbinic Judaism.* Boston: Academic Studies Press

"Declaration of Principles" ("The Pittsburgh Platform"). 1885. Available at: www.ccarnet.org

Downs, David J. 2016. *Alms: Charity, Reward, and Atonement in Early Christianity.* Waco: Baylor University Press

Fishman, Joel. 2013. *Jewish Political Studies Review* 25:3–4. Special Issue: Tikkun Olam

Friedman, Shamma. 1978. "'Al Derekh Heker Hasugya." In: H.Z. Dimitrovsky, ed. *Mehkarim U-mekorot I.* New York: Jewish Theological Seminary of America, pp. 283–321 (in Hebrew)

Galinsky, Judah. 2004. "'And It Is for the Glory of the Great That Their Name Be Remembered': Commemorating the Dead and the Practice of Establishing a *Hekdesh* in Christian Spain." *Masechet* 2:113–131 (in Hebrew)

Galinsky, Judah. 2004. "Jewish Charitable Trusts and the Hekdesh Trust in Thirteenth-Century Spain." *Journal of Interdisciplinary History* 33:423–440

Galinsky, Judah. 2005. "Commemoration and Heqdesh in the Jewish Communities of Germany and Spain in the 13th Century." In: Michael Borgolte, ed. *Stiftungen in Christentum, Judentum und Islam vor der Moderne.* Berlin: Akademie, pp. 191–204

Gardner, Gregg E. 2015. *The Origins of Organized Charity in Rabbinic Judaism.* New York and Cambridge: Cambridge University Press

Garrison, Roman. 1993. *Redemptive Almsgiving in Early Christianity.* Sheffield: Sheffield Academic Press

Gray, Alyssa M. 2005. *A Talmud in Exile: The Influence of Yerushalmi Avodah Zarah on the Formation of Bavli Avodah Zarah.* Providence: Brown Judaic Studies

Gray, Alyssa M. 2007. "Amoraim." *Encyclopedia Judaica,* 2nd ed., 2, pp. 89–95

Halivni, David. 2009. *Introduction to "Sources and Traditions": Studies in the Formation of the Talmud.* Jerusalem: Magnes (in Hebrew)

Halivni, David. 2013. *The Formation of the Babylonian Talmud.* Introduced, translated, and annotated by Jeffrey L. Rubenstein. New York and Oxford: Oxford University Press

Halkin, Hillel. 2008. "How Not to Repair the World." *Commentary* 126:1:22–23

Hallamish, Moshe. 2000. *Kabbalah: In Liturgy, Halakhah and Customs.* Ramat-Gan: Bar-Ilan University (in Hebrew)

Hurvitz, Avi. 1987. "Reshitam Ha-Miqra'it shel Munahim Talmudiyyim—Le-Toldot Tzemichato shel Musag Ha-Tzedakah." *Mehkarim be-Lashon* 2–3:155–160

Jacobs, Jill. 2008. *There Shall Be No Needy: Pursuing Social Justice through Jewish Law and Tradition.* Woodstock: Jewish Lights

Juster, Jean. 1914. *Les Juifs Dans L'Empire Romain: Leur Condition Juridique, Économique et Sociale*, vol. 1. Paris: Librairie Paul Geuthner

Kalmin, Richard. 1994. *Sages, Stories, Authors, and Editors in Rabbinic Babylonia.* Atlanta: Scholars Press

Kalmin, Richard. 2006. *Jewish Babylonia between Persia and Roman Palestine.* New York and Oxford: Oxford University Press

Kalmin, Richard. 2014. *Migrating Tales: The Talmud's Narratives and Their Historical Context.* Oakland: University of California Press

Kanarek, Jane L. 2007. "What Does *Tikkun Olam* Actually Mean?" In: Rabbi Or N. Rose, Jo Ellen Green Kaiser and Margie Klein, eds. *Righteous Indignation: A Jewish Call for Justice.* Woodstock: Jewish Lights

Kliksberg, Bernardo. 2003. *Social Justice: A Jewish Perspective.* New York and Jerusalem: Gefen

Kochen, Madeline. 2014. *Organ Donation and the Divine Lien in Talmudic Law.* New York: Cambridge University Press

Kohler, Kaufmann. 1906. "Alms." In: *Jewish Encyclopedia* 1, pp. 435–436

Lieberman, Saul. 1946. "Two Lexical Notes." *Journal of Biblical Literature* 65:67–72

Loewenberg, Frank M. 2001. *From Charity to Social Justice: The Emergence of Communal Institutions for the Support of the Poor in Ancient Judaism.* New Brunswick and London: Transaction Publishers

Mishkan Hanefesh: Mahzor for the Days of Awe; Yom Kippur. 2015. New York: CCAR Press

Neusner, Jacob. 1989. *Making the Classics in Judaism.* Atlanta: Scholars Press

Przybylski, Benno. 1980. *Righteousness in Matthew and his World of Thought.* Cambridge: Cambridge University Press

Rosenthal, Franz. 1950–1951. "Sedaka, Charity." *Hebrew Union College Annual* 23(Part I):411–430

Rosen-Zvi, Ishay. 2017. "Pauline Traditions and the Rabbis: Three Case Studies." *Harvard Theological Review* 110:169–194

Satlow, Michael L. 2010. "'Fruit and the Fruit of Fruit': Charity and Piety among Jews in Late Antique Palestine." *Jewish Quarterly Review* 100:244–277

Schwartz, Marcus Mordecai. 2011. *Rewriting the Talmud: The Fourth-Century Origins of Bavli Rosh Hashanah.* Ph.D. diss. Jewish Theological Seminary of America

Schwartz, Marcus Mordecai. 2015. "As They Journeyed from the East: the Nahotei of the Fourth Century and the Construction of the Rabbinic Diaspora." *Hebrew Union College Annual* 86:63–99

Segal, Eliezer. 2005. "Rabbi Eleazar's *Perutah.*" *The Journal of Religion* 85:25–42

The Shluchim Office. 2004. "Tzedaka: A Coin a Day Keeps the World Spinnin' Round." p. 5

Sorek, Susan. 2010. *Remembered for Good: A Jewish Benefaction System in Ancient Palestine.* Sheffield: Sheffield Phoenix Press

Strack, H.L. and Günter Stemberger. 1996. *Introduction to the Talmud and Midrash.* Minneapolis: Fortress

Sussmann, Yaacov. 1990. "V'Shuv le-Yerushalmi Nezikin." In: Yaacov Sussmann and David Rosenthal, eds. *Mehkerei Talmud: Talmudic Studies I.* Jerusalem: Magnes, pp. 55–133

Ulmer, Rivka and Moshe Ulmer. 2014. *Righteous Giving to the Poor:* Tzedakah *("Charity") in Classical Rabbinic Judaism.* Piscataway: Gorgias

Vidas, Moulie. 2014. *Tradition and the Formation of the Talmud.* Princeton: Princeton University Press

Vorspan, Albert and David Saperstein. 1998. *Jewish Dimensions of Social Justice: Tough Moral Choices of Our Time.* New York: UAHC Press

Weinfeld, Moshe. 1995. *Social Justice in Ancient Israel and in the Ancient Near East.* Jerusalem and Minneapolis: Magnes Press and Fortress Press

Wilfand, Yael. 2014. *Poverty, Charity and the Image of the Poor in Rabbinic Texts from the Land of Israel.* Sheffield: Sheffield Phoenix Press

Wilfand, Yael. 2015. "From the School of Shammai to Rabbi Yehuda the Patriarch's Student: The Evolution of the Poor Man's Tithe." *Jewish Studies Quarterly* 22:36–61

Wilfand Ben-Shalom, Yael. 2017. *The Wheel that Overtakes Everyone: Poverty and Charity in the Eyes of the Sages of the Land of Israel.* Tel Aviv: Hakibbutz Hameuchad (in Hebrew)

Yanklowitz, Shmuly. 2014. *The Soul of Jewish Social Justice.* Jerusalem: Urim

Zion, Noam. 2012. *From Each According to One's Ability: Duties to Poor People from the Bible to the Welfare State and* Tikkun Olam. Cleveland: Zion Holiday Publications

2 God as the true recipient of *tzedaqah*

In his *Mishnat Hakhamim* R. Moses Hagiz (*c*.1671–1750)[1] recounts a story he claims to have heard from "the tellers of truth" and the "elders of that generation of knowledge in the days of the Ari (= R. Isaac Luria), of blessed memory."[2] In Hagiz's version, a Portuguese *converso* and his wife settled in the mystical northern city of Safed. The man's religious zeal was kindled by a homily he heard in the synagogue about the twelve loaves of showbread (literally, the "*lehem ha-panim*," or "bread of the face") that the priests were commanded to set out on a table before God each Sabbath day. According to Pentateuchal law, the loaves would remain on the table for a week, after which the priests would replace them and eat the week-old bread "in the sacred precinct," these loaves being now the property of the priests.[3] The man asked his wife to prepare two loaves on a weekly basis, so that he might offer them before the "*heikhal Adonai*," or "sanctuary of God." Each week the man would bring the loaves and place them before the synagogue ark and pray and beseech God to accept them. The synagogue sexton, a poor man, would take the loaves without wondering how or by whom they were left, and this state of affairs went on for some time.

Eventually the synagogue's rabbi became aware of what the pious *converso* was up to and became enraged at the *converso*'s ascription of gross physicality to the divine. The great kabbalist Isaac Luria sent a messenger to communicate God's wrath at the rabbi's reaction; God was said to have derived great satisfaction from the *converso*'s piety in presenting the weekly bread offering and prayers. The story ends on the note that the rabbi died as a punishment for his reaction, just as Luria had foretold.

This story is a rich storehouse of cultural treasures, notably a notion of misguided *converso* piety[4] and the conflict between the rabbi's rationalist Maimonidean understanding of God and the warmly anthropomorphic image of God that vanquishes it.[5] Tamar Alexander-Frizer points out that the use of bread in the story is likely a deliberate evocation of the sacrament of the Eucharist, part of the *converso* experience in Spain and Portugal.[6] Other versions of the story bear the title "God Loves the Heart"; instead of Sabbath loaves being placed in the synagogue Ark each week, the protagonist places a cooked sheep's heart, a pious action based on a (mis)interpretation of the traditional saying that "God desires the (human) heart" (*rahamana liba ba'ei*).[7] In describing the religious impulse underlying the story, Alexander-Frizer states that it "expresses the wish of the common listeners, who … need unmediated contact with God."[8] Not only then, but "in every age, including today, people have struggled with this abstract notion, which robs them of the living, personal God to whom one can turn and with whom one can speak."[9]

Alexander-Frizer has put her finger on a core feature of the continuing appeal of this story, which is a beloved piece of Jewish folklore. But the story's significance goes beyond the issue of struggle with an abstract notion of the divine. Hagiz's *converso* wishes to serve God as the priests of old had done in the Jerusalem Temple. His excitement upon learning about the showbread is an excitement that he has found a way to worship God, even to offer sacrifice to God, in a way that he knows to be real, unlike, say, the offering of the Eucharist that he left behind in Portugal. What he intends as sacrifice to God becomes (unbeknownst to him for many years) *tzedaqah* for the indigent synagogue sexton. A sacrifice to God became a gift for the poor or, viewed from the opposite end, *tzedaqah for the poor is the very same thing as a sacrifice to God*. Placing the bread in the Ark was not incidental to the drama; placing the bread in the Ark is the way to offer sacrifice to God in a world lacking a Holy Temple in Jerusalem. And again, this sacrifice to God is *tzedaqah*.

This narrative has been transmitted in many versions, and the identity of the simple Jew who leaves the gift for God changes in accord with whatever other cultural issues are at play in the storytellers' environment. Although always portrayed as possessing a simple and naïve faith, the Jew is at times portrayed as a *converso* (as in Hagiz's tale), at times as a synagogue beadle, and at times as a wealthy yet religiously unsophisticated Jew. The gift can be two or twelve loaves of bread, or, again, a heart. At times the simple donor embarks on his gift-giving deliberately, after hearing and misinterpreting a rabbi's sermon; at other times, he does so after putting together scattered ideas filtered through the haze of a doze in the synagogue. There are also narrative variations on the rabbi's reaction and fate: while the versions in *Mishnat Hakhamim* and the early modern Ladino compilation *Me'am Lo'ez* are exceedingly harsh on the rabbi, other, particularly contemporary, versions end on the note that he was forgiven, or else he takes an active role in educating the donor and recipient of the "divine" food about the holy significance of their actions. And as noted, God's own role varies in different versions of the story: whereas in the versions of *Mishnat Hakhamim* and *Me'am Lo'ez* God is pleased with the men's exchange and angry with the rabbi, in other versions, God does not actually appear at all.

Whatever form this story takes, its very existence depends upon the ancient idea—found in both Israelite and Jewish religion, both pre-rabbinic and rabbinic—that *tzedaqah* is literally a gift, a form of sacrifice, to God, with God as its true recipient. In his important study *Charity: The Place of the Poor in the Biblical Tradition* Gary Anderson demonstrates the biblical roots of this idea and its reception in Jewish literature of the Second Temple period, while Peter Brown illuminates aspects of the idea's reception in Christian circles in the late Roman Empire.[10] Anderson also touches on the idea's afterlife in Roman

Catholic teaching and the skepticism and rejection of it in the West in the wake of the emergence first of Protestantism and then Enlightenment philosophy. Peter Brown also notes this Catholic-Protestant disagreement, further pointing out that "[m]odern Catholic authors have been … reserved when confronted with this notion."[11]

Brown's observation that the same reservation is found in "Jewish circles" is accurate but requires greater nuance.[12] This chapter will provide that nuance in relation to two very particular "Jewish circles," the late antique rabbis of Palestine and Babylonia. The analytic journey being long, a brief summary of the findings may be helpful. T. *Megillah* 2:15 is an important exception to what is in fact a mostly untroubled tannaitic acceptance of the idea. *Amoraim* in both rabbinic centers tend toward skepticism and retreat from too close an identification of charity as a gift to God. *Amoraim* display awareness that no one benefits from such a too-close identification: not the living, breathing poor, nor the communities that support them, nor the rabbis themselves. The poor may not benefit because to the extent that *tzedaqah* is seen as donors' gifts to God, it may become entangled in laws governing other gifts to God that may delay its conveyance to them. Communities may not benefit because to the extent that *tzedaqah* is seen as donors' gifts *to* God, the poor may see it as gifts to them *from* God. The poor—especially the well-born and formerly wealthy poor, who retain a sense of personal entitlement based on their erstwhile social status—may then view *tzedaqah* as their due and be heedless of the possible financial burdens on the local communities that collect and provide the support. Finally, *amoraim* in both rabbinic centers portray themselves as active "players" in *tzedaqah* collection and distribution. This portrayal indicates a rabbinic wish to construct themselves as important and indispensable leaders in wider Jewish society. To the extent that *tzedaqah* is identified too closely as a gift to God, the mediating role assigned to God (either directly or as the domain of *heqdesh*, or sacred, dedicated property) has the potential to shift attention away from the importance of the rabbis' mediating role.

God as the mediator between donors and recipients in pre-amoraic sources

M. *Sheqalim* 5:6 and T. *Sheqalim* 2:16 model a triangulated charitable transaction similar to that described colorfully in Hagiz's narrative of the bread in the ark and its many retellings.[13] The *mishnah* opens with the "recollection" that there were two halls in the Temple, one called the "hall of secrets" and the other the "hall of vessels." As to the "hall of secrets" the *mishnah* points out: "Fearers of sin (*yir'ei heit*) would put into it secretly, and poor of good family (*aniyyim b'nei tovim*) would be sustained from it secretly." The *mishnah* describes the hall of vessels as functioning in a parallel manner: whoever wished to donate a vessel to the Temple would deposit it there, and once every thirty days the Temple overseers would examine the contents of the hall. Vessels for which they saw a use would be retained, while others would be sold and the proceeds used for the

Temple's upkeep. The parallel descriptions of the halls of secrets and of vessels show that the *aniyyim b'nei tovim* are the analogue to the Temple, and their sustenance is the analogue to the Temple's upkeep.[14] The well-born poor receive the anonymously deposited gifts, and the anonymous donors are (somehow) relieved of their "fear" of their "sins."

The *Tosefta* contributes the observation that such "halls of secrets" existed in every city, not only the Temple, although precisely where they were located is unspecified. Given the conceptual work the Temple is made to do in M. *Sheqalim* 5:6 as a mediator between donors and the well-born poor, the location of the local halls may well be the synagogue, a local holy place.[15] T. *Sheqalim* 2:16 may therefore be a tannaitic re-presentation of a pre-70 CE phenomenon known from Philo, Josephus, and epigraphic evidence: Diaspora synagogues as repositories of funds, even as way-stations for the storage of Temple tax funds prior to their transfer to Jerusalem. The funds kept at synagogues may well have included charitable funds. Much literary, archaeological, and epigraphic evidence suggests just such a link between charity and synagogues. Beggars were known to ply their trade near synagogues as well as other religious environments, such as Roman temples.[16] Menahem Stern reports that in the latter half of the second century CE, Artemidorus mentioned the synagogue as a place where paupers received support.[17] Excavations at a synagogue at Arbel in northern Israel led investigators to determine that they had found a *quppah*, or basket for the collection of money.[18] An inscription in a fourth-century synagogue at Hammath-Tiberias states that everyone who gives to charity will be blessed, and that the community should continue to make such donations in order to continue to receive divine blessings.[19]

Reading a text's silence is famously ill advised. But T. *Sheqalim* 2:16's silence about whether its local "halls of secrets" are synagogues may be a hint that its tannaitic authors wished to place some distance between the synagogue and *tzedaqah*. This hypothesized rabbinic uncoupling of *tzedaqah* collection and distribution from the synagogue calls out for explanation, given the archaeological evidence just noted and the juxtaposition of religious giving to synagogues and charitable giving in T. *Megillah* 2:13–16 and parallels. One explanation may be that T. *Sheqalim* 2:16's emphasis is different from that of M. *Sheqalim* 5:6. The *mishnah*'s description of the triangulated charitable transaction in the Jerusalem Temple's hall of secrets and its similarity to transactions in the Temple's hall of vessels shows that its interest lies precisely in demonstrating this triangulation: the Temple is the intermediary between donors and well-born poor; the latter get charity and the former are relieved of the fear of their sins. The Toseftan pericope's silence about the location of the local "halls of secrets" suggests that its interest may lie more in emphasizing the *anonymity* of the charitable transaction: what matters is that donors and recipients not interact with each other anywhere, anytime. Susan Sorek supplies a plausible reason for this focus on anonymity: giving to God is an act of piety, and piety requires anonymity. God knows what the donor has done and it is God who will reward her, not other people.[20] This idea was nicely captured a little more than a century before the *Tosefta* in Matthew 6:4, where Jesus explains to his disciples that anonymous giving is a sign of true piety. The anonymous giver has no expectation of worldly reward, and her thus disinterested gift is an act of piety. Piety as the absence of expectation of reward—in this next case, divine reward— is also found in the very different rabbinic context of M. *Avot* 1:3. Antigonos of Socho counsels his audience to be like slaves who serve the Master without expectation of reward. Antigonos's counsel follows immediately upon M. *Avot* 1:2's declaration that the world stands on Torah, Temple service, and reciprocal acts of kindness (*gemilut hasadim*). Without putting too fine a point on it, *Mishnah Avot*'s juxtaposition of acts of kindness and the advice to serve the Master without expectation of reward suggests that the performance of (*inter alia*) such acts of kindness should be without expectation of reward—precisely what anonymous giving to a "hall of secrets" would accomplish.

Nothing like the tannaitic "hall of secrets" appears in the Hebrew Bible. But on the most basic level, the equation of religious giving and provision for the poor found in *Mishnah* and *Tosefta Sheqalim* has biblical roots. Gary Anderson directs our attention to Deuteronomy 12:5's centralization of Israel's worship in *only ... the site that the Lord your God will choose amidst all your tribes as His habitation, to establish His name there* (Deuteronomy 12:5).[21] Tithes are to be brought to this *place where the Lord your God will choose to establish His name* (Deuteronomy 26:2), and the Deuteronomist juxtaposes his discussion of tithes to be brought to priests with the tithe to be separated out in the third year of the seven-year sabbatical cycle for distribution to the *Levite, the stranger, the fatherless, and the widow* (Deuteronomy 26:12–15). Anderson's striking insight is that despite Deuteronomy's repeated insistence on bringing sacrifices and tithes to the central sanctuary, it makes a notable exception for the tithe separated every third year for the Levite, stranger, fatherless, and widow:

> *Every third year you shall bring out the full tithe of your yield of that year, but leave it within your settlements. Then the Levite, who has no hereditary portion as you have, and the stranger, the fatherless, and the widow in your settlements shall come and eat their fill, so that the Lord your God may bless you in all the enterprises you undertake.*
>
> (Deuteronomy 14:28–29)

Like other tithes, this gift to these socially marginalized persons is still a *sacred* gift and is called a *consecrated portion* (Deuteronomy 26:13) by the farmer when he recounts to the priest how he correctly distributed it. Although a consecrated portion, the tithe for the poor was set aside and distributed locally, not at the central place of worship in Jerusalem. Having placed the central sanctuary at a distance, the Deuteronomist brought into being "forms of religious devotion that did not require a temple."[22] One such form was the tithe for the poor. Anderson points out that this construction of giving to the poor as a form of religious giving—indeed, as a form of sacrifice—is found as well in the books of Tobit and Ben Sira. Tobit was distinguished while at home by service at the altar, and while abroad by acts of charity—which the book's author equates.[23] Ben Sira makes clear that charity to the poor was the equivalent of temple sacrifice even while the Temple was still standing.[24]

A major difference between Deuteronomy 14:28–29's tithe for the poor and the gifts left anonymously in M. *Sheqalim* 5:6's "hall of secrets" is that the latter is located in the sacred precincts of the Temple while the former was retained locally in people's homes for distribution. Even T. *Sheqalim* 2:16's "halls of secrets," although local, were outside of people's homes. Nevertheless, Anderson's insight about how the Deuteronomist created a way to express religious devotion at a distance from the central sanctuary may shed additional light on the relationship between the tannaitic pericopes. M. *Sheqalim* 5:6 may be a literary construct expressing the ideal practice—giving to the Temple's hall of secrets—while T. *Sheqalim* 2:16 responds to the loss of M. *Sheqalim* 5:6's idealized Temple by describing a local way to perpetuate that practice.

Charity as a loan made to God

The tannaitic "hall of secrets" is not further discussed in tannaitic or post-tannaitic sources. The notion that *tzedaqah* is somehow given to God, God being the indispensable intermediary between the donor and recipient, takes another form as an application of Proverbs 19:17 (*He who is generous to the poor makes a loan to the Lord; He will repay him his due*). Here the generosity to the poor is not a gift or sacrifice to God, but a loan to him. The verse turns a generous donor into God's creditor, assuring the donor that God will make good on his "debt" to the donor. This is a different (albeit related) model of the relationship between the donor, God, and the recipient. On the model of *tzedaqah* as a gift to God, God is under no obligation to repay the giver. Any repayment to the donor would be God's own expression of *tzedaqah*, righteousness, a gift to the donor to which the latter really has no inherent entitlement. On Proverbs 19:17's model of giving to the poor as a loan to God, however, God—like any other debtor—is indeed obligated to repay the charitable giver.

Gary Anderson has expanded upon the significance and widespread use of Proverbs 19:17 in late antique Christian sources, averring that it is "difficult to exaggerate" the importance of this verse for Judaism, Christianity, and eventually, Islam.[25] But as applied to Judaism this claim requires adjustment. There are likely only two relevant exegeses of Proverbs 19:17 in late antique rabbinic literature. *Leviticus Rabbah* 34:2 brings Proverbs 19:17 together with Proverbs 22:7 (*And the borrower is a slave to the lender*).[26] This juxtaposition suggests the radical idea—to which the *midrash* strongly alludes without stating outright—that God is actually a "slave" to the one who becomes God's creditor by giving to the poor. The Palestinian *amora* R. Yohanan openly expresses astonishment at this combined idea: "What is the meaning of [Proverbs 19:17]? Were the verse not written it would be impossible to say it, as it were the borrower [God] is slave to the lender" (B. *Baba Batra* 10a). R. Yohanan is astonished at the implication that God is like any other debtor, bound to pay back the lender, and hence bound *to* the lender. Yet while R. Yohanan appears to accept that the verse means what it says, there is nothing else either in his statement or the surrounding Talmudic context that points to the verse's being of particular importance to him or others. Even if he accepts the verse's radical implication, his astonishment may at the very least indicate some ambivalence about it. In sum, R. Yohanan's ambivalent take on Proverbs 19:17, taken together with the scant number of references to the verse, suggest that caution is warranted in asserting its importance to the rabbis. *Leviticus Rabbah*'s straightforward acceptance of the radical implications of Proverbs 19:17 is not widely shared in the rabbinic corpus, and certainly not by the *Bavli*.

Vows and *tzedaqah*: amoraic skepticism about a tannaitic certainty

If *tzedaqah* is a gift to God, then it may be dedicated to him by means of a vow like any other gift to God. Moshe Benovitz distinguishes between two sorts of vows in rabbinic literature. A votary can take a "prohibitive vow" to ban the use of specific property "by the votary himself or by another person mentioned in the vow."[27] A "dedicatory vow" is "a promise to devote something or someone to the Temple." The votary "can either devote his property to the Temple outright or *liken* his property to dedicated property with formulae such as '*qorban*' ..."[28] Speaking of such dedicatory vows, Madeline Kochen avers

> The rabbis set in motion a system that preserved the phenomenon entailed in sacrifice with more than just priestly gifts. With the practice of vows in general, and the giving of *tsedakah* in particular, the idea of sacrifice/gifts to God was thought to continue well beyond the destruction of the Temple.[29]

She summarizes: "For the rabbis, every vow is (or is tantamount to) giving a sacrifice or gift to God's domain."[30] As we will see, this very point as applied to *tzedaqah*—fairly unproblematic for the *tannaim*—is problematized by *amoraim* in both rabbinic centers and by the *Bavli* narrator. We will begin our examination of this problematization with *Sifre Deuteronomy*.

Sifre Deuteronomy *264–265 and its Talmudic afterlife*

Sifre Deuteronomy 264–265 is a midrashic elaboration of Deuteronomy 23:22–24:

> *When you make a vow to the Lord your God, do not put off fulfilling it, for the Lord your God will require it of you, and you will have incurred guilt; whereas you incur no guilt if you refrain from vowing. You must fulfill what has crossed your lips and perform what you have voluntarily vowed to the Lord your God, having made the promise with your own mouth.*

The *Sifre* characteristically parses each scriptural phrase.[31] In *pisqa* 264 the first "*to the Lord your God*" is said to refer to "personal valuations,"[32] "dedications," and "*sacra*." "*For the Lord your God*" is said to refer to property "dedicated for the upkeep of the Temple," "*will require it*" refers to "sin-" and "guilt-offerings," and "*of you*" refers to the three principal agricultural gifts for the poor: gleanings, forgotten sheaf, and corners of the field.[33] In *pisqa* 265 the second "*to the Lord your God*" is interpreted the same way as the first was in *pisqa* 264, while "*having made the promise*" refers to property "dedicated for the upkeep of the Temple." Finally, *pisqa* 265 interprets "*with your own mouth*" as a reference to *tzedaqah*. The association of *with your own mouth* and *tzedaqah* reflects an old Palestinian interpretation found in the Aramaic *targum* Pseudo-Jonathan, which says "and [give] charity (*tzidqata*) to the poor as you said with your mouths."[34] The linkage of *tzedaqah* and the "mouth" is understood to imply a *tzedaqah* vow.

In its exegesis of Deuteronomy 23:22–24, the *Sifre* equates the biblical agricultural gifts to the poor and *tzedaqah*. The *Sifre* roots the agricultural gifts in the scriptural phrase "*of you*," which appears in a verse that begins "*When you make a vow*." We have just seen that *tzedaqah* is similarly rooted in "*with your own mouth*," also understood as implying a vow. But nothing in the Pentateuch's commands about the agricultural gifts links them to vows. The obligation to give the agricultural gifts to the poor is triggered upon a successful harvest. Vows seem more properly associated with the voluntary demonstration of righteousness that characterizes *tzedaqah*.[35] But the *Sifre*'s equation of the agricultural gifts and *tzedaqah* reveals a key commonality between the two and between those two and the other sacred gifts: none of the *Sifre*'s examples of religious giving have *both* a fixed amount *and* a fixed obligation to give the gift at a fixed time. "Valuations" have a fixed amount but a person need not ever dedicate his own value. There is no fixed time to offer sin- or guilt-offerings, and one might conceivably choose never to vow to dedicate property to the Temple. *Tzedaqah* is also not fixed in either amount or time. This lack of fixity is true to some extent of the agricultural gifts as well: while there will always be "corners of the fields" to leave for the poor's own harvest, it is unclear how much the corners will yield for them and even how generous the farmer will be in leaving expansive "corners."[36] As to "gleanings" and "forgotten sheaf," it is possible that there will be none at all for the farmer to leave for the poor. This lack of fixity distinguishes all these gifts from (for example) the "poor man's tithe," which is also a biblically mandated agricultural gift to the poor, and *one that is noticeably missing from the Sifre*. The poor man's tithe differs from the other items on the *Sifre*'s list of religious giving because it is both fixed in amount *and* to be given at a fixed time (the third year of every sabbatical cycle). The *Sifre*'s equation of *tzedaqah* and its other listed examples of religious giving thus reveals something important about the tannaitic embrace of the notion that giving to the poor is a gift to God. All these "gifts to God" are *gifts* because all involve an element of human volition: a choice to give or not to give, and/or a choice of whether to give lavishly or stingily.

The *Yerushalmi*'s treatment of its version of the *Sifre* does not mention *tzedaqah* at all.[37] The two *Sifre* passages are treated extensively—and in the same order as they are found in the *Sifre*—on B. *Rosh Hashanah* 4a–4b, which also incorporates relevant material from T. *Arachin* 3:17–18. The latter includes "*tzedaqot*" among a list of *sacra* that once dedicated must be given immediately, although it also presents a number of views on what constitutes tolerable delay in conveyance of the sacred items such that the votary will not violate Deuteronomy 23:22's command *do not put off fulfilling it* (one's vow).

The *Bavli* re-presents the Toseftan list and its views more clearly (and with some differences). We learn in the *Bavli* that: (1) delay may mean a failure to convey the gifts by the time three pilgrimage festivals have elapsed; (2) delay may mean a failure to convey the sacred donations by the time three pilgrimage festivals beginning with the Passover have passed (R. Shimon); (3) delay may mean the passage of (even) one pilgrimage festival (R. Meir); (4) delay may mean the passage of two pilgrimage festivals (R. Eliezer b. Ya'aqov); or (5) delay may mean the passage of the *Sukkot* festival (R. Eliezer b. R. Shimon). The lesson thus far is that like other dedicated items, there is a certain period of tolerable delay in the conveyance of *tzedaqot* (although ideally there should be none). Depending on which interpretation one adopts of *do not put off fulfilling it*, the delay between a votary's dedication of *tzedaqah* and its conveyance to the poor could be very long. Assuming, for example, that one follows the view of R. Shimon, one who dedicates *tzedaqah* right after Passover (the first pilgrimage festival) would not violate *do not put off fulfilling it* until *Shavuot*, *Sukkot*, and the next Passover, *Shavuot*, and *Sukkot* had elapsed—quite a long period of time.

The tannaitic toleration of a delayed conveyance of *tzedaqot* is perhaps odd given that the point of *tzedaqah* is presumably the care of the poor. Tolerance of a delayed conveyance of *tzedaqah* highlights the fact that it really is not at all different from any other gift to God, as to which the same toleration of delay applies. The toleration of delayed conveyance of *tzedaqah* erases the suffering reality of the flesh-and-blood poor by subsuming a *tzedaqah* gift to them to other religious giving and the rules that govern the latter. This particular example of Toseftan erasure of the poor is not unique. T. *Peah* 4:18's colorful account of King Monbaz's "scattering" of his patrimony as *tzedaqah* lacks any mention of the poor, as does T. *Peah* 4:21, which proclaims *tzedaqah* and *gemilut hasadim* to be a "great intercessor" between Israel and their "father in heaven."[38] The conclusion is inescapable that in tannaitic literature, seeing *tzedaqah* as no different from any other gift to God correlates with a tendency to erase the poor. This should not be understood as a lack of sympathy for the poor; tannaitic literature is replete with such concern.[39] But other evidence shows that the *tannaim* do not portray themselves as interacting with the chronically poor, or organizing efforts to relieve chronic poverty.[40] The *tannaim* portray themselves as disconnected from chronic poverty. M. *Peah* 8:5–9's descriptions of the communal *quppah* (fund) and *tamhui* (platter of food collected by donors for distribution) do not mention rabbis. References in tannaitic literature to the undifferentiated *gabbai* ("collector") or specialized *"gabbai quppah"* or *"gabbai tzedaqah"* do not link these communal functions to the rabbis in any way.[41] Lacking such direct engagement in charitable collection and distribution, the *tannaim* could view *tzedaqah* as a sacrifice to God and even allow for a period of delay in the fulfillment of a charity vow without being compelled to confront the practical difficulties for the living, breathing poor that all this might entail.

Moving on in the *Bavli*, B. *Rosh Hashanah* 5b clearly affirms the identity of *tzedaqah* and *heqdesh* (the sacred realm of items dedicated for God's use in the Temple) in its interpretation of Deuteronomy 23:22's *the Lord your God* (B. *Rosh Hashanah* 5b). The *Bavli* interprets *the Lord your God* as "charities (*tzedaqot*), tithes, and firstborn [animals]," rather than the *Sifre*'s "property dedicated for the upkeep of the Temple." The *Bavli* thus sees *tzedaqah* as equivalent to the *Sifre*'s "property dedicated for the upkeep of the Temple." *Tzedaqah* is thus *heqdesh* and, as established on B. *Rosh Hashanah* 4a–4b, this identity means that *tzedaqah*, like *heqdesh*, can bear a certain amount of delay in its conveyance by the votary.

Something changes, however, when the *Bavli* discusses *Sifre Deuteronomy* 265's *"with your own mouth*—this is *tzedaqah*" (B. *Rosh Hashanah* 6a).

1   Rava said: "As to *tzedaqah*, he is liable for [giving] it immediately."
2   What is the reason? Because the poor are right there.
3   This is obvious! What would you have said? [You might have said:] Since this [*with your own mouth*] is written within the topic of sacrifices, [a dilatory *tzedaqah* votary] would not be liable until three festivals had passed, just as with sacrifices. This comes to teach us [that in the case of *tzedaqah*, a person is liable immediately for failing to fulfill his vow]. It is there [in the case of sacrifices] that the Merciful One hangs the matter [of delay] on the festivals. But here, no—because the poor are commonly found.

We will separate Rava's statement (1) from the *Bavli* narrator's commentary on it (2–3). Rava straightforwardly changes the law on the delayed conveyance of *tzedaqah* as it appears in T. *Arachin* 3:17–18 and B. *Rosh Hashanah* 4a–4b and thereby also alters its nature. To be sure, Rava does not deny that *tzedaqah* is like the other sacred conveyances among which it was listed. But Rava drives a wedge between *tzedaqah* and the other dedications by doing away with any tolerable period of delay in its conveyance. Something about the notion of *tzedaqah* as a sacrifice to God is no longer workable for Rava, and a closer look at other Rava charity traditions illuminates why this is so. Rava is strikingly portrayed as the protagonist in a narrative that pits the financial interest of a community against a rigid ideology of seeing charity as a gift to the poor directly from God (B. *Ketubot* 67b):

1   There was one [man] who came before Rava.
2   [Rava] said to him, "On what do you dine?"

3   He said to him, "On a fat chicken and old wine."

4   [Rava] said to him, "And aren't you concerned about the burden on the community?"

5   He said to him, "And am I eating of what is theirs? I am eating of what is God's! As it was taught (Psalm 145:15): *The eyes of all look to You expectantly, and You give them their food in his own time*—this teaches that the Holy Blessed One gives his sustenance to each and every one in his own time."[42]

6   Just then, Rava's sister—whom he had not seen for thirteen years—came, bringing him a fat chicken and old wine.

7   He said, "What is this before us?"

8   [Rava] said to him, "I submit to you, rise up and eat."[43]

This story nicely illustrates the Bavli's ambivalence about too close an identification of charity with religious giving, from the perspective of the local community. Rava and the formerly wealthy poor man stand for distinct perspectives: Rava stands for the perspective that the resources the community uses to support the indigent are in fact its own, and the man stands for the perspective that these resources actually come from God, not the community. The man seems to see the community as an incidental and inconsequential conduit for sustenance that he receives directly from God. Thus the man cleverly dismisses Rava's question about the burden on the community by pointing to Psalm 145:15, which pithily makes the point that God (and not other human beings) is all created beings' real source of support. The verse says that God gives each being its required sustenance *in his own time* and not the community's time; according to the man's interpretation, this makes the community a mere cipher, an escrow account, as it were, for monies passing from God to the needy. A closer look at the formerly wealthy man's position shows that it is a logical development of the notion that *tzedaqah* is a gift to God. If a donor is making a gift *to* God, then a *tzedaqah* recipient is taking the gift *from God*. The fact that the money may be collected and held for distribution by a local community is inconsequential; the money does not belong to the community, but to God, and the community therefore has (or should have) little to no say in its distribution. B. *Ketubot* 67b demonstrates how the poor may press—and possibly even abuse—the idea that *tzedaqah* is a gift to God, to the detriment of the embodied, local community that must actually provide support to the poor.

Notwithstanding Rava's ambivalence and hesitation, he is portrayed as unconditionally surrendering to the poor man.[44] God seems to make his own view of the matter known through the serendipitous arrival after thirteen long years of Rava's long-lost sister, who comes bearing the exact opulent meal the man desired. But note that the source of the meal is Rava's sister—a *private* source—and not the community. The message seems to be that those like the anonymous formerly wealthy poor man can indeed expect to receive from God the lavish food to which they are entitled, but that lavish support may come serendipitously, not necessarily from communal funds. God will provide, but the gift the formerly wealthy poor receive from God may not necessarily be the *tzedaqah* that the community *qua* community collects. Moreover, the *Bavli* contextualizes this story along with another about a formerly wealthy poor man who dies after eating R. Nehemiah's simple food; tellingly, the *Bavli* narrator criticizes R. Nehemiah's interlocutor for having previously pampered himself to such an extent that he could not survive on simple food. The juxtaposition of these stories suggests that, despite Rava's defeat, the *Bavli* does not see Rava's poor man as an entirely unproblematic character.

B. *Ketubot* 67b sheds abundant light on Rava's weakening of the identification of *tzedaqah* with other *heqdesh* on B. *Rosh Hashanah* 6a. While Rava's specific concern in *Ketubot* is the community, and in *Rosh Hashanah* the poor, his overall concern is the same: too close an identification of *tzedaqah* as *heqdesh* is problematic. Rava drives a wedge between *tzedaqah* and *heqdesh* that may redound, depending upon the context, either to the benefit of the poor (*Rosh Hashanah*) or the giving community (*Ketubot*).

Rava's overall portrayal reveals a more intricate pattern of his de-emphasizing the vertical, divine–human aspect of the *tzedaqah* transaction in favor of the horizontal, inter-human aspect. Rava's hard-nosed behavior on B. *Baba Batra* 8b is illustrative: he is said to have "compelled" Rav Natan bar Ami to donate the large sum of 400 *zuz* for *tzedaqah*. In that same context, Rava also praises *tzedaqah* collectors who use aggressive methods in exacting *tzedaqah* from reluctant wealthy givers. Palestinian rabbis may understand *tzedaqah* as a donor's demonstration of righteousness before God by giving to a recipient who lacks a clear moral entitlement to that demonstration, but Rava clearly holds in *Bavli Baba Batra* that the this-worldly goal of ensuring sufficient communal *tzedaqah* funds justifies the employment of this-worldly aggressive tactics.

We now return to the *Bavli* narrator's explanation of Rava on B. *Rosh Hashanah* 6a. The *Bavli* narrator provides a social rationale for a retreat from a complete identification of *tzedaqah* as a sacrifice to God: vows to give *tzedaqah* are different from other vows because the poor are right there and in need of immediate help. Consequently, although the scriptural phrase (*with your own mouth*) that refers to *tzedaqah* is written in the same sacrificial context as other vows and sacred gifts, *tzedaqah* is clearly and critically different. The *Bavli* narrator makes the same point on B. *Ketubot* 106b. M. *Sheqalim* 4:3 is quoted there as part of an extensive discussion of *heqdesh*; the *mishnah*'s topic is what may be done with leftover, unneeded *sheqalim* collected for Temple purposes. R. Aqiva makes the point in the *mishnah* that custodians of either *heqdesh* funds or poor's funds may not conduct financial transactions with them. The *Bavli* narrator in *Ketubot* explains why such transactions may not be conducted with poor's funds: "perhaps a poor person will come up to them, and there will be nothing to give to him."[45] As in B. *Rosh Hashanah* 6a, then, *Bavli Ketubot* at first implicitly equates *heqdesh* and funds for the poor, only to illustrate at the end how they are critically different. In sum, as the *Bavli* narrator concisely puts the matter on B. *Arachin* 6a: *tzedaqah* "is not like *heqdesh*."[46]

Amoraic ambivalence about *tzedaqah* as a gift to God and their self-fashioning as mediators between donors and the poor

The *Bavli* narrator cannot be dated with precision, but the *Bavli* narrator interventions we have been following thus far must be either contemporaneous with or subsequent to Rava. The obvious question is why the views of Rava and the *Bavli* narrator display this observable shift away from the idea that charity is a gift to God. The answer lies (at least partly) in a shift in the portrayals of *tannaim* and *amoraim* in both rabbinic centers vis-à-vis charitable collection and distribution. Unlike *tannaim, amoraim* are portrayed as engaging in charitable collection and distribution. The amoraic interest in serving as and appointing *parnasim* (Palestine) and in serving as charity collectors and distributors (Babylonia) is a notable shift from the tannaitic lack of interest, and likely indicates an amoraic desire to bid for influence in Jewish society outside the narrow circles of rabbis and disciples.[47] Returning to Michel Foucault's notion of "problematization," we may say that this shift makes a "problem" of the notion of charity as a gift to God. Lacking involvement in the communal collection and distribution of charity, the *tannaim* did not need to ponder how the notion of *tzedaqah* as a gift to God might work (or not) in the context of a reality of administering a communal mechanism for providing for the flesh-and-blood poor. *Amoraim* in both rabbinic centers, by contrast, did need to ponder that complexity. Moreover, for the *amoraim,* we may hypothesize that too strong an assertion that *tzedaqah* is a gift to God could undermine their efforts to portray *themselves* as indispensable to its collection and distribution. In order for the *amoraim*'s role in *tzedaqah* collection and distribution to be useful in their self-fashioning as important players in Jewish society, the importance of their mediating role in *tzedaqah* requires enhancement and a perception of God's unmediated involvement requires reduction.

The shift from tannaitic lack of involvement in communal charitable collection and distribution to amoraic involvement is readily demonstrated. In Palestine, R. Ya'aqov b. Idi and R. Yitzhaq b. Nahman are described as *parnasim,* communal officials with some responsibility for social welfare.[48] R. Berechiah is portrayed as taking up a collection for the support of a hapless Babylonian *mamzer* (offspring of an illicit union).[49] R. Haggai and R. Yose are also described as appointing certain unnamed people as *parnasim.*[50] The former is even portrayed as encouraging his appointees to see their role as *parnasim* in religious terms, quoting to them from Proverbs 8:15: *Through me* (Torah) *kings reign and rulers decree just laws.* Other examples of *amoraim* playing such a role include R. Imi, who is portrayed as having authority over the collection and disposition of charity in Sepphoris[51] and R. Hinena b. Papa, described in *Yerushalmi Sheqalim* as "distributing the *mitzvah.*"[52] One reason Palestinian *amoraim* may have embraced a role in charity collection and distribution may have been its utility in helping them spread their particular approach to Torah among non-rabbinic Jews.[53] *Genesis Rabbah* 49:4, which we examined in

Chapter 1, is suggestive. Recall that Abraham would invite his guests to bless God after their meal using the quasi-rabbinic formula "Blessed be the God of the world of whose bounty we have eaten." *Genesis Rabbah* illustrates how *tzedaqah* can be a means through which rabbinic Torah can be propagated among non-rabbinic Jews. Abraham's food is the bait, while rabbinic Torah (exemplified by Proverbs 8:15) is what is really on the menu.

In the *Bavli*, the Babylonian *amoraim* Rav Huna, Rav Yosef, Rabbah (all of whom precede Rava), Ravina, and Rav Ashi (who follow him) are unambiguously portrayed as collectors and distributors of *tzedaqah*. Rava's own portrayal is somewhat ambiguous, although he does appear on B. *Ketubot* 67b to be a sort of mediator between the community and the formerly wealthy poor man analogous to the Temple (M. *Sheqalim* 5:6).[54] Although that story ends with Rava's unconditional surrender, the *Bavli* does not erase his concerns about the poor man's view that his sustenance comes directly from God. The notion that *tzedaqah* is a gift to (and from) God thus persists in Babylonian rabbinic culture yet is problematic; it is a view held by some—notably the poor, who clearly benefit from it—but one that may be troubling to and inconsistent with the interests of others, especially the local community. Rava's singular importance in the *Bavli* renders him a most useful *amora* for the *Bavli* to deploy in thinking about this tension.

Rav Yosef is also portrayed as such a mediator in the previous amoraic generation; before attending to his portrayal, we must briefly examine the *Yerushalmi* source on which it is based. The *Yerushalmi* ponders M. *Ma'aser Sheni* 5:9, in which Rabban Gamliel declares that a tithe he will in future measure out will be given to Aqiva ben Yosef, who will give it to the poor.[55] The anonymous *Yerushalmi* asks how R. Aqiva could take possession of the tithe (since he was wealthy), and the answer given is that the transaction described in the *mishnah* took place *before* he acquired his wealth. Another anonymous interpolation posits that R. Aqiva could even have accepted the tithe after he became wealthy because he was the *parnas* and "the hand of the *parnas* is like the hand of the poor." That is, the *parnas* is like the poor's agent, so that whatever comes into his hands for the benefit of the poor enters the poor's possession immediately.[56] Rav Yosef is constructed on the model of R. Aqiva on B. *Baba Qama* 36b. He is said to have adjudicated a case in which a man was awarded a half-*zuz*. The man initially declared his willingness that the paltry amount be given to the poor, but then changed his mind. Rav Yosef declared that the half-*zuz* must go to the poor, since they already became entitled to it when the man first said they should get it. Even though no poor people were present, Rav Yosef claimed authorization to accept the half-*zuz* on their behalf, because "we—we are the hand of the poor" ("*anan—yad aniyyim anan*").

Rav Yosef's application of the "*yad aniyyim*" principle is critically different from the *Yerushalmi*'s. The *Yerushalmi*'s "*yad aniyyim*" explains the direct transfer of a freely given (although obligatory) tithe for the poor through the charity collector/distributor. Rav Yosef broadens the application of "*yad aniyyim*" beyond the tithing context in order to secure *other* monies for the poor that might otherwise have been lost to them through an *unwilling* donor's change of heart. Rav Yosef's authoritarian bent on behalf of the poor is demonstrably characteristic of other Babylonian *amoraim*. We earlier pointed out that Rava "compelled" R. Natan bar Ami, taking 400 *zuz* from him for *tzedaqah*. Rav Huna, of the previous amoraic generation, is described as "imposing" (*ramah*) *tzedaqah* on his and Rav Hana bar Hanilai's townspeople.[57] Rabbah imposed a condition on his townspeople that he could give charity to whatever poor person—local or not—he found deserving (B. *Baba Batra* 9a). Elsewhere Rabbah is said to have "imposed" (*rama*) charity on the orphans of the house of Bar Meryon despite a *baraita*'s disallowance of such an imposition (B. *Baba Batra* 8a). Rav Ashi later took Rabbah's position to an extreme, asserting that he had a free hand to act as he saw fit with the local charity purse, even without imposing a condition on the townspeople (B. *Baba Batra* 9a).

Babylonian *amoraim* thus "impose" and "compel" *tzedaqah*. This construction has the effect of turning them all into local Babylonian embodiments of the "halls of secrets" of M. *Sheqalim* 5:6 and T. *Sheqalim* 2:16. *Tzedaqah* is or should be given to them (whether willingly or under duress) and they, in turn, distribute it to the poor. Too strong an ideational emphasis on *tzedaqah* as *heqdesh*, on *tzedaqah* as a gift directly to God and to the poor directly from God, could crowd out their role and undermine this aspect of their self-fashioning. The less *tzedaqah* is associated directly with *heqdesh* and the more it is associated directly with the Babylonian *amoraim*, the more they can use it to build their religious and social capital in their local communities.[58]

Religious giving to synagogues and religious giving as charity: more evidence of amoraic reticence about *tzedaqah* as a sacrifice to God

T. *Megillah* 2:13, 14, and 16 discuss fashioning, dedicating, or preparing items for synagogues, while 2:15 discusses *tzedaqah*.[59] The juxtaposition of these topics is (by now) unsurprising, but what deserves close attention is the common vocabulary and literary structure used for these various dedications. Paragraph 13 states that once the "High One" uses a chest or cloth covers that have been "made" for him (or it), these items can no longer be used for non-sacred purposes (literally, for a "layperson," or *hedyot*). "High One" (*gavoha*) refers to God, or, more generally, to a sacred purpose, notably use in and by the Temple. Similarly, paragraph 16 bookends this contrast between *gavoha* and *hedyot* by its ruling about a "sacred vessel" (*kli gavoha*) which may be used for a non-sacred purpose (*hedyot*) so long as it has not yet been used for its intended sacred purpose. Paragraph 15, referring to *tzedaqah*, rules similarly that one who stipulates (*poseq*) a *tzedaqah* amount may change the use of the money so long as the charity collectors (*parnasin*) have not yet "merited" (*zakhu*) it, that is, come into possession of it. If they have done so, then their knowledge and consent is required before the hypothetical donor can change the use of the money.

Paragraph 15's *tzedaqah* is thus constructed similarly to the other items described as being dedicated for synagogue or Temple use in paragraphs 13 and 16. The role played by paragraph 15's *parnasin* is structurally similar to the *gavoha* of paragraphs 13 and 16, and to the synagogue of paragraph 16. Finally, paragraph 15's use of the trilateral Hebrew root *p-s-q* to refer to a donor's stipulating a *tzedaqah* amount is the structural equivalent of paragraph 13's "making" of items for synagogues, and paragraph 16's "dedicating" (*hiqdish*) such items.[60] But the *Tosefta* highlights a critical difference between the dedication of *tzedaqah* and of other items for a sacred purpose. In T. *Megillah* 2:15, the donor may change the purpose of the dedicated monies even when the *parnasin* have acquired them, provided they know and consent to that change. T. *Megillah* 2:15's ruling is strikingly realistic, dealing with the very same subject that gave pause to both Rava and the *Bavli* narrator in *Ketubot* and *Rosh Hashanah*: communal collection and distribution of *tzedaqah*. To T. *Megillah* 2:15 *tzedaqah* both is and is not like other sacred dedications: its embodied, social context may bend, deflect, or in other ways alter its (undoubted) sacred character.

Both Talmuds re-present and analyze parts of T. *Megillah* 2:13–16. Y. *Megillah* 3:1, 74a appears to be a Palestinian amoraic elaboration of T. *Megillah* 2:15–16.[61] The *Yerushalmi* recounts that R. Hiyyah bar Ba "went to Hamatz and they [unspecified donors] gave him coins to distribute to widows and orphans. He went out and distributed them to the rabbis." The passage presents different views about R. Hiyyah bar Ba's unilateral decision to switch recipients, the question being whether he was obligated to make good on that amount to the widows and orphans. The *Yerushalmi* passage ends with a series of amoraic tradents transmitting a tradition similar to part of T. *Megillah* 2:15: as long as (presumably *tzedaqah*) monies have not been given to the *gizbarin* (treasurers), the purpose for which they were given may be changed. "*Gizbar*" refers to the Temple treasurer, and the *Yerushalmi*'s use of this term in place of the *Tosefta*'s "*parnasin*" is itself noteworthy. What is even more noteworthy is how R. Hiyyah bar Ba changes the purpose for which he was given the monies, and how the *Yerushalmi* implicitly sees what he did as consistent with the law on changing the purpose of dedicated monies. Presumably R. Hiyyah bar Ba was not himself the *gizbar*; whether or not he was, the *Yerushalmi*'s attitude toward his action might allow for even more leeway in handling charity monies than the *Tosefta* allows, especially when the support of rabbis is at issue. And, significantly, by discussing R. Hiyyah bar Ba's distribution of the charity to rabbis instead of widows and orphans in the context of an explicit discussion of *tzedaqah*, the *Yerushalmi* indicates that giving to rabbis—whether or not they are described as materially poor—is, in a sense, *tzedaqah*.[62] Put differently, the *Yerushalmi* does not privilege *tzedaqah* to the materially poor over *tzedaqah* to rabbis, whether materially poor or not; the *Yerushalmi* portrays a complex balancing of different types of giving in which giving to the poor, the rabbis, and even the Temple (represented by the "*gizbar*") blend one into the other.[63]

Like Y. *Megillah* 3:1, 74a, B. *Arachin* 5b–6b also appears to be a commentary of sorts on T. *Megillah* 2:15–16. This extended passage moves from the topics of (dedications to the) Temple, dedications to the synagogue, and then to *tzedaqah*. Specifically, the passage opens with discussion of Gentiles' contributing to the upkeep of the Temple (based on Ezra 4:3), moves into Gentiles' offerings of *terumah* for the priests, then their dedications of items for the upkeep of synagogues, and finally, toward the bottom of 6a, a discussion (not limited to Gentiles) of dedicating *tzedaqah*. This progression demonstrates the *Bavli*'s disinclination (not unlike *Yerushalmi Megillah*) to draw hard and fast distinctions between donating to the Temple, donating to the synagogue, and donating to *tzedaqah*. But after building up this equivalence, the *Bavli* draws a clear distinction between *tzedaqah* and *heqdesh*. The *Bavli* observes that *tzedaqah* resembles vows in that a delay in fulfilling the vow will violate Deuteronomy 23:22 (*do not put off fulfilling it*) but is not like *heqdesh* in that *tzedaqah* may be used for a non-sacred purpose. As we have already pointed out, the *Bavli* narrator clearly and concisely observes on B. *Arachin* 6a "*tzedaqah* is not like *heqdesh*." *Bavli Arachin* illustrates this point (6b) with the example of R. Yannai, who would engage in financial transactions with *tzedaqah* monies he had collected, notwithstanding T. *Megillah* 2:15's rule that this cannot be done once the money comes into the hands of the "*gabbai*." The *Bavli* justifies R. Yannai's action on the ground that the poor were amenable to it; they accepted his action because the delay caused by his use of the funds resulted eventually in the availability of even more funds for their support. But there is more. Rava, as interpreted by the *Bavli* narrator (B. *Rosh Hashanah* 6a), had insisted that *tzedaqah* had to be conveyed to the poor immediately, unlike other sacred dedications as to which there is a period of tolerable delay. R. Yannai's story illustrates that, *contra* Rava, there *is* tolerable delay in the conveyance of *tzedaqah* to the poor; that tolerable delay is not based on the principles governing *heqdesh* and is tolerable only if the poor are amenable to it and the delay redounds to their benefit. The *Bavli*'s portrayal of R. Yannai's social welfare role is thus not in principle inconsistent with Rava. Moreover, it is highly significant that the *Bavli*'s separation of *tzedaqah* from *heqdesh* in *Bavli Arachin* is made in the concrete context of a story about R. Yannai's providing for the living, breathing, poor. The point is clear: too close an association of *tzedaqah* with *heqdesh* and too consistent an application to *tzedaqah* of the laws associated with *heqdesh* can be detrimental to the poor. But this point raises a question: if *tzedaqah* is not *heqdesh*, what do we make of the link between *tzedaqah* and the law of vows? What then is a *tzedaqah* vow?

Ambivalence about charity as a gift to God and the ambiguous nature of the charity vow

The discernible amoraic unwillingness to affirm robustly and without equivocation that charity is a gift to God leaves fingerprints on their understanding of votive dedications of money as *tzedaqah*. If *tzedaqah* is not necessarily understood to be a gift to God in the full sense of the term, then the *tzedaqah* vow—despite its dedicatory formula—is not quite a votive dedication, but something a bit different. Tracing that bit of difference discloses another aspect of amoraic ambivalence about the idea that charity is a gift to God.

In tannaitic literature the trilateral root *p-s-q* clearly means a votive dedication equal in force and gravity to other votive dedications. For example, in T. *Megillah* 2:15, *p-s-q* as applied to *tzedaqah* is the equivalent of T. *Megillah* 2:16's "*hiqdish*" ("dedicated") as applied to dedicating a beam for use in synagogue construction. *P-s-q* is thus a votive dedication of *tzedaqah*, one that makes it *heqdesh*. The *Tosefta*'s equation of "*p-s-q*" with sacred dedications is borne out by archaeological evidence of inscriptions from Beth Alfa and Isifyah, in which "*pasaq*" refers to a person's making a vow.[64]

Given the votive context of "*p-s-q*," the tannaitic and Palestinian amoraic linkage of this activity to the sacred space of the synagogue is unsurprising. Rabban Shimon ben Gamliel rules that one may not stipulate ("*posqin*") *tzedaqah* for the poor in the synagogue on the Sabbath (T. *Shabbat* 16:22).[65] The linkage of this votive activity to the public space of the synagogue creates a slippage between "*p-s-q*" as denoting an individual votive activity and as denoting a more public activity of pledging *tzedaqah*, something more akin to fundraising. We also see this slippage in *Leviticus Rabbah* 32:7, the story of how R. Berechiah was approached by a Babylonian *mamzer* for whom he arranged a "*pesiqa b'tzibbura*" (a public stipulation and collection) in the synagogue the following day.

Palestinian rabbinic sources display distress over those who "*p-s-q*" *tzedaqah* but fail to make good on their pledge, with a suggestive terminological difference between tannaitic and amoraic sources. The *Tosefta* declares that confiscation of Jewish homes by Rome will be a consequence of those who *posqin tzedaqah v'ein notnin* (stipulate *tzedaqah* and do not give it).[66] The *Yerushalmi* cautions that drought will result from this failure, which it describes as the failure to give on the part of those who *posqei* (or *posqin*) *tzedaqah b'rabim*, those who stipulate *tzedaqah publicly* but fail to give it. The *Yerushalmi* specifically points out that drought will result from the failure to fulfill *tzedaqah* pledges made *b'rabim*, in *public*.[67] Palestinian sources in the *Bavli* also refer to a failure to give *tzedaqah* that was dedicated *b'rabim*, in public.[68]

Two points emerge from these sources. The first is that the many references to punishments for failures to fulfill the pledges show that these "votive dedications" were not always taken seriously by those making them, and Palestinian rabbis were somewhat at a loss for what to do about that. Those engaging in the votive activity described by the root *p-s-q* did not necessarily see their stipulations of *tzedaqah* as full-fledged vows requiring fulfillment. The second point is that Palestinian amoraic literature states clearly that failure to fulfill pledges made *in public* will lead to dire consequences; presumably failure to fulfill votive pledges made *privately* will not lead to such consequences. The amoraic emphasis on "public" implies a change from a tannaitic perspective that failure to fulfill *any* pledges, whether public or private, will lead to these dire consequences. The difference perhaps reflects Palestinian amoraic abandonment of any attempt to regulate private votive dedications of *tzedaqah* and resignation to the possibility that individuals might well not fulfill vows undertaken in private. The *amoraim* limit themselves instead to predicting dire public consequences for failure to fulfill publicly undertaken votive commitments—commitments that can be witnessed and are widely known to have been undertaken. But as the need for any sort of promise of dire consequences shows, Palestinian *amoraim* were disturbed by failures to fulfill even those public commitments.

Leviticus Rabbah 16:5 is another case in point.[69] R. Yehoshua ben Levi says that one who fails to make good on a public *tzedaqah* pledge violates Ecclesiastes 5:5 (*Don't let your mouth bring you into disfavor*). Later in that same pericope R. Mani interprets Ecclesiastes 5:5 as referring to vows (*nedarim*), but *Leviticus Rabbah* does not bring R. Mani's interpretation together with the public *tzedaqah* pledge described by R. Yehoshua ben Levi. *Leviticus Rabbah*'s distinction between the institutions of the public *tzedaqah* pledge and vows ("*nedarim*") generates ambiguity about whether the negligent *tzedaqah* pledge-maker has indeed committed the serious religious infraction of failing to fulfill a *vow*. This ambiguity may be another example of the hypothesized tacit rabbinic response to the ubiquity of failures to fulfill these pledges and the *amoraim's* consequent legal concern not to create a large class of unintentional vow-breakers.

The case of *p-s-q* illustrates interplay between non-rabbis' behavior and rabbis' response to that behavior. Notwithstanding the inherited understanding, discernible in both material and rabbinic literary culture, that undertakings described by *p-s-q* are votive in nature, the rabbis are aware that people do not always fulfill those undertakings. Perhaps anxious not to create a large class of vow-breakers, the *amoraim* ignore failures to fulfill privately made *tzedaqah* votive stipulations and suffice with pointing out the dangerous consequences for the public of failing to fulfill publicly announced stipulations. Non-rabbis may have taken the first step in driving this particular wedge between *tzedaqah* and other votive dedications, but the rabbis' reaction widens it: Palestinian *amoraim* see the failure to fulfill such a vow as sinful, as one that may lead to dire personal and societal consequences, and yet they do not stigmatize it as a violation of Deuteronomy 23:22.

The Hebrew root "*p-s-q*" is attributed exclusively to Palestinian sages in the *Bavli*; no Babylonian sage or non-rabbi is described as dedicating *tzedaqah* using the root *p-s-q*. Nevertheless, there is evidence of a change in the Babylonian rabbis' own understanding of the votive *tzedaqah* pledge. B. *Nedarim* 6b–7a discusses short-form votive formulae called *yadot* (literally, "hands"). The relevant part of the passage begins with Rav Papa's question about whether there is "*yad*" for corners of the field. That is, should a farmer designate a given field in its entirety as "corners of the field" and then say "and this" about a second field, what is the law? Is the second field also to be considered "corners of the field" or not? After discussion of this question the *Bavli* narrator moves on to ask the same question about *tzedaqah*. Should a person have declared that a certain coin was *tzedaqah* and then declared "and this" about another, is the latter dedicated for *tzedaqah* or not? After some more discussion the *Bavli* narrator also asks the same question about *hefqer* (declaring property to be ownerless) and *beit ha-kissei* (declaring a spot to be a privy). *Hefqer* and privies are certainly not *heqdesh*—notwithstanding the inclusion of these designations within the law of vows—and their presence on a list that begins with corners of the field and *tzedaqah* strongly suggests that vows to dedicate these do not necessarily create *heqdesh* either. Put another way, the *Bavli* retains enough of the tannaitic and pre-rabbinic identification of *tzedaqah* as a gift to God to maintain the institution of the *tzedaqah* vow, but the *tzedaqah* vow is now subtly different. Not really a vow that dedicates a gift to God, the *tzedaqah* vow formula now seems to invoke the Temple realm in order to create a binding expression of an irrevocable obligation to donate the designated (and dedicated) property as *tzedaqah*. In brief, the *tzedaqah* vow seems to be reconstructed as a solemn, binding promise, but it is something other than a votive dedication of a gift to God. This would also seem to be an implication of B. *Arachin* 6a, which maintains *tzedaqah*'s inclusion in the category of vows, while explicitly removing it from that of *heqdesh*. Whatever the *tzedaqah* vow is, it is a very serious acceptance of obligation, but one that does not necessarily create *heqdesh*.[70]

Conclusion

Tannaitic literature by and large straightforwardly represents *tzedaqah* as a gift to God. *Amoraim* of both centers do not reject the old linkage of *tzedaqah* and religious giving *tout court* (with the exception of B. *Arachin* 6a), but they challenge and complicate it. These challenges take three forms in the *Bavli*: (1) concern about the burden on the community that may come from the (well-born) poor's pressing the notion that the bountiful *tzedaqah* to which they are legally entitled comes directly from God and not the community (B. *Ketubot* 67b); (2) awareness that too literal an application of the "*tzedaqah* as *heqdesh*" metaphor might lead to a *tzedaqah* regimen too inflexible to assist the poor (B. *Rosh Hashanah* 6a; B. *Arachin* 6a, b); and (3) contextualizing the votive *tzedaqah* formula among other examples of "dedications" of items that could not possibly have been dedicated to the Jerusalem Temple (B. *Nedarim* 6b–7a).

Palestinian rabbis, both *tannaim* and *amoraim*, were aware that people did not always fulfill vows to give *tzedaqah*. Such behavior indicates a tacit rejection on the part of people outside the rabbinic circle of the notion that *tzedaqah* pledged by a votive means is a gift made to God. *Amoraim* limit their predictions of dire consequences for failure to fulfill those pledges to those that were made in public, thereby tacitly conceding both that public pledges were not being fulfilled and their own resignation to the futility of issuing any warnings about failures to fulfill privately made pledges. Factoring in the *Bavli*'s contribution to this issue as well, we see that votive undertakings to give *tzedaqah* subtly change: these undertakings may perhaps continue to be understood as serious, even irrevocable undertakings, but they definitely lack the full force of the law of vows.

Amoraim in both centers—but more noticeably in Babylonia—break the link between *tzedaqah* and religious giving in order to deploy *tzedaqah* as a vehicle for discursive constructions of their own authority. The *tzedaqah*-collecting and distributing Babylonian *amora* occupies the position occupied by the "hall(s) of secrets" in M. *Sheqalim* 5:6 and T. *Sheqalim* 2:16. Structurally, the Babylonian *amora* is the *heqdesh* realm, mediating between donors and recipients who are unknown to one another. Should *tzedaqah* remain too firmly linked to *heqdesh*, it would be difficult for the rabbis to make the case for their own indispensability to its collection and distribution, and for their own social importance and religious indispensability.

But why should people give *tzedaqah*, whether individually or to funds collected and distributed by rabbis? What is the reward for their demonstrations of righteousness, what can they "buy" with their accumulated merits? It is to a consideration of the changing representations of *tzedaqah*'s role in atonement and its rewards in rabbinic literature that we now turn.

Notes

1 Moses Hagiz (1672–1751) was born in Jerusalem and educated by his grandfather, the well-known scholar Moses Galante. Hagiz himself became known for his passionate opposition to Sabbateanism and his conflict with the Sabbatean Nehemiah Hayon. He published *Mishnat Hakhamim*, his major work, in 1733. According to Elisheva Carlebach, the purpose of the work was to deal with what Hagiz reasonably saw as the two major crises of Jewish faith of the day: Sabbateanism and Marranism. See Elisheva Carlebach, *The Pursuit of Heresy: R. Moses Hagiz and the Sabbatean Controversies* (New York: Columbia University Press, 1990), 257 and *passim*.

2 According to Dan Ben-Amos, this story "has been in print since the eighteenth century." See Dan Ben-Amos, *Folktales of the Jews: Tales from the Sephardic Dispersion* (2 vols.; Philadelphia: Jewish Publication Society, 2006), 1:209. While a similar story appears in a fifteenth-century Ashkenazic manuscript (prior to the 1492 expulsion from Spain), it first appears in print in Hagiz's *Mishnat Hakhamim* (1733), and then in the Ladino compilation *Me'am Lo'ez*. Thanks largely to *Me'am Lo'ez* the story was of particular importance in the Sefardic diaspora. See also Tamar Alexander-Frizer, *The Heart is a Mirror: The Sephardic Folktale* (Detroit: Wayne State University Press, 2008), 258–271, esp. 264.

3 See Exodus 25:30; Leviticus 24:5–9.

4 Living between two worlds and encountering Judaism the religion through written sources, without a connection to a Jewish community, some *conversos* had a rather fraught relationship with their ancestral faith. See, e.g., Yosef Kaplan, *From Christianity to Judaism: The Story of Isaac Orobio de Castro* (Portland: The Littman Library of Jewish Civilization, 2004); and José Faur, *In the Shadow of History: Jews and Conversos at the Dawn of Modernity* (Albany: State University of New York Press, 1992) (notably Faur's treatment of Uriel da Costa).

5 As part of the rabbi's rant, he is said to point out that God *"ein lo d'mut ha-guf v'eino guf"* ("has no bodily likeness and is not a body"), a phrase found in the thirteenth-century hymn known as *"Yigdal,"* composed by Daniel ben Judah of Rome based on Maimonides' so-called "thirteen principles" of belief. The literature on Maimonides' thirteen principles is vast. See, e.g., Admiel Kosman, "Maimonides' Thirteen Principles in his *Commentary on the Mishnah*, in *Yigdal*, and in *Ani ma'amin*," in Itamar Warhaftig, editor, *Minchah L'ish* (Jerusalem, 1991), 337–348 (in Hebrew); Menahem Kellner, *Must a Jew Believe Anything?* (London: Littman Library of Jewish Civilization, 1999).

6 See Tamar Alexander-Frizer, *The Heart is a Mirror*, 267.
7 This is the version published by Dan Ben-Amos. See also Tamar Alexander-Frizer, *The Heart is a Mirror*, 259–260.
8 Tamar Alexander-Frizer, ibid., 262.
9 Ibid.
10 Gary Anderson, *Charity*; see also Peter Brown, *The Ransom of the Soul: Afterlife and Wealth in Early Western Christianity* (Cambridge and London: Harvard University Press, 2015).
11 Peter Brown, *Ransom of the Soul*, 28.
12 Anderson calls attention to Protestant polemics against the idea that charity is a gift made to God, one that also may result in the forgiveness of sin, even entering the lists himself to contend against too strict an application to charity of Immanuel Kant's notion that no act is moral if motivated in any way by self-interest. See Gary Anderson, *Charity*, 6–11, 66–69. Brown has noted the absence of discussion about charity as a gift to God in some contemporary Jewish treatments of charity. See Peter Brown, *Ransom of the Soul*, 28–29. Contemporary treatments of *tzedaqah* as a gift to God in scholarship on Jewish religious culture include Madeline Kochen, "'It Was Not for Naught that They Called It *Hekdesh*': Divine Ownership and the Medieval Charitable Foundation," in Joseph Fleishman, editor, *Jewish Law Association Studies* XVIII (2008): 131–142; and ibid., *Organ Donation and the Divine Lien in Talmudic Law*, 60–177. In addition to Kochen, legal and social historians of medieval Judaism have also paid closer attention to the legal and ideational manifestations of linkages between *tzedaqah* and God. See, e.g., the studies listed in Chapter 1, n. 5).
13 On these two tannaitic pericopae, see, e.g., Gregg Gardner, *Origins of Organized Charity*, 16–19, 152; Yael Wilfand, *Poverty, Charity*, 133, 160; Susan Sorek, *Remembered for Good*, 219–220. Sorek's discussion suffers from a tendency to assume that these texts transparently reflect social history. Gardner more reasonably points out that these passages are tannaitic constructions that shed light more on their attitudes than on social history. We will examine these pericopes for what they reveal about the tannaitic representation of redemptive almsgiving in Chapter 3. M. *Sheqalim* 5:6 and T. *Sheqalim* 2:16 (ed. Lieberman, 211), along with *Sifre Deuteronomy* 117 (ed. Finkelstein, 176), which alludes to M. *Sheqalim* 5:6, are—to the best of my knowledge—the only references in late antique rabbinic literature to the "hall of secrets."
14 On changing attitudes in classical rabbinic literature to the "well-born poor" as well as other formerly wealthy poor (whether or not well-born), see my "The Formerly-Wealthy Poor: From Empathy to Ambivalence in Rabbinic Literature of Late Antiquity," *Association for Jewish Studies Review* 33:1 (2009): 101–133. Tannaitic literature demonstrates empathy toward these poor, and amoraic literature is largely (although not entirely) characterized by ambivalence toward them.
15 Gregg Gardner claims that T. *Sheqalim* 2:16 is an allusion to the *quppah*, or communal fund. See Gregg Gardner, *Origins of Organized Charity*, 152. Susan Sorek points out that Philo and Josephus both identified Diaspora synagogues as repositories of funds, most notably the Temple tax; it was stored in the synagogue prior to its transfer to Jerusalem. See Susan Sorek, *Remembered for Good*, 65 and n. 12. This reality may underlay T. *Sheqalim* 2:16's representation of a local "hall of secrets."
16 See Gregg Gardner, *Origins of Organized Charity*, 5 and n. 25.
17 See Yael Wilfand, *Poverty, Charity*, 277.
18 See Susan Sorek, *Remembered for Good*, 65, citing Z. Ilan, *Ancient Synagogues in Israel* (Tel-Aviv: Ministry of Defence, 1991), 116–119.
19 Z. Ilan, ibid., 112; see also M. Dothan, *Hammath Tiberias: Early Synagogues and the Hellenistic and Roman Remains. Final Excavation Report 1* (Jerusalem: Israel Exploration Society, 1983), 53.
20 Susan Sorek, *Remembered for Good*, 157.
21 See Gary Anderson, *Charity*, 26–28.

22 Ibid., 28.
23 Ibid., 20.
24 Ibid., 21.
25 Ibid., 30 and n. 18. Anderson relies in this discussion on a passage found in David Zvi Hoffmann's 1908 *Midrash Tannaim zum Deuteronomium*. Hoffmann produced the text he called "*Midrash Tannaim*" by extracting from a Yemenite compilation named *Midrash HaGadol* all the material that seemed in his scholarly judgment to be authentically tannaitic. More recent scholarship demonstrates that the materials in *Midrash Tannaim* cannot be unproblematically assumed to be authentically tannaitic. For a thorough and careful analysis, see M. Bar-Asher Siegal, "Parashat Ma'aserot in the Mechilta le-Devarim" (M.A. thesis; Hebrew University, 2006), *passim* (in Hebrew).
26 *Leviticus Rabbah* 34:2 (ed. Margulies, 774–775).
27 Moshe Benovitz, *Kol Nidre: Studies in the Development of Rabbinic Votive Institutions* (Atlanta: Scholars Press, 1998), 3.
28 Ibid. On pp. 123–124, Benovitz explains how the prohibitive vow "*konam*" could "paradoxically" (as he puts it) turn into a donation to charity. The details need not concern us; what is of interest is Benovitz's recognition of the link between vows and charity.
29 Madeline Kochen, *Organ Donation*, 120.
30 Ibid., 123.
31 *Sifre Deuteronomy* 264–265 (ed. Finkelstein, 285–286). On *Sifre Deuteronomy*, see, e.g., Steven D. Fraade, *From Tradition to Commentary: Torah and its Interpretation in the Midrash Sifre to Deuteronomy* (Albany: State University of New York Press, 1991), and relevant essays in ibid., *Legal Fictions: Studies of Law and Narrative in the Discursive Worlds of Ancient Jewish Sectarians and Sages* (Supplements to the *Journal for the Study of Judaism* 147; Leiden and Boston: Brill, 2011).
32 See Leviticus 27:1–9. The reference is to a person's vowing to give to the Temple an amount of money equal to the Torah's set valuation of what such a human being is worth; for example, a male Israelite between the ages of twenty and sixty has a valuation of fifty shekels while an Israelite woman is valued at thirty shekels. This is the topic of *Mishnah*, *Tosefta*, and *Bavli Arachin*.
33 See Leviticus 19:9–10; Leviticus 23:22; Deuteronomy 24:19–22.
34 On Targum Pseudo-Jonathan, see, e.g., Paul V.M. Flesher and Bruce D. Chilton, *The Targums: A Critical Introduction* (Leiden and Boston: Brill, 2011).
35 Yet there is a link between the agricultural gifts, vows, and charity. Taking "corners of the field" as an example, the rabbis do discuss in *Mishnah* and *Tosefta Peah* how big a "corner" should be. There is thus a degree of discretion left to the farmer, who can choose either to meet a minimal legal standard or be more generous. This discretion lessens the gap between charity and the agricultural gifts.
36 See M. *Peah* 1:1–2. Although "corners of the field" is said not to have any limit (1:1), the very next *mishnah* acknowledges that all goes according to the size of the field, the number of the poor, and the field's yield. The farmer may not leave less than one-sixtieth of his field's yield as "corners of the field" (1:2).
37 Y. *Rosh Hashanah* 1:1, 56a–56c (ed. Academy, 659–662). See Madeline Kochen, *Organ Donation*, 126 n. 17.
38 See the discussion of T. *Peah* 4:18 (ed. Lieberman, 60) in Chapter 1; further discussion of it and T. *Peah* 4:21 (ed. Lieberman, 61) are found in Chapters 3 and 4.
39 See, e.g., T. *Megillah* 1:4 (ed. Lieberman, 344); T. *Niddah* 9:17 (ed. Zuckermandel, 651–652); Gregg Gardner, *Origins of Organized Charity*, 83 (on the importance to the *tannaim* of protecting the poor from the "indignity of begging").
40 I emphasize "chronic poverty" because the *tannaim* are noticeably empathetic toward the shame-faced "formerly wealthy poor." See my "The Formerly-Wealthy Poor" as well as the further discussion of this point in Chapter 3.

41 For earlier discussions of this point, see Alyssa M. Gray, "Redemptive Almsgiving and the Rabbis of Late Antiquity," *Jewish Studies Quarterly* 18:2 (2011): 153–154; ibid., "The Formerly-Wealthy Poor": 121–122. As to the *gabbai* in his various guises see, e.g., M. *Demai* 3:1; M. *Qiddushin* 4:5; T. *Peah* 4:15 (ed. Lieberman, 59); T. *Demai* 3:16, 17 (ed. Lieberman, 77); T. *Baba Qama* 11:6 (ed. Lieberman, 59); T. *Baba Metzia* 3:9 (ed. Lieberman, 74); T. *Baba Batra* 10:5 (ed. Lieberman, 164); *Sifre Deuteronomy* 47 (ed. Finkelstein, 106). What literary evidence there is of tannaitic social welfare leadership is found exclusively in Palestinian amoraic compilations. See also Shaye J.D. Cohen, "The Rabbi in Second-Century Jewish Society," in William Horbury, W.D. Davies, and John Sturdy, *The Cambridge History of Judaism, Vol. 3* (Cambridge: Cambridge University Press, 1999), 935; Gregg Gardner, *Origins of Organized Charity*, 185–192.

42 I have altered the JPS translation's *when it is due* to *in his own time* in the interest of the unfolding analysis.

43 B. *Ketubot* 67b. For another reading of this story see my "The Formerly-Wealthy Poor": 125–126.

44 Rava apologizes using the phrase "*ne'eneti lakh*" ("I humble myself"). This phrase also indicates a rabbi's complete capitulation to another person in its three other occurrences: Y. *Ta'anit* 4:1, 67d (ed. Academy, 727); B. *Berachot* 28a, and B. *Ta'anit* 20b.

45 This rationale is clearly that of the *Bavli* narrator; it is not found in *Mishnah Sheqalim* and is in Aramaic, a sure sign of its being an addendum to the view of R. Aqiva.

46 Although the "poor man's tithe" (*ma'aser ani*) is not *tzedaqah*, it is also noteworthy that the *Bavli* narrator applies the principle "one who would take money from his fellow must bring proof" to a situation of doubt as to whether that tithe had been appropriately separated (B. *Yoma* 9a). This is significant because the poor man's tithe is then considered by the *Bavli* narrator to be, in some sense, a (mere) matter of money, not entirely the *consecrated portion* it is styled in Deuteronomy 26:13. If doubts about this tithe are to be adjudicated using a principle common in the adjudication of monetary cases, then one may presume that doubts about *tzedaqah*, which Gregg Gardner describes as "an obligation for a non-poor individual to give—not a right for the poor to receive" should be similarly adjudicated and *tzedaqah* similarly considered to be a matter of money, not a gift to God. On the distinction between the poor man's tithe and *tzedaqah* and for the quote, see Gregg Gardner, *Origins of Organized Charity*, 31–32.

47 Gregg Gardner has made this point about the Palestinian *amoraim* specifically. See Gregg Gardner, *Origins of Organized Charity*, 185–192.

48 Y. *Peah* 8:9, 21b (ed. Academy, 112). On the role and institution of the *parnas*, see Steven Fraade, "Local Jewish Leadership in Roman Palestine: The Case of the *Parnas* in Early Rabbinic Sources in Light of Extra-Rabbinic Evidence," in ibid., *Legal Fictions*, 555–576; Gregg Gardner, *Origins of Organized Charity*, 158–163 and *passim*.

49 *Leviticus Rabbah* 32:7 (ed. Margulies, 752–753). See Deuteronomy 23:3: *No one misbegotten ("mamzer") shall be admitted into the congregation of the Lord; none of his descendants, even in the tenth generation, shall be admitted into the congregation of the Lord.* The Pentateuch does not define the "*mamzer*." Tannaitic literature defines this individual as one born of a union between a man and a woman who legally cannot enter into the marital tie of "*qiddushin*" ("betrothal") due to their consanguinity or because the woman is already legally married to another man (see, e.g., M. *Qiddushin* 3:12). The offspring of this forbidden union is consequently a social outsider, and that vulnerable status is undoubtedly what underlies this *mamzer*'s need for material support.

50 Y. *Peah* 8:7, 21a (ed. Academy, 111).

51 Y. *Megillah* 3:2, 74a (ed. Academy, 764).

52 Y. *Sheqalim* 5:6, 49b (ed. Academy, 622).

53 See Gregg E. Gardner's pertinent observations in *Origins of Organized Charity*, 180–194. Gardner also recognizes the Palestinian amoraic shift in portraying their active involvement in the collection and distribution of charity.

54 See, e.g., B. *Megillah* 27a–27b (Rav Huna); B. *Baba Batra* 8a–8b (Rav Yosef);
   B. *Baba Batra* 8b–9a (Rabbah); B. *Baba Batra* 8b; B. *Ketubot* 67b (Rava); B. *Baba
   Qama* 119a (Ravina); B. *Baba Batra* 9a (Rav Ashi).
55 Y. *Peah* 4:9, 18c (ed. Academy, 97).
56 On the *parnas*, see n. 48. Although the named sages in this passage are both *tannaim*,
   the discussion of *parnas* is a tip-off that the passage reflects an amoraic, not a tannaitic, context. No confirmed tannaitic source describes a *tanna* as having been a
   parnas. Apropos, note that M. *Ma'aser Sheni* 5:9 itself does not specify Aqiva's role;
   the anonymous *Yerushalmi* identifies him as a *parnas*. R. Aqiva, together with R.
   Eliezer, is also described as a *parnas* on Y. *Peah* 8:7, 21a (ed. Academy, 111). The
   Yerushalmi's interest in describing leading *tannaim* as *parnasim* reflects a change in
   the rabbinic (amoraic) perspective on rabbis' undertaking the *parnas* role.
57 See Y. *Megillah* 3:2, 74a (ed. Academy, 764) and its parallel on B. *Megillah* 27a–27b.
58 We will examine another crucial aspect of Babylonian amoraic self-fashioning
   vis-à-vis *tzedaqah* on B. *Baba Batra* 10a–10b in Chapter 4.
59 T. *Megillah* 2:13–16 (ed. Lieberman, 351–352).
60 See Michael Sokoloff, *A Dictionary of Jewish Palestinian Aramaic: Third Revised
   and Expanded Edition* (Ramat-Gan: Bar-Ilan University Press, 2017), 499, for the
   definition of "*p-s-q*" as "to make a charitable pledge."
61 Y. *Megillah* 3:1, 74a (ed. Academy, 764).
62 Gregg Gardner also understands the *amoraim* to have expanded the definition of
   "*tzedaqah*" to include gifts to rabbis, not only the poor. See Gregg Gardner, *Origins
   of Organized Charity*, 32 and n. 116.
63 Apropos, Y. *Megillah* 3:2, 74a (ed. Academy, 764) goes on right away to discuss,
   inter alia, the emperor "Antolinus's" donation of a *menorah* to a synagogue. Again,
   the juxtaposition of charity for the poor, the (re)distribution of that charity to rabbis,
   and synagogue dedications, marks all of these as somehow conceptually equivalent.
64 See L. Robert, *Nouvelles inscriptions de Sardes* (Paris: A Maisonneuve, 1964), 39,
   nos. 3, 5, cited in Susan Sorek, *Remembered for Good*, 117 and n. 26. Sorek discusses
   the reference to "*pasaq*" in the Isyfiah inscription further on p. 143.
65 T. *Shabbat* 16:22 (ed. Lieberman, 79–80).
66 T. *Sukkah* 2:5 (ed. Lieberman, 262).
67 Like T. *Sukkah* 2:5, a reference to "public" is also missing from Rabban Shimon ben
   Gamliel's ruling in T. *Shabbat* 16:22 that *tzedaqah* is not to be dedicated to the poor
   on the Sabbath in the synagogue.
68 See Y. *Ta'anit* 3:3, 66c (ed. Academy, 719) and parallels, including B. *Ta'anit* 8b and
   B. *Yebamot* 78b. Indeed, rabbinic compilations in both centers are filled with sources
   that condemn those who fail to fulfill public *tzedaqah* pledges. In addition to the
   sources cited, see, e.g., Y. *Qiddushin* 4:1, 65b (ed. Academy, 1179); Y. *Sanhedrin*
   6:7, 23d (ed. Academy, 1294); B. *Sukkah* 29a–29b.
69 *Leviticus Rabbah* 16:5 (ed. Margulies, 356–360).
70 See also B. *Baba Batra* 148b. There we find a question about a person lying on his
   death bed who either dedicated (*hiqdish*), declared ownerless (*hifqir*) or distributed as
   tzedaqah to the poor all of his possessions, whereupon he recovered and survived. Is
   he permitted to revoke his dedication, declaration, or *tzedaqah*? Note the Bavli's
   equation of these three; ultimately, the question is declared to be unresolved (*teyqu*).

Bibliography

Primary sources, critical editions, and dictionaries

Albeck, Chanoch. 1978. *Shishah Sidre Mishnah: With New Commentary, Introductions,
   Additions, and Completions.* Tel-Aviv: Dvir

Babylonian Talmud. 1975 (repr.). Vilna-Romm edition with standard commentaries. Jerusalem: n.p.

Finkelstein, Louis. 1969. *Sifre on Deuteronomy.* New York: The Jewish Theological Seminary of America

Lieberman, Saul. 1955. *The Tosefta: According to Codex Vienna, with Variants from Codex Erfurt, Genizah Mss. And Editio Princeps (Venice 1521). The Order of Zera'im.* New York: The Jewish Theological Seminary of America

Lieberman, Saul. 1962. *The Tosefta: According to Codex Vienna, with Variants from Codex Erfurt, Genizah Mss. And Editio Princeps (Venice 1521). The Order of Mo'ed.* New York: The Jewish Theological Seminary of America

Lieberman, Saul. 1988. *The Tosefta: According to Codex Vienna, with Variants from Codex Erfurt, Ms. Schocken and Editio Princeps (Venice 1521). The Order of Nezikin.* New York: The Jewish Theological Seminary of America

Margulies, Mordecai. 1993. *Midrash Wayyikra Rabbah: A Critical Edition Based on Manuscripts and Genizah Fragments with Variants and Notes.* New York and Jerusalem: The Jewish Theological Seminary of America

Sokoloff, Michael. 2017. *A Dictionary of Jewish Palestinian Aramaic: Third Revised and Expanded Edition.* Ramat-Gan: Bar-Ilan University Press

Talmud Yerushalmi: According to Ms. Or. 4720 (Scal. 3) of the Leiden University Library with Restorations and Corrections. 2005. Introduction by Yaacov Sussman. Jerusalem: The Academy of the Hebrew Language

Tanakh: *A New Translation of the Holy Scriptures According to the Traditional Hebrew Text.* 1985. Philadelphia, New York, Jerusalem. The Jewish Publication Society

Zuckermandel, M.S. 1970. *Tosephta: Based on the Erfurt and Vienna Codices.* Jerusalem: Wahrmann Books

Scholarly studies

Alexander-Frizer, Tamar. 2008. *The Heart is a Mirror: The Sephardic Folktale.* Detroit: Wayne State University Press

Anderson, Gary A. 2013. *Charity: The Place of the Poor in the Biblical Tradition.* New Haven: Yale University Press

Bar-Asher Siegal, M. 2006. "Parashat Ma'aserot in the Mechilta le-Devarim." M.A. thesis. Hebrew University (in Hebrew)

Ben-Amos, Dan. 2006. *Folktales of the Jews: Tales from the Sephardic Dispersion,* 2 vols. Philadelphia: Jewish Publication Society

Benovitz, Moshe. 1998. *Kol Nidre: Studies in the Development of Rabbinic Votive Institutions.* Atlanta: Scholars Press

Brown, Peter. 2015. *The Ransom of the Soul: Afterlife and Wealth in Early Western Christianity.* Cambridge and London: Harvard University Press

Carlebach, Elisheva. 1990. *The Pursuit of Heresy: R. Moses Hagiz and the Sabbatean Controversies.* New York: Columbia University Press

Cohen, Shaye J.D. 1999. "The Rabbi in Second-Century Jewish Society." In: William Horbury, W.D. Davies, and John Sturdy, eds. *The Cambridge History of Judaism,* vol. 3. Cambridge: Cambridge University Press, pp. 922–990

Dothan, M. 1983. *Hammath Tiberias: Early Synagogues and the Hellenistic and Roman Remains. Final Excavation Report 1.* Jerusalem: Israel Exploration Society

Faur, José. 1992. *In the Shadow of History: Jews and Conversos at the Dawn of Modernity.* Albany: State University of New York Press

Flesher, Paul V.M. and Bruce D. Chilton. 2011. *The Targums: A Critical Introduction.* Leiden and Boston: Brill

Fraade, Steven D. 1991. *From Tradition to Commentary: Torah and its Interpretation in the Midrash Sifre to Deuteronomy.* Albany: State University of New York Press

Fraade, Steven D. 2011. *Legal Fictions: Studies of Law and Narrative in the Discursive Worlds of Ancient Jewish Sectarians and Sages.* Supplements to the *Journal for the Study of Judaism* 147. Leiden and Boston: Brill

Fraade, Steven D. 2011. "Local Jewish Leadership in Roman Palestine: The Case of the *Parnas* in Early Rabbinic Sources in Light of Extra-Rabbinic Evidence." In: *Legal Fictions: Studies of Law and Narrative in the Discursive Worlds of Ancient Jewish Sectarians and Sages* Supplements to the *Journal for the Study of Judaism* 147. Leiden and Boston: Brill, pp. 555–576

Gardner, Gregg E. 2015. *The Origins of Organized Charity in Rabbinic Judaism.* New York and Cambridge: Cambridge University Press

Gray, Alyssa M. 2009. "The Formerly-Wealthy Poor: From Empathy to Ambivalence in Rabbinic Literature of Late Antiquity." *Association for Jewish Studies Review* 33:101–133

Gray, Alyssa M. 2011. "Redemptive Almsgiving and the Rabbis of Late Antiquity." *Jewish Studies Quarterly* 18:144–184

Ilan, Z. 1991. *Ancient Synagogues in Israel.* Tel-Aviv: Ministry of Defence

Kaplan, Yosef. 2004. *From Christianity to Judaism: The Story of Isaac Orobio de Castro* Portland: The Littman Library of Jewish Civilization

Kellner, Menahem. 1999. *Must a Jew Believe Anything?* London: Littman Library of Jewish Civilization

Kochen, Madeline. 2008. " 'It Was Not for Naught that They Called It *Hekdesh*': Divine Ownership and the Medieval Charitable Foundation." In: Joseph Fleishman, ed. *Jewish Law Association Studies* XVIII:131–142

Kochen, Madeline. 2014. *Organ Donation and the Divine Lien in Talmudic Law.* New York: Cambridge University Press

Kosman, Admiel. 1991. "Maimonides' Thirteen Principles in his *Commentary on the Mishnah*, in *Yigdal*, and in *Ani ma'amin*." In: Itamar Warhaftig, ed. *Minchah L'ish.* Jerusalem: n.p., pp. 337–348 (in Hebrew)

Sorek, Susan. 2010. *Remembered for Good: A Jewish Benefaction System in Ancient Palestine.* Sheffield: Sheffield Phoenix Press

Wilfand, Yael. 2014. *Poverty, Charity and the Image of the Poor in Rabbinic Texts from the Land of Israel.* Sheffield: Sheffield Phoenix Press

3 Redemptive almsgiving and charity's rewards in the land of Israel

Overview

In a brief essay entitled "The Politics and Ethics of Street Tzedakah," Letty Cottin Pogrebin describes her transformation from conscience-stricken assessor of the sincerity of charity supplicants on the streets of New York to open-handed giver. Pogrebin credits this change to her being inspired by a fellow congregant at Manhattan's Congregation B'nai Jeshurun, who saw homeless people as God's way of calling out to him; his response—open-handed giving—was his way, in turn, of responding "*hineni*," "here I am," the fundamental biblical declaration of readiness to act at the summons of God or other human beings.[1] Pogrebin closes by remarking on the minimal impact practicing this "unwavering street *tzedakah*" has had on her finances, and highlighting how it yields her dividends in another, more profound way:

> Practicing this minimal but unwavering street
> *tzedakah* has had a relatively small impact on my
> cash outflow, but it has returned to me a thousand
> blessings—literally. When I give, I almost always get
> three words back. Not "Here I am," but "God bless you."[2]

Knowingly or not, Pogrebin taps in these two sentences into the ancient notion "redemptive almsgiving," the idea that giving to the poor is a particularly efficacious way of obtaining God's favor, notably, the expunging, scrubbing, forgiveness, and atonement of and for sins and the donor's accumulation of heavenly merits. The prayerful "God bless you" of those to whom she gives echoes some related ancient and medieval Jewish and Christian portrayals of the poor praying for their benefactors, to the latter's spiritual benefit. Redemptive almsgiving is the first and largest of this chapter's topics. Tannaitic literature represents charity straightforwardly as a way to remit sins and accrue heavenly merits. Palestinian amoraic literature perpetuates this idea but differs from tannaitic literature in its new thematic emphasis on charity's power to rescue a donor from death or guarantee him a longer life (whether in this world or the next). These consequences of charity are not at all unrelated to the remitting of sin (the punishment for which can be death or a shortened life), but the amoraic emphasis on longer life and rescue from death is notably distinct.

Moving on from redemptive almsgiving, tannaitic literature identifies involuntary loss of wealth as a consequence of sin (or divine displeasure generally). This idea is unrelated to redemptive almsgiving, but Palestinian amoraic literature spins a gossamer strand of connection between them by its representation that an involuntary loss of wealth may expunge sin, or even substitute for a death penalty at the hand of heaven. Loss of wealth is even represented in one Palestinian amoraic source as a critical feature of a charitable strategy: one can preemptively donate as charity property one is already fated to lose, and thereby earn religious merit.

Tannaitic literature also hints at this-worldly rewards for religious giving. M. *Peah* 1:1 famously teaches that *gemilut hasadim* earns the doer unspecified "fruits" in this world; R. Aqiva also ambiguously teaches (M. *Avot* 3:13) "tithes are a fence to wealth." Palestinian amoraic literature expands on charity's this-worldly rewards, notably charity's consequence of securing or even augmenting donors' wealth. This chapter will close with an examination of the relationship between these various heavenly and earthly consequences of charity and changing tannaitic and amoraic constructions of the image of the chronically poor and their own roles vis-à-vis donors and the poor.

A brief survey of redemptive almsgiving outside of rabbinic literature

The rabbis most certainly do not invent redemptive almsgiving. Early attestations of redemptive almsgiving are found in a late stratum of the Hebrew Bible and in Jewish literature of the Second Temple period.[3] Daniel 4:24 (LXX 4:27)'s advice to *Redeem your sins by beneficence and your iniquities by generosity to the poor; then your serenity may be extended* seems to be one.[4] Gary Anderson has examined redemptive almsgiving's further development in the apocryphal books of Tobit and Ben Sira.[5] The point is made in Tobit (*inter alia*) that "charity will save a man from death; it will expiate any sin" (Tobit 12:9). Roman Garrison points out Ben Sira's straightforward expression of redemptive almsgiving: just as "water extinguishes a blazing fire, so does charity atone for sin" (Ben Sira 3:30).[6]

New Testament passages in Luke and Acts also became key foundations of late antique Christian redemptive almsgiving. Jesus states (Luke 11:41): *So give for alms those things that are within; and see, everything will be clean for you.*[7] Both Garrison and Anderson call attention to the story of the angel's call to the Roman centurion Cornelius in Acts 10:1–4:

At Caesarea there was a man named Cornelius...
He was a devout man who feared God ... he gave alms generously to the people and prayed.... One afternoon at about three o'clock he had a vision in which he clearly saw an angel of God coming in and saying to him,

"Cornelius..." "He answered, "Your ... alms have ascended as a memorial before God..." He said, "Cornelius, your prayer has been heard and your alms have been remembered before God."

Cornelius's alms—like his prayers—are a form of service "remembered" by God, a "heavenly investment."[8]

The second-century *Didache* establishes redemptive almsgiving as the social core of Christian almsgiving: *If the labor of your hands has been productive, your giving will be a ransom for sins ... share all your possessions with your brother, and do not claim that anything is your own.*[9] A related notion, well known from both the New Testament and Second Temple literature, is that giving alms on earth stocks a donor's treasury of heavenly merits. In the middle of the Sermon on the Mount, Matthew's Jesus states (Matthew 6:19–21):

Do not store up for yourselves treasures on earth,
where moth and rust consume and where
thieves break in and steal; but store up for yourselves treasures in heaven,
where neither moth nor rust consumes, and where thieves do not break in
and steal.
For where your treasure is, there your heart will
be also.

Luke's Jesus likewise teaches (Luke 12:33–34):

Sell your possessions, and give alms. Make purses for
yourselves that do not wear out, an unfailing treasure
in heaven, where no thief comes near and no
moth destroys. For where your treasure is, there your heart
will be also.

Helen Rhee traces the further elaboration of the notion that charitable giving piles up treasure in heaven (what she terms the "dualism" of heavenly and earthly riches) into the *Shepherd of Hermas* (first-second centuries), Cyprian's *On Works and Alms* (third century), the *Acts of Thomas* (third century), and Lactantius's *Divine Institutes* (fourth century).[10]

Roman Garrison has argued that redemptive almsgiving can also be effective in easing social tensions. The poor receive the charity they need to live, the wealthy receive salvation, and the result is social peace.[11] Helen Rhee likewise observes: "as the rich meet the material needs of the poor through alms, the poor ... intercede for the salvation of the rich."[12] Peter Brown has similarly pointed out that Christian writers' and preachers' emphasis on redemptive almsgiving calls the attention of both rich and poor to their common sinfulness; the rich consequently cannot see themselves as special or superior to the poor.[13] John Chrysostom (fourth century) would quite agree; thundering to the wealthy auditors among his audience in *Homily XVII* to 2 Corinthians he proclaims that "if there were no poor, the greater part of our salvation would be overthrown, in that we should not have where to bestow our wealth."[14] Helen Rhee draws on colorful imagery from the *Shepherd of Hermas* in highlighting the theological partnership redemptive almsgiving creates between donors and recipients: "[t]he elm and the vine, representing the rich and the poor, bear much fruit only when they are attached to each other and function together, not on their own."[15]

This partnership between rich and poor leads to an unsurprising conceptual development: as redemptive almsgiving grows in importance in the fourth and fifth centuries, the charitable exchange comes increasingly to be described in terms of gift exchange. The poor's acceptance of charity and prayer on the donor's behalf is a "gift" to the donor (who thereby earns the redemptive benefit).[16] "Promoters" of redemptive almsgiving in these centuries "all but universally advanced the view" that almsgiving would redeem post-baptismal sins[17] and, as Peter Brown has observed, "poor now flooded the churches."[18] The fourth-century intertwining of redemptive almsgiving's soteriological and social consequences is also evidenced by Brown's observation that Christian almsgiving preaching at this time (by Augustine and others) was about more than inspiring the wealthy to toss a few coins to the poor; the point was to overturn the inherited Greco-Roman notion of civic euergetism. Christian preachers and writers turned from euergetism toward a Christian social–religious ethic according to which the most important social division is not that between the citizens of one's own city and outsiders, but that between rich and poor. The "faceless mass of the poor," not simply one's fellow citizens, are to be favored as beneficiaries of donors' largesse.[19] In sum, redemptive almsgiving binds together the rich and poor in mutually beneficial ties of reciprocity; the poor need the material support, and the rich need the salvation.[20]

Spiritual dignity through the preaching of redemptive almsgiving could come at the expense of recognizing (let alone alleviating) the poor's embodied, suffering, human reality. Susan R. Holman describes how the poor could be characterized in third-century and even later Christian writing and preaching as merely a means to the end of redemption from sin for their donors:

> The recipients of alms are essentially symbols, their
> bodies representing holy containers by which the
> *donor* may be lifted up to God. The poor are thus
> rendered with a profound, if inert, liturgical
> identity.[21]

Susan Holman's description of the poor as "holy containers by which the *donor* may be lifted up to God" aptly describes the ringing rhetoric of Clement of Alexandria (third century) as quoted by Richard Finn:

> Use your money to acquire bodyguards like these
> [= the poor] to protect you body and soul ... people
> through whom a sinking ship is buoyed up, steered

> only by the prayers of the saints ... and through whom
> the attacking robbers are disarmed, stripped of their
> weapons by devout prayers; people through whom the
> violence of the demons is smashed ...[22]

Other Christian writers, by contrast, were quite aware that the living, breathing poor might not embody the lofty spiritual qualities of "saints." Pointing to Origen as well as Clement of Alexandria himself, Helen Rhee identifies their awareness that mere poverty alone does not make for an exalted spiritual state: how the poor choose to endure their poverty—be it with prayerful acceptance or rebellion and anger—is a factor that helps determine whether they might indeed be "blessed and beloved of God."[23]

The recent surge in scholarship on redemptive almsgiving in the Hebrew Bible, Second Temple literature, and late antique Christianity is at least partly responsible for increased attention to its presence in late antique rabbinic literature and beyond.[24] There are undeniable similarities between Christian and rabbinic redemptive almsgiving discourses, but also some critical differences. Unlike some Christian writers and theologians, Palestinian rabbis do not assign redemptive almsgiving religious and ideational pride of place; the idea is scantily attested in tannaitic and amoraic literature. There are subtle changes in its representation between the tannaitic and amoraic periods, and redemptive almsgiving coexists in both periods with the simultaneously developing concept of *teshuvah* ("repentance") which is constructed as a, if not the, preferred rabbinic way to atone for sin.[25] We will now follow into Palestinian rabbinic literature four fruitful themes highlighted in our brief survey of redemptive almsgiving outside of that literature: (1) charity atones for sin, (2) charity funds a heavenly bank of merits, (3) redemptive almsgiving creates a partnership between rich and poor, and (4) redemptive almsgiving may have a bearing on how the poor are portrayed.

Redemptive almsgiving in tannaitic literature[26]

Charity relieves the burden of sin and stocks a bank of heavenly merits

Tannaitic references to redemptive almsgiving are few: M. *Sheqalim* 5:6; *Mekhilta de-Rabbi Ishmael* (*Mishpatim*; *Neziqin* 10); T. *Peah* 4:18; and T. *Peah* 4:21.[27] Chapter 2 introduced M. *Sheqalim* 5:6, which describes the so-called "hall of secrets" and "hall of vessels" in the Jerusalem Temple. The "fearers of sin" ("*yir'ei heit*") would make deposits into the hall of secrets, and *aniyyim b'nei tovim* (poor of good family) would be supported by what they would secretly take from it.[28] It was pointed out earlier that calling donors to the hall of secrets "fearers of sin" implies that their giving (or their giving in this surreptitious fashion) somehow relieves them of their "fear" of their "sins"—but how? M. *Sheqalim* 5:6's vague formulation leaves unclear both what "sin" the *yir'ei heit* "fear" and how their generosity relieves that fear. Reading the passage on its own terms may yield an answer: the *yir'ei heit*'s "fear" is of unspecified "sin" in general (not any specific transgression), and their secret giving somehow mitigates that sin, thereby alleviating their "fear."[29] In a word, M. *Sheqalim* 5:6's "*yir'ei heit*" may be an allusion—however opaque—to redemptive almsgiving.

The following passage from the *Mekhilta de-Rabbi Ishmael* more clearly illustrates charity's sin-effacing power.[30]

R. Yishmael says,

> Come and see the mercy of the One Who spoke and the world came into being on flesh and blood. For a human being can acquire himself by money from the hands of heaven, as it says (Exodus 30:12) *When you take a census of the Israelite people according to their enrollment, each shall pay the Lord a ransom* (*kofer*) *for himself*, and it says (II Kings 12:5) *any money a man may pay as the money equivalent of persons* and it says (Proverbs 13:8) *Riches are ransom* (*kofer*) *for a man's life*, and it says (Daniel 4:24) *Therefore O king ... Redeem your sins by beneficence* (*tzidqah*) *and your iniquities by generosity to the poor*, and it says (Job 33:23) *If he has a representative, one advocate against a thousand to declare the man's uprightness*, and it says (Job 33:24) *Then He has mercy on him and decrees, "Redeem him from descending to the Pit, for I have obtained his ransom* (*kofer*)."

The *Mekhilta* anthologizes verses that allegedly illustrate R. Yishmael's dictum that God's mercy on human beings may be seen through his allowing a person to "acquire himself" through money "from the hands of heaven." R. Yishmael's teaching is ambiguous on its own terms (what does "acquire himself" mean?), but the verses, taken together, suggest that the person's money buys him a ransom from the punishment to which his sins would otherwise condemn him, an expunging and erasure of those sins. The passage's clustering of verses suggests that no one verse on its own is seen as an adequate source for redemptive almsgiving; the verses likely are not *sources* of redemptive almsgiving so much as *post facto* justifications of a known idea.

The six verses fall into two sets of three. The first set establishes that the payment of money to the sanctuary or Temple (Exodus 30:12; II Kings 12:5) is a person's "ransom" ("*kofer*," Exodus 30:12); the point is driven home by the last verse of this set according to which "riches" are again described as a "ransom" ("*kofer*") for one's life (Proverbs 13:8). The second set opens with Daniel 4:24 and moves roughly in the chronological order of a person's life: Daniel 4:24 gives guidance for the duration of a person's life (as might Job 33:23), while Job 33:24 clearly provides that a person's "ransom" will save him from the "pit" after death. The *Mekhilta* thus juxtaposes the themes of paying money to the holy sanctuary as "ransom" and "redeeming sins" through charity. Charity is thus constructed as a sort of replacement for the expiatory sacrifices in the Jerusalem Temple.

A related theme is that charity stockpiles a donor's heavenly merits. Our examination of this theme is yet another illustration of the multivalence of *tzedaqah*, specifically the interplay of the term's general signification of religious "merit" ("*zekhut*") and the concrete manifestation of that religious "merit" in the form of "charity." In Genesis 15:6, Abraham is said to have *put his trust in the Lord*, which God accounted to *his merit (tzedaqah)*. *Mekhilta de-Rabbi Ishmael* explains this "*tzedaqah*": "Abraham our father only inherited this world and the world to come through *merit (zekhut)* of [his] faith ..."[31] The *Mekhilta*'s understanding of "*tzedaqah*" as (heavenly) merit reflects an even earlier tradition found in the second-century *targum* literature: *Targum Onqelos* renders Deuteronomy 6:25's "*tzedaqah*" (*It will therefore be to our merit* [*tzedaqah*] *before the Lord our God*) as "*zakhuta*" ("merit"), and *Targum Jonathan* expands on the specifically heavenly nature of this merit by noting that "and merit (*z'khu*) will be kept for us for the world to come." Apropos, M. *Peah* 1:1 famously declares that *gemilut hasadim* are among the meritorious acts for which the principal is preserved for the doer in the next world; the "principal" so "preserved" may reasonably be understood as accumulated heavenly merits.

Deuteronomy 24:13 and 15 are also relevant:

> Verse 13: *You must return the pledge to him at sundown, that he may sleep in his cloth and bless you; and it will be to your merit (tzedaqah) before the Lord your God.*

> Verse 15: *You must pay him his wages on the same day, before the sun sets, for he is needy and urgently depends on it; else he will cry to the Lord against you and you will incur guilt (heit).*

Verse 13 refers to the poor debtor. The creditor is commanded to return by nightfall a cloak he has taken as a pledge to secure the loan so that the debtor has a garment in which to sleep. The creditor's reward is that the poor man will "bless" him, which will be to his "merit" (*tzedaqah*) before God. Verse 15 refers to an impoverished day laborer. The employer is commanded to pay him his day's wages right away, before the day ends. Should this not happen the poor laborer "will cry to the Lord against" you and the employer will incur "guilt" ("*heit*"). Note the pairs of opposites: "blessing" (v. 13) is paralleled by "cry ... against you" (v. 15) and *tzedaqah* ("merit") (v. 13) by "guilt" ("*heit*") (v. 15).[32] The opposite of receiving a "blessing" is that the poor person will "cry ... against you"; the opposite of accumulating heavenly merit, "*tzedaqah*," is accumulating guilt, "*heit*." Presumably, then, the way to expiate that *heit* is through the earning of "merit," "*tzedaqah*." *Sifre Deuteronomy* 277 comments on Deuteronomy 24:13 as follows:[33]

> *That he may sleep in his cloth and bless you:* This teaches that he is commanded to bless you. Can it be that you are blessed if he blesses you, but not if he does not bless you? Scripture says: *And it will be to your merit (tzedaqah)*—you do *tzedaqah* on your own. *And it will be to your merit (tzedaqah)*—this teaches that *tzedaqah* ascends before the Throne of Glory. And thus it says (Psalm 85:14): *Justice (tzedeq) goes before Him as he sets out on his way.*

"*Tzedaqah* ascends before the Throne of Glory"—"*tzedaqah*" as "merit" stands before God as a reminder of the donor's righteousness, righteousness that accumulates in heaven and expiates the donor's *heit*.[34]

Thus far we have followed the entwining of the distinct literary threads "*zekhut*" and "*tzedaqah*" (as "merit"). While Deuteronomy 24:13's "*tzedaqah*" is not "charity" per se, that verse most certainly means charity in the narrative of King Monbaz (T. *Peah* 4:18).

1   It once happened that King Monbaz scattered his treasuries [to the poor] in years of drought. His (fathers) brothers sent [a message] to him: "Your fathers hid away treasuries and augmented those of their fathers, and you have stood up and scattered all your treasuries—yours and those of your fathers?!"

2   He said to them: "My fathers hid treasuries below, and I have hidden [treasuries] up above, as it is said, *Truth springs up from the earth; justice (tzedeq) looks down from heaven* (Psalm 85:12). My fathers hid treasuries in a place in which the hand can have dominion over them, and I hid [treasuries] in a place in which the hand cannot have dominion over them, as it is said, *Righteousness (tzedeq) and justice are the base of your throne* (Psalm 89:15). My fathers hid treasuries that do not yield fruits, and I hid treasuries that do yield fruits, as it is said, *Hail the just man (tzadiq), for he shall fare well, etc.* (Isaiah 3:10). My fathers hid treasuries of money and I hid treasuries of living souls, as it is said, *The fruit of the righteous (tzadiq) is a tree of life* (Proverbs 11:30). My fathers hid treasuries for others and I hid [treasuries] for myself, as it is said, *and it will be to your merit (tzedaqah)* before *the Lord your God* (Deuteronomy 24:13). My fathers hid treasures in this world, and I hid for myself for the world to come, as it is said, *Your Vindicator (tzidqecha) shall march before you* (Isaiah 58:8)."[35]

Monbaz's skeptical relatives argue that he has wasted his (and their) patrimony, which their mutual ancestors had carefully preserved and augmented in value. Monbaz offers six scriptural responses in which he essentially argues that his "scattering" of these treasures to the poor is a superior "investment strategy" to that which his ancestors had pursued. His penultimate argument is an ironic inversion of his relatives' complaint. They complain that he dissipated assets accumulated for his (and their) benefit; he argues that, to the contrary, his "scattering" of the possessions to "others" was in fact the ultimate preservation of the assets for "himself," while his fathers' "hiding" of the assets for the benefit of "others" (presumably their own descendants, including himself and his angry relatives) in fact brought them no benefit at all.[36]

Monbaz's scriptural proofs all include variations of the trilateral root *tz-d-q* and, taken separately, none is a perfect proof for his basic argument. The accumulation of these verses suggests that for the Palestinian rabbinic editors of the Monbaz narrative—just like the editors of the Mekhiltan passage—redemptive almsgiving was an idea with some currency in their circles, despite their inability to locate it precisely in the Hebrew Bible.[37] Monbaz's scriptural references make two principal points. First, his generous "scattering" of treasures to the poor is in fact an accumulation of treasures in heaven. Second, his giving "justifies," or makes him righteous, before God. That is, charity is called "*tzedaqah*" because it is a way one demonstrates righteousness before God.

Monbaz's final two prooftexts (Deuteronomy 24:13 and Isaiah 58:8) are most illuminating. Monbaz uses Deuteronomy 24:13 to demonstrate that he has hidden (heavenly) treasures for himself; his use of the verse is one, very particular concretization as "charity" of *Sifre Deuteronomy* 277's "*and it will be a merit for you*—this teaches that *tzedaqah* ascends before the Throne of Glory ...*" Thus however one does "*tzedaqah*," be it through the righteous act of returning the debtor's cloak at nightfall or through giving charity, that *tzedaqah* will "ascend[] before the Throne of Glory," accumulate, and expiate *heit*. *Sifre Deuteronomy* helps us more precisely locate where in heaven Monbaz's treasures are kept—before the Throne of Glory. Isaiah 58:8 is a fitting capstone to the passage's presentation of redemptive almsgiving and the funding of a heavenly bank of merits. *Your Vindicator* is Monbaz's charity, his righteousness before God, which will march before him. Charity is the ultimate concretization of "*tzedaqah*" as "merit," which ascends to and accumulates before God.[38]

Redemptive almsgiving revised in Palestinian amoraic literature

Palestinian amoraic literature retains the notion that charity atones for sin and stockpiles a donor's heavenly merits while introducing a new, related theme: charity rescues the donor from death; he is rewarded with longer life either in this world or the next. Y. *Shabbat* 6:10, 8d colorfully illustrates rescue from death as charity's redemptive reward:

1   Two students of R. Haninah went out to cut wood. They saw an astrologer. [He said:] "One of these two will go out and not come back."

2   When they went out, an old man encountered them. He said to them: "Acquire merit through me (*zekhun imi*), for I haven't tasted anything in three days."

3   They had with them one loaf. They cut it in half and gave to him.

4   He ate and prayed over them, saying to them: "May your lives be preserved for you this day just as you have preserved my life this day."

5   The students went out in peace and returned in peace. And there were people who had heard his [= the astrologer's] voice. They said to him: "Didn't you say that [one of] these two would go out and not come back?"

6   He said: "Woe! There is a man of lies here [= referring to himself] whose astrology is lies."

7   They went, examined, and found a snake: half in this [student's] pack, and half in this [student's] pack. They said: "What good [deed] did you do this day?" And the students told them of the interaction.

8   [The astrologer] said: "And what can this man [= me] do? For the God of the Jews is mollified by half a loaf."[39]

Three key aspects of this rich narrative deserve closer attention: (1) the poor man's invitation to the students "*zekhun imi*," "acquire merit through me"; (2) his prayer on their behalf; and (3) the reward the students earn for their generosity—rescue from death.

"Zekhun imi"—"acquire merit through me"

The simple phrase "*zekhun imi*" signals the reciprocity, the partnership, of charitable donors and recipients that contemporary scholars of late antique Christianity have discerned in those sources. "*Zekhun imi*" is a shorthand reference to redemptive almsgiving attested elsewhere in Palestinian amoraic literature. An unnamed man similarly asks one of R. Yannai's relatives for charity using the similar formula "*zekhei imi*" ("gain merit for yourself with me"), and a Babylonian *mamzer* asks R. Berechiah for charity by inviting him to "*zekhi imi*" ("gain merit for yourself with me").[40] R. Ze'ira underscores the religious significance of this formula in his teaching that Jews' quotidian speech teaches Torah; the poor say "*zekhi bi*" ("acquire merit through me"), "*izdakhei bi*" ("be merited through me"), or "*zekhi garmach bi*" ("gain merit for yourself through me").[41] R. Ze'ira's point is that even the poor know and teach through their requests for charity that the giver will earn heavenly merits by fulfilling their request. Although the word "*tzedaqah*" appears in none of these examples, we have already observed the intertwining of "*tzedaqah*" and "*zekhut*" in *Mekhilta de-Rabbi Ishmael* and *Sifre Deuteronomy* 277 (on Deuteronomy 24:13) and the further linkage of "*tzedaqah*" as "merit" to "*tzedaqah*" as "charity" through Deuteronomy 24:13's appearance in T. *Peah* 4:18. Taken all together, then, the poor's invitation to a potential donor to acquire heavenly "merit" for himself in Palestinian amoraic literature is functionally equivalent to his invitation to a potential donor to do "*tzedaqah*" with him. That is, the poor person is inviting the potential donor to demonstrate his righteousness by performing that righteousness as the giving of charity.

Prayers by the poor on behalf of the donors

The Hebrew Bible well documents God's heightened sensitivity and responsiveness to the call of the poor and downtrodden. We have seen Deuteronomy 24:13's promise that upon receiving back his pledged cloak for the night, the poor man will *bless you; and it will be to your merit (tzedaqah) before the Lord your God.* Deuteronomy 24:15 warns that a worker's wages must be paid the same day, *else he will cry to the Lord against you and you will incur guilt.*

The power of the oppressed widow's and orphan's cry to God is even more forcefully presented in Exodus 22:21–22: *I will heed their outcry as soon as they cry out ... and My anger shall blaze forth and I will put you to the sword....* Psalm 12:6 quotes God as saying: *Because of the groans of the plundered poor and needy, I will now act, says the Lord.*

Deuteronomy 24:13's *you must return the pledge ... that he may sleep in his cloth and bless you; and it will be to your merit before the Lord your God* permits the inference that the poor person's "blessing" is what will be to your "merit" ("*tzedaqah*") before God. How one defines the scriptural word "*it*" determines whether this inference is merely permitted or compelled. If "*it*" is understood to be the poor person's blessing of the pious creditor, then the blessing is a *sine qua non* for the creditor's earning "*tzedaqah*." If "*it*" is merely the pious act of returning the cloak, then the creditor can earn "*tzedaqah*" even without the poor person's blessing. *Sifre Deuteronomy* 277 opts for the latter interpretation: "Can it be that you are blessed if he blesses you, but not if he does not bless you? Scripture says: *And it will be to your merit (tzedaqah)*—you do *tzedaqah* on your own."[42] Faced with the choice of making the poor person's "blessing" a *sine qua non* for the creditor's earning of "*tzedaqah*" or uncoupling the two, *Sifre Deuteronomy* opts for the latter. This choice strikingly erases the agency that Deuteronomy 24:13 assigns to the poor, and the *Sifre*'s message to the creditor is clear: "you do *tzedaqah* on your own"—"on your own," *without* the poor's prayerful intercession.

But in *Yerushalmi Shabbat* the grateful old man responds with prayer on the students' behalf, expressing the wish that their lives be preserved that day just as they had preserved his. There is another description of prayer by grateful recipients of charity in *Yerushalmi Peah*, where a group of the poor are said to have eaten at R. Eliezer's house in his absence. In response to the sage's subsequent query to his household about the day's happenings, they reported that a group of poor people had come, eaten, and prayed for him.[43]

A key difference between *Yerushalmi Shabbat* and *Yerushalmi Peah* is that in the former the old man's prayer is a key cause of the students' eventual reward, while in *Yerushalmi Peah* the *tanna* R. Eliezer proclaims that the poor's prayer on his behalf is "not a good reward." R. Eliezer's negative assessment of the poor's prayer is consistent with *Sifre Deuteronomy* 277's elimination of the necessity of the poor's blessing; taken together, the two sources suggest a tannaitic tendency to minimize the importance to donors of the poor's prayers. But there is also a key commonality between the two *Yerushalmi* tractates: in neither does the *Yerushalmi prescribe* such prayers as an obligation of the poor. The recipients offer those prayers on their own initiative.[44] The *Yerushalmi* thus perpetuates the tannaitic view that donors' earning of merit through charity is not contingent on the prayers of the poor; the poor may pray for their benefactors, but such prayers are neither required of the poor nor essential for the donors' amassing of heavenly merits. Observe the contrast between the *Yerushalmi* and the fourth-century western Syrian *Apostolic Constitutions*:

for it becomes them, when one of their fellow-
widows is clothed by anyone, or receives money, or
meat, or drink, or shoes, at the sight of the
refreshment of their sister to say: Thou are blessed,
O God, who hast refreshed my fellow-widow. Bless,
O Lord, and glorify him that has bestowed these things
upon her, and let his good work ascend in truth to Thee,
and remember him for good in the day of his
visitation.... In the same manner, let the widow who
has received the alms join with the other in praying
for him who ministered to her.[45]

The *Apostolic Constitutions* instructs widows to ask that the donor be "glori-
fied" and that his good work ascend to God, who should remember the donor
"for good in the day of his visitation," presumably after death. Elsewhere in
the *Apostolic Constitutions* the bishop is charged to tell the needy the donor's
identity, "so that they may *pray for him or her by name*"[46] (emphasis added).
Recall Clement of Alexandria's colorful use of martial imagery to tell donors
to "[u]se your money to acquire bodyguards ... to protect you body and soul
... through whom the attacking robbers are ... stripped of their weapons *by
devout prayers*; people through whom the violence of the demons is
smashed..."[47] (emphasis added). To Clement, part of the job of these "bodyguards" is to provide "devout prayers."

It must be emphasized that not all late antique Christian writing and preaching on the poor echoes the *Apostolic Constitutions* and Clement of Alexandria;
other writers portray the poor as unworthy or off-putting, and not all describe
prayer on behalf of donors.[48] But even Palestinian amoraic literature's warmest
portrayals of the poor (some of which we will survey at the end of this chapter)
fall short of the effusive, exalted portrayals we see in these Christian texts, and
nowhere in Palestinian amoraic literature are the poor *instructed* or *expected* to
pray for donors. Yes, the poor may teach the Torah of redemptive almsgiving in
their everyday speech ("*z'khei imi*"); and yes, they are individuals whose plight
is of special concern to God and whose acceptance of charity will cause God to
act on behalf of their donors. But in Palestinian amoraic literature the poor are
by no means the exalted intercessors with God described in the *Apostolic Constitutions* and by Clement of Alexandria. In *Sifre Deuteronomy* 277's words: "You
do *tzedaqah* on your own."

The redemptive reward for charity in Yerushalmi Shabbat: rescue from death

Yerushalmi Shabbat's story of R. Haninah's two students, the astrologer, and the
unnamed poor old man ends on the note that the students receive a real-world
reward for their charity, a reward of which they were not even aware until the
end of the story: rescue from the violent death by snakebite to which they had

been fated. *Yerushalmi Shabbat* thus signals an interest in a different reward for charity than sin remission and accumulation of heavenly merits: rescue from death and longer life in *this* world.

Genesis Rabbah 59:1 also represents long life as *tzedaqah*'s reward.[49] R. Meir is said to have gone to Mamla, where he encountered dark-haired (= younger) people. He asked their family name and learned that they were descendants of the House of Eli, and thus fated to die young (cf. I Samuel 2:33). The dark-haired people asked him to pray for them, but he demurred, urging them instead to engage in *tzedaqah* and thereby "merit" ("*zokhim*") old age. His scriptural proofs are Proverbs 16:31 (*Gray hair is a crown of glory; it is attained by the way of righteousness* ([*tzedaqah*]) and the deduction that thanks to Abraham's instructing his children to do the "*just*" (*tzedaqah*; Genesis 18:19) he merited attaining the status of *Abraham was now old, advanced in years* (Genesis 24:1). The "merit" the people of Mamla will acquire through their *tzedaqah* is thus not heavenly in nature, but a this-worldly reward of long life. *Tzedaqah* will rescue, "redeem," them from premature death.

What accounts for Palestinian amoraic literature's interest in charity's power to rescue a donor from death and lead to his longer life? Recall how the tannaitic redemptive almsgiving anthologies (*Tosefta Peah* and *Mekhilta de-Rabbi Ishmael*) draw their persuasive power from their sheer accumulation of verses. No one verse alone in *Tosefta Peah* unequivocally supports redemptive almsgiving; the *Mekhilta*'s Daniel 4:24 appears to, but the *Mekhilta* does not rely on it alone, likely for a reason we will suggest later in this chapter. Few though the amoraic examples are, I suggest that their discernible focus on charity's power to rescue from death and extend life is due to an amoraic perception that this redemptive reward is more securely anchored in the Hebrew Bible than charity's power to atone for sin. This suggestion is consistent with Ephraim E. Urbach's observation that "[t]he fundamental reward for the observance of the commandments ... *in a man's lifetime* [is] stated again and again in the Torah and reiterated in the Prophets and Hagiographa"[50] (emphasis added). Urbach points out that this message would be reinforced by the quotidian performance of the rabbinic liturgy; as an example, recitation of the *Shema* would teach a worshipper "to link the blessing of the land and its produce, *his own length of days and that of his children*, with the keeping of the Lord's precepts ..."[51] (emphasis added).

The admitted difficulty with this suggestion is that neither *Yerushalmi Shabbat* nor *Genesis Rabbah* cites what seems to be the strongest biblical proof in its support: Proverbs 10:2 and/or the similar Proverbs 11:4 (*tzedaqah saves from death*). As a thought experiment, consider how Proverbs 10:2/11:4 might have worked perfectly as a capstone to *Yerushalmi Shabbat*'s story of R. Haninah's students. In fact, the *Yerushalmi* introduces Proverbs 10:2/11:4 into its re-presentation of the Toseftan story of King Monbaz, as a replacement for the *Tosefta*'s Isaiah 58:8 at the end of the narrative (*Your Vindicator* [*tzidqecha*] *shall march before you*).[52] In *Yerushalmi Peah* Monbaz says:

my fathers gathered in this world, and I gathered
for the world to come, as it says, *and tzedaqah saves from
death.*

The anonymous *Yerushalmi* immediately raises and answers a question about
Monbaz's quotation of Proverbs 10:2/11:4:

And didn't he die? Rather, [Proverbs 10:2/11:4 comes to
teach] that he will not die a death in the coming future.

Yerushalmi Peah's assignment to Monbaz of Proverbs 10:2/11:4 rather than
Isaiah 58:8 suggests that it is more interested in charity's power to conquer death
than in the accumulation of heavenly merits. But this assignment suggests more.
The anonymous *Yerushalmi* likely inherited a narrative in which the substitution
of Proverbs 10:2/11:4 had already been made; the *Yerushalmi* is therefore left to
grapple with the puzzling question: Didn't Monbaz, in fact, eventually die? How
could he say that his *tzedaqah saves from death*? The anonymous *Yerushalmi*'s
question presumes an a priori refusal to understand the verse according to its
literal meaning. Given that refusal, the *Yerushalmi*'s sensible—but by no means
inevitable—response to its own question is that Monbaz is referring not to a
physical death, but to a "death" in the "coming future" (the "world to come").[53]
Yerushalmi Peah's interpretive move explains why *tzedaqah saves from death* is
missing from *Yerushalmi Shabbat* and *Genesis Rabbah*: despite Palestinian
amoraic literature's heightened interest in charity's power to rescue a donor from
death, it sees *tzedaqah saves from death* as applicable only to rescue from death
and longer life in the *next* world.

But whether it applies to this world or the next, Proverbs 10:2/11:4 is a bewil-
dering capstone to the *Yerushalmi*'s Monbaz narrative. Monbaz quotes it as
support for his having "gathered for the world to come." But how does *tzedaqah
saves from death* in any way pertain to, let alone support, Monbaz's having
"gathered for the world to come"? Isaiah 58:8 seems to support that idea better
with its suggestion of the "Vindicator" (= Monbaz's "gathered" heavenly merits)
"marching before" him. I suggest that *Yerushalmi Peah*'s substitution of Proverbs 10:2/11:4 for Isaiah 58:8 bridges the gap between the tannaitic notion that
charity accumulates heavenly merits and the Palestinian amoraic notion of rescue
from death and longer life in this world. The *Yerushalmi*'s reference to the
"coming future" echoes M. *Peah* 1:1: *gemilut hasadim* is one of the things for
which the "principal" is preserved for the doer in the "world to come." The substitution of Proverbs 10:2/11:4 for Isaiah 58:8 as the capstone of the Monbaz
narrative thus results in an innovative hybrid of tannaitic and amoraic ideas.
Yerushalmi Peah maintains ideational continuity with the tannaitic focus on the
next world, but its own emphasis is on *not dying* (and hence living longer) in
that "coming future" rather than accumulating a "principal" of merits that is preserved in the "world to come."

Redemptive almsgiving for Gentiles(?)

We will round out our survey and analysis of redemptive almsgiving in Palestinian rabbinic literature with the vexed issue (for the rabbis) of whether Gentiles can atone for their own sins through charity. We have seen that Daniel advises King Nebuchadnezzar (Daniel 4:24) to *redeem your sins by beneficence and your iniquities by generosity to the poor.* The verse is infrequently quoted in Palestinian rabbinic literature; we have noted its solitary appearance in *Mekhilta de-Rabbi Ishmael,* and it also appears once in *Leviticus Rabbah* and twice in *Pesiqta deRav Kahana.*[54] In *Leviticus Rabbah* and *Pesiqta deRav Kahana* 26:1 the verse's scope is limited to Nebuchadnezzar himself. In *Pesiqta deRav Kahana* 2:5 Rabban Gamliel applies the verse broadly to the "nations" as confirmation for his exegesis of Proverbs 14:34 (*righteousness exalts a nation; sin is a reproach to any people*). Rabban Gamliel's exegesis of Proverbs 14:34 is based on a creative misreading employed by other sages as well throughout the passage. The Hebrew word JPS renders as "*sin*" is "*hesed,*" which *Pesiqta deRav Kahana* creatively misreads as "kindness." The Hebrew word JPS renders as "*reproach*" is "*hatat,*" which the *midrash* understands straightforwardly as a "sin-offering" (e.g., Leviticus 4:1–3). "*Tzedaqah*" is, naturally, "*righteousness.*" Rabban Gamliel consequently reads Proverbs 14:34 as teaching redemptive almsgiving for Gentiles: *righteousness* (*tzedaqah*) exalts *a nation* (Israel), while the *hesed* that the Gentiles do is a *hatat* (sin-offering) for them. Rabban Gamliel's use of Daniel 4:24 strongly suggests that the Gentiles he (and *Pesiqta deRav Kahana*) has in mind are Christians, as the verse was a staple of late antique Christian writing and preaching on redemptive almsgiving.[55] But crucially, R. Yohanan ben Zakkai decisively rejects Rabban Gamliel's view (among others). The suggestion that *Pesiqta deRav Kahana*'s Gentiles are Christians explains in turn why Palestinian rabbinic literature does not highlight Daniel 4:24 as a or the key biblical source for Jewish redemptive almsgiving: Palestinian rabbis may well have been reluctant to rely on a verse so important to Christian writers and preachers.

Loss of wealth as expiation; earning merit for giving as charity money that one is already fated to lose

This section's theme is redemptive almsgiving's distant cousin. Tannaitic literature perpetuates the Hebrew Bible's representation that loss—of property, wealth, and land—is a sign of divine displeasure.[56] R. Shimon Shizuri recalls in *Tosefta Baba Qama* that his father's house was one among the prosperous Galilean households; his family lost its wealth due to the transgressions of adjudicating monetary cases with one judge and raising small cattle in the land of Israel.[57] Palestinian amoraic literature's associations of loss of wealth with sin leave the "sin" undefined; *Leviticus Rabbah,* for example, teaches that "householders" lose their wealth because they "did not stretch out their hands in *mitzvoth*" and did not "do the will of their heavenly Father."[58] Apropos, R. Shimon ben Laqish counsels a worried Rabbi Judah the Prince not to take property from others so that he will not have to give anything to Rome.[59] Cryptic though the advice is, R. Shimon ben Laqish seems delicately to be referring to inappropriate conduct on Rabbi's part toward others' property that results in Rabbi's having to part with his own to Rome (as a form of expiation).

Loss of wealth in Palestinian amoraic literature may also play the productive role (for the one losing it) of expiating sin or it may discharge the property owner's liability for a much greater punishment at heaven's hand. R. Yitzhaq teaches in *Pesiqta deRav Kahana* 24:17 that loss of property or a small-scale physical calamity atones for a sin the punishment for which would otherwise be death at heaven's hand.[60] Rav Huna advises those who have committed sins that entail death at the hands of heaven to expiate those sins through Torah study; if they are unable to do so, they will live if they are appointed as *parnasim* over the community or "*gabba'im* of *tzedaqah*."[61] *Leviticus Rabbah* 17:4 teaches that God, the "master of mercies," strikes at a person's property before touching his life.[62] The role played in all these sources by a loss of wealth resembles but is not at all the same as redemptive almsgiving: the "giving" is most certainly involuntary, but it does the productive work for the "giver" of atoning for sin.

From here it is a short leap to the notion that *pre-emptive giving* can earn the donor a religious reward for parting with wealth he was in any case destined to lose. This is a striking feature of a narrative about R. Shimon ben Yohai and his nephews, the point of which is that money the nephews are fated to lose can earn them religious merit (in this case, release from imprisonment) if they pre-emptively give it away as *tzedaqah*.[63] R. Shimon ben Yohai dreamed on the night of *Rosh Hashanah* that his nephews would be fined 600 *dinars* by Rome. *Rosh Hashanah* is a day of judgment for life or death[64] and, significantly, the day on which a person's sustenance for the coming year is set.[65] In light of the date, then, the significance of R. Shimon ben Yohai's dream is the foreknowledge it gives him that, one way or another, his nephews are fated to lose 600 *dinars* in the coming year. He compelled them to accept communal appointments as *parnasim*, telling them to keep a written record of their expenditures for which he would compensate them at the end of the year. Rumor and political intrigue resulted in the nephews' being imprisoned when they had only managed to spend 594 *dinars* as *tzedaqah*. R. Shimon ben Yohai told them to give him the remaining six, which he appears to have used to bribe a guard to release them. The nephews tell him of their suspicion that he had known of their plight in advance; had he told them, they say, they would have given the additional six *dinars* as *tzedaqah* right away. R. Shimon ben Yohai admits his advance knowledge but defends his concealing it by pointing out to his nephews that they would have not believed him, and he would consequently have had to provide all 600 *dinars* himself, an amount he appears doubtful he could raise.

The reward of retaining or augmenting one's wealth

According to M. *Peah* 1:1 *gemilut hasadim* are among those things the "fruits" of which are eaten in this world while the "principal" is preserved for the world to come. *Yerushalmi Peah* tacitly defines "fruits" by way of R. Abba, according to whom God will protect one "who gives *tzedaqah* from your pocket" from four types of involuntary financial outlays: required debt or other kinds of payments (*pisin*), fines (*zimiyot*), head-taxes (*gulgaliyot*), and in-kind taxes (*annona*).[66] R. Abba's teaching immediately precedes the story of King Monbaz, and the literary juxtaposition nicely illustrates in order the two clauses of M. *Peah* 1:1: the "fruits" one eats in this world (R. Abba) followed by the "principal" preserved for the world to come (Monbaz).

But exactly what R. Abba means by his claim that God will "protect" the *tzedaqah* donor from these various outlays is unclear. One possibility is that the protection is someone else's coming forward to pay the *tzedaqah* donor's various tax obligations or fines (as in the story of R. Shimon ben Yohai and his nephews). Another possibility is that the protection is the *tzedaqah* donor's retention or even augmentation of his wealth; this will allow in turn for his continued or even increased expenditures on both *tzedaqah* and these unwelcome financial obligations. *Leviticus Rabbah* 34:13 illustrates the latter possibility in two interpretive steps. It claims initially that householders' failure to "extend their hands in the performance of *mitzvoth*" and to "do the will of their heavenly Father" will result in a loss of wealth.[67] Later in the same passage *Leviticus Rabbah* uses Isaiah 58:7 (*and to take the wretched poor into your home*) to teach that householders should take Torah scholars into their home who will teach them, *inter alia*, to "do the will of their heavenly Father." The implicit combined message is that by supporting Torah scholars who teach them how to do their heavenly Father's will, these householders will successfully perform that will and hence not be punished by a loss of wealth. In brief, householders will be repaid for their support of Torah scholars by their retention of their wealth.

The story of the rabbinic benefactor Abba Yudan colorfully makes a similar point.[68] Abba Yudan had been a generous donor to the rabbis but fell on hard times and was embarrassed when he had nothing to give three rabbis who approached him for funds. His wife advised him to take the risky step of selling half of his one remaining field and giving the proceeds to the rabbis. He did so, and miraculously found a treasure in the half-field remaining to him, which made him fantastically wealthy. Upon their return the rabbis told him they had anticipated his serendipitous reversal of fortune, quoting Proverbs 18:16 (*A man's gift eases his way and gives him access to the great*).[69] The rabbinic interpretation of Proverbs 18:16 sheds light on *Yerushalmi Peah*'s R. Abba: charity "eases the giver's way" because the donor is rewarded for his charitable giving by his retention or augmentation of wealth. The message to potential donors is both comforting and incentivizing of continued giving.[70]

Although not about *tzedaqah* per se, *Pesiqta deRav Kahana* 10:10's discussion of Deuteronomy 14:22 (*You shall set aside every year a tenth part of all the yield of your sowing that is brought from the field*) is also relevant.[71] The original Hebrew of *you shall set aside ... a tenth part* is "*aser t'aser*," a untranslatable doubling of the trilateral root *a-s-r* (ten) which can more literally be rendered as "you shall (or must) surely tithe." Responding to the doubling of the verb root, the *midrash* states that "in order that you not be lacking, *aser t'aser* (you shall surely tithe)." Tithing is (as it were) an insurance policy for maintaining one's property. Another interpretation of the doubled verb root *aser t'aser* invokes the similar-sounding but unrelated root *a-sh-r* ("rich"): "Tithe (*aser*) in order that you become rich (*titasher*)." Apropos God is made to say: "Tithe (*aser*) what is Mine (i.e., what I have given you) and I will enrich (*m'asher*) what is yours." *Pesiqta deRav Kahana* then briefly pivots to Deuteronomy 14:22's "*all the yield of your sowing,*" specifically, the meaning of "*all.*" R. Abba bar Kahana explains that "tithe what is Mine and I will enrich what is yours" is a "hint" that business travelers would give one-tenth to "those who labor in Torah." R. Abba bar Kahana thus sees Deuteronomy 14:22 as pertaining even to gains from commercial ventures. The business travelers' distribution of a tenth of their non-agricultural gains to "those who labor in Torah" blurs the boundary between this tithing and *Leviticus Rabbah* 34:13's giving to rabbis, which was also said to be a way to preserve wealth. Tithing for "those who labor in Torah" also blurs into *tzedaqah* since, as we saw in *Yerushalmi Megillah,* giving to rabbis can also be considered *tzedaqah* (Chapter 2).[72]

Redemptive almsgiving, charity's rewards, and portrayals of the poor in Palestinian amoraic literature

Helen Rhee identifies in the Hebrew Bible and Second Temple literature what she terms "the notion of 'the pious poor and the wicked rich.'"[73] Prophets and psalmists tend to see "poor," "pious," and "righteous" as parallel, synonymous concepts, as contrasted with wicked, oppressive, wealthy folk. The Qumran sect is a paradigmatic example of this tendency: the members of the sect identify themselves as "poor" as a badge of sectarian honor and identity, not because of material deprivation. Rhee notes the disappearance of the "pious poor"/"wicked rich" dichotomy from late antique Christian redemptive almsgiving texts; redemptive almsgiving as a spiritual partnership of the rich and poor is simply inconsistent with the notion that the rich are always and absolutely wicked.[74] Rhee's observation about the disappearance of the "pious poor"/"wicked rich" dichotomy from Christian sources holds true as well for Palestinian rabbinic literature. This is not to say that Palestinian rabbinic literature never represents the poor as pious or the rich as wicked, but that differences of wealth in these literatures are not mapped onto a "good versus evil" binary. This commonality between tannaitic and amoraic literature acknowledged, we move on to an exploration of some salient differences.

Tannaitic redemptive almsgiving and the invisible (chronically) poor

Susan R. Holman observes that "[i]n most early Christian texts the poor exist primarily as a passive tool for redemptive almsgiving," with a "profound, if inert, liturgical identity."[75] The same might be said of those unidentified, unnamed, indeed, entirely unmentioned, poor to whom King Monbaz "scattered" his and his ancestors' earthly treasures (T. *Peah* 4:18). The poor are likewise nowhere in evidence in *Mekhilta de-Rabbi Ishmael*'s anthology of redemptive almsgiving verses. The poor are similarly missing from T. *Peah* 4:21:

> From where do we know that *tzedaqah* and *gemilut hasadim* are peace and a great intercessor between Israel and their Father in heaven? As it says, (Jeremiah 16:5) *For thus said the Lord: Do not enter a house of mourning, do not go to lament and to condole with them; For I have withdrawn My favor from that people ... My kindness and compassion.* "*Kindness*" is acts of kindness. "*Compassion*" is *tzedaqah*. This teaches that *tzedaqah* and *gemilut hasadim* are a great peace between Israel and their Father in heaven.[76]

The poor's absence from this passage is striking; *tzedaqah* and *gemilut hasadim* are said to be "peace[makers]" and "intercessors" between Israel and God, with nary a mention of the poor who are the recipients of that *tzedaqah* and acts of kindness. We also saw how *Sifre Deuteronomy* 277 strikingly mutes the agency that Deuteronomy 24:13 assigns the poor with its observation to the donor: "You do *tzedaqah* on your own." To the *Sifre* the poor man has the "profound, if inert" identity (Holman) of being the passive stage on which the creditor performs his drama of righteousness. This all being so, it is unsurprising that *tannaim* do not portray themselves as engaged in organized charitable efforts on the poor's behalf.[77]

On the other hand, M. *Sheqalim* 5:6 and T. *Sheqalim* 2:16 call attention to the "*aniyyim b'nei tovim*" (the "poor of good family") who derive support from what *yir'ei heit* anonymously deposit into the "halls of secrets." The *Sheqalim* tractates' singling-out of the *aniyyim b'nei tovim* in the context of their allusion to redemptive almsgiving is linked to what I have elsewhere described as a discernible and distinctive tannaitic empathy for the "formerly-wealthy" poor.[78] I suggest that three phenomena are related: the *Sheqalim* tractates' explicit reference to the *aniyyim b'nei tovim*, the total erasure of the (chronically) poor from other tannaitic redemptive almsgiving sources, and the general tannaitic empathy for the formerly wealthy, that is, the high status, poor. The scarlet thread that links these phenomena is the importance in tannaitic literature of hierarchy and high social status.[79] As Shaye J.D. Cohen has pointed out, tannaitic literature contains approximately ten lists of social hierarchies, which signals the importance to them of status, class, and social position. Commenting on these lists, Cohen observes that they demonstrate a tannaitic view that "birth determined social status," a view that persisted alongside their notion of a "hierarchy ... based on intellectual and spiritual attainments."[80] *Tannaim* demonstrably empathize with the formerly wealthy poor, people of good family or otherwise high social standing who have fallen from wealth into poverty. While not unsympathetic to the chronically poor, *tannaim* do not *empathize* with them, not "seeing" them in redemptive almsgiving sources.[81]

Palestinian amoraic warmth toward the chronically poor and their social welfare role

Palestinian *amoraim* portray themselves as intermediaries between donors and the poor.[82] This difference from the *tannaim* is bound up with another: whereas tannaitic redemptive almsgiving sources erase the chronically poor, Palestinian amoraic literature is replete throughout with warm portrayals of the chronically poor, including but not limited to redemptive almsgiving contexts. The lesson for us is that the teaching of redemptive almsgiving does not inexorably lead to any particular manner of portraying the poor. Tannaitic redemptive almsgiving erases the chronically poor and focuses almost exclusively on the donor; Palestinian amoraic redemptive almsgiving focuses much more on the poor, who invite donors to "acquire merit" through them. The amoraic self-portrayal as intermediaries between donors and poor and the literature's warm portrayals of the poor are related: the latter may serve to spur charitable donations, and, to the extent these donations are made to charity funds administered by the *amoraim*, the *amoraim*'s profile is raised as visible and consequential players in Palestinian Jewish society.[83]

Palestinian amoraic literature constructs the poor as a special group of whose welfare God is particularly solicitous. Song of Songs 7:6 reads: *The locks (dalat) of your head are like purple. Leviticus Rabbah* 31:4 plays on the word *dalat, dal* being one of the biblical terms for the poor.[84] God says "even the *dalim* (poor) among you are as beloved to me as (King) David." According to R. Luliani "of the south," quoting R. Yehudah b. R. Simon, God has four types of people in his house just as we have four types in our own. We have sons, daughters, and male and female servants whom we must cause to rejoice on festival days, while God's house consists of the landless Levite, the stranger, orphans, and widows. God promises that if we see to the happiness of his charges on festival days, he will see to the happiness of our charges as well as his own.[85]

R. Shimon ben Laqish points out that a person is quick to acknowledge a wealthy relative and to deny a poor relative. Yet God, he adds, is not at all like that: even if Israel has fallen to its lowest point and cannot fall any lower, God still calls them *my kin and friends* (Psalm 122:8).[86] Apropos, Psalm 22:25 (*For He did not scorn, He did not spurn the plea of the lowly*) is said to yield a telling contrast between the way God works and the way human society works. In the human world, a judge naturally inclines toward a rich man when the latter and a poor man enter the courtroom. But Psalm 22:25 shows that God is inclined instead to turn toward the poor.[87]

R. Shila of Naveh interprets the term *ha-evyon* (the "indigent one"), to mean "this poor man—be careful (*hav honakh*; a near homonym of *haevyon*) of him." Apropos R. Avin points to Psalm 109:31 (*because He stands at the right hand of the needy*) as proof that when a poor person stands at one's door, God is at his right hand, ready to reward the one who gives to him, or to exact punishment from one who does not.[88]

God is said to prefer the handful of cereal brought by the poor as a freewill offering over the fine incense offered by the entire community.[89] R. Yohanan explains that although the smell of burning birds is distasteful and unpleasant, Leviticus 1:17 commands that the poor man's bird offering (see also Leviticus 1:14) be burned on the altar so that the altar can be ornamented with it.[90] This is immediately followed by a story in which King Agrippa orders a priest to offer no sacrifices but his own on a given day. The priest thereupon refuses to offer up a poor man's offering of two turtledoves. This refusal panics the poor man who explains that he typically catches four birds per day; he keeps two and offers two in thanks to God. The priest's refusal to offer his daily two-bird offering would cause God to diminish his catch the next day. The priest relents, and his recounting of the poor man's plight to King Agrippa assuages the latter's wrath. The poor man's humble daily offering of two turtledoves thus has greater religious value than King Agrippa's likely more lavish offerings.

In another story, a man was unsuccessfully attempting to lead his ox to sacrifice at the same time as a poor person was bringing a bunch of vegetation as an offering. The poor man extended the vegetation to the ox, who ate and disgorged a needle that would otherwise have torn his insides and rendered him unfit for sacrifice. The ox's owner was later informed about this in a dream: "the offering of a poor person preceded you." Unbeknownst to both, the poor man performed a valuable religious service for the ox's owner.[91]

Warm portrayals of the poor such as these can incentivize charity by neutralizing antipathy toward the poor and consequently softening potential donors' reluctance to part with their property. Palestinian amoraic literature is replete with evidence of hostility toward the poor. *Leviticus Rabbah* 34:4 is an imagined diatribe launched by a rich man against a poor man based on Proverbs 29:13 (*A poor man and a fraudulent man meet; the Lord gives luster to the eyes of both*).

> If the rich man says to this same poor man: "Why do you not
> go work and get food? Look at those hips! Look at those legs!
> Look at that fat body! Look at those lumps of flesh!," the Holy One,
> Blessed be He, says to him: "It is not enough that you have not given
> him anything of yours, but you must set an evil eye upon what I
> have given him, must you?" …[92]

Leviticus Rabbah's striking portrayal of alienation between the poor and others is not unique in Palestinian amoraic literature. The poor are described as excluded from even family celebrations,[93] and as too ashamed to be seen even by friends.[94] There are also portrayals of the poor as ungrateful or resentful. Recall that a group of the poor cursed R. Eliezer despite the bounty they received at his home.[95] Elsewhere in *Leviticus Rabbah* a poor man is described as complaining: "What am I and what is So-and-so? So-and-so lives in his house and I live 'here.' So-and-so sleeps on his bed, and I sleep on the ground."[96] These narrative details are a telling reminder to these stories' audiences that the living, breathing poor do not necessarily conform to the idealized image of the poor as conveyor belts of redemptive benefits between God and donors. Potential donors must be motivated to overcome the antagonism that may exist between the poor and their donors and, in Palestinian amoraic literature, redemptive almsgiving may be one such motivation.[97] And, to the extent that Palestinian *amoraim* construct themselves as mediators between donors and the poor, then they—either directly or through modalities of charity collection and distribution that they supervise—will absorb some of the poor's "bad behavior," which may also serve to incentivize giving to the poor by way of the rabbis.

In light of all this evidence, one should hardly be surprised that Palestinian *amoraim*—not *tannaim*—are portrayed as engaging in organized collections for the poor, in appointing their own candidates to fill positions such as that of *parnas*, and in offering scriptural rationales for the religious significance of those positions.[98] Turning our attention to the east, we may ask: how, and to what extent, do these various ideas about charity, atonement, and reward persist in the Talmud *Bavli*? What if any new forms do they take? We now turn to an exploration of these questions and to the *Bavli*'s unique transformations of these ideas.

Notes

1 See, e.g., Genesis 22:1, 37:13; 1 Samuel 3:4; Isaiah 6:8.
2 Letty Cottin Pogrebin, "The Politics and Ethics of Street Tzedakah," www.moment-mag.com/opinion-politics-ethics-street-tzedakah/ (2014).
3 The literature on redemptive almsgiving is vast. Key sources include Roman Garrison, *Redemptive Almsgiving in Early Christianity* (Sheffield: Sheffield Academic Press, 1993); Gary A. Anderson, "3. Redeem Your Sins Through Works of Charity," in Robin Darling Young and Monica J. Blanchard, editors, *To Train His Soul in Books: Syriac Asceticism in Early Christianity* (Washington, DC: Catholic University of America Press, 2011), 57–65; ibid., "A Treasury in Heaven: The Exegesis of Proverbs 10:2 in the Second Temple Period," *Hebrew Bible and Ancient Israel* 1:3 (September 2012): 351–367; ibid., "How Does Almsgiving Purge Sins?," in Steven E. Fassberg, Moshe Bar-Asher and Ruth A. Clements, editors, *Hebrew in the Second Temple Period: The Hebrew of the Dead Sea Scrolls and Other Contemporary Sources* (Leiden and Boston: Brill, 2013), 1–14; ibid., *Charity*; ibid., *Sin: A History* (New Haven and London: Yale University Press, 2009); Peter Brown, *The Ransom of the Soul*; and David J. Downs, *Alms*. There are also important discussions of redemptive almsgiving in Richard Finn, *Almsgiving in the Later Roman Empire: Christian Promotion and Practice; 313–450* (Oxford: Oxford University Press, 2006), *passim*; Susan R. Holman, *The Hungry are Dying: Beggars and Bishops in Roman Cappadocia* (Oxford: Oxford University Press, 2001); and Helen Rhee, *Loving the Poor, Saving the Rich: Wealth, Poverty, and Early Christian Formation* (Grand Rapids: Baker Academic, 2012), *passim*.
4 David Downs has very recently questioned the emerging scholarly consensus that Daniel 4:24 (LXX 4:27) is about charity; see David J. Downs, *Alms*, 50–56.
5 See Gary Anderson, *Charity*, 60–61, 70–103. For David Downs's discussion of Tobit and Ben Sira see ibid., *Alms*, 57–81.
6 Roman Garrison, *Redemptive Almsgiving in Early Christianity*, 54–55.
7 New Testament quotes in this chapter are taken from *The Holy Bible: New Revised Standard Version* (Nashville: Thomas Nelson Publishers, 1989).
8 The phrase "heavenly investment" is Roman Garrison's; see Roman Garrison, *Redemptive Almsgiving in Early Christianity*, 63–68. See also Gary Anderson, *Charity*, 184–185.

9 *The Didache* (trans. Maxwell Staniforth; trans. revised Andrew Louth), in Andrew Louth, editor, *Early Christian Writings: The Apostolic Fathers* (London: Penguin, 1987), 192–193. On the *Didache*'s treatment of atoning charity, see also David J. Downs, *Alms*, 235–240.

10 Helen Rhee, *Loving the Poor, Saving the Rich*, 64–70. David Downs notes that Cyprian's *On Works and Alms* "stands as a preeminent contribution to early Christian discourse about the atoning value of almsgiving, not least because it offers the first systematic discussion of the topic." See David J. Downs, *Alms*, 95.

11 See Roman Garrison, *Redemptive Almsgiving in Early Christianity*, 132–133 and *passim*. David Downs has recently questioned Garrison's social–historical assumption that Rome and Corinth were in fact rent by class conflict in the first and early second centuries CE; whatever the socioeconomic reality may have been, at the very least redemptive almsgiving's assignment of complementary roles to donors and poor calls the attention of each class to the other's indispensability. See David J. Downs, *Alms*, 280–281.

12 See Helen Rhee, *Loving the Poor, Saving the Rich*, 76.

13 Peter Brown, *The Ransom of the Soul*, 103.

14 John Chrysostom, *Homily XVII* to II Corinthians, in Philip Schaff, editor, *A Select Library of the Nicene and Post-Nicene Fathers*, 1st series, vol. 12 (Grand Rapids: Eerdmans, repr. 1983), 361.

15 Helen Rhee, *Loving the Poor, Saving the Rich*, 65.

16 Richard Finn, *Almsgiving in the Later Roman Empire*, 179–182.

17 Ibid., 179.

18 Peter Brown, *Ransom of the Soul*, 43. Helen Rhee also calls attention to the heightened significance of redemptive almsgiving in the fourth century especially, see her *Loving the Poor, Saving the Rich*, 76 ("[i]n the fourth century and onward, 'redemptive almsgiving' would be one of the most consistent elements in the sermons and teachings of church leaders").

19 Peter Brown, *Ransom of the Soul*, 83–91. The mention of "faceless mass of the poor" is on p. 87.

20 It bears emphasizing that not *all* late antique Christian writers and preachers embraced redemptive almsgiving. David Downs discusses the interesting case of the *Gospel of Thomas*, a second-century work that "shows not merely the dismissal but the disparagement of care for the poor." Downs quotes remarkable language from *Gospel of Thomas* 14:3: "and if you give alms, you will do harm to your spirits." See David J. Downs, *Alms*, 206, 207, and *passim*. But again, note Richard Finn's observation that by the fourth and fifth centuries, redemptive almsgiving was very widely preached and accepted. See Richard Finn, *Almsgiving in the Later Roman Empire*, 179–182.

21 Susan R. Holman, *The Hungry Are Dying*, 54 (emphasis in original).

22 See Richard Finn, *Almsgiving in the Later Roman Empire*, 180.

23 See Helen Rhee, *Loving the Poor, Saving the Rich*, 85 and *passim*.

24 See, e.g., see my "Redemptive Almsgiving and the Rabbis of Late Antiquity," *Jewish Studies Quarterly* 18:2 (2011): 144–184 and the work of other scholars cited in Chapter 1, n. 5. My work in this chapter and the next revises some of that essay's earlier conclusions.

25 We will take up the tension between *tzedaqah* and *teshuvah* as "competing" or "complementary" modes of atonement in Chapter 5.

26 The study of redemptive almsgiving in rabbinic sources is methodologically complex. First, as is also true of many other topics, rabbinic statements on redemptive almsgiving are neither organized into, nor reflective of, a systematic rabbinic view of the topic. Consequently, we do well to bear in mind Yaakov Elman's warning that we "avoid the danger of producing systems of theology which never existed," a warning he attributed to the late E.P. Sanders. See Yaakov Elman,

"Righteousness as its Own Reward: An Inquiry into the Theologies of the Stam," *PAAJR* 57 (1990/1991): 40 n. 14 and source cited. For more on the methodological difficulties of sorting rabbinic sources into thematically coherent sets, see, e.g., Alexander Samely, *Forms of Rabbinic Literature and Thought: An Introduction* (Oxford: Oxford University Press, 2007), 38, 48, 50–52 and *passim*. Another difficulty in identifying rabbinic redemptive almsgiving sources is that the concept can appear in sources that really deal with something else. One such example to which we will shortly return is M. *Sheqalim* 5:6.

27 Roman Garrison claims that "it is … difficult to establish that [redemptive almsgiving] existed in rabbinic thought during the tannaitic period." See Roman Garrison, *Redemptive Almsgiving in Early Christianity*, 59. We might say that redemptive almsgiving is *attested* in tannaitic compilations, although lacking in the prominence it has in contemporaneous Christian writing and preaching. Garrison's implicit assumption that redemptive almsgiving should be as prominent in tannaitic compilations as it is in Christian sources is unwarranted. Peter Brown also exaggerates the importance of redemptive almsgiving in "Jewish" thought, without sufficiently distinguishing between different strata within the rabbinic period. See, e.g., *Ransom of the Soul*, 96–98 (especially 97): "we realize that we have passed one of the most significant frontiers in the history of ancient Judaism." There is no doubt that the emergence of redemptive almsgiving in Jewish sources is the passing of a "significant frontier," but that "frontier" must be more precisely demarcated. We must be skeptical of the idea that sea changes in Christian theological emphases must also be sea changes in rabbinic understandings. The textual evidence reveals a more complex picture.

28 Who are the "*yir'ei heit*"? The few other tannaitic occurrences of the moniker yield the general impression that *yir'ei heit* need not be religious elites, just anyone who fears the snares of sin. See M. *Sotah* 9:15; T. *Ta'anit* 3:7–8 (ed. Lieberman, 339–340); *Sifre Deuteronomy* 311, 323 (ed. Finkelstein 352, 374). The term can, of course, refer to rabbis; the sage R. Shimon ben Netanel is referred to as a "*yir'e heit*" in M. *Avot* 2:8. The general observation is made in M. *Avot* 2:5 that the uncouth person ("*bor*") cannot be a *yir'e heit*; a "couth" person may be, but need not necessarily be, a rabbi. See the discussion in Ephraim E. Urbach, *The Sages: Their Concepts and Beliefs* (2nd enlarged ed.; Jerusalem: Magnes Press, 1979), 1:415–416.

29 Gregg Gardner posits that M. *Sheqalim* 5:6 (and the related T. *Sheqalim* 2:16) are representative of a tannaitic preference for anonymous giving to a communal source, which will both alleviate the problem of begging and protect the dignity of the poor. One might argue, then, that the "sin" that the donors to the hall of secrets fear is the sin of embarrassing the poor to whom they might give face-to-face. But there is no clear indication that this is the sin of concern in these two pericopes; the "sin" is undefined. See Gregg E. Gardner, *Origins of Organized Charity*, 152–153.

30 *Mekhilta de-Rabbi Ishmael* (*Mishpatim*; *Neziqin* 10) (ed. Horovitz-Rabin, 285–286). See also David J. Downs's observations about this passage in *Alms*, 88.

31 *Mekhilta de-Rabbi Ishmael* (*B'shalach*; *Vayehi* 6) (ed. Horovitz-Rabin, 114).

32 David J. Downs also notes the oppositional pairing of "*tzedaqah*" with "*heit*" in *Alms*, 33 n. 13.

33 *Sifre Deuteronomy* 277 (ed. Finkelstein, 295).

34 See also David J. Downs, *Alms*, 33:

> One interpretative tradition understands [*tzedakah*] in Deut. 24:13 as a reward from God granted on the basis of one's compassion for the poor, a "merit" accrued through charity … [it] is a concrete embodiment of "righteous," or rightly ordered, social relations within the covenant community.

35 T. *Peah* 4:18 (ed. Lieberman, 60). I have adapted this translation from my earlier one in "Redemptive Almsgiving and the Rabbis of Late Antiquity": 150–151. For a

detailed comparison of the parallel versions of the Monbaz narrative in the *Tosefta* (= *Bavli*) and *Yerushalmi Peah*, see ibid.:150–153. Other treatments of the Monbaz narrative include, e.g., Gregg E. Gardner, "Competitive Giving in the Third Century C.E.: Early Rabbinic Approaches to Greco-Roman Civic Benefaction," in Jordan D. Rosenblum, Lily C. Vuong, and Nathaniel P. DesRosiers, editors, *Religious Competition in the Third Century C.E.: Jews, Christians, and the Greco-Roman World* (Supplements of Journal of Ancient Judaism: Vandenhoeck & Ruprecht, 2014), 81–92; Yael Wilfand, *Poverty, Charity*, 50–52; Rivka Ulmer and Moshe Ulmer, *Righteous Giving to the Poor*, 84; David J. Downs, *Alms*, 88–91; Yael Wilfand Ben-Shalom, *The Wheel that Overtakes Everyone*, 56–59 and *passim* (in Hebrew).

36 A word is in order about the broader cultural resonance of the Hebrew root "*b-z-b-z*," translated here as "scattered." Peter Brown points out that the Gallic aristocracy had not learned "to redeem sins by means of scattered coins." Peter Brown, *Ransom of the Soul*, 118 and 231 n. 6. In his earlier *Poverty and Leadership in the Later Roman Empire* (Hanover and London: University Press of New England, 2002) Brown discusses an image in a mosaic floor in a sixth-century church in the Negev, in which a woman named Silthous is portrayed with an outstretched right hand from which coins cascade. Brown compares this image to an illustration of *sparsio* (the scattering of money) in Constantius II's *Calendar of 354*. See Peter Brown, *Poverty and Leadership in the Later Roman Empire*, 28, 121.95. Monbaz is thus portrayed in the *Tosefta* as "scattering" his monies in an aristocratic manner befitting his royal rank.

37 There are also interesting discursive overlaps between the Monbaz narrative and pre-rabbinic Jewish as well as Greek sources. For a survey of these, see A.A. Halevi, *Ha-Aggadah Ha-Historit Biographit: L'Or Mekorot Yevaniyyim V'latiniyyim* (Tel-Aviv: Niv, 1975), 160–162. Echoes of Monbaz's contrast between earthly and heavenly treasures are also found in Christian sources. Helen Rhee points out how the *Acts of Thomas* later presents a contrast between "corruptible, transient" this-worldly riches and "incorruptible, everlasting" heavenly treasures. She describes a similar contrast in *Shepherd of Hermas*, specifically, *Similitude* 1:8 (*instead of fields buy souls that are in distress*). I note that this specific contrast echoes Monbaz's observation that he hid "treasuries of souls" unlike the "treasuries of money" hidden by his fathers. See Helen Rhee, *Loving the Poor, Saving the Rich*, 65, 67. These discursive overlaps further support the suggestion that ideas like these found in Christian sources had some currency in the Palestinian rabbis' time and place.

38 T. *Peah* 4:21's teaching that *tzedaqah* and *gemilut hasadim* are a great peacemaker and intercessor between God and Israel is entirely consistent with this: these two religiously meritorious practices intercede and make peace between God and Israel because they are a memorial, a demonstration, a march of merit, that intercedes and makes peace with God.

39 Y. *Shabbat* 6:10, 8d (ed. Academy, 400). On this story, see Yael Wilfand, *Poverty, Charity*, 179–180; Yael Wilfand Ben-Shalom, *The Wheel that Overtakes Everyone*, 118, 200, 292. A comparison of this story with its *Bavli* parallel (B. *Shabbat* 156a–156b) and a survey of relevant scholarship on that comparison will be undertaken in Chapter 4.

40 Y. *Ta'anit* 1:4, 64b (ed. Academy, 707); *Leviticus Rabbah* 32:7 (ed. Margulies, 752–753).

41 *Leviticus Rabbah* 34:7 (ed. Margulies, 783–784). The redemptive benefit afforded the donor through the giving of charity also underlies the teaching that *Leviticus Rabbah* 34:8 (ed. Margulies, 791) attributes to the *tanna* R. Yehoshua: the poor person does more for the householder than the latter does for him, presumably because the poor person makes possible the practice of charity, which brings redemptive benefits in its wake.

42 *Sifre Deuteronomy* 277 (ed. Finkelstein, 295).

43 Y. *Peah* 8:7, 21a (ed. Academy, 111).

44 Nor, for that matter, does Palestinian amoraic literature elsewhere mention prayer by the poor on donors' behalf. See also Yael Wilfand Ben-Shalom, *The Wheel that Overtakes Everyone*, 292 n. 44, who also correctly notes the paucity of prayer by the poor on behalf of donors in Palestinian amoraic literature.

45 *The Constitutions of the Holy Apostles*, in Alexander Roberts and James Donaldson, editors, *The Ante-Nicene Fathers* (Grand Rapids: Eerdmans; repr. 1985), 7:430.

46 Quoted in Richard Finn, *Almsgiving in the Later Roman Empire*, 180.

47 Ibid., 180.

48 See Helen Rhee's pertinent discussion of Origen's views on the "ignoble" poor in *Loving the Poor, Saving the Rich*, 85; and Susan R. Holman's discussion of Clement of Alexandria's ambivalence about the involuntary poor, some of whom may be "ignorant" or "carnal" and "have not tasted the righteousness of God" in ibid., *The Hungry are Dying*, 52–53.

49 *Genesis Rabbah* 59:1 (ed. Theodor-Albeck, 630–631). Although the *tanna* R. Meir is the protagonist of the story, it is otherwise unattested in tannaitic compilations.

50 Ephraim E. Urbach, *The Sages*, 1:436.

51 Ibid. In Chapter 5 we will explore another likely explanation: the amoraic weighting of *teshuvah* as the superior way to atone for sin than charity.

52 Y. *Peah* 1:1, 15b (ed. Academy, 79). Proverbs 10:2/11:4, with its declaration that *tzedaqah saves from death*, also appears in pre-rabbinic and later Christian sources. As an example of the former, Ben Sira 29:12 paraphrases it in the advice to "Store up almsgiving in your treasury, and it will rescue you from every disaster." Gary Anderson observes that Ben Sira points up "the power of almsgiving to save the generous soul from any imaginable danger that might confront him in this world"; see Gary Anderson, "A Treasury in Heaven": 366. For a Christian example, Polycarp quotes Tobit 12:9's paraphrase of Proverbs 10:2/11:4 in chapter 11 of his Letter to the Philippians; on this source see David J. Downs, *Alms*, 230–231.

53 Cf. Rivka Ulmer and Moshe Ulmer, *Righteous Giving to the Poor*, 83–87.

54 See *Leviticus Rabbah* 20:1 (ed. Margulies, 443–444); *Pesiqta deRav Kahana* 2:5 (ed. Mandelbaum, 20–21); *Pesiqta deRav Kahana* 26:1 (ed. Mandelbaum, 384). On *Pesiqta deRav Kahana* 2:5 see my "The People, Not the Peoples: The Talmud Bavli's 'Charitable' Contribution to the Jewish-Christian Conversation in Mesopotamia," *Review of Rabbinic Judaism* 20 (2017): 137–167. See also Yael Wilfand, *Poverty, Charity*, 209–212; Yael Wilfand Ben-Shalom, *The Wheel that Overtakes Everyone*, 251–254.

55 After a thorough discussion in my "The People, Not the Peoples": 152 n. 47 I take the position that *Pesiqta deRav Kahana*'s "Gentiles" are most likely Christians (certainty of course being unattainable). Peter Brown has also pointed out that this verse (LXX Daniel 4:27) was widely cited by Christian writers and preachers. See Peter Brown, *The Ransom of the Soul*, 97. The Christian engagement with the verse makes it unlikely that *Pesiqta deRav Kahana* is referring primarily to adherents of traditional Roman religion.

56 See, e.g., Deuteronomy 11:13–17; Deuteronomy 28:30–31, 38–42, 49–51; and the assumptions made by Job's companions in the eponymous biblical book.

57 T. *Baba Qama* 8:14 (ed. Lieberman, 40). On the proper number of judges for adjudicating monetary cases, see, e.g., M. *Sanhedrin* 1:1; on the interdiction of raising small cattle, see M. *Baba Qama* 7:7; M. *Demai* 2:3; T. *Shevi'it* 3:13 (ed. Lieberman, 177); T. *Bikkurim* 2:16 (ed. Lieberman, 293).

58 *Leviticus Rabbah* 34:13 (ed. Margulies, 800). "*Mitzvoth*" in this passage may include, yet not necessarily be limited to, the giving of charity. On "*mitzvah*" as charity, see Chapter 1.

59 *Genesis Rabbah* 78:12 (ed. Theodor-Albeck, 931).

60 *Pesiqta deRav Kahana* 24:17 (ed. Mandelbaum, 376).

61 *Leviticus Rabbah* 25:1 (ed. Margulies, 568–569).

62 *Leviticus Rabbah* 17:4 (ed. Margulies, 378–379). For a related notion attributed to the Babylonian Rav Hisda, see B. *Pesachim* 118a.

63 *Leviticus Rabbah* 34:12 (ed. Margulies, 796–799).
64 Y. *Rosh Hashanah* 1:3, 57a (ed. Academy, 665).
65 *Leviticus Rabbah* 30:1 (ed. Margulies, 688).
66 Y. *Peah* 1:1, 15b (ed. Academy, 79). Neither R. Abba nor the *Yerushalmi* clarifies whether these four involuntary payments are those made (exclusively) to Roman authorities. *Yerushalmi Shevi'it*'s literary context for the same list of outlays in the same order clearly implies that taxes to Rome are intended. See Y. *Shevi'it* 4:3, 35b (ed. Academy, 191). These involuntary outlays are also mentioned separately, or at least not always as this unit of four. The *"annona"* is linked to Rome in a poignant interpretation of Psalm 103:20 in *Leviticus Rabbah* 1:1 (ed. Margulies, 4). *"Pasin"* (= *pisin*) can refer to internal Jewish financial obligations (Y. *Baba Batra*, 1:5, 12d [ed. Academy, 1239]; *Genesis Rabbah* 17:3 [ed. Theodor-Albeck, 153]; and *Leviticus Rabbah* 34:14 [ed. Margulies, 804]). *"Zimiyot"* seems primarily to refer to fines paid to Rome, see *Leviticus Rabbah* 34:12 (ed. Margulies, 796–799). *"Galgulyot"* are demanded by Rome (= "Esau the evil one"); see *Pesiqta deRav Kahana* 2:2 (ed. Mandelbaum, 17).
67 *Leviticus Rabbah* 34:13 (ed. Margulies, 800–801).
68 *Leviticus Rabbah* 5:4 (ed. Margulies, 110–113).
69 For another colorful story about a charitable man, see *Leviticus Rabbah* 37:2 (ed. Margulies, 856) and Ephraim E. Urbach's discussion of it in *The Sages*, 1:440–441. On the Palestinian amoraic notion that giving to rabbis is a way to preserve and augment one's wealth, see my "Wealth and Rabbinic Self-Fashioning in Late Antiquity," in Leonard J. Greenspoon, editor, *Wealth and Poverty in Jewish Tradition* (West Lafayette: Purdue University Press, 2015), 53–81.
70 We cannot fail to observe that the two *Leviticus Rabbah* sources we have just examined are about donors giving to *rabbis*, not to the poor generally. Gregg Gardner also points out that Palestinian *amoraim* alter the meaning of *"tzedaqah,"* innovatively teaching that giving to rabbis, not just the materially poor, can be *"tzedaqah."* See Gregg Gardner, *Origins of Organized Charity*, 32 and *passim*. Apropos, *Leviticus Rabbah* 34:13 applies Isaiah 58:7 to the rabbis and thus discursively constructs them as the "poor," a category that may be of religious significance and not necessarily indicative of material want. This amoraic-era construction of the rabbis as a category of the "poor" requires more research, including careful comparison with contemporaneous Christian developments. See, e.g., Peter Brown, *Treasure in Heaven: The Holy Poor in Early Christianity* (Charlottesville and London: University of Virginia Press, 2016). For Palestinian amoraic ambivalence about *tzedaqah* for rabbis, see the discussion of R. Hiyyah bar Ba in Chapter 2.
71 See *Pesiqta deRav Kahana* 10:10 (ed. Mandelbaum, 172–174). As noted earlier in this chapter, R. Aqiva teaches enigmatically that "tithes are a fence to wealth" in M. *Avot* 3:13.
72 On Y. *Ma'aser Sheni* 5:6, 56b (ed. Academy, 307) three sages are described as not accepting agricultural tithes for themselves, while R. Yonah is said to have wished R. Aha bar Ulla to accept them, precisely because he engages in Torah. R. Shmuel bar Nahman is asked whether a sage should accept tithes, and he answers affirmatively. Palestinian *amoraim* were thus clearly divided over the issue of whether rabbis should accept agricultural tithes; this division of opinion makes it all the more interesting that R. Abba bar Kahana asserts without demurral that "those who labor in Torah" would accept tithes from non-agricultural gains. Some rabbis might have seen the acceptance of agricultural tithes as an encroachment on priestly prerogatives, unlike the acceptance of non-agricultural tithes.
73 Helen Rhee, *Loving the Poor, Saving the Rich*, 27–32. The quote is on p. 29.
74 Ibid., 59 and *passim*.
75 Susan R. Holman, *The Hungry are Dying*, 54.
76 T. *Peah* 4:21 (ed. Lieberman, 25).
77 As noted in Chapter 2, we do find such portrayals of *tannaim* in Palestinian amoraic literature. But as Shaye J.D. Cohen has already pointed out, this portrayal of tannaitic

activity is nowhere mirrored in tannaitic literature itself. Consequently, these portrayals cannot be taken at face value as descriptions of tannaitic activity. See Shaye J.D. Cohen, "The Rabbi in Second-Century Jewish Society," in William Horbury, W.D. Davies, and John Sturdy, editors, *The Cambridge History of Judaism*, vol. 3 (Cambridge: Cambridge University Press, 1999), 3:935.

78 I explain how the *aniyyim b'nei tovim* are a subset of a larger group called "the formerly-wealthy poor" in my "The Formerly-Wealthy Poor." I demonstrate there how empathy for the formerly wealthy poor runs like a scarlet thread throughout tannaitic literature while the *Yerushalmi* and *Bavli* (the latter especially) are noticeably ambivalent about them.

79 For the tannaitic sense of the importance of high social status, see my "The Formerly-Wealthy Poor" and the sources cited therein. Apropos, the question of whether the *tannaim* were mostly wealthy or of diverse socioeconomic backgrounds has recently been reopened. Prior to the 2015 publication of his *Origins of Organized Charity* Gregg Gardner had gathered evidence demonstrating "[n]ot all rabbis … were necessarily wealthy," a claim which he appears to have revised later; see his "Who is Rich? The Poor in Early Rabbinic Judaism," *Jewish Quarterly Review* 104:4 (Fall 2014): 515–536, especially 518–521; and ibid., *Origins of Organized Charity*, 125. Yael Wilfand argues that tannaitic evidence supports neither an assumption that "most … were well-to-do landlords who studied Torah while supporting themselves from the profits of their land" nor that "most of them were poor." She concludes after a characteristically careful assessment of admittedly scant evidence that the *tannaim* were of a "diverse" socioeconomic background. See Yael Wilfand, *Poverty, Charity*, 90–100; ibid., *The Wheel that Overtakes Everyone*, 100–108 and *passim*. But Wilfand acknowledges that a moniker such as "Rabbi Yohanan the Sandal-Maker" may mean either that he was "the craftsman who makes sandals or *the owner of the factory*." See Yael Wilfand, *Poverty, Charity*, 94–95 (emphasis added); ibid., *The Wheel that Overtakes Everyone*, 103. It also bears noting that when tannaitic literature wishes to call attention to the socioeconomic status of *tannaim*, it tends to emphasize wealth (see, e.g., the examples in Gregg Gardner, "Who is Rich?": 518–521; and M. *Baba Metzia* 7:1's implicit description of R. Yohanan ben Matya). One apparent example of a poor *tanna* is R. Yohanan ben Hahoranit (T. *Eduyyot* 2:2 [ed. Zuckermandel, 457]; T. *Sukkah* 2:3 [ed. Lieberman, 261]), who is portrayed as eating "*pat harevah*" ("dry bread") during "years of drought" and as refusing a gift of olives out of concern about eating ritually impure food. But this example does not necessarily establish R. Yohanan ben Hahoranit's poverty. His eating "dry bread" during years of drought may have been motivated by a concern to behave modestly during a time of communal economic distress. Indeed, no other *tanna* is described as eating "*pat harevah*," a term that appears in only these two places in tannaitic literature. The *Tosefta*'s reference to "*pat harevah*" may in fact be a literary borrowing from Proverbs 17:1 (*better a dry crust [pat harevah] with peace than a house full of feasting with strife*), which supports the idea that his eating this bread is a discursive creation rather than a straightforward behavioral description. Shaye J.D. Cohen's observations that *tannaim* are not by and large portrayed as poor and are demonstrably interested in social hierarchy and rank remain valid. The *tannaim*'s interest in social hierarchy and rank at the very least accounts for their greater sense of identification with higher rather than low status persons such as *aniyyim b'nei tovim*; it is difficult to imagine that persons of modest means would have an interest in emphasizing social stratification. See Shaye J.D. Cohen, "The Rabbi in Second-Century Jewish Society," 3:922–990.

80 Shaye J.D. Cohen, ibid., 3:941–942, 950.

81 But *tannaim* are not hostile to the chronically poor. See, e.g., M. *Baba Qama* 8:6; M. *Baba Metzia* 7:5. In the context of discussing the agricultural laws, tannaitic literature also expresses concern about landowners' (not) "robbing the poor." But this concern does not translate to direct tannaitic engagement with the poor to

alleviate their plight; moreover, the concern about "[not] robbing the poor" is as much about the proper application of the relevant agricultural laws as it is about proper treatment of the poor. Another interesting phenomenon is the tannaitic warmth toward the *working* poor, see, e.g., M. *Baba Metzia* 7:11. We will explore the working poor further in Chapter 4 along with the Talmud *Bavli*'s own elaboration of this particular display of warmth.

82 See the evidence cited about Palestinian *amoraim* in Chapter 2.

83 See also Gregg E. Gardner, *Origins of Organized Charity*, 185–192.

84 *Leviticus Rabbah* 31:4 (ed. Margulies, 718). For *dal*, see, e.g., Exodus 23:3 (*nor shall you show deference to a poor man [dal] in his dispute*).

85 See *Pesiqta deRav Kahana* 10:10 (ed. Mandelbaum, pp. 173–174).

86 Y. *Berakhot* 9:1, 13b (ed. Academy, 68). This notion—that the poor are identified as God's "brothers" and "friends," does not recur per se in late antique Palestinian literature or in the *Bavli*. The notion does recur in the later midrashic compilations *Exodus Rabbah* and *Midrash Tanchuma*, as noted by Ephraim E. Urbach, "Megamot Datiyot V'Hevratiyyot B'Sifrut Hazal," *Zion* 16 (1951): 19 nn. 135–136.

87 *Leviticus Rabbah* 3:2 (ed. Margulies, 61).

88 *Leviticus Rabbah* 34:9 (ed. Margulies, 791–792). I have translated the phrase *hav honakh* in accordance with Margulies' n. 8.

89 *Leviticus Rabbah* 3:1 (ed. Margulies, 59).

90 *Leviticus Rabbah* 3:5 (ed. Margulies, 65–66).

91 *Leviticus Rabbah* 3:5 (ed. Margulies, 67).

92 "Fraudulent man" may alternatively be rendered as "contentious man." The passage is found in *Leviticus Rabbah* 34:4 (ed. Margulies, 780). The translation here is taken from *Midrash Rabbah: Leviticus* (trans. Judah J. Slotki; London and New York: Soncino, 1983), 430.

93 *Leviticus Rabbah* 34:3 (ed. Margulies, 777–778).

94 *Genesis Rabbah* 91:5 (ed. Theodor-Albeck, 1120–1121).

95 Y. *Peah* 8:7, 21a (ed. Academy, 111).

96 *Leviticus Rabbah* 34:16 (ed. Margulies, 814). Helen Rhee also points out the early church's willingness to "rebuke[] the poor just as harshly as the wicked rich for their apparent envy and fretting about the rich as well as their ingratitude to the Lord…" See Helen Rhee, *Loving the Poor, Saving the Rich*, 87.

97 While Palestinian amoraic portrayals of God's warmth toward the poor may do some of that work, we should note that tannaitic erasure of the chronically poor may also be a strategy that encourages giving, precisely because the (possibly disagreeable) poor are thereby hidden from view! Richard Finn has made the point that Christian writers in late antiquity simultaneously both hid and revealed the poor in order to "make them attractive as recipients of alms." See Richard Finn, "Portraying the Poor: Descriptions of Poverty in Christian Texts from the Late Roman Empire," in Margaret Atkins and Robin Osborne, editors, *Poverty in the Roman World* (Cambridge: Cambridge University Press, 2006), 134.

98 See, e.g., Y. *Peah* 8:7, 21a (ed. Academy, 111) and the sources cited in Chapter 2.

Bibliography

Primary sources, critical editions, and translations

Albeck, Chanoch. 1978. *Shishah Sidre Mishnah: With New Commentary, Introductions, Additions, and Completions.* Tel-Aviv: Dvir

Babylonian Talmud. 1975 (repr.). Vilna-Romm edition with standard commentaries. Jerusalem: n.p.

Chrysostom, John. 1983 (repr.). *Homily XVII* to II Corinthians. In: Philip Schaff, ed. *A Select Library of the Nicene and Post-Nicene Fathers*, 1st series, vol. 12. Grand Rapids: Eerdmans, pp. 359–363

The Constitutions of the Holy Apostles. 1985 (repr.). In: Alexander Roberts and James Donaldson, eds. *The Ante-Nicene Fathers*, vol. 7. Grand Rapids: Eerdmans, pp. 385–505

The Didache. 1987. Translated by Maxwell Staniforth. Revised translation by Andrew Louth. In: Andrew Louth, ed. *Early Christian Writings: The Apostolic Fathers*. London: Penguin, pp. 187–199

Finkelstein, Louis. 1969. *Sifre on Deuteronomy*. New York: The Jewish Theological Seminary of America

The Holy Bible: New Revised Standard Version. 1989. Nashville: Thomas Nelson Publishers

Horovitz, H.S. and I.A. Rabin. 1970. *Mechilta D'Rabbi Ismael*. Jerusalem: Wahrmann Books

Lieberman, Saul. 1955. *The Tosefta: According to Codex Vienna, with Variants from Codex Erfurt, Genizah Mss. And Editio Princeps (Venice 1521). The Order of Zera'im*. New York: The Jewish Theological Seminary of America

Lieberman, Saul. 1962. *The Tosefta: According to Codex Vienna, with Variants from Codex Erfurt, Genizah Mss. And Editio Princeps (Venice 1521). The Order of Mo'ed*. New York: The Jewish Theological Seminary of America

Mandelbaum, Bernard. 1962. *Pesikta de Rav Kahana: According to an Oxford Manuscript; With Variants*. New York: The Jewish Theological Seminary of America

Margulies, Mordecai. 1993. *Midrash Wayyikra Rabbah: A Critical Edition Based on Manuscripts and Genizah Fragments with Variants and Notes*. New York and Jerusalem: The Jewish Theological Seminary of America

Slotki, Judah J., trans. 1983. *Midrash Rabbah: Leviticus*. London and New York: Soncino

Talmud Yerushalmi: According to Ms. Or. 4720 (Scal. 3) of the Leiden University Library with Restorations and Corrections. 2005. Introduction by Yaacov Sussman. Jerusalem: The Academy of the Hebrew Language

Tanakh: *A New Translation of the Holy Scriptures According to the Traditional Hebrew Text*. 1985. Philadelphia, New York, Jerusalem. The Jewish Publication Society

Theodor, Judah and Chanoch Albeck. 1996 (repr.). *Midrash Bereschit Rabbah*. Berlin and Jerusalem: Akademie für die Wissenschaft des Judentums

Zuckermandel, M.S. 1970. *Tosephta: Based on the Erfurt and Vienna Codices*. Jerusalem: Wahrmann Books

Scholarly studies and other contemporary works

Anderson, Gary A. 2009. *Sin: A History*. New Haven and London: Yale University Press

Anderson, Gary A. 2011. "3. Redeem Your Sins Through Works of Charity." In: Robin Darling Young and Monica J. Blanchard, eds. *To Train His Soul in Books: Syriac Asceticism in Early Christianity*. Washington, DC: Catholic University of America Press, pp. 57–65

Anderson, Gary A. 2012. "A Treasury in Heaven: The Exegesis of Proverbs 10:2 in the Second Temple Period." *Hebrew Bible and Ancient Israel* 1:351–367

Anderson Gary A. 2013. *Charity: The Place of the Poor in the Biblical Tradition*. New Haven: Yale University Press

Anderson, Gary A. 2013. "How Does Almsgiving Purge Sins?" In: Steven E. Fassberg, Moshe Bar-Asher and Ruth A. Clements, eds. *Hebrew in the Second Temple Period: The Hebrew of the Dead Sea Scrolls and Other Contemporary Sources*. Leiden and Boston: Brill, pp. 1–14

Brown, Peter. 2002. *Poverty and Leadership in the Later Roman Empire*. Hanover and London: University Press of New England

Brown, Peter. 2015. *The Ransom of the Soul: Afterlife and Wealth in Early Western Christianity*. Cambridge and London: Harvard University Press

Brown, Peter. 2016. *Treasure in Heaven: The Holy Poor in Early Christianity*. Charlottesville and London: University of Virginia Press

Cohen, Shaye J.D. 1999. "The Rabbi in Second-Century Jewish Society." In: William Horbury, W.D. Davies, and John Sturdy, eds. *The Cambridge History of Judaism. Vol. 3*. Cambridge: Cambridge University Press, pp. 922–990

Downs, David J. 2016. *Alms: Charity, Reward, and Atonement in Early Christianity*. Waco: Baylor University Press

Elman, Yaakov. 1990/1991. "Righteousness as its Own Reward: An Inquiry into the Theologies of the Stam." *Proceedings of the American Academy for Jewish Research* 57:35–67

Finn, Richard. 2006. *Almsgiving in the Later Roman Empire: Christian Promotion and Practice; 313–450*. Oxford: Oxford University Press

Finn, Richard. 2006. "Portraying the Poor: Descriptions of Poverty in Christian Texts from the Late Roman Empire." In: Margaret Atkins and Robin Osborne, eds. *Poverty in the Roman World*. Cambridge: Cambridge University Press, pp. 130–144

Gardner, Gregg E. 2014. "Competitive Giving in the Third Century C.E.: Early Rabbinic Approaches to Greco-Roman Civic Benefaction." In: Jordan Rosenblum, Lily C. Vuong, and Nathaniel P. DesRosiers, eds. *Religious Competition in the Third Century C.E.: Jews, Christians, and the Greco-Roman World*. Supplements of Journal of Ancient Judaism. Vandenhoeck & Ruprecht, pp. 81–92

Gardner, Gregg E. 2014. "Who is Rich? The Poor in Early Rabbinic Judaism." *Jewish Quarterly Review* 104:515–536

Gardner, Gregg E. 2015. *The Origins of Organized Charity in Rabbinic Judaism*. New York and Cambridge: Cambridge University Press

Garrison, Roman. 1993. *Redemptive Almsgiving in Early Christianity*. Sheffield: Sheffield Academic Press

Gray, Alyssa M. 2009. "The Formerly-Wealthy Poor: From Empathy to Ambivalence in Rabbinic Literature of Late Antiquity." *Association for Jewish Studies Review* 33:101–133

Gray, Alyssa M. 2011. "Redemptive Almsgiving and the Rabbis of Late Antiquity." *Jewish Studies Quarterly* 18:144–184

Gray, Alyssa M. 2015. "Wealth and Rabbinic Self-Fashioning in Late Antiquity." In: Leonard J. Greenspoon, ed. *Wealth and Poverty in Jewish Tradition*. West Lafayette: Purdue University Press, pp. 53–81

Gray, Alyssa M. 2017. "The People, Not the Peoples: The Talmud Bavli's 'Charitable' Contribution to the Jewish-Christian Conversation in Mesopotamia." *Review of Rabbinic Judaism* 20:137–167

Halevi, A.A. 1975. *Ha-Aggadah Ha-Historit Biographit: L'Or Mekorot Yevaniyyim V'latiniyyim*. Tel-Aviv: Niv

Holman, Susan R. 2001. *The Hungry are Dying: Beggars and Bishops in Roman Cappadocia*. Oxford: Oxford University Press, 2001

Pogrebin, Letty Cottin. 2014. "The Politics and Ethics of Street Tzedakah." Available at: www.momentmag.com/opinion-politics-ethics-street-tzedakah/

Rhee, Helen. 2012. *Loving the Poor, Saving the Rich: Wealth, Poverty, and Early Christian Formation*. Grand Rapids: Baker Academic

Samely, Alexander. 2007. *Forms of Rabbinic Literature and Thought: An Introduction* Oxford: Oxford University Press

Ulmer, Rivka and Moshe Ulmer. 2014. *Righteous Giving to the Poor:* Tzedakah *("Charity") in Classical Rabbinic Judaism.* Piscataway: Gorgias

Urbach, Ephraim E. 1951. "Megamot Datiyot V'Hevratiyyot B'Sifrut Hazal." *Zion* 16:1–27

Urbach, Ephraim E. 1979. *The Sages: Their Concepts and Beliefs*, 2nd enlarged ed. Jerusalem: Magnes Press

Wilfand, Yael. 2014. *Poverty, Charity and the Image of the Poor in Rabbinic Texts from the Land of Israel.* Sheffield: Sheffield Phoenix Press

Wilfand Ben-Shalom, Yael. 2017. *The Wheel that Overtakes Everyone: Poverty and Charity in the Eyes of the Sages of the Land of Israel.* Tel Aviv: Hakibbutz Hameuchad (in Hebrew)

4 Redemptive almsgiving and charity's rewards in the Talmud *Bavli*

Overview

The *Bavli* is our major (although not exclusive) source for rabbinic culture in Sasanian Iran.[1] We do well to bear in mind that the *Bavli* contains various and even conflicting ideas about charity; sharp discontinuities from Palestinian rabbinic literature are not always in evidence. Different expressions of ideas about charity's role in atoning for sin and its rewards are found throughout the corpus, sometimes within the same passage; at other times, they are discernible only after painstaking intertextual detective work. Steven Fraade's observations, made in the context of different research, are apt: the development of ideas about charity in the *Bavli* is "*progressive* rather than sudden and *dialectical* rather than linear." Fraade's continuation is equally relevant: "The combination of seemingly incommensurate (but not necessarily rhetorically incompatible) expressions within single texts ... may be editorial expressions of cultural and theological ambivalence ... rather than sedimentary layers to be separated and historicized ..."[2]

These methodological cautions acknowledged, we can discern in the *Bavli* six broad patterns of continuity and discontinuity vis-à-vis the Palestinian rabbinic legacy. The *Bavli* anthologizes and adapts three Palestinian ideas about charity. First, redemptive almsgiving: the *Bavli* largely attributes redemptive almsgiving to Palestinian sages and represents only the Babylonian *amoraim* Rav Yosef and Abaye as teaching some version of it. And apropos, although in one place the *Bavli* re-presents T. *Peah* 4:18 nearly verbatim (the Toseftan Monbaz narrative),[3] in another passage it follows the lead of *Yerushalmi Peah*'s altered ending of that narrative and fashions the uniquely Babylonian formulation that giving charity saves one from the adverse heavenly decree of "*dinah shel Gehinnom*" (the "judgment of *Gehinnom*").[4] The *Bavli* also follows the Palestinian amoraic lead in teaching that *tzedaqah* may be rewarded by rescue from death and/or longer life, although it displays an unresolved tension over whether "rescue from death" means rescue from an "unusual" (that is, unnatural) death or from "death itself." Third, like Palestinian rabbinic literature (but with some differences), the *Bavli* teaches that *tzedaqah* may be rewarded by the retention or augmentation of wealth.

The *Bavli* uniquely presents three entirely new ideas. First, donors are only rewarded for giving charity to "worthy" ("*mehuganin*") recipients. Second, *tzedaqah* given under compulsion is (nevertheless) considered religiously valid *tzedaqah* entitling the donor to a reward. Third, the *Bavli* displays an unresolved tension between advocating doing *tzedaqah* "*lishmah*" ("for its own sake") and allowing for the religious validity of *tzedaqah* a donor does for the express purpose of earning reward. We begin (again) with redemptive almsgiving.

The Talmud *Bavli*'s transformation of redemptive almsgiving

The extant evidence of Zoroastrian beliefs and practices in Sasanian Iran, although stemming from after the Islamic conquest, suggests that the Babylonian *amoraim* lived in a cultural and religious environment that may have been conducive to redemptive almsgiving. Zoroastrianism fostered a strong sense of the virtue of charity, as well as a concern for the fate of souls after death, whether one's own or those of others. Zoroastrian concern about the postmortem fates of souls manifested itself in Sasanian Iran in part through the establishment of "pious foundations" by people on their own or others' behalf, for purposes set out by the founder. Endowments could be made "for religious services for the soul" (*ruwān yazišn rāy*), or more simply "for the soul" (*ruwān rāy* or *pat ruwān*), in which case the foundation's administrator had wide latitude to provide for the soul in any way he saw fit, including public works and/or charity for the poor.[5] The *Bavli* does not mention these Zoroastrian religious endowments, nor does it adopt the Zoroastrian notion that charity benefits the souls of the dead—an idea that appears in Jewish religious writing after the *Bavli*.[6] Nor do Babylonian *amoraim* establish religious foundations like those of the Zoroastrians.

Sasanian Iran was also home to a Christian religious minority. One of a series of twenty-three discourses authored by a fourth-century Christian intellectual and polemicist named Aphrahat (the *Demonstrations*) is entitled "On the Support of the Poor" ("*Demonstration 20*").[7] Aphrahat likely wrote his *Demonstrations* between 339–379 CE, corresponding to the third and fourth Babylonian amoraic generations. Aphrahat teaches redemptive almsgiving in several places in *Demonstration 20*. Quoting Sirach (according to the version of the Syriac Peshitta), Aphrahat instructs: *Store up almsgiving and make a treasure [of it], for this is better for you than all treasures.*[8] Aprahat also quotes Daniel 4:27 (LXX): *Atone for your sins through almsgiving, and your iniquity through compassion for the poor*, introducing it by observing that "It is also written that the offences of the one who sins are wiped out through almsgiving."[9] Naturally, Aphrahat rounds out his presentation of redemptive almsgiving with an extensive quotation from Matthew 6:19–21, in which Jesus notably says: *store up for yourselves a treasure in heaven, a treasure that will not decrease, [in] a place where no worm corrupts and no thieves steal.*[10]

Recent scholarship has detailed clear evidence of overlapping discourses and even "polemic by omission" between Aphrahat and Babylonian rabbis.[11] Is redemptive almsgiving one of these "overlapping discourses"? What forms does redemptive almsgiving take in the *Bavli*? Analytic precision will be enhanced by a heuristic separation of the different threads of which redemptive almsgiving is woven: charity as atonement for sin, the accumulation of heavenly merits, rescue from *dinah shel Gehinnom* and/or "life" or "merit" of the world to come, and the gift of rescue from death/longer life in this world. The *Bavli* subtly adapts and transforms each of these, which must be examined separately (to the extent possible) so that its contributions may come fully into view.

Does charity atone for sin?

The *Bavli* sees redemptive almsgiving overall, in all its forms, as essentially a Palestinian idea, and attributes it to Palestinian sages in numerous places. Some of these attributed positions are attested in Palestinian compilations, some not. The *Bavli* attributes a view to R. Eleazar b. R. Yose that is indeed attributed to him in a Palestinian compilation: *tzedaqah* is a great intercessor between Israel and God, presumably due to its power to reconcile the two by effacing Israel's sins.[12] The *Bavli* attributes to R. Dostai b. R. Yannai a position unattested in Palestinian compilations: one who gives a gift (*doron*) to a human king cannot be certain the gift will earn him an audience; by contrast, one who gives a coin to a poor person will merit receiving the divine presence. Giving the coin to the poor "buys" access to the king, presumably by effacing sins that would otherwise prevent it.[13]

For its own part, the *Bavli* has a discernible tendency to lessen the importance and lower the profile of the Palestinian notion that charity atones for sin. There are only two discernible attributions to Babylonian sages (Rav Yosef and Abaye) of such a view, and their positions are strikingly different from the *Bavli's* portrayals of a robust Palestinian embrace of the idea. In *Bavli Sanhedrin* Rav Yosef rejects Rav Nahman's contention that the biblical King Ahab's merits and demerits were equally balanced.[14] Rav Yosef acknowledges that Ahab's wife Jezebel had a penchant for spending lavishly on idolatry, but points out that Ahab, for his part, was lavish in his support of Torah sages. He describes Ahab as a "*vatran b'mamono*," someone expansive and open-handed with his money, whose support of sages atoned for half his grave sins.

Rav Yosef's perspective on Ahab is unique to the *Bavli*. Palestinian amoraic discussions of Ahab—including the *Yerushalmi Sanhedrin* parallel—do not mention Ahab's alleged support of sages.[15] Significantly, Rav Yosef's claim is that Ahab's giving to sages (= to the rabbis) atoned for sin; he does not claim that these sages were materially poor, nor does he claim that half of Ahab's sins were atoned for through provisions to the non-rabbinic poor. Rav Yosef's claim that Ahab's providing for the sages atoned for half his sins is reminiscent of the valorization of providing for rabbis in Palestinian amoraic literature, but the consequences for the donor are strikingly different: Palestinian amoraic literature claims that giving to rabbis is rewarded by the donor's retention or augmentation of wealth, not by atonement for sin.[16]

If giving to the rabbis atones for sin, then giving to the rabbis is analogous to offering the appropriate atoning sacrifices in the Temple. And, if this is so, then giving to the rabbis is broadly analogous to religious giving to the Jerusalem Temple priests. This hypothesized analogy between the Babylonian rabbis and the Jerusalem Temple priests is indeed embraced by some second- and fourth-generation Babylonian *amoraim*. Rav Anan refused to hear the legal case of a litigant who brought him a gift of fish, but he accepted the gift as "*bikkurim*," an offering of first-fruits given to the priests.[17] Rava expressly analogizes support for rabbis to gifts to priests in the Jerusalem Temple.[18] Crucially, neither Rav Anan nor Rava (nor Rav Yosef for that matter) characterizes giving to rabbis as *tzedaqah*, or links it to *tzedaqah* in any way.[19] Putting together these various data, then, Rav Yosef's point may be less about the idea that charity (to anyone) can atone for (anyone's) sin than it is about incentivizing wealthy non-rabbinic elites' giving to Babylonian rabbis, the contemporary analogue to the Jerusalem priesthood.

Abaye's teaching of redemptive almsgiving puts him at odds with Rabbah as to the proper interpretation of I Samuel 3:14 (*the iniquity of the House of Eli will never be expiated* [*yitkapeir*; of the trilateral root *k-p-r*] by *sacrifice or offering*).[20] This dispute is a *Bavli* reworking of *Genesis Rabbah* 59:1, in which R. Meir advised the unhappy descendants of the House of Eli to prolong their lives through engagement in *tzedaqah*. Rabbah observes that engagement in Torah will supply the expiation that "sacrifice or offering" cannot, while Abaye affirms that Torah together with *gemilut hasadim* will atone. R. Meir's "*tzedaqah*" becomes Abaye's "*gemilut hasadim*."[21] And while R. Meir's point is that the reward for *tzedaqah* is longer life, Abaye's is that *gemilut hasadim* (in addition to Torah) atones for sin.[22] The *Bavli* narrator goes on to point out that both Rabbah and Abaye were descended from the House of Eli; Rabbah, who engaged in Torah, lived for forty years, while Abaye, who engaged in *gemilut hasadim* as well as Torah, lived for sixty years. But the *Bavli* buttresses Rabbah's rather than Abaye's position with a story immediately following this genealogical note. Rabban Yohanan ben Zakkai was said to have advised a Jerusalem family with a genetic tendency to early death that they might be descendants of the House of Eli; he advises them to engage in Torah and live, and they do so—with nary a mention of *gemilut hasadim*.

It may be observed that Rabbah and Abaye represent, respectively, a "Babylonian" and a "Palestinian" perspective on Torah, *gemilut hasadim*, and the atoning role each plays. Rabbah represents the Babylonian rabbinic perception of the overriding importance of Torah, a perspective elsewhere attributed to Rava. On B. *Menachot* 110a, Rava stands out from a series of tradents (largely, but not exclusively Palestinian) in teaching that one "who engages in Torah" has no need of the sacrificial offerings. The other tradents compare the study of the sacrifices to the act of offering them. "Sin-" and "guilt-offerings" are among the sacrifices Rava presumably sees as "unneeded" and in place of which Torah study provides satisfaction.[23] Abaye's pairing of Torah and *gemilut hasadim* is found in the *Yerushalmi* and *Pesiqta deRav Kahana*, as well as in Palestinian-attributed sources elsewhere in the *Bavli*.[24] The *Bavli*'s substitution of "*gemilut hasadim*" for *Genesis Rabbah*'s "*tzedaqah*" may therefore be explicable (at least in part) by the ubiquitous linkage of "*gemilut hasadim*" and "Torah" in Palestinian rabbinic compilations and the *Bavli*. As a literary matter, once the *Bavli* reworks *Genesis Rabbah* to introduce a dispute about whether Torah or acts of righteousness toward others are more efficacious in extending one's mortal existence, it makes sense that the *Bavli* would pair "Torah" with its usual companion "*gemilut hasadim*" rather than "*tzedaqah*." The replacement of "*tzedaqah*" with "*gemilut hasadim*" is, however, no mere literary matter. Given both rabbinic cultures' construction of *gemilut hasadim* as superior to *tzedaqah*, the replacement has the effect of dimming the latter's luster in comparison with the former.[25] Abaye's substitution of "*gemilut hasadim*" for "*tzedaqah*" thus tacitly raises doubt about whether *tzedaqah* alone—which is only one way to practice *gemilut hasadim*—can atone for sin.[26]

Additional evidence attests to the *Bavli*'s tendency to lessen redemptive almsgiving's importance. B. *Baba Batra* 10a presents three interpretations of Psalm 17:15 (*Then I, justified* [*b'tzedeq*] *will behold Your face*). R. Dostai b. R. Yannai and R. Eleazar clearly understand "*b'tzedeq*" as a reference to "*tzedaqah*." R. Dostai b. R. Yannai interprets Psalm 17:15 to mean that one who gives a *perutah* to a poor person will "merit" (*z-k-h*) receiving the Divine Presence, and R. Eleazar is said to have relied on Psalm 17:15 for his practice of giving a *perutah* to a poor person prior to prayer.[27] The attribution of Psalm 17:15 to these Palestinian sages reflects its importance as a charity verse in Palestinian amoraic literature; it is quoted in four places spread over three compilations as a prooftext that helps support the idea that *tzedaqah* (along with prayer and repentance) "nullifies the harsh decree."[28] The *Bavli* juxtaposes Rav Nahman bar Yitzhaq's Torah study-oriented interpretation of the latter part of Psalm 17:15 to these Palestinian interpretations (*awake, I am filled with the vision of You*). Rav Nahman bar Yitzhaq understands the verse as a reference to Torah scholars, who deprive themselves of sleep in this world and so enjoy the radiance of the Divine Presence in the next. The *Bavli* thereby signals that Psalm 17:15 need not be understood (solely) as a redemptive almsgiving verse; it may bear that significance for Palestinian scholars, but for Babylonian rabbis, it supports their engagement in Torah. Redemptive almsgiving is thus "a" value, but one that must share the stage with—indeed, even literarily give way to—Torah study.

Finally, Rava's list of questions a person will be asked "when they bring him in for [postmortem] judgment" notably omits questions about *tzedaqah*, *gemilut hasadim*, or any other demonstration of care for the poor (or anyone else, for that matter); he posits no question that is in any way redolent of redemptive almsgiving.[29] Rava's questions are: whether a person has transacted business ethically, fixed times for Torah study, engaged in procreation, lived in hopeful anticipation of the redemption, engaged in dialectical study with wisdom, attained an understanding of "one thing from another" (also a study concept), and, most of all, had "fear of heaven." Rava's silence about *tzedaqah* or *gemilut hasadim* or anything redolent of redemptive almsgiving contributes to the lessening of the latter's importance.

Ambivalence about redemptive almsgiving and "tzedaqah lishmah"

The *Bavli*'s tendency to lessen the importance of redemptive almsgiving is the tip of an iceberg of ambivalence about the idea. The "iceberg" is well-represented by a lengthy passage quoting R. Meir and an alleged dialogue between "R. Aqiva" and the Roman general "Tineius Rufus" (B. *Baba Batra* 10a).[30] The protagonists' names are enclosed in quotation marks because this narrative is not found in Palestinian compilations and contains anachronisms that are clues to its Babylonian provenance. The *Bavli* narrator chose its protagonists well, and its choice lends the passage verisimilitude: R. Meir and R. Aqiva are tannaitic icons, and R. Aqiva especially plays a prominent role in sources dealing with wealth, poverty, and charity in both Palestinian rabbinic literature and the *Bavli*.[31]

1   It was taught: R. Meir used to say, "[One's] opponent in
     court will answer and say to you: 'If your God is a lover of
     the poor, why doesn't he provide for them?' Say to him: 'In
     order that we might be saved through them from the
     judgment of *Gehinnom*.'"

2   And Tineius Rufus the wicked one asked this very question
     of R. Aqiva. "If your God is a lover of the poor, why doesn't he
     provide for them?" [R. Aqiva] said to him, "In order that we
     might be saved through them from the judgment of *Gehinnom*."

3   [Tineius Rufus] said to him: "To the contrary! This [giving
     charity to the poor] is what will make them liable for *Gehinnom*.[32]
     I will tell you a parable; to what may this be compared? To a
     mortal king who became angry at his slave and imprisoned him,
     commanding about him that he neither be fed nor given to drink.
     A man came and fed him and gave him to drink. When the king
     hears [of it], won't he be angry at that man?

4   [Tineius Rufus continues:] You are called 'slaves,' as it is said
     For it is to me that the Israelites are slaves (Leviticus 25:55)."[33]

5   R. Aqiva said to him: "I will tell you a parable; to what may this
     be compared? To a mortal king who became angry at his son and
     imprisoned him, commanding about him that he neither be fed
     nor given to drink. A man came and fed him and gave him to drink.
     When the king hears, won't he send him a gift?[34] And we are called
     'sons,' as it is written, *You are sons of the Lord your God*
     (Deuteronomy 14:1)."[35]

6   [Tineius Rufus] said to him: "You are called 'sons' and you are
     called 'slaves.' When you do the will of the Place [= God], you
     are called 'sons.' And when you do not do the will of the Place,
     you are called 'slaves.' And now, you are not doing the will of the
     Place."

7   [R. Aqiva] said to him: "Behold it says, *It is to share your bread with
     the hungry, and to take the wretched poor into your home* (Isaiah 58:7).
     When do you *take the wretched poor into your home*? Right now![36]
     And it says, *It is to share your bread with the hungry*."

R. Meir (a student of R. Aqiva, according to rabbinic tradition) opens by observing that "one's opponent in court" will object that the God of Israel cannot be a "lover of the poor." If he is, why does he not support them? R. Meir's prescribed response to the "opponent" is that the poor are the means through whom we—the givers of charity—will be saved from *dinah shel Gehinnom*. R. Meir's implicit portrayal of the poor as the means through which "we" may be saved from the "judgment of Gehinnom" assigns them a particular role in the divine scheme as living martyrs whose role is to suffer in order to provide the occasion for others to receive salvation. This notion is reminiscent both of the absence of the chronically poor from tannaitic redemptive almsgiving passages (e.g., T. *Peah* 4:18) as well as Palestinian amoraic portrayals of God's warmth toward the poor.[37] The *Bavli*'s building the passage around R. Aqiva signals the importance of the topic and the arguments attributed to him, while its attribution of challenges to redemptive almsgiving to "the wicked" Tineius Rufus signals its self-distancing from those arguments.[38]

But there is something odd about the notion that "God loves the poor." The passage does not—indeed, it cannot—provide any scriptural support for the proposition, as none exists. God is simply not described anywhere in the Hebrew Bible as "loving" the poor. Palestinian amoraic literature comes closer to this idea with its moving portrayals of God's warmth toward the poor, yet none of even those sources represents that God *loves* the poor. Moreover, the passage as a whole broadcasts anachronism to those on a wavelength to discern it. R. Meir's use of the phrase "*dinah shel Gehinnom*" ("judgment of *Gehinnom*") is clearly anachronistic; this expression is only found in the *Bavli* and post-*Bavli* literature.[39] And although R. Aqiva and Tineius Rufus are depicted in *Genesis Rabbah* as engaging in debate, that debate is not nearly as well-developed literarily as this one, and J. Theodor points out there that other examples of debate between the two are only found in post-*Bavli* midrash compilations.[40] These data suggest that the *Bavli* narrator played a key role in the fashioning of this passage, which should therefore be taken as more representative of a Babylonian than a Palestinian perspective.

Tineius Rufus's challenge to R. Aqiva's first answer (paragraphs 2–4) is a lesson based on a parable linked to Leviticus 25:55. Far from saving one from the judgment of *Gehinnom*, Tineius Rufus argues, providing for the poor should condemn the giver to that very fate. Just as a human master would be angry if someone tried to thwart his punishment of his slave through imprisonment and starvation, so would God be angry if someone tried to thwart his imposition of those punishments on his slave—and Israel *is* God's slave, as per Leviticus 25:55. To Tineius Rufus, poverty is a punishment, not a martyr-like status imposed so as to make the sufferer the vehicle through which another might come to grace. His construction of the relationship of God and Israel and of Israel's relationship one to the other is one of domination, submission, suffering, and alienation—a relationship reminiscent of the relations of Roman masters to their slaves.[41] To Tineius Rufus charity for the poor is impious and the premise of the initial question therefore simply and utterly wrong: God does not provide sustenance for the poor because God does *not* love the poor.

R. Aqiva fights parable with parable (paragraph 5). To R. Aqiva, the poor person is more properly understood as the king's *son*. While R. Aqiva accepts the premise that poverty is a punishment, his understanding of the (punished) poor person as the king's son introduces a subtle and delicate psychological and theological dynamic that Tineius Rufus entirely lacks. Just as a human father— however angry at his child—would be moved from anger to mercy and love by witnessing a loving deed done for his wayward child, so would God be moved to compassion at the sight of one person providing charity to a needy other.[42] Far from making God angry, that charitable act would arouse God's mercy toward the person who was charitable toward his son (the impoverished Israelite).

R. Aqiva's parable accomplishes several things. He answers the initial question (God does not support the poor because poverty is indeed a punishment) and buttresses his own initial expression of redemptive almsgiving (God rewards the giver with the gift of salvation from *Gehinnom* because his mercy and gratitude are aroused at the sight of the giver's compassion). He also alters the premise of Tineius Rufus's initial question. God loves, but that love is aroused and activated *after* human attempts to support the poor are undertaken. Significantly, God's love is *not* directed toward the poor (whose poverty is a punishment), but toward those who show them compassion and give them sustenance. There is therefore an interesting dissimilarity between the "Babylonian" R. Aqiva's representation of the donor–recipient relationship and what we find in Palestinian literature: to the "Babylonian" R. Aqiva God grants the donor the redemptive benefit because God is moved by the act of giving, *not* because the poor person earns the redemptive benefit for the donor by accepting the gift. The "Babylonian" R. Aqiva's parable thus subtly erases the poor even as he accords the poor person the exalted status of "king's son."

Tineius Rufus responds to R. Aqiva by acknowledging the validity of both of their constructions (paragraph 6). Although Israel may be the "king's son," they are so only when Israel is doing God's will—which they are not, as indicated implicitly by the destruction and continuing lack of a Temple. Faced with the apparent contradiction between Leviticus 25:55 and Deuteronomy 14:1, R. Aqiva reaches in paragraph 7 for Isaiah 58:7 (*It is to share your bread with the hungry, and to take the wretched poor into your home*). He asks rhetorically when it is that one is to take the wretched poor into one's home and responds that according to the verse the time is *now*. And, in this present time, Israel is further instructed *to share your bread with the hungry*. R. Aqiva's subtle omission of redemptive almsgiving at the end of the passage is as significant as his exegesis of Isaiah 58:7.

What does that omission mean? R. Aqiva's interpretation of Isaiah 58:7 may be read as an insistence that even if Tineius Rufus's understanding of Israel's current alienation from God is correct (meaning that no redemptive benefits for almsgiving are forthcoming) the proper course of action for Israel to follow is to take care of the poor "now," regardless. The *Bavli* narrator's attribution of Isaiah 58:7 to R. Aqiva closes the passage with artful ambiguity. In the Hebrew Bible Isaiah 58:7 is followed by Isaiah 58:8 (*Your Vindicator* [*tzidqecha*] *shall march before you*), a ringing declaration of charity as heavenly merit that is the capstone to the Monbaz narrative in T. *Peah* 4:18 (= B. *Baba Batra* 11a). But R. Aqiva is not represented anywhere—whether printed edition or manuscripts—as quoting Isaiah 58:8 here, only 58:7.[43] One point therefore stands out clearly: supporting the poor *today* is the right thing to do, *regardless* of the status of the divine reward to earned by doing so.[44]

On the very same folio the *Bavli* takes the short step to the logical, but by no means inevitable, next point that doing *tzedaqah* should be "*lishmah*," "for its own sake" (literally, "for its [own] name") (B. *Baba Batra* 10a). This is a unique conceptual development in the *Bavli*, which proceeds in two stages. The first stage follows immediately upon the R. Akiva/Tineius Rufus dialogue; R. Yehudah b. R. Shalom represents that one's losses for the year are determined on *Rosh Hashanah*, and if one "merits" (*zakah*), one will be able to "lose" that money by giving it to the poor. In the second stage the *Bavli* illustrates R. Yehudah b. R. Shalom with a reworking of *Leviticus Rabbah*'s narrative of R. Shimon ben Yohai and his nephews.[45] This reworking introduces the notion of doing *tzedakah* "*lishmah*."

1	This is like the case of the nephews of Rabban Yohanan ben Zakkai. He saw in a dream that they were to lose 700 *denarii* (in the coming year). He compelled them and took [money] from them for *tzedaqah* until only 17 [*denarii*] were left.
2	When *Yom Kippur* eve came, the house of Caesar seized them [the 17 *denarii*]. Rabban Yohanan ben Zakkai said to them: "Don't worry, they've [only] taken from you the 17 *denarii* you have."
3	They said to him, "How did you know [that all this would happen]?"
4	He said to them, "I saw a dream about you."
5	They said to him: "And why didn't you tell us, so that we might have given all [the money to *tzedaqah*]?" He said to them: "In order that you might do the *mitzvah* for its own sake (*lishmah*)."

Rabban Yohanan ben Zakkai sees in a dream that his nephews are destined to lose the enormous sum of 700 *denarii*. He discerns two alternatives: his nephews can "lose" the money in a religiously meritorious way to *tzedaqah* or lose it (anyway) in some other way lacking in religious merit. He therefore compels them to give money for *tzedaqah*, and they manage to give away all but seventeen of the ill-fated 700 *denarii* by the next *Yom Kippur* eve. At this point, the finger of fate intervenes as the house of Caesar seizes all their assets. Thanks to the nephews' assiduous practice of *tzedaqah* over the preceding months the house of Caesar is only able to seize (the remaining) seventeen *denarii* (with which it is apparently satisfied). Questioned by his nephews as to why he hadn't told them all this in advance so that they might have worked harder to give away all 700 *denarii* by *Yom Kippur* eve, Rabban Yohanan responds that he had kept silent so that they would do *tzedaqah* for pure motives, "*lishmah*," "for its own sake."

The divergent endings of the two narratives are what is of interest to us here. R. Shimon ben Yohai (*Leviticus Rabbah*) tells his nephews that he had kept the details of their fate to himself because he would not have been believed and hence would have had to pay out the entire sum. Rabban Yohanan ben Zakkai (*Bavli*) says instead that he concealed the true facts "in order that you might do the *mitzvah* (= give charity) for its own sake." Had Rabban Yohanan ben Zakkai's nephews known everything in advance, they would have zealously worked to spend the money on charity out of a self-interested and hence improper motive. Rabban Yohanan ben Zakkai does not claim that this improper motive would have entirely vitiated the religious value of their spending, but implies that, not being *lishmah*, the spending would have been somehow flawed.

The *Bavli* certainly does not create the idea of performing commandments *lishmah*, which was already a tannaitic value.[46] Even absent the term "*lishmah*," the idea of performing a commandment without the expectation of reward also underlies the *tanna* Ben Azzai's teaching that "the reward of a *mitzvah* is a *mitzvah*."[47] The *Bavli* is, however, the first and only rabbinic compilation to single out *tzedaqah* in particular as a commandment that should be done "*lishmah*." Apropos, B. *Baba Batra* 10a's two-stage development of the *tzedaqah lishmah* idea subtly undermines the older Palestinian amoraic notion of a pre-emptive strategy of giving as *tzedaqah* monies one is already fated to lose (Chapter 3). R. Yehudah b. R. Shalom says that one will be able to spend one's "losses" on provision for the poor "if one merits"; presumably there is no way to plan strategically for something that hinges on "merit." In addition, while both Rabban Yohanan ben Zakkai (*Bavli*) and R. Shimon ben Yohai (*Leviticus Rabbah*) intentionally practiced the pre-emptive spending strategy, the former undermines the strategy *qua* strategy by his emphasis on the importance of doing *tzedaqah lishmah*.

The *Bavli*'s advocacy of *tzedaqah lishmah* is in tension with its thrice-repeated affirmation of the religious value of doing *tzedaqah* for unmistakable and entirely self-regarding motives—including redemptive almsgiving.[48] According to an otherwise-unattested *baraita* "one who says, 'This *sela* is for *tzedaqah* in order that my sons might live, or that in order I may merit the world to come'—this is a complete *tzaddiq*."[49] In *Bavli Pesachim*, the *baraita* is used to support the proposition that a person on a *mitzvah* errand (called a "*mitzvah* messenger") is considered to be a valid "*mitzvah* messenger" even if he incidentally does something to benefit himself while on the mission. Presumably this is because his personal benefit is incidental to the mission, which remains his primary task and focus. *Bavli Pesachim* understands the *baraita* the same way: the religious value of the person's primary mission (doing *tzedaqah*) is not vitiated by any incidental personal benefit earned while doing it. The doer remains a "complete *tzaddiq*."[50] Whatever the harmonization, there remains an undeniable tension between the *baraita*'s frank acceptance of the religious legitimacy of self-interested *tzedaqah* and the *Bavli*'s innovation that *tzedaqah* should really be done "*lishmah*." Neither position therefore can be characterized as "the" position of the *Bavli*.

Does charity result in the accumulation of treasure in heaven?

We have observed that the *Bavli* anthologizes the Toseftan Monbaz narrative, the very point of which is the giver's accumulation of a treasury of heavenly merits through charity.[51] But an examination of a wider set of sources points in a different direction: the *Bavli* uncouples heavenly treasure from charity.

Four other *Bavli* narratives about heavenly treasure of some sort present those heavenly treasures as sages' reward for living pious lives of poverty and deprivation—not for doing *tzedaqah*.[52] Three of these (*Bavli Ta'anit*, *Bavli Baba Metzia*, and *Bavli Qiddushin*) are of most relevance. All three stories allow for the sages' drawing-down of heavenly treasure during this life, but with a critical difference. The Palestinian R. Hanina ben Dosa's doing so is implicitly criticized (*Bavli Ta'anit*),[53] while the two Babylonian sages benefit—indeed, even become wealthy—through access to the heavenly treasure laid up as rewards for their poverty. Rabbah bar Abuha (*Bavli Baba Metzia*) complains to the prophet Elijah that his poverty interferes with his ability to study. Upon being brought to Eden and given permission to collect fragrant leaves (his heavenly reward), Rabbah bar Abuha is stunned to hear a voice commenting disapprovingly on his collection. He responds by scattering the leaves and abandoning them in Eden. But Rabbah bar Abuha's handling of these flora leaves behind a heavenly and ultimately lucrative residue: his cloak absorbs the leaves' heavenly fragrance and he later sells it for 12,000 *dinars*, which he gives away to his sons-in-law. Rav Kahana (*Bavli Qiddushin*) was an impoverished and socially vulnerable basket-seller whom a "*matrona*" ("great lady") pestered with illicit sexual demands. In desperation Rav Kahana thought about ending his life, but the prophet Elijah appeared and alleviated his poverty by giving him a utensil filled with *dinars*. While the narrative does not explicitly identify these *dinars* as being of heavenly origin, their conveyance by the prophet Elijah provides such a link.

All three *Bavli* narratives see these heavenly treasures as literal treasures (not as treasuries of merits), and all uncouple them from *tzedaqah*. The stories about the Babylonian *amoraim* Rabbah bar Abuha and Rav Kahana even suggest a Babylonian view that one's heavenly treasure may be enjoyed on earth if it is drawn down through indirect means: Rabbah bar Abuha does so by monetizing his newly fragrant cloak, and Rav Kahana by benefiting from *dinars* the prophet Elijah somehow obtains for him. The *Bavli*'s disapproval of R. Hanina ben Dosa's early withdrawal of heavenly treasure may perhaps be due to his having made his withdrawal *directly*, in the form of a golden table-leg from the table at which he would dine in the next world. But again, the significant point is that none of these narratives links heavenly treasure with *charity*.

We have seen thus far (and *inter alia*) that Babylonian *amoraim* do not clearly or unequivocally represent that charity atones for sin and that the *Bavli* uncouples charity and heavenly treasure. The *Bavli* also lessens the importance of redemptive almsgiving by comparison with Torah study and by its new emphasis on *tzedaqah lishmah*, although redemptive almsgiving remains a viable motivation for giving. We will now examine the *Bavli*'s transformation of the ideas that charity atones for sin and accumulates heavenly merits into related, albeit differently formulated, heavenly consequences: rescue from "*dinah shel Gehinnom*" and/or the "meriting" (using the trilateral root "*z-k-*') of a "portion," or of "life," in the "world to come."

Charity and a portion in the world to come or rescue from dinah shel Gehinnom

We saw in Chapter 3 that the *Yerushalmi*'s Monbaz narrative ends with Monbaz's quoting Proverbs 10:2/11:4 (*tzedaqah saves from death*) rather than Isaiah 58:8 (*Your Vindicator shall march before you*).[54] The anonymous *Yerushalmi* reconciles *tzedaqah saves from death* with the inconvenient fact of Monbaz's eventual physical death by applying the verse to a "death" in the "coming future." *Tzedaqah* thus does indeed rescue donors from death and extend their lives—albeit not in *this* world, but in a world and life beyond this one.

The *Bavli* adopts the notion that *tzedaqah* results in the reward of a felicitous post-mortal existence but not necessarily in the *Yerushalmi*'s terms. While select individuals are indeed "invited" in the *Bavli* to the "*life* of the world to come,"[55] the *Bavli* also tends to reach over the *Yerushalmi* back to tannaitic expressions such as "having" or "meriting" a "portion in the world to come."[56] "Having" or "meriting" a "portion" in the "world to come" is reminiscent of M. *Peah* 1:1's "principal" that remains "in the world to come"; M. *Peah* 1:1's "principal" *is* a "portion in the world to come." While uncoupling actual heavenly treasures of gold and precious items from charity, the *Bavli* thus does nevertheless perpetuate the idea that the charitable donor does accumulate heavenly merits. What this "portion" looks like is unclear; what is clear is that the *Bavli* does not represent it as literal "treasure." The *Bavli* also differs from the *Yerushalmi* in its tendency—aspects of which we have already examined in this chapter—to refer to rescue from "*dinah shel Gehinnom*," which implies forgiveness of the sins that would otherwise doom the sinner to *Gehinnom*. The following sources illustrate these *Bavli* tendencies.

A *tanna* of the House of R. Yishmael creatively interprets Nahum 1:12 (*Even so are they over* [*nagozu*] *and gone; As surely as I afflicted you, I will afflict you no more*) to mean that whoever "shears" (*gozez*, a play on the verse's "*nagozu*") his possessions and does *tzedaqah* with them will be saved from the "*dinah shel Gehinnom*."[57] The metaphor is two sheep crossing a river (i.e., two people crossing over from this life into the next): only the one "sheared" (of his possessions) is able to cross and thereby be saved from "*dinah shel Gehinnom*." The "sheared sheep's" demonstration of righteousness through its "doing" of *tzedaqah* (= shearing away of possessions) results in the redemptive reward of its being saved from that terrible judgment.[58]

R. Abba interprets Hosea 7:13 (*For I was their Redeemer; Yet they have plotted treason against* me) to refer to God's disappointment that he had planned to "redeem them [Israel] through their money" in this world so that Israel would "merit the world to come" (*yizku l'olam ha-ba*), but Israel instead "plotted treason against me."[59] Note God's hope that through its money Israel would "merit" (of the trilateral root *z-k-'*) the coming world. Moving on, Rava asks Rabbah bar Mari why the biblical Micah (Judges 17) was not included in M. *Sanhedrin* 10:1's list of those who have no "portion in the world to come." Rabbah bar Mari responds by quoting a Palestinian tradition that Micah was generous with travelers; his bread was freely available to passersby. His hospitality (analogous to *tzedaqah*) ensured his portion in the world to come, notwithstanding his sponsorship of an idol.[60] Micah's reward is not expressed in the language of a postmortem rescue from death and grant of longer life; his reward is expressed in the language of having a "portion" in the coming world. As with R. Abba, the result here may be the same as *Yerushalmi Peah*'s stress on Monbaz's rescue from death in the "coming world," but the *Bavli*'s hint at the enjoyment of accumulated heavenly merit in the next world is subtly different from the *Yerushalmi*'s focus on extended life; indeed, it hearkens back to tannaitic formulations.[61]

Charity and rescue from death or grant of longer life

Like Palestinian amoraic literature, the *Bavli* advances the notion that charity results in the donor's rescue from death and longer life in this world. This message comes through clearly in a narrative found only in the *Bavli* about a communal *tzedaqah* collector/distributor named "Benjamin the *tzaddiq*," who uses his own resources to provide for a widow and her seven children in a time of drought when the communal *tzedaqah* pouch was empty (B. *Baba Batra* 11a). Benjamin subsequently falls mortally ill; after the ministering angels plead on his behalf, God grants him twenty-two more years of life. The narrative does not rely on the verse *tzedaqah saves from death* (as one might expect), likely for reasons we will explain later.

In three other places the *Bavli* subtly reworks sources that ostensibly teach or imply that charity atones for sin in order to emphasize instead that charity leads to rescue from death, longer life. Recall R. Yishmael's teaching in the *Mekhilta*:

> Come and see the mercy of the One Who spoke and the world came into being on flesh and blood. For a human being can acquire himself by money from the hands of heaven, as it says, (Exodus 30:12) *When you take a census of the Israelite people according to their enrollment, each shall pay the Lord a ransom (kofer) for himself.*[62]

As discussed in Chapter 3 this is straightforward redemptive almsgiving: one's paying the *ransom* to God results in one's acquisition of oneself. In the *Bavli*'s re-presentation of this source, R. Yishmael (son of R. Yohanan ben Beroqah) is said to teach that those liable on earth for a death penalty at the hands of heaven may atone and evade that heavenly death penalty through the giving of money. Unlike the *Mekhilta*'s R. Yishmael, the *Bavli*'s R. Yishmael relies on Exodus 21:30 (*If ransom [kofer] is laid upon him, he must pay whatever is laid upon him to redeem his life*).[63] The *Bavli*'s R. Yishmael clarifies the *Mekhilta*'s ambiguity about what "acquiring himself" means: in the *Bavli* the "giving of money" atones for those "liable for a death penalty at the hand of heaven." The benefit earned by the paying of the "ransom" is thus clearly stated to be the rescue from death and consequent longer life on this earth.

B. *Megillah* 28a illustrates a similar transformation. R. Nehunya ben HaQanah's students ask him by what virtues he merited his long life; among his merits he points out his being a *"vatran b'mamono"* ("generous with his money") like the biblical Job.[64] Later in the same passage R. Aqiva asks the same question of R. Nehunya the Great, who includes *"vatran b'mamono"* among his own virtues, along with his willingness not to seek retribution against anyone who wronged him. The *Bavli* narrator then makes a chronological and geographical leap and quotes a statement by Rava in support of the merit of not seeking retribution. Rava teaches that the sins of one who does not seek retribution are forgiven; the prooftext is Micah 7:18 (*Who is a God like You, forgiving iniquity and remitting transgression*). Rava's interpretation is that the one who "remits transgression" (i.e., foregoes retribution) is the one whose "iniquity" is "forgiven." A careful examination of the progression of opinions in this passage shows that being a *vatran b'mamono* contributes to enjoyment of a longer life in this world, but the only one whose sins are forgiven is the one who foregoes retribution. In other words, charity leads to longer life; foregoing retribution—and not charity—atones for sin.

The *Bavli* narrator also illustrates that rescue from death and longer life result from charity by its intervention into an amoraic source. Rav Yehudah states that extending one's time at the table is one of three things that "lengthens a man's days and years," but the connection between the two is opaque.[65] The *Bavli* narrator explains that "perhaps a poor person will come and he will give to him." The *Bavli* narrator bases its explanation on Ezekiel 41:22, to which it attaches a rabbinic tradition jointly attributed to R. Yohanan and R. Eleazar. Ezekiel 41:22 opens with mention of the Jerusalem Temple altar (*a wooden altar*) and closes with mention of a table (*And he said to me, "This is the table that stands before the Lord"*). R. Yohanan and R. Eleazar teach that the Temple altar atoned for Israel as long as the Temple stood, but in the present, "a man's table atones for him."[66] The *Bavli* narrator creates meaning through its juxtaposition of sources: Rav Yehudah says nothing about the poor, Ezekiel 41:22 says nothing about eating, and even if R. Yohanan and R. Eleazar themselves (or other *amoraim*) attached their tradition to Ezekiel 41:22, the meaning of "a man's table atones for him" is ambiguous. But the *Bavli* narrator brings the verse and all these traditions together, thereby creating new meaning: one's table can be one's means of atonement if one lingers long enough there to encounter and give food to a poor person. The form the atonement takes is not the forgiveness of sin and accumulation of heavenly treasure, but the lengthening of "a man's days and years." The *Bavli* narrator thus draws on the language of atonement to teach instead that *tzedaqah* leads to longer life.[67]

The Bavli*'s harmonization of a tension in the* Yerushalmi *and its internal polemic against itself*

In Chapter 3 we noted the *Yerushalmi*'s unremarked tension around *tzedaqah*'s consequence of rescue from death and longer life. In *Yerushalmi Shabbat* R. Haninah's students are saved from death, although *tzedaqah saves from death*, which seems to apply perfectly to their situation, goes unmentioned.[68] *Yerushalmi Peah*'s version of the story of King Monbaz ends with the king's quotation of *tzedaqah saves from death*, which the anonymous *Yerushalmi* refuses to understand literally; the verse is seen as applicable exclusively to a rescue from death "in the coming future." We hypothesized earlier that the *Yerushalmi*'s position seems to be that *tzedaqah saves from death* applies only to life or death in the next world, not this one; it therefore applies to Monbaz, but not to R. Haninah's students. We now add the observation that *Yerushalmi Peah* does not even acknowledge, let alone grapple with, the doubling of *tzedaqah saves from death* in Proverbs 10:2 and Proverbs 11:4. Why does the identical scriptural phrase appear twice? Do (or can) both refer exclusively to rescue from death in the coming future?

The *Bavli* (B. *Baba Batra* 10a–10b) weaves an intricate intertextual web that improves on the *Yerushalmi* by explaining Proverbs' doubling of *tzedaqah saves from death*. This explanation does the additional work of revealing the *Bavli*'s obviously different understanding that one occurrence of *tzedaqah saves from death* is indeed applicable to rescue from death in this world. The two occurrences of *tzedaqah saves from death*, one of which refers to terrestrial death and the other to the next world, enable the *Bavli* in *Baba Batra* to offer its own implicit harmonization of *Yerushalmi Peah* and *Yerushalmi Shabbat*. In a further turn of the screw, we will see that B. *Shabbat* 156a–156b polemicizes against a key part of the *Baba Batra* harmonization. We begin the unraveling of the intertextual web with *Bavli Baba Batra*:

1   R. Hiyya bar Abba said: "R. Yohanan juxtaposed
    [two verses]. It is written: *Wealth is of no avail
    on the day of wrath, but tzedaqah saves from death*
    (Proverbs 11:4), and it is written: *Ill-gotten wealth
    is of no avail, but tzedaqah saves from death* (Proverbs 10:2).[69] Why
    these two [mentions of] '*tzedaqot*'? One saves [the donor] from an
    unusual death, and one saves him from *dinah shel Gehinnom*."

2   And which one saves him from *dinah shel Gehinnom*? The one in con-
    nection with which "wrath" is written, as it is written: *That day shall be
    a day of wrath* (Zephaniah 1:15).

3   And which one saves him from an unusual death? [If]
    he gives, and does not know to whom he gives; [if] he
    takes, and does not know from whom he takes.

4   He gives, and does not know to whom he gives—this
    excludes [the story of] Mar Uqba. He takes, and does

not know from whom he takes—this excludes [the story
of] R. Abba.

5   How should [the donor] act? Let [the donor] give to the *tzedaqah* pouch.

At first glance this entire passage appears to be attributed to R. Hiyya bar
Abba in the name of R. Yohanan, but the *Bavli* narrator's fingerprints are discernible throughout. The first and most important of these fingerprints is this
passage's harmonization of the *Yerushalmi*'s just-recounted unresolved tensions.
Such harmonization of material found in two places in the *Yerushalmi* requires
the harmonizer to have a bird's eye view of a large amount of edited material;
the *Bavli* narrator likely has such a view, but not a sage as early as R. Hiyya bar
Abba. The *Bavli* narrator applies Proverbs 10:2's *tzedaqah saves from death* to
rescue from an *unusual* death and Proverbs 11:4's to salvation from "*dinah shel
Gehinnom.*" "Unusual death" is reminiscent of the violent fate that had awaited
R. Haninah's students, while the characteristic *Bavli* phrase "*dinah shel
Gehinnom*" echoes the anonymous *Yerushalmi*'s reference to Monbaz's avoid-
ance of "death in the coming future" (*Yerushalmi Peah*).[70]

A second discernible fingerprint of the *Bavli* narrator is the representation that
Proverbs 10:2 means that *tzedaqah* saves from an unusual death only when the
donor and recipient are unaware of each other. In an explicit display of intertextuality, the *Bavli* narrator ties this point to stories about Mar Uqba and R. Abba
now found on B. *Ketubot* 67b. "Giving and not knowing to whom one gives" is
declared preferable to the approach of Mar Uqba, who is described in *Bavli
Ketubot* as giving to a poor person whose identity was known to him (which led
to Mar Uqba's embarrassment and physical injury). "Taking and not knowing
from whom one takes" is proclaimed preferable to the approach of R. Abba,
whom *Bavli Ketubot* describes as providing charity to people whose identity he
did not know, although they were aware of his. B. *Baba Batra* 10b presents these
intertextual references in the same order in which they are found in *Bavli
Ketubot*, a display of awareness of ordering of material more characteristic of
the *Bavli* narrator than of an individual amora.

The *Bavli* narrator's third fingerprint follows its exclusion of the examples of
Mar Uqba and R. Abba. The *Bavli* narrator asks: "How should [the donor] act?"
The question is sensible; if Proverbs 10:2 only saves from an unusual death if
the donor and recipient do not encounter one another, then how is the donor to
give to the recipient? The *Bavli* narrator's answer is: "Let [the donor] give to the
tzedaqah pouch," and it goes on to impose the condition that the pouch be
administered by a sage of the stature of the tannaitic icon R. Hananya ben
Teradyon. *Bavli Baba Batra* thus concludes with a new, distinctively Babylonian
notion: *tzedaqah* can yield the redemptive benefit of rescue from (an unusual)
death (Proverbs 10:2) or from "*dinah shel Gehinnom*" (Proverbs 11:4) when a
donor gives anonymously to a (communal) *tzedaqah* pouch administered by a
highly reputable rabbinic sage. *Pace* the received Palestinian tradition *face-to-
face* charity does *not* yield these redemptive results, but *anonymous giving* to a
rabbinically administered fund does.[71]

The *Bavli* narrator in *Baba Batra* has thus elegantly harmonized *Yerushalmi Shabbat* and *Yerushalmi Peah*. *Tzedaqah saves from* [unusual] *death* (Proverbs 10:2) in this world *and* rescues from *dinah shel Gehinnom* (Proverbs 11:4). Proverbs 10:2 is applicable to R. Haninah's students and Proverbs 11:4 to Monbaz. But the *Bavli* narrator is not a monolith, and *Bavli Shabbat* rejects this harmonization in part. In *Bavli Shabbat* the first generation *amora* Shmuel and the *tanna* R. Aqiva are both said to teach that "*tzedaqah saves from death*" in two of three stories that form part of an extended passage on astrology.[72] The first story is about Shmuel, the second about R. Aqiva's daughter, and the third about the fourth-generation *amora* Rav Nahman bar Yitzhaq. Only the first story is of direct relevance.

1   And from [the story] of Shmuel also, [we learn]
    there is no astrological determinism for Israel.

2   For Shmuel and Ablat were sitting, and certain
    people were headed to the lake. Ablat said to
    Shmuel: "This man will go and not return; a snake
    will bite him and he will die."

3   Shmuel said to him: "If he is a son of Israel,
    he will go and return."

4   As they were sitting there, he went and returned.
    Ablat rose, threw down his pack, and found a snake
    that was divided and tossed in the two sides [of the pack].

5   Shmuel said [to the man]: "What did you do?"

6   He said: "Every day we would pool our bread and eat.
    Today, one of us did not have bread, and he was embarrassed.
    I said to them: 'I will stand up and toss in the bread.' When
    his turn came, I pretended that I was taking
    from him, in order that he not be embarrassed."

7   Shmuel said to him: "You did a *mitzvah*!"

8   Shmuel went out and expounded: "*And tzedaqah
    saves from death*; and not from an
    unusual death, but from death itself."[73]

The important point to note is that Shmuel allegedly adds the gloss "and not from an unusual death, but from death itself" to *tzedaqah saves from death*. This gloss insists upon the very understanding of *tzedaqah saves from death* that the anonymous *Yerushalmi* in *Peah* refused even to entertain—that *tzedaqah* saves the donor from a physical death in this world. Moreover, the gloss is oddly placed: the death from which the charitable character was saved was a death by snakebite—an "unusual," unnatural death. How then is the gloss "and not from an unusual death, but from death itself" appropriate? The likely answer is that the gloss is not properly attributable to Shmuel at all, but to the *Bavli* narrator of tractate *Shabbat*. The gloss is a precisely aimed polemical dart pointed directly at *Bavli Baba Batra*'s conclusion that Proverbs 10:2's *tzedaqah saves from death* applies (only) to rescue from "an unusual death."

We can even take the further step of attributing the entire narrative to the *Bavli* narrator, not just this gloss. The attribution to Shmuel is demonstrably unreliable. The discerning reader may already have noticed the strong literary similarity between the Shmuel narrative and *Yerushalmi Shabbat's* story of R. Haninah's woodcutting students. Indeed, other contemporary scholars have independently recognized that *Bavli Shabbat* is probably a reworking of *Yerushalmi Shabbat*, one meant to fit the story into the extended astrology passage. Gregg Gardner has observed that the *Yerushalmi's* "R. Haninah" needed to be replaced with another sage; R. Haninah's endorsement of astrology at the beginning of the *Bavli Shabbat* passage renders him unsuitable as a character in this anti-astrology story. In turn, Richard Kalmin explains why R. Haninah and the *Yerushalmi's* anonymous astrologer would have been replaced with the duo of Shmuel and Ablat: the *Bavli* identifies Shmuel with astronomy (a rabbinically appropriate pursuit), and the Gentile Ablat with astrology (a rabbinically inappropriate pursuit). Kalmin also points to a reference to the cutting of wood in a *genizah* fragment of this story, a small detail that brings the two versions of the story even closer.[74]

At bottom, then, the *Bavli* narrator likely selected and fitted Shmuel into place as it refashioned *Yerushalmi Shabbat's* R. Haninah story into the story we now find in *Bavli Shabbat*. Three other narrative details solidify the case. First, consider Shmuel's exclamation to the charitable man: "You have done a *mitzvah*!" In context, "*mitzvah*" can only refer to the man's charitable act; no other "commandment" is at issue. We observed in Chapter 1 that the term "*mitzvah*" was well known in Palestinian rabbinic and even Christian circles as a term signifying "charity monies." Babylonian sages do not use "*mitzvah*" this way, so its appearance in these stories is likely a remnant of an earlier Palestinian version of the story. Second, *Bavli Shabbat's* linkage of charity and a concern about the *tzedaqah* recipient's embarrassment (indicated by the trilateral root "*k-s-f*") is also found elsewhere in the *Bavli*.[75] Third, the other four quotations in the *Bavli* of *tzedaqah saves from death* are all attributed to Palestinian sages, rendering the attribution of the verse to the Babylonian *amora* Shmuel suspect.[76]

In sum, the *Bavli* narrator in *Baba Batra* harmonizes *Yerushalmi Shabbat* and *Yerushalmi Peah*, teaching that *tzedaqah* rescues the donor from an "unusual" death (Proverbs 10:2), and/or from *dinah shel Gehinnom* (Proverbs 11:4).[77] But we can discern another layer of Babylonian cultural tension about how to understand Proverbs 10:2's "*tzedaqah saves from death*." We may now understand why *Bavli Baba Batra* does not quote *tzedaqah saves from death* in connection with God's granting Benjamin the *tzaddiq* twenty-two extra years of life for his support of a hungry woman and her seven sons. In *Bavli Baba Batra* Proverbs 10:2 only applies to "unusual" death; Benjamin's death may have been premature, but it was natural, in no way "unusual." Proverbs 11:4 refers to rescue from *dinah shel Gehinnom*, which was not at issue in Benjamin's case. In brief, there is no understanding of *tzedaqah saves from death* that could apply to Benjamin in *Bavli Baba Batra*. By contrast, had his story appeared in *Bavli Shabbat*, the *Bavli* narrator there might well added Proverbs 10:2 to it because of its view that *tzedaqah saves from death* applies even to "death itself."

Does charity atone for Gentile sin?

The last topic to be explored under the general heading of redemptive almsgiving in the *Bavli* is whether Gentiles' charity atones for *their* sins and accumulates heavenly merits for *them*. This inevitably brings us back (again) to Daniel 4:24 (*Redeem your sins by beneficence and your iniquities by generosity to the poor*). According to Rav Yehudah in the name of Rav (or R. Yehoshua ben Levi) the biblical Daniel was punished for providing this counsel to Nebuchadnezzar, who demonstrably benefited from the advice (Daniel 4:25–27). The *Bavli* narrator inquires about the biblical proof that Daniel was indeed punished, and two suggestions are proffered. The first is that the Queen Esther's eunuch Hathach (Esther 4:5) is really Daniel, so renamed because he had been "cut down from his greatness" (a play on the trilateral root *ch-t-ch*, "cut"), a double entendre hinting at Hathach's being a physical eunuch as well as a rather unimportant person at the royal court. The second suggestion is that Daniel's punishment was his well-known fate of being cast into the lions' den, which happened later under King Darius (Daniel 6).[78]

The *Bavli*'s unambiguous message is that Daniel should not have revealed to Nebuchadnezzar the truth that charity indeed atones for (even Gentiles') sins. The *Bavli*'s insistence that Daniel was punished makes of him a cautionary tale: highly placed, politically connected powerful Jews should not offer such advice to their royal masters. Gentile rulers' charity *will* atone for their sins and nullify any disasters headed their way; charity's atoning efficacy for them is precisely the reason Jewish courtiers should keep silent.[79]

B. *Baba Batra* 4a's message is echoed with striking consistency on 10b–11a, in an extended reworking of a passage found in *Pesiqta deRav Kahana*.[80] The verse at issue is again Proverbs 14:34 (*Righteousness* [*tzedaqah*] *exalts a nation; sin* [*hesed*] *is a reproach* [*hatat*] *to any people*). Two aspects of the passage reinforce B. *Baba Batra* 4a; one is Rabban Yohanan ben Zakkai's change of heart about Gentile redemptive almsgiving, and the other the view of R. Ami. After hearing a number of interpretations of Proverbs 14:34, Rabban Yohanan ben Zakkai opts for that of Rabbi Nehunya ben HaQanah, who ascribes "*tzedaqah*" and "*hesed*" (the latter in the sense of "kindness") to Israel, and "*hatat*" (sin) to the nations of the world. The *Bavli* narrator's antennae are sensitive to Rabban Yohanan ben Zakkai's declaration that Rabbi Nehunya ben HaQanah's words are "*nir'in*" (they "appear" correct); this implies that Rabban Yohanan ben Zakkai may have held a view that he now feels compelled to reject. As the *Bavli* narrator puts it:

> From this it may be inferred that [Rabban Yohanan ben Zakkai] also said [something]! What is it? As it was taught in a *baraita*: Rabban Yohanan b. Zakkai said to them, "Just as the sin-offering [*hatat*] atones for Israel, so does *tzedaqah* atone for the nations of the world."[81]

Because of Rabbi Nehunya ben HaQanah, Rabban Yohanan ben Zakkai reverses his previously held position that charity atones for Gentile sin. *Pesiqta deRav*

Kahana's Rabban Yohanan ben Zakkai is not said to reject Gentile redemptive almsgiving with such directness.

A later unit within this large passage describes a misunderstanding between Rava and R. Ami about money the Sasanian King Mother Ifra Hormiz wished to give them (for an unspecified purpose). R. Ami rejected the money, and was angered to hear that Rava accepted it. R. Ami wondered: "Does [Rava] not hold (Isaiah 27:11), *When its crown is withered, they break; Women come and make fires with them*"? R. Ami's use of Isaiah 27:11 is unique in late antique rabbinic literature. He implies a link between Rava's acceptance of Ifra Hormiz's money and the perpetuation of Gentile rule; presumably, refusing the monies will cause the Sasanian *crown* to *wither* and *break*, as a result of which *fires* can be made *with them*. The medieval northern French commentator Rashi's understanding of R. Ami makes good sense: when the "merit" [*z'chut*] that is in "their" (= Gentiles') hand is "used up" and the "moistness" of their charitable actions is "dried up," then "they will be broken."[82]

I have argued elsewhere that this novel interpretation of Isaiah 27:11 is likely a response to the Christian sage Aphrahat's wielding against the Jews of fire imagery such as that in Ezekiel 15:4 (*Now suppose it was thrown into the fire as fuel and the fire consumed its two ends and its middle was charred—is it good for any use?*).[83] Isaiah 27:11 as attributed to R. Ami is the *Bavli*'s response to Aphrahat's fire polemic: If Jews (rabbis) stop accepting Gentile money (charity), the "crown" will "wither" and "break." Women will then use it to "make fires," signifying the final destruction of the Gentile empires. B. *Baba Batra* 10b–11a's fire polemic is entirely consistent with B. *Baba Batra* 4a: Gentile charity *is* redemptive for them and does indeed prolong their imperial rule. Politically connected Jewish courtiers should therefore not counsel Gentile rulers to do *tzedaqah*; withholding such counsel will hasten the withering-up and destruction of these Gentile empires.

Finally, B. *Baba Batra* 10b–11a improves upon its Palestinian parallel by making explicit how *Righteousness exalts a nation* (Proverbs 14:34)—Israel.

> R. Abbahu said: "Moses said before the Holy One, blessed be He: 'By what means will Israel's horn be exalted?' He said to him: 'By means of *ki tissa* [*when you take a census*](Exodus 30:12).'"

Israel's national exaltation is linked to its offering of Exodus 30:12's "*kofer*," ("ransom"), that is, to its doing of charity.[84] In the *Bavli*, then, charity is key to a critical distinction between the ultimate fates of Israel and the Gentile nations.[85]

The reward of retaining or augmenting one's wealth

The *Bavli* follows Palestinian amoraic literature in teaching that *tzedaqah* is rewarded by the retention or augmentation of wealth. R. Yitzhaq says "the one who gives a small coin to a poor person is blessed with six blessings, and the one who commiserates [with him] is blessed with eleven (citing Isaiah 58:7–11)."[86] Moreover:

> And R. Yitzhaq said: "What is the meaning of the
> verse *He that pursues tzedaqah and kindness*
> *will find life, tzedaqah, and honor* (Proverbs 21:21)?[87]
> He will find *tzedaqah* because he pursued *tzedaqah*?!
> Rather, this tells you: whoever pursues *tzedaqah*, the
> Holy Blessed One will provide him monies by
> which to do *tzedaqah*."

R. Yitzhaq's unambiguous point is that doing *tzedaqah* will be rewarded with more money with which to do *tzedaqah*.[88] Other pertinent evidence of this reward abounds: R. Yehoshua ben Levi likewise relies on Proverbs 21:21 to teach that the reward for "regularly" doing *tzedaqah* is the birth of sons who will be masters of wealth (along with masters of wisdom and masters of *aggadah*).[89] In *Bavli Makkot* Rami bar Hama re-presents an interpretation of Malachi 3:10 we find in *Leviticus Rabbah*: giving the mandated tithes to the Temple will result in God's bountiful granting of agricultural plenty.[90] R. Yohanan links tithing to *tzedaqah* in a delightful wordplay that echoes an idea found earlier in *Pesiqta deRav Kahana*: one should "tithe" (*t'aser*) in order that one become wealthy (*titasher*).[91]

Rav Yosef teaches the similar idea that a poor person who does *tzedaqah* will no longer display signs of poverty; in other words, his doing of *tzedaqah* will improve his material circumstances.[92] In *Bavli Ketubot* the daughter of Naqdimon ben Gurion asks R. Yohanan ben Zakkai about a proverb oft-repeated in Jerusalem that "the one who wishes to salt his money should diminish it" (or, in another version) "the one who wishes to salt his money should do *hesed* (kindness) with it."[93] The literary context of the proverb is the recollection that Naqdimon ben Gurion's family lost all their wealth because they did not "diminish" the wealth (through charity) or "do *hesed* with it." "Salting" (i.e., "preserving") one's money is thus best accomplished by lessening it through charitable expenditures. The apparent paradox that preservation of wealth is assured by charitable giving is precisely the point: charitable giving indeed results in the replenishing and maintenance of one's wealth.

Donors only receive reward for giving to "worthy" (*mehuganin*) recipients

This chapter has thus far examined the *Bavli*'s adaptations and creative reworking of demonstrably Palestinian ideas. We now turn to charity concepts and ideas in the *Bavli* that lack a discernible Palestinian precedent, beginning with the idea first mentioned in Chapter 1 that only donors to "worthy" recipients will be rewarded. In Chapter 1 we touched on this idea and that of the Bavli's thematization of financial (and *tzedaqah*) compulsion in order to demonstrate how the

Bavli's understanding of *"tzedaqah"* differs from the Palestinian idea of *"tzedaqah"* as a donor's self-motivated demonstration of righteousness before God. In this section we will explore the emergence and development of these ideas on their own terms.

The *Bavli* juxtaposes two Babylonian amoraic teachings to R. Yitzhaq's reading of Proverbs 21:21 (*He that pursues* tzedaqah *and kindness will find life,* tzedaqah, *and honor).*[94] As we saw, R. Yitzhaq's declared meaning is that the doer of *tzedaqah* will be rewarded with more money with which to do it. Significantly, the Babylonian *amoraim* qualify this by introducing the idea of "worthy" *tzedaqah* recipients:

1   Rav Nahman bar Yitzhaq said: "The Holy Blessed One
will provide him worthy (*mehuganin*) persons with whom to do
tzedaqah in order that he may receive his reward
for them."

2   [Rav Nahman bar Yitzhaq's view comes] to exclude
what? [It comes] to exclude [those about whom] Rabbah expounded.
For Rabbah expounded: "What is the meaning of the verse, *They are
made to stumble in their ways*
(Jeremiah 18:15)? Jeremiah said before the Holy
Blessed One: 'Master of the World! Even at the time
they subdue their inclination and wish to do *tzedaqah*
before you, cause them to stumble with unworthy persons,
so that they will not receive reward for them.' "

Rav Nahman bar Yitzhaq (paragraph 1) reinterprets Proverbs 21:21; what God will provide is not more money with which to do *tzedaqah*, but "worthy" persons with whom to do *tzedaqah* and thereby earn its reward. The *Bavli* narrator points out that Rav Nahman bar Yitzhaq's "worthy" recipients excludes the "unworthy" recipients about whom Rabbah expounded (paragraph 2), but this observation is not entirely helpful in making sense of the category. "Unworthy" recipients might be those who are not actually needy.[95] As appealing as this hypothesis is, a survey of occurrences of *"mehugan"* ("worthy") in the *Bavli* does not necessarily support it.[96] At bottom, the *Bavli's* insistence on "worthy" recipients signals that a donor's good intentions to act on his righteousness before God by doing *tzedaqah* (in the form of charity) are not enough: giving to an unworthy recipient is of no religious value. The donor needs not just any recipient, but a *worthy* recipient.

The *Bavli's* requirement of "worthy" recipients sheds light on a tradition attributed to the Palestinian *amora* R. Eleazar and unattested as such in Palestinian compilations.[97] R. Eleazar ranks *gemilut hasadim* higher than *tzedaqah* on the basis of Hosea 10:12: *Sow righteousness* (tzedaqah) *for yourselves; reap the fruits of goodness* (hesed). As R. Eleazar understands the verse, one who "sows" (*tzedaqah*) is uncertain of whether he will be able to eat. One who "reaps" (*hesed*) will certainly eat. Doing *tzedaqah* alone does not guarantee reward;

doing *hesed* (= *gemilut hasadim*) does. I suggest that R. Eleazar's uncertainty about the consequences of "sowing" *tzedaqah* is linked to the *Bavli's* larger uncertainty about the "worthiness" of potential *tzedaqah* recipients. R. Eleazar's greater certainty about being rewarded for doing *hesed* may be due to the broader range of people to whom *gemilut hasadim* applies (e.g., the dead, the rich), and the consequent greater likelihood that one will indeed encounter "worthy" beneficiaries of one's *hesed.*

Money taken for *tzedaqah* by force is still considered valid *tzedaqah* worthy of reward

The *Bavli* also uniquely affirms the religious merit of (even) *tzedaqah* given under duress.

> And R. Eleazar said: "At the time the Temple was standing a man would weigh out his *sheqel* and it would atone for him. Now that the Temple is not standing: if they do *tzedaqah* it is well, and if not, the idolaters will come and take it by force. Nevertheless, that will be considered *tzedaqah* for them, as it says (Isaiah 60:17), *Those who take from you by force, it is* tzedaqah."[98]

R. Eleazar re-presents the old equation of religious giving to the Temple and *tzedaqah*, stressing the equal sin-remitting powers of both. But he also makes the novel point that "*tzedaqah*" need not be given voluntarily to be considered as such; even the despoliation of one's property by idolaters can be "*tzedaqah.*" This idea may be a Babylonian twist on the Palestinian amoraic notion that giving as *tzedaqah* monies one is otherwise fated to lose is still religiously meritorious. But the *Bavli's* linkage of "compulsion" and *tzedaqah* is not found in Palestinian compilations in quite this form; moreover, the *Bavli* elsewhere thematizes a link between compulsion and money generally.[99] As to *tzedaqah* specifically, Rava exerts compulsion on R. Natan bar Ami and exacts the large sum of 400 *zuz* for *tzedaqah*, a form of legally sanctioned despoliation that nevertheless qualifies as "*tzedaqah.*"[100] R. Eleazar points out that the one who "compels" (*'a-s-y*) others to give *tzedaqah* is greater than the one who actually gives it.[101] Rabbah "imposed" ("*ramah*") *tzedaqah* on the orphans of the House of Bar Maryon.[102] And we have seen how Rabban Yohanan ben Zakkai "compels" his nephews to give *tzedaqah* after dreaming they would lose 700 *dinars* by the next *Yom Kippur* eve.[103]

The *Bavli's* emphasis on *tzedaqah* compulsion is vividly if subtly on display in *Bavli Megillah's* reworking of its *Yerushalmi Megillah* parallel.[104] The *Yerushalmi* portrays R. Imi as being in control of charity collection in Sepphoris. The visiting R. Helbo followed tannaitic prescription and participated along with the Sepphoreans in a public stipulation of charity. R. Helbo later wished, also in accordance with tannaitic precedent, to receive back his stipulated charity for distribution in his own town. R. Imi refused to give it back, saying: "You are an

individual [and thus must leave the stipulated charity in Sepphoris]." The protagonists in the *Bavli* are Rav Huna, who "imposes" a charity assessment on his
town, and the visiting Rav Hana bar Hanilai, who has come to Rav Huna's town
together with his own townspeople.[105] Rav Hana bar Hanilai and his fellow
townspeople participate in Rav Huna's charity assessment and like the *Yerushalmi*'s R. Helbo, he later seeks its return for distribution back in his own town.
Like R. Imi, Rav Huna refuses, but the reason is clearly and critically different.
R. Imi insists on retaining R. Helbo's *tzedaqah* because R. Helbo is (merely) one
individual. Rav Huna insists on retaining the *tzedaqah* of Rav Hana bar Hanilai
and his fellow townspeople because he, Rav Huna, is the unique individual (the
haver ir, or "town scholar") on whom both his and Rav Hana bar Hanilai's
towns depend.

Rav Huna's is an unprecedented interpretation of the term *hever ir*. In M.
Berachot 4:7 "*hever ir*" refers to a collectivity (a "town fraternity"), not an individual. The *Bavli*'s crafting of Rav Huna's position is a creative misreading of
the *Yerushalmi* parallel which functions to heighten the local authority of Rav
Huna and, by extension, Babylonian *amoraim* more widely.

Babylonian amoraic assertion of control over charity is also a feature of Rav
Yosef's, Rabbah's, and Rav Ashi's charitable activities in succeeding amoraic
generations. Rav Yosef is represented as being in charge of the "*arneqa
d'tzedaqah*" in Pumbedita, which he placed in another person's care, thus clearly
exercising a communal charitable leadership role.[106] We saw earlier that Rav
Yosef declares himself authorized to accept a coin on behalf of the poor because
"we—we are the hand of the poor" ("*anan—yad aniyyim anan*").[107] Rabbah and
Rav Ashi are also portrayed as having unilateral control over their local *tzedaqah*
pouches.[108]

The *Bavli*'s portrayals of the poor and of rabbis' involvement in the collection and distribution of *tzedaqah*

Ambivalence about redemptive almsgiving and portrayals of the poor

The *Bavli* is hardly unsympathetic to the plight of the poor, and movingly—
albeit indirectly—calls attention to the soul-destroying impact of extreme
poverty. A *baraita* unattested in Palestinian rabbinic literature includes "*diqduqei aniyyut*" (the "finer points" of poverty) as one of the things that "drives a
person out of his mind and from a knowledge of his Creator."[109] But the *Bavli*'s
ambivalence about redemptive almsgiving correlates with a demonstrably negative attitude toward the poor who accept charity and even the acceptance of
charity itself. "Correlates," not "causes": its ambivalence about redemptive
almsgiving cannot readily be identified as the cause of these negative attitudes or
vice versa, but the imbrication of the two is readily demonstrable.

We begin with the *Bavli*'s negative evaluation of accepting charity. Ulla
states that a person who supports himself through work is better than one who
fears heaven (and presumably relies on heaven for support from others); he

derives this from a comparison of Psalm 112:1 (*Happy is the man who fears the Lord*) with Psalm 128:2 (*Happy are you when you eat the fruit of your labors; you shall be happy and you shall prosper*).[110] Eating the "fruit of your labors" earns the toiler the additional promise "*you shall prosper*" in addition to "*you shall be happy.*"

The *Bavli*'s repetition of "*al tiztareikh la-briyot*" ("do not have need of other created beings") is also relevant.[111] R. Aqiva holds that one should treat the Sabbath like an ordinary day of the week rather than "have need of other created beings," that is, accept charity. The *Bavli* adds this caution about avoiding "need of other created beings" to its prescription that one ought not to give away more than one-fifth of one's wealth annually as charity. This caution is missing from the *Yerushalmi* parallel.[112] R. Yose teaches that one should not fast too much lest he come to have need of other people and find none to come to his aid.[113] R. Yose's meaning seems to be that excessive fasting weakens a person physically and makes him vulnerable, thereby inevitably necessitating his reliance on others.

Apropos, the *Bavli* also tends to illustrate the importance of charity by means of negative examples rather than positive portrayals of warm interactions between donors and the poor. Nahum Ish Gam Zu's apparently slight delay in assisting a poor man has dire consequences for the sage.[114] Rav Papa declines to help a beggar, whereupon Rav Sama b. deRav Yeba scolds him: "If the master does not attend to him, no one else will attend to him! Shall he die?"[115] In another story, Rav Papa almost suffers a fatal fall from a ladder. Hiyya bar Rav Midifti speculates that perhaps Rav Papa's near miss was due to his having failed to give charity to a poor person.[116] Finally, we have seen how the importance of providing lavishly for (even) a (demanding) formerly wealthy poor man is established through the negative example of Rava.[117]

We now move on to the *Bavli*'s ambivalent and even negative portrayals of the poor who need and accept charity. Mar Uqba was in the habit of leaving four *zuzim* for a poor person in the latter's doorpost. The poor man became curious about his benefactor's identity and followed Mar Uqba and his wife when the couple left the money on a certain day. Mar Uqba and his wife ran from the man and hid in a hot, recently used oven.[118] The *Bavli* narrator glosses this story with an interpretation that suggests Mar Uqba's desire to avoid embarrassing the poor man. Yet shorn of the *Bavli* narrator's gloss, Mar Uqba seems to have run away from the poor man simply to avoid contact with him.[119]

There is other, related evidence of the potential for danger in face-to-face encounters between potential donors and recipients. Imma Shalom was said to have prevented her husband R. Eliezer's "falling on his face" in prayer out of fear that his prayer would cause harm to her brother Rabban Gamliel, who claimed responsibility for R. Eliezer's excommunication.[120] One day R. Eliezer succeeded in "falling on his face"; one reason given for Imma Shalom's lapse in vigilance was that a poor man came to the door and Imma Shalom brought out bread to him, during which time the fateful prayer was uttered.[121] However unwittingly, Imma Shalom's charitable act set the stage for her brother's death.

Similarly, the Angel of Death disguised himself as a poor man at the door in order to seize R. Hiyya, who had hitherto successfully evaded him.[122] Plimo was humiliated by the Satan disguised as a demanding, entitled, socially graceless poor man.[123]

Rava explains that the saying *"batar anya azla aniyuta"* ("poverty follows the poor") is based on Leviticus 13:45, which requires the leper to warn people away by calling out: "Unclean! Unclean!" Rava's scriptural derivation is striking: poverty is, as it were, a form of "leprosy," a persistent, mute cry of "Unclean! Unclean!" Just as people naturally tend to flee from the presence of a leper, so presumably, (according to Rava), people naturally tend to flee from the presence of the poor.[124]

The *Bavli* also displays its ambivalence and even negativity toward the poor who accept charity by its refusal to characterize as "poor" (using some form of "*ani*") the very few rabbis it describes as enduring straitened material circumstances. The *Bavli*'s typical way of expressing such material deprivation is through some variation of the euphemistic phrase "*dehiqa leih* (or *l'hu*) *milta* [*tuva*]" ("he [or they] were [very] pressed").[125] Poor Babylonian rabbis are simply not called "*aniyyim*." Two cases in which the root *a-n-i* is in fact employed are instructive. Rav Kahana tells the prophet Elijah that he took desperate measures because "poverty (*aniyuta*) caused me" to do so; he does not identify himself as an *ani*, but as someone motivated by *aniyuta*, someone to whom poverty happened.[126] Rav Yosef states that no Torah scholar becomes impoverished (*m'anei*), but the *Bavli* narrator immediately objects that there are indeed poor Torah scholars (again using "*m'anei*"). The *Bavli* narrator explains Rav Yosef's meaning to be that poor Torah scholars do not beg from door to door.[127] Rav Yosef's statement seems too easily belied by reality and the *Bavli* narrator's explanation of it seems forced, yet taken together, the two reinforce the larger point: a Torah scholar may live in straitened circumstances, but he is not an "*ani*," meaning that he does not engage in characteristic "*ani*" behavior such as begging.[128]

On the other hand, the *Bavli*'s warmth toward the working poor who presumably do not support themselves through charity is striking.[129] Rav tells Rav Kahana to "flay a carcass in the marketplace" rather than refuse the menial job on the ground that he is a "great man."[130] Before his rise to scholarly prominence Hillel is famously described as working for a menial wage each day, half of which he would use for his family's support and half as the entrance fee to the house of study.[131] In Chapter 1 we examined the story of Rav's ordering Rabbah bar Rav Huna to return the cloaks and even pay the wages of the clumsy workers who broke Rabbah bar Rav Huna's jugs of wine.[132] Among the late antique rabbinic compilations only the *Bavli* derives from Leviticus 25:55's *For it is to Me that the Israelites are slaves* the notion that day laborers may walk off the job at any time, because they—like all human beings—are God's slaves, and not "slaves to slaves," that is, to other human beings.[133]

The *Bavli*'s disfavoring the acceptance of charity, its negative portrayals of the poor who do, and its warm, positive portrayals of the working poor are all consistent with a discernible *Bavli* preference for financial independence for rabbis as well as the poor.[134] The *Bavli*'s preference for rabbinic financial independence manifests itself in two bodies of evidence: the traditions about the rise from poverty to wealth of certain Babylonian *amoraim*, and descriptions of Babylonian amoraic hostility to the non-rabbinic wealthy in Babylonia, which are bound up with expressions of rabbinic preferences for financial independence.[135] One example of the *Bavli*'s preference for rabbinic financial independence is Rava's interpretation of I Samuel 7:17 (*Then he would return to Ramah, for his home was there*) to mean that the biblical prophet Samuel's home was wherever he was traveling; that is, he maintained self-sufficiency and independence in his travels, not taking anything from anyone.[136] Apropos, Abaye (or R. Yitzhaq) teaches that whoever wishes to benefit from others should do so like the biblical prophet Elisha (that is, minimally); those who wish not to benefit at all from others should do so like the prophet Samuel.[137] The Babylonian amoraic preference for financial independence also sheds light on the *Bavli's* portrayal of the impoverished sages Rabbah bar Abuha and Rav Kahana's benefiting on earth in some way from their heavenly treasures.[138] The importance of achieving financial independence in this world allows for an indirect drawing-down of some benefits of the heavenly treasure of the next. Rav Anan's, Rav Yosef's, and Rava's analogy of giving to rabbis as giving to the Jerusalem Temple priests is not inconsistent with an emphasis on rabbinic independence.[139] The analogy permits an implicit construction of the rabbis as a distinct social group entitled to accept these gifts as their divinely provided due—when they are offered. Unlike Palestinian *amoraim*, who solicit contributions from non-rabbis, Babylonian *amoraim* do not—but they will accept them if offered.

Taken all together, these many and varied sources make sense of why Rav Yosef teaches that Ahab's giving to sages (not the materially poor) atoned for half his sins, why Abaye states that Torah and *gemilut hasadim* (not *tzedaqah* alone) atone for sin,[140] and why *Bavli Baba Batra* leaves redemptive almsgiving's status as a religious idea rather ambiguous, with an added healthy dose of ambivalence.[141] Negative attitudes toward the acceptance of charity and the poor who do so, combined with positive attitudes toward the working poor and financial independence, are simply inconsistent with a robust, full-throated embrace of redemptive almsgiving in all its manifestations.

The Bavli's *focus on "worthy" charity recipients, the religious validity of charity given under compulsion, and a role for Babylonian rabbis*

Negative attitudes toward the acceptance of charity and the poor who do so also evince distrust of those poor. This distrust sheds light in turn on the *Bavli*'s unique focus on limiting *tzedaqah*'s rewards to those who give to "worthy" (*mehuganin*) recipients. Not all who seek charity may be presumed "worthy."[142]

The *Bavli* narrator is quite clear (B. *Baba Batra* 10b) that in order to avoid the mistakes of both Mar Uqba and R. Abba, a prospective donor should give to "the *arneqi shel tzedaqah*" (the "*tzedaqah* pouch"). The *Bavli* narrator goes on to point out that one should only give to a *tzedaqah* pouch under the supervision of a sage as reliable as the tannaitic hero R. Hananya ben Teradyon. The *Bavli*'s careful construction of the importance, even indispensability, of rabbinic control over the communal *tzedaqah* pouch is arguably related to its emphasis on "worthy" *tzedaqah* recipients. An individual donor may not be able to tell who is "worthy" and who not, but by delegating this responsibility (and headache) to a reputable rabbi, the donor is relieved of that burden. The Babylonian rabbinic sage will mediate between the donor and the poor, ensuring that charity money only goes to "worthy" recipients. The donor may therefore rest assured that her *tzedaqah* will produce for her the requisite divinely bestowed benefits.

The *Bavli*'s discouragement of face-to-face encounters between donors and the poor and its correlative stress on donating to a communal *tzedaqah* pouch under rabbinic supervision is also related to the *Bavli*'s thematization of compulsion and *tzedaqah*. Compelling charitable contributions makes good sense as Babylonian rabbinic policy: compulsion reliably fills the *tzedaqah* pouch the rabbis control with funds they can distribute as they see fit.

Our work in Chapters 3 and 4 has, *inter alia*, explored the various aspects and transformations of redemptive almsgiving in both Palestinian rabbinic compilations and the *Bavli*, and various displays of ambivalence about it. But one major, related topic requires exploration: the coexistence in the literatures of both rabbinic centers of redemptive almsgiving and *teshuvah* (repentance), the latter a more extensively treated and even valorized mode of atonement. It is to an exploration of *teshuvah* and its arguably uneasy relationship with *tzedaqah* that we turn in Chapter 5.

Notes

1 Scholars are becoming increasingly aware of the significance of Jewish material culture in Sasanian Iran. See, e.g., Shai Secunda, *The Iranian Talmud: Reading the Bavli in its Sasanian Context* (Philadelphia: University of Pennsylvania Press, 2014), 16, 34–38, 40, 46, and *passim*. As to seals, see, e.g., Moshe Beer, "Three Seals of Babylonian Jews and Their Date," *Tarbiz* 52 (1983): 435–445 (in Hebrew); Shaul Shaked, "Jewish Sasanian Sigillography," in Rika Gyselen, editor, *Au Carrefour des Religions: Melanges offerts a Philippe Gignoux* (Bures-sur-Yvette: Groupe pour l'etude de la civilization du Moyen-Orient, 1995), 239–255; Daniel M. Gridenberg, *Sasanian Jewry and Its Culture: A Lexicon of Jewish and Related Seals* (Urbana: University of Illinois Press, 2009). As to incantation bowls, see, e.g., Michael Morony, "Religion and the Aramaic Incantation Bowls," *Religion Compass* 1 (2007): 414–442; Shaul Shaked, "Form and Purpose in Aramaic Spells: Some Jewish Themes," in Shaul Shaked, editor, *Officina Magica: Essays on the Practice of Magic in Antiquity* (Leiden, Brill, 2005), 1–30. Secunda usefully calls attention to scholarship that links Sasanian Jewish material and rabbinic culture in *The Iranian Talmud*, 155 n. 46–156 n. 51 and *passim*.
2 See Steven D. Fraade, "Rabbinic Polysemy and Pluralism Revisited: Between Praxis and Thematization," *Association for Jewish Studies Review* 31:1 (2007): 1–40, especially 39–40 (emphasis in original).
3 B. *Baba Batra* 11a.

4 See B. *Baba Batra* 10a. The phrase *"dinah shel Gehinnom"* is found in the *Bavli* and post-*Bavli* compilations. It is not found in the *Yerushalmi* or *Genesis* or *Leviticus Rabbah.* It is found on B. *Berachot* 61a (two occurrences); B. *Shabbat* 118a (twice); B. *Erubin* 18b (twice); B. *Yebamot* 102b (twice); B. *Nedarim* 40a (twice); B. *Sotah* 4b (three occurrences); B. *Sotah* 5a; B. *Gittin* 7a; and B. *Baba Batra* 10a (four occurrences). This evidence suggests that *"dinah shel Gehinnom"* is not of Palestinian origin; its appearance in Palestinian traditions in the *Bavli* is likely the result of the "Bavlicization" of these traditions.

5 See Mary Boyce, *Zoroastrianism: Its Antiquity and Constant Vigour* (Costa Mesa: Mazda Publishers and Bibliotheca Persia, 1992); J.P. de Menasce, "Feux et Fondations Pieuses dans le Droit Sassanide," *Travaux de l'Institut d'études iranniennes de l'Université de Paris* (Paris: Librairie C. Klincksieck, 1964), 2:59–62; Mary Boyce, "The Pious Foundations of the Zoroastrians," *Bulletin of the School of Oriental and African Studies* 31:2 (1968): 270–289; ibid., *Zoroastriaism: Its Antiquity and Constant Vigour,* 141; Anahit Perikhanian, "Iranian Society and Law," in Ehsan Yarshater, editor, *The Cambridge History of Iran: Volume 3(2): The Seleucid, Parthian and Sasanian Periods* (Cambridge: Cambridge University Press, 1983), 661–665; Maria Macuch, "Charitable Foundations," in Ehsan Yarshater, editor, *Encyclopedia Iranica* (Costa Mesa: Mazda Publishers, 1992), V:380–385. Mention should be made of the late Yaakov Elman, who was a trailblazer in the study of Middle Persian and Sasanian law and culture and their utility in shedding light on the *Bavli.*

6 See Chapter 7. The *Bavli* does, however, represent that charity given at the time of the donor's own death may be of utility in easing his path in the journey from life into death. See Mar Uqba's deathbed bequest (B. *Ketubot* 67b).

7 All references herein to Aphrahat's *Demonstrations* are to the excellent translation by Adam Lehto. See Adam Lehto, *The Demonstrations of Aphrahat, the Persian Sage* (Piscataway: Gorgias Press, 2010).

8 Aphrahat, *Demonstrations* (ed. Lehto, 426).

9 Aphrahat, *Demonstrations* (ed. Lehto, 430).

10 Aphrahat, *Demonstrations* (ed. Lehto, 433).

11 See my "The People, Not the Peoples: The Talmud Bavli's 'Charitable' Contribution to the Jewish-Christian Conversation in Mesopotamia."

12 B. *Baba Batra* 10a (= T. *Peah* 4:21).

13 B. *Baba Batra* 10a.

14 B. *Sanhedrin* 102b.

15 Y. *Sanhedrin* 10:2, 28b (ed. Academy, 1318–1319); *Pesiqta deRav Kahana* 24:11 (ed. Mandelbaum, 358–368).

16 See, e.g., *Leviticus Rabbah* 5:4 (ed. Margulies, 110–113); *Leviticus Rabbah* 34:13 (ed. Margulies, 800–801).

17 B. *Ketubot* 105b (based on Deuteronomy 26:1–11).

18 B. *Hullin* 133a; cf. Y. *Ma'aser Sheni* 5:6, 56b (ed. Academy, 307).

19 We will return later in this chapter to the *Bavli*'s tendency not to construct giving to rabbis as *tzedaqah.* For the Palestinian willingness to do so, see, e.g., Y. *Megillah* 3:1, 74a (ed. Academy, 764) and the pertinent observations of Gregg E. Gardner, *Origins of Organized Charity,* 32 and *passim.*

20 B. *Rosh Hashanah* 18a. The question of whether Abaye's interlocutor is "Rabbah" or "Rava" requires consideration of manuscripts of both B. *Rosh Hashanah* 18a and its parallel on B. *Yebamot* 105a. As to B. *Rosh Hashanah* 18a: Mss. Munich 95, Munich 140, London—BL Harl. 5508 (140), and the Spanish print (1516) read "Rava" throughout the narrative. Ms. Oxford Opp. Add. Fol. 23 attributes to "Rava" the statement that Torah atones, but says that "Rabbah" was, along with Abaye, a descendant of the House of Eli, as do Ms. JTS Rab. 1608 (ENA 850) and the Pesaro Print (1514). Ms. JTS Rab. 218 (EMC 270) reads inversely: "Rabbah" teaches that

Torah atones, and "Rava" is said to have been a descendant of the House of Eli along with Abaye. As to B. *Yebamot* 105a: the Pesaro Print (1508), Ms. Moscow—Guenzberg 594, and Ms. Moscow—Guenzberg 1017 have "Rava" throughout the narrative, while Ms. Munich 141 has "Rabbah" throughout the narrative. Ms. Jerusalem Michael Krupp 3894/10 attributes to "Rava" the teaching that Torah atones and identifies "Rabbah" as the descendant of the House of Eli, while Ms. Munich 95 does exactly the opposite. Ms. Oxford Opp. 248 (367) and Ms. Vatican III identify "Rava" as the descendant of the House of Eli; the former attributes the teaching that Torah atones to "R. Shmuel bar Nahmani," while the latter leaves the tradent unclear. The manuscript evidence is so obviously divided that relying on it alone to choose the proper attribution is practically impossible. "Rabbah" makes most sense as the correct reading in both tractates for the entire narrative. The reasons are: (1) Given Rabbah's and Abaye's uncle-nephew relationship as described in the *Bavli*, a reference to their shared genealogical misfortune is apt; (2) "Rabbah" is elsewhere described as having had a short life (B. *Moed Qatan* 28a), which dovetails with this narrative; and (3) while Rava might be expected to teach that Torah atones, he is nowhere else described in the *Bavli* as a descendant of the House of Eli.

21 *Genesis Rabbah* 59:1 (ed. Theodor-Albeck, 630–631). See the discussion of this passage in Chapter 3.

22 See Yaakov Elman's comments on B. *Rosh Hashanah* 18a in "Righteousness as its Own Reward": 65.

23 As Richard Kalmin puts the matter: "For Babylonian rabbis, Torah study was the *summum bonum* of human existence. For Palestinian rabbis, Torah study was only one among many important religious observances and practices…" See Richard Kalmin, *Jewish Babylonian between Persia and Roman Palestine* (New York and Oxford: Oxford University Press, 2006), 20–29, 31–36. See also his earlier study "Rabbinic Traditions about Roman Persecutions of the Jews: A Reconsideration," *Journal of Jewish Studies* 54:1 (2003): 21–50; Ephraim E. Urbach, *The Sages*, 1:611.

24 See Y. *Ta'anit* 4:2, 68a (ed. Academy, 729), which provides scriptural support for M. *Avot* 1:2 (the world stands on "Torah," "*avodah*," [Temple service], and *gemilut* hasadim)." Indeed, M. *Avot* 1:2 may be the basis for the amoraic pairing of "Torah" and "*gemilut hasadim*" in both rabbinic centers, "*avodah*" being of obvious irrelevance in a Temple-less world. See also the parallel at *Pesiqta deRav Kahana* 19:6 (ed. Mandelbaum, 309) (Torah and *gemilut hasadim* make one worthy to sit in the shadow of God's hand). See also B. *Berachot* 8a (God says that whoever engages in Torah, *gemilut hasadim*, and communal prayer redeem him and Israel from among the nations of the world); B. *Yoma* 9b (the Second Temple was destroyed because of causeless hatred despite the prevalence at that time of engagement in "Torah, *mitzvoth*, and *gemilut hasadim*"); B. *Avodah Zarah* 5b (the pairing of Torah and *gemilut hasadim* is attributed to R. Yohanan in the name of R. Bana'ah); B. *Avodah Zarah* 17b–18a (Torah and *gemilut hasadim* are paired in the account of R. Hanina ben Teradyon's life and martyrdom).

25 See Y. *Peah* 1:1, 15c (ed. Academy, 79) and the parallel on B. *Sukkah* 49b.

26 Apropos, B. *Sotah* 4b–5a quotes R. Yohanan's interpretation of Proverbs 16:5, which literally reads *hand to hand, he will not go unpunished.* R. Yohanan's interpretation is that giving charity secretly ("*hand to hand*") will not expunge the sin of intercourse with a married woman and the malefactor will be punished with "*dinah shel Gehinnom.*" If charity cannot expunge this singular, particularly heinous sin, then one certainly cannot assume it can expunge sin *tout court.* In Chapter 5 we will explore how the *Bavli* perceives *teshuvah* to be a more effective mode of atonement overall than charity.

27 On some aspects of the afterlife of R. Eleazar's teaching in Jewish religious culture, see Eliezer Segal, "R. Eliezer's *Perutah*," *The Journal of Religion* 85:1 (2005): 25–42. From a source-critical perspective R. Eleazar's statement is a creation of the

Bavli. R. Eleazar is the tradent of three of the four Palestinian representations of the triad *"tefillah, tzedaqah, teshuvah"* and its scriptural derivations. The derivation of *"tefillah"* from Psalm 17:15 is common to all four. See Y. *Ta'anit* 2:1, 65b (ed. Academy, 712); Y. *Sanhedrin* 10:2, 28c (ed. Academy, 1319–1320); *Genesis Rabbah* 44:12 (ed. Theodor-Albeck, 434–435); *Pesiqta deRav Kahana* 28 (ed. Mandelbaum, 425). The *Bavli* narrator pulls out this derivation of *"tefillah"* and presents it as a stand-alone tradition of R. Eleazar on B. *Baba Batra* 10a.

28 See the sources cited in n. 27. We will examine these traditions in Chapter 5.

29 B. *Shabbat* 31a.

30 I draw here on my previously published version of this translation in my "Redemptive Almsgiving and the Rabbis of Late Antiquity." The translation is of the printed edition. Significant manuscript variations will be noted.

31 See my "Wealth and Rabbinic Self-Fashioning," 56–57 and nn. 30–32; Azzan Yadin, "Rabbi Akiva's Youth," *Jewish Quarterly Review* 100:4 (2010): 573–597.

32 Ms. Vatican (Biblioteca Apostolica Ebr. 115) instead reads *"v'zo hi davar!,"* which can be rendered as "Is this an argument?"

33 I have altered the JPS translation's *"servants"* to "slaves."

34 Ms. Vatican eliminates the mention of a gift, reading instead that the king will consider the charitable man as having done him a good turn.

35 In keeping with R. Aqiva's gendered parable, I have altered the JPS translation's *"children"* to "sons."

36 Ms. Vatican reads *bazman ha-zeh* (at this time) and does not quote the rest of the verse.

37 See Chapter 3.

38 Apropos of rabbinic attributions of positions to different sorts of characters, see Christine Hayes, "Displaced Self-Perceptions: the Deployment of 'Minim' and Romans in B. Sanhedrin 90b–91a," in Hayim Lapin, editor, *Religious and Ethnic Communities in Later Roman Palestine* (Bethesda: University Press of Maryland, 1998), 249–289.

39 See n. 4.

40 Circumstantial evidence of the *Bavli*'s own fashioning of this "dialogue" between R. Aqiva and Tineius Rufus is revealed by a look at other references to these figures. "Tineius Rufus" in any form of the name is missing from tannaitic literature. The *Yerushalmi* does not mention "Tineius Rufus," although Y. *Ta'anit* 4:5, 69b (ed. Academy, 736) says that a "Rufus" plowed over the sanctuary (the parallel on B. *Ta'anit* 29a reads "Tineius Rufus"). Y. *Berachot* 9:5, 14b (ed. Academy, 75) says that R. Aqiva was judged and martyred by "Turnus Trufus." B. *Nedarim* 50a–50b and B. *Avodah Zarah* 20a associate the two in non-judicial, non-polemical settings. Among the late antique compilations, only *Genesis Rabbah* 11:5 (ed. Theodor-Albeck, 92–94) represents R. Aqiva and Tineius Rufus as engaged in debate (about the Sabbath); as pointed out in the main text, J. Theodor points to other, post-*Bavli* examples of their debates. This literary evidence is further support for our contention that B. *Baba Batra* 10a is anachronistic, likely the work of the *Bavli* narrator.

41 For a description of Roman slavery, see, e.g., Keith Hopkins, *Death and Renewal* (Cambridge: Cambridge University Press, 1983), 10, 12, 27–28, and *passim.*

42 This notion attributed to "R. Aqiva" may be based on *Genesis Rabbah* 33:3 (ed. Theodor-Albeck, 304) (R. Abba says that when God sees people showing mercy to each other in a time of drought, He in turn is filled with mercy for them).

43 Apropos, note Richard Finn's interesting observation about Augustine: "Augustine avoids texts which emphasize redemptive almsgiving in atonement for sin. Among the texts most frequently cited by him to promote almsgiving is ... Isaiah 58.7..." Richard Finn, "Portraying the Poor," 139. Augustine's use of Isaiah 58:7 buttresses our conclusion that the verse's quotation in this passage is part of a rhetorical undermining of redemptive almsgiving.

44 Bar Kappara is said to have drawn a similar ethical conclusion in *Leviticus Rabbah* 34:14 (ed. Margulies, 802). He observes that everyone experiences poverty, if not a person himself, then his son or grandson. His ethical conclusion is that one should consider the flesh of the poor as one's own (and hence act appropriately in providing clothing to one who needs it). On this point see also Yael Wilfand, *Poverty, Charity,* 69–70; Yael Wilfand Ben-Shalom, *The Wheel that Overtakes Everyone,* 77.

45 *Leviticus Rabbah* 34:12 (ed. Margulies, 796–799).

46 For a brief, useful summary of sources, see Ephraim E. Urbach, *The Sages,* 1:393–395 and *passim.*

47 M. *Avot* 4:2. See also the usage of "*lishmah*" and "*lishman*" in the sacrificial contexts of *Mishnah Zebachim* and *Menachot.*

48 See B. *Baba Batra* 10b and the parallels on B. *Rosh Hashanah* 4a and B. *Pesachim* 8a–8b.

49 The translation is of B. *Baba Batra* 10b. The second condition is worded slightly differently on B. *Rosh Hashanah* 4a: "in order that I merit through it the life of the world to come." B. *Pesachim* 8a–8b does not include use of the trilateral root "*z-k-'*," reading instead: "in order that I be a son of the world to come."

50 See *Rashi* to B. *Pesachim* 8b, s.v. "*harei zeh tzaddiq gamur.*"

51 B. *Baba Batra* 11a (= T. *Peah* 4:18).

52 Eliezer Diamond collects and discusses three of these stories as a unit (he does not discuss B. *Qiddushin* 40a) in his *Holy Men and Hunger Artists: Fasting and Asceticism in Rabbinic Culture* (New York: Oxford University Press, 2004), 68–71. The stories are found on B. *Ta'anit* 24b–25a (R. Hanina ben Dosa); B. *Ta'anit* 25a (R. Eleazar ben Pedat); and B. *Baba Metzia* 114b (Rabbah bar Abuha). As Diamond points out, the R. Eleazar ben Pedat narrative in *Bavli Ta'anit* is a difficult text; it establishes that a heavenly treasure awaits the ascetically inclined rabbi, but otherwise is irrelevant here.

53 R. Hanina ben Dosa sees and makes an early withdrawal of some of his accumulated heavenly treasure in the form of a golden table-leg from the "table" at which he will dine in the next world. Upon learning that the premature withdrawal and use of this golden table-leg would leave her husband in the next world with only a rickety two-legged table, his wife asks him to pray and return it to heaven.

54 Y. *Peah* 1:1, 15b (ed. Academy, 79).

55 See, e.g., B. *Berachot* 61b; B. *Avodah Zarah* 10b and 18a.

56 See, e.g., M. *Sanhedrin* 10:1. In the *Yerushalmi,* the notion of a "portion in the coming world" is found either in the *Mishnah* or other tannaitic sources. To the best of my knowledge the solitary exception is Y. *Hagigah* 2:1, 77c (ed. Academy, 785), where the term is attributed to the *amora* R. Yose ben Haninah.

57 B. *Gittin* 7a.

58 The Christian text *Shepherd of Hermas* makes the same point with a stone carving metaphor. The "carving" of the "stones" is a metaphor for the "cutting away" of wealth through charity. See Helen Rhee, *Loving the Poor, Saving the Rich,* 60.

59 B. *Avodah Zarah* 4a.

60 B. *Sanhedrin* 103b.

61 See Gary A. Anderson, *Charity,* 179 and 213 n. 24. As noted earlier, however, there are indeed *Bavli* references to "life" in the world to come, although these are not directly connected to charity. As Mar Uqba lay dying, he asked for his *tzedaqah* accounts to be brought before him. He saw written there that he had given 7,000 *dinars* of good coinage. He observed: "a small provision for a long journey!" and gave away (literally, "scattered") half his money on the spot. But he is not described as earning "life" in the "world to come. The martyr Qetiah bar Shalom (B. *Avodah Zarah* 10b) "outs" himself as a philo-Semite and saves the Jews from the Roman emperor's planned genocide, only to be condemned to death for having bested the emperor in oral combat. As he is being taken out for execution, a lady observes

"Woe to the one who sails without paying the tax!" Qetiah immediately divines her intention, and circumcises himself, whereupon he states: "I have paid the tax. I will pass." A heavenly voice declares that Qetiah "is invited to the life of the world to come"; Rabbi weeps, noting that some "acquire their world" over many years and some (like Qetiah) in one "moment." Although Qetiah divides his possessions among "R. Aqiva and his companions," this bequest is not how he earns the life of the world to come—he earns that through his martyrdom.

62 See Chapter 3.
63 B. *Ketubot* 37b.
64 On Job as a "*vatran b'mamono*," see also B. *Baba Batra* 15b.
65 B. *Berachot* 54b.
66 B. *Berachot* 55a.
67 The partial parallel on B. *Menachot* 97a does indeed have R. Yohanan and R. Eleazar's tradition attached to Ezekiel 41:22, but it lacks both the larger context of Rav Yehudah's teaching about what will lengthen a person's life and the statement by the *Bavli* narrator that lengthened time at table will accomplish this because "perhaps a poor person will come and he will give to him." That charity context is entirely the creation of the *Bavli* narrator on B. *Berachot* 54b–55a.
68 See Y. *Peah* 1:1, 15b (ed. Academy, 79); Y. *Shabbat* 6:10, 8d (ed. Academy, 400), and the earlier discussion in Chapter 3.
69 A reminder: I have altered the JPS translation by leaving "*tzedaqah*" untranslated.
70 The phrase "*arneqi shel tzedaqah*" (*tzedaqah* pouch) is also unique to the *Bavli*; see also B. *Ketubot* 67b; B. *Baba Qama* 93a.
71 Note that this is also a *Bavli* reinvention of the *Sheqalim* tractates' "hall of secrets." We will return later to contextualize this innovation in light of other *Bavli* evidence.
72 B. *Shabbat* 156a–156b. The passage opens on B. *Shabbat* 156a with the conflicting views of R. Hanina and R. Yohanan as to whether or not there is "*mazal*"—astrological determinism—for Israel. This passage has received a great deal of attention in contemporary scholarship. See, e.g., Richard Kalmin, *Jewish Babylonia between Persia and Roman Palestine*, 173–186, 249–254; ibid., "A Late Antique Babylonian Treatise on Astrology," in Shai Secunda and Steven Fine, editors, *Shoshannat Yaakov: Jewish and Iranian Studies in Honor of Yaakov Elman* (Leiden and Boston: Brill, 2012), 165–184; Gregg Gardner, "Astrology in the Talmud: An Analysis of Bavli Shabbat 156," in Eduard Iricinschi and Holger M. Zelentin, editors, *Heresy and Identity in Late Antiquity* (Tübingen: Mohr Siebeck, 2008), 314–388; Jeffrey L. Rubenstein, "Talmudic Astrology: *Bavli Šabbat* 156a–156b," *Hebrew Union College Annual* 78 (2009): 109–148.
73 Again, I have altered the JPS translation, leaving "*tzedaqah*" untranslated.
74 See Gregg Gardner, "Astrology in the Talmud," 334–336; Richard Kalmin, "A Late Antique Babylonian Rabbinic Treatise," 173–176.
75 B. *Ketubot* 67b, B. *Hagigah* 5a.
76 B. *Baba Batra* 10a (two occurrences; R. Yehudah [the *tanna*] and R. Yohanan); B. *Rosh Hashanah* 16b (R. Yitzhaq); B. *Shabbat* 156b (two occurrences; Shmuel [as noted] and R. Aqiva).
77 Cf. Yaakov Elman's observations about a similar phenomenon in his study of theodicy in the *Bavli*:

> the *Bavli* presents a number of independent explanations of the problem of theodicy—an embarrassment of riches—the exact applicability of which is not clear … it is impossible to determine how each redactor would have viewed the solution offered by others.

> See Yaakov Elman, "Righteousness as its Own Reward: An Inquiry into the Theologies of the Stam": 66. In this case we are afforded a glimpse of how the *Bavli Shabbat* narrator responds to *Bavli Baba Batra*, but not the reverse.

78 B. *Baba Batra* 4a.

79 The *Bavli*'s limitation of Daniel 4:24 to Nebuchadnezzar himself may also be a tacit polemic against a view like that of the Persian Christian sage Aphrahat, who quotes Daniel 4:27 (LXX) in his *Demonstration* 20 to illustrate that, as to *all* Christians, "it is also written that the offences of the one who sins are wiped out through almsgiving." The message of the tacit polemic would be that Daniel 4:24 does not in fact apply to all Gentiles. See Aphrahat, *Demonstrations* (ed. Lehto, 430).

80 See *Pesiqta deRav Kahana* 2:5 (ed. Mandelbaum, 20–21) and the pertinent discussion in Chapter 3. On B. *Baba Batra* 10b–11a see my "The People, Not the Peoples"; Yael Wilfand, *Poverty, Charity*, 212–216; Yael Wilfand Ben-Shalom, *The Wheel that Overtakes Everyone*, 254–257.

81 Mss. Oxford Opp. 249 (360) and Escorial G-I-3 read that just as the sacrifices atone for Israel "in this world" so does *tzedaqah* atone for the nations "in this world." Mss. Florence II-I-9, Hamburg 165, Munich 95, and possibly Vatican 115 distinguish between the sacrificial atonement for Israel "in the world to come" and the consequences of *tzedaqah* for the nations "in this world." Ms. Paris 1337, like the Pesaro (1511) and Vilna-Romm printed editions, refers simply to atonement.

82 *Rashi* to B. *Baba Batra* 10b, s.v. "*b'vosh qetzirah tishavarnah.*"

83 See my "The People, Not the Peoples": 158–160.

84 Exodus 30:12. The verse continues: *each shall pay the Lord a ransom for himself on being enrolled...*" We saw in Chapter 3 that this *ransom* (Heb.: *kofer*) is identified with charity in *Mekhilta de-Rabbi Ishmael* (*Neziqin* 10) (ed. Horovitz-Rabin, 285–286).

85 Apropos of redemptive almsgiving for Gentiles, mention should be made of B. *Sukkah* 55b. R. Yohanan laments for the idolatrous nations who do not realize what they lost upon the destruction of the Jerusalem Temple. While the Temple stood "the altar atones for them," but in the absence of the Temple, "what (or who) atones for them"? On B. *Baba Batra* 9a the point is made that charity atones for Jews in the absence of the Temple, but a similar representation that charity will likewise atone for the Gentile nations is missing from B. *Sukkah* 55b. The latter is thus entirely consistent with the overall thrust of B. *Baba Batra* 4a and 10b–11a.

86 B. *Baba Batra* 9b. "Six" and "eleven" come from counting up the blessings the verses heap upon the giver; for purposes of our analysis, these need not be spelled out.

87 The partial translation of the verse is my own.

88 See *Leviticus Rabbah* 34:13 (ed. Margulies, 800–801); *Leviticus Rabbah* 5:4 (ed. Margulies, 110–113). See also my "Wealth and Rabbinic Self-Fashioning in Late Antiquity," and the earlier discussion in Chapter 3.

89 B. *Baba Batra* 9b.

90 Malachi 3:10: *Bring the full tithe into the storehouse ... I will surely open the floodgates of the sky for you and pour down blessings on you.* See B. *Makkot* 23b (= *Leviticus Rabbah* 35:12 [ed. Margulies, 832]).

91 B. *Ta'anit* 9b (= *Pesiqta deRav Kahana* 10:10 [ed. Mandelbaum, 172]); see also Deuteronomy 14:22. On these sources see the discussion in Chapter 3. The very same wordplay attributed to R. Yohanan in *Bavli Ta'anit* is elsewhere attributed to R. Yishmael b. R. Yose (B. *Shabbat* 119b). Apropos, Rav Nahman bar Yitzhaq is also represented as teaching that proper tithing will result in much wealth. His prooftext is Numbers 5:10 (*And each shall retain his sacred donations*), which he interprets against the grain of the plain meaning to say that the giver of the tithe will "retain" what he gives to the priest, in that he will "retain" and suffer no diminution of wealth.

92 B. *Gittin* 7a–7b.

93 B. *Ketubot* 66b.

94 B. *Baba Batra* 9b; see also B. *Baba Qama* 16b.

95 See, e.g., B. *Ketubot* 67b–68a and my discussion of "frauds" in "The Formerly-Wealthy Poor."

96 An examination of *"mehugan"* in the *Bavli* shows that in some contexts, what is "inappropriate" depends upon what the person so described has or has not done. A person who is *"eino mehugan"* may misuse knowledge of the Temple service for purposes of idolatry (B. *Yoma* 38a), or mislead the sages about the appearance of the new moon in order to corrupt the calendar (B. *Rosh Hashanah* 22b). In other cases the term is more ambiguous; for example, it is used to describe inappropriate marriage partners for a woman, without clearly indicating how they are inappropriate (e.g., B. *Yebamot* 108a, B. *Ketubot* 22a, B. *Ketubot* 54a, B. *Baba Qama* 80a). Reference is also made to people "worthy" to accompany Ruth the Moabite and other gleaners in the fields—although again, there is no clarification of what makes them so (B. *Shabbat* 113b). In two cases, the term is used broadly to refer to people of generally inappropriate character (B. *Nedarim* 20a; B. *Qiddushin* 70a). All this ambiguity suggests that *"einam mehuganin"* in the charity context may include, but not be limited to, the notion that the taking of charity is "inappropriate" because unnecessary, but this remains speculative.

97 B. *Sukkah* 49b.

98 B. *Baba Batra* 9a. The translation of the verse is my own.

99 E.g., B. *Hagigah* 5b, B. *Avodah Zarah* 65a, B. *Sanhedrin* 109a, B. *Ketubot* 67b, and B. *Bava Batra* 8b. This is related to the *Bavli*'s thematization of rabbinic control over the collection and distribution of *tzedaqah*, to which we will shortly return.

100 B. *Baba Batra* 8b.

101 B. *Baba Batra* 9a.

102 B. *Baba Batra* 8a.

103 B. *Baba Batra* 10a.

104 B. *Megillah* 27a–27b; Y. *Megillah* 3:2, 74a (ed. Academy, 764).

105 B. *Megillah* 27a–27b. Alone among the textual witnesses, Oxford Opp. Add. Fol. 1.23 reads "פסקו עליו," using the older Palestinian term, rather than a form of the trilateral root *"r-m-',"* "imposed." See Michael Sokoloff, *A Dictionary of Jewish Babylonian Aramaic of the Talmudic and Geonic Periods* (Ramat-Gan: Bar-Ilan University Press, 2002), 1086, for the meaning of *"r-m-h"* as "imposed" in the context of financial obligations including charity.

106 B. *Baba Qama* 93a.

107 Rav Yosef is unique among Babylonian *amoraim* in his tendency eisegetically to read poverty-oriented interpretations into earlier sources on B. *Megillah* 4b and B. *Ketubot* 107b. In the former, he explains that the reason the reading of the Esther scroll must be moved up to the market day when Purim falls on the Sabbath is "because the eyes of the poor are raised to the reading of the scroll"; that is, the poor live in anticipation of receiving their statutory "gifts to the poor" which are not distributed on the Sabbath. In the latter, he identifies as *"tzedaqah"* the ambiguous *"davar aher"* ("another thing") in a *baraita* about court-ordered maintenance for a woman whose husband is away on a trip. In these cases, Rav Yosef's strong identification with charity is demonstrated not only through action, but through his preferences in interpretation. For other of his poverty-oriented interpretations see B. *Baba Qama* 108b–109a and the *Bavli* narrator's intervention into a statement of Rav Yosef's with a "poverty-oriented" interpretation on B. *Baba Qama* 56b.

108 B. *Baba Batra* 8b–9a.

109 B. *Erubin* 41b.

110 B. *Berachot* 8a. I have deviated from the JPS translation by rendering the first half of the verse literally in order to underscore the parallelism between its two parts.

111 B. *Shabbat* 118a; B. *Pesachim* 112a; B. *Ketubot* 50a; B. *Ta'anit* 22b.

112 B. *Ketubot* 50a; Y. *Peah* 1:1, 15b (ed. Academy, 78).

113 B. *Ta'anit* 22b.

114 B. *Ta'anit* 21a; compare the parallel on Y. *Peah* 8:9, 21b (ed. Academy, 113).

115 B. *Baba Batra* 9a.

116 B. *Baba Batra* 10a.

117 B. *Ketubot* 67b.

118 B. *Ketubot* 67b.

119 This point was first suggested by Richard Kalmin. See Richard Kalmin, *The Sage in Jewish Society of Late Antiquity*, 43.

120 B. *Baba Metzia* 59b.

121 Cf. the discussion of this narrative detail in Jeffrey L. Rubenstein, *Talmudic Stories: Narrative Art, Composition, and Culture* (Baltimore: Johns Hopkins University Press, 1999), 51–53.

122 B. *Moed Qatan* 28a.

123 B. *Qiddushin* 81a–81b.

124 B. *Baba Qama* 92a–92b. Abaye uses the phrase "*batar anya azla aniyuta*" on B. *Hullin* 105a and B. *Baba Batra* 174b. Apropos, see B. *Nedarim* 64a's classification of the poor as among those who are considered to be dead, presumably a reference to a form of social death.

125 See B. *Ta'anit* 25a; B. *Baba Metzia* 114b; B. *Baba Batra* 174b (= B. *Arachin* 23a); B. *Ta'anit* 21a; B. *Avodah Zarah* 35b; B. *Baba Qama* 18b. Rabbah's poverty is described without reference to this expression but also without his being labeled an "*ani*"; see B. *Moed Qatan* 28a.

126 B. *Qiddushin* 40a.

127 B. *Shabbat* 151b.

128 For the *Bavli*'s perspective that begging from door to door is a characteristic behavior of the *ani*, see, e.g., B. *Qiddushin* 22a (it is unseemly for a man's wife to beg from door to door, but not for his children).

129 The *Bavli* likely derives its sympathy for the working poor from tannaitic literature. As an example, R. Yohanan b. Matya stresses to his son that the working poor the son hired are the noble descendants of the patriarchs Abraham, Isaac, and Jacob. (M. *Baba Metzia* 7:1). The *Bavli*'s similarity to the *Mishnah* in this respect is hardly an isolated case.

130 B. *Baba Batra* 110a.

131 B. *Yoma* 35b.

132 B. *Baba Metzia* 83a.

133 See B. *Qiddushin* 22b; B. *Baba Qama* 116b; B. *Baba Metzia* 10a. I have altered the JPS's "*servants*" to "slaves."

134 B. *Menachot* 85b is an interesting example of the *Bavli*'s interest in financial independence (even) for the poor. Proverbs 13:7 reads: *One man pretends to be rich and has nothing; another professes to be poor and has much wealth.* The verse is illustrated by a story of a man rich in olive oil but cash-poor, who behaves like a poor laborer, much to the confusion of a purchasing agent who comes with a great deal of cash in order to buy a large quantity of oil. Ultimately the "rich" agent comes to owe a great deal of money to the "poor" olive-dealer. The *Bavli*'s portrayal of a cash-poor "rich" man and his financial independence is an interesting additional datum relevant to its preference for financial independence.

135 For a closer look at all this material, see my "Wealth and Rabbinic Self-Fashioning in Late Antiquity." While Palestinian compilations and the *Bavli* do represent Palestinian rabbis' voluntary poverty (e.g., *Leviticus Rabbah* 30:1 [ed. Margulies, 688–689]); B. *Ta'anit* 21a), the very few examples of Babylonian amoraic poverty are noticeably *involuntary* (e.g., B. *Moed Qatan* 28b [Rabbah]; B. *Qiddushin* 40b [Rav Kahana]; B. *Baba Batra* 174b [Rav Huna bar Moshe bar Atzri]).

136 B. *Nedarim* 38a.

137 B. *Berachot* 10b. For Elisha's acceptance of support from the Shunemite woman, see II Kings 4:8–11.
138 B. *Baba Metzia* 114b (Rabbah bar Abuha); B. *Qiddushin* 40b (Rav Kahana). There is more to say about these narratives' thematization of financial independence. Eliezer Diamond includes in his discussion of these narratives a story about the *tanna* R. Yehudah, who refuses the gift of a cloak from the Patriarch despite his extreme poverty (B. *Nedarim* 49b–50a). This portrayal of the *tanna* is consistent with the *Bavli*'s larger tendency to portray sages (notably, but not only, Babylonian *amoraim*) as financially independent, and its related tendency to praise and strongly encourage such rabbinic independence. Again, see my "Wealth and Rabbinic Self-Fashioning in Late Antiquity," 66–72.
139 See B. *Ketubot* 105b; B. *Hullin* 133a; B. *Sanhedrin* 102b; and the discussion at the beginning of this chapter.
140 B. *Rosh Hashanah* 18a.
141 B. *Baba Batra* 10a.
142 B. *Baba Batra* 9b. Both Talmuds are keenly concerned about the possibility of charlatans' posing as the needy in order to collect charity money. See my "The Formerly-Wealthy Poor" for a discussion of the Talmuds' treatments of that issue.

Bibliography

Primary sources, critical editions, translations, and dictionaries

Albeck, Chanoch. 1978. *Shishah Sidre Mishnah: With New Commentary, Introductions, Additions, and Completions.* Tel-Aviv: Dvir

Babylonian Talmud. 1975 (repr.). Vilna-Romm edition with standard commentaries. Jerusalem: n.p.

Horovitz, H.S. and I.A. Rabin. 1970. *Mechilta D'Rabbi Ismael.* Jerusalem: Wahrmann Books

Lehto, Adam. 2010. *The Demonstrations of Aphrahat, the Persian Sage.* Piscataway: Gorgias Press

Lieberman, Saul. 1955. *The Tosefta: According to Codex Vienna, with Variants from Codex Erfurt, Genizah Mss. And Editio Princeps (Venice 1521). The Order of Zera'im.* New York: The Jewish Theological Seminary of America

Mandelbaum, Bernard. 1962. *Pesikta de Rav Kahana: According to an Oxford Manuscript; With Variants.* New York: The Jewish Theological Seminary of America

Margulies, Mordecai. 1993. *Midrash Wayyikra Rabbah: A Critical Edition Based on Manuscripts and Genizah Fragments with Variants and Notes.* New York and Jerusalem: The Jewish Theological Seminary of America

Saul and Evelyn Henkind Talmud Text Databank. Saul Lieberman Institute of Talmudic Research. The Jewish Theological Seminary of America

Sokoloff, Michael. 2002. *A Dictionary of Jewish Babylonian Aramaic of the Talmudic and Geonic Periods.* Ramat-Gan: Bar-Ilan University Press

Talmud Yerushalmi: According to Ms. Or. 4720 (Scal. 3) of the Leiden University Library with Restorations and Corrections. 2005. Introduction by Yaacov Sussman. Jerusalem: The Academy of the Hebrew Language

Tanakh: A New Translation of the Holy Scriptures According to the Traditional Hebrew Text. 1985. Philadelphia, New York, Jerusalem. The Jewish Publication Society

Theodor, Judah and Chanoch Albeck. 1996 (repr.). *Midrash Bereschit Rabbah.* Berlin and Jerusalem: Akademie für die Wissenschaft des Judentums

Scholarly studies and other contemporary works

Anderson Gary A. 2013. *Charity: The Place of the Poor in the Biblical Tradition.* New Haven: Yale University Press

Beer, Moshe. 1983. "Three Seals of Babylonian Jews and Their Date." *Tarbiẓ* 52:435–445 (in Hebrew)

Boyce, Mary. 1968. "The Pious Foundations of the Zoroastrians." *Bulletin of the School of Oriental and African Studies* 31:270–289

Boyce, Mary. 1992. *Zoroastrianism: Its Antiquity and Constant Vigour.* Costa Mesa: Mazda Publishers and Bibliotheca Persia

de Menasce, J.P. 1964. "Feux et Fondations Pieuses dans le Droit Sassanide." In: *Travaux de l'Institut d'études iranniennes de l'Université de Paris*, vol. 2. Paris: Librairie C. Klincksieck, pp. 59–62

Diamond, Eliezer. 2004. *Holy Men and Hunger Artists: Fasting and Asceticism in Rabbinic Culture.* New York: Oxford University Press

Elman, Yaakov. 1990/1991. "Righteousness as its Own Reward: An Inquiry into the Theologies of the Stam." *Proceedings of the American Academy for Jewish Research* 57:35–67

Finn, Richard. 2006. "Portraying the Poor: Descriptions of Poverty in Christian Texts from the Late Roman Empire." In: Margaret Atkins and Robin Osborne, eds. *Poverty in the Roman World.* Cambridge: Cambridge University Press, pp. 130–144

Fraade, Steven D. 2007. "Rabbinic Polysemy and Pluralism Revisited: Between Praxis and Thematization." *Association for Jewish Studies Review* 31:1–40

Gardner, Gregg. 2008. "Astrology in the Talmud: An Analysis of Bavli Shabbat 156." In: Eduard Iricinschi and Holger M. Zelentin, eds. *Heresy and Identity in Late Antiquity.* Tübingen: Mohr Siebeck, pp. 314–388

Gardner, Gregg E. 2015. *The Origins of Organized Charity in Rabbinic Judaism.* New York and Cambridge: Cambridge University Press

Gray, Alyssa M. 2009. "The Formerly-Wealthy Poor: From Empathy to Ambivalence in Rabbinic Literature of Late Antiquity." *Association for Jewish Studies Review* 33:101–133

Gray, Alyssa M. 2011. "Redemptive Almsgiving and the Rabbis of Late Antiquity." *Jewish Studies Quarterly* 18:144–184

Gray, Alyssa M. 2015. "Wealth and Rabbinic Self-Fashioning in Late Antiquity." In: Leonard J. Greenspoon, ed. *Wealth and Poverty in Jewish Tradition.* West Lafayette: Purdue University Press, pp. 53–81

Gray, Alyssa M. 2017. "The People, Not the Peoples: The Talmud Bavli's 'Charitable' Contribution to the Jewish-Christian Conversation in Mesopotamia." *Review of Rabbinic Judaism* 20:137–167

Gridenberg, Daniel M. 2009. *Sasanian Jewry and Its Culture: A Lexicon of Jewish and Related Seals.* Urbana: University of Illinois Press

Hayes, Christine. 1998. "Displaced Self-Perceptions: The Deployment of 'Minim' and Romans in B. Sanhedrin 90b–91a." In: Hayim Lapin, ed. *Religious and Ethnic Communities in Later Roman Palestine.* Bethesda: University Press of Maryland, pp. 249–289

Hopkins, Keith. 1983. *Death and Renewal.* Cambridge: Cambridge University Press

Kalmin, Richard. 1999. *The Sage in Jewish Society of Late Antiquity.* London and New York: Routledge

Kalmin, Richard. 2003. "Rabbinic Traditions about Roman Persecutions of the Jews: A Reconsideration." *Journal of Jewish Studies* 54:21–50

Kalmin, Richard. 2006. *Jewish Babylonia between Persia and Roman Palestine.* New York and Oxford: Oxford University Press

Kalmin, Richard. 2012. "A Late Antique Babylonian Treatise on Astrology." In: Shai Secunda and Steven Fine, eds. *Shoshannat Yaakov: Jewish and Iranian Studies in Honor of Yaakov Elman.* Leiden and Boston: Brill, pp. 165–184

Macuch, Maria. 1992. "Charitable Foundations." In: Ehsan Yarshater, ed. *Encyclopedia Iranica.* Vol. V. Costa Mesa: Mazda Publishers, pp. 380–385

Morony, Michael. 2007. "Religion and the Aramaic Incantation Bowls." *Religion Compass* 1:414–442

Perikhanian, Anahit. 1983. "Iranian Society and Law." In: Ehsan Yarshater, ed. *The Cambridge History of Iran. Vol. 3:2. The Seleucid, Parthian and Sasanian Periods.* Cambridge: Cambridge University Press, pp. 661–665

Rhee, Helen. 2012. *Loving the Poor, Saving the Rich: Wealth, Poverty, and Early Christian Formation.* Grand Rapids: Baker Academic

Rubenstein, Jeffrey L. 1999. *Talmudic Stories: Narrative Art, Composition, and Culture.* Baltimore: Johns Hopkins University Press

Rubenstein, Jeffrey L. 2009. "Talmudic Astrology: *Bavli Šabbat* 156a–b." *Hebrew Union College Annual* 78:109–148

Secunda, Shai. 2014. *The Iranian Talmud: Reading the Bavli in its Sasanian Context.* Philadelphia: University of Pennsylvania Press

Segal, Eliezer. 2005. "R. Eliezer's *Perutah.*" *The Journal of Religion* 85:25–42

Shaked, Shaul. 1995. "Jewish Sasanian Sigillography." In: Rika Gyselen, ed. *Au Carrefour des Religions: Melanges offerts a Philippe Gignoux.* Bures-sur-Yvette: Groupe pour l'etude de la civilization du Moyen-Orient, pp. 239–255

Shaked, Shaul. 2005. "Form and Purpose in Aramaic Spells: Some Jewish Themes." In: Shaul Shaked, ed. *Officina Magica: Essays on the Practice of Magic in Antiquity.* Leiden: Brill, pp. 1–30

Urbach, Ephraim E. 1979. *The Sages: Their Concepts and Beliefs.* 2nd enlarged ed. Jerusalem: Magnes Press

Wilfand Ben-Shalom, Yael. 2017. *The Wheel that Overtakes Everyone: Poverty and Charity in the Eyes of the Sages of the Land of Israel.* Tel Aviv: Hakibbutz Hameuchad (in Hebrew)

Wilfand, Yael. 2014. *Poverty, Charity and the Image of the Poor in Rabbinic Texts from the Land of Israel.* Sheffield: Sheffield Phoenix Press

Yadin, Azzan. 2010. "Rabbi Akiva's Youth." *Jewish Quarterly Review* 100:573–597

5 *Tzedaqah* and *teshuvah*
Partially overlapping magisteria

This chapter's title is inspired by the paleontologist Stephen Jay Gould's coinage of the phrase "non-overlapping magisteria" to describe his view of the relationship between "religion" and "science."[1] Gould describes each has having a legitimate "magisterium," or teaching authority: religion's is the realm of values and meaning, science's the realm of developing and coordinating facts about the natural world. My interest is in Gould's phrase, not the disputed use to which he puts it; the phrase is a useful if imperfect metaphor for the relationship of *tzedaqah* and *teshuvah* ("repentance") in Palestinian rabbinic literature and the Talmud *Bavli*.[2] Aside from the obvious lack of equivalence between "religion" and "science" and "*tzedaqah*" and "*teshuvah*," the imperfection lies in the fact that the latter two intersect in a way that Gould's "religion" and "science" do not: both are portrayed in various contexts as doing the same thing—atoning for sin. Despite this commonality, however, the two do not at all overlap in tannaitic literature and coexist uneasily despite their overlap in Palestinian amoraic literature and the Talmud *Bavli*. This chapter argues that rabbinic literature evinces a tension between *teshuvah* and *tzedaqah* as modes of atonement, with the rabbinic "thumb" (both Palestinian and Babylonian) pressed down on the scale in favor of *teshuvah*.

Tzedaqah and *teshuvah* in tannaitic literature

The interiority of teshuvah *(unlike* tzedaqah*)*

Tzedaqah and *teshuvah* occupy distinct, non-overlapping literary niches in tannaitic literature. *Teshuvah* and its related acts of prayer and fasting, as well as *Yom HaKippurim* (the Day of Atonement) and its attendant rituals of affliction and confession, are discussed—and much more extensively than *tzedaqah*—as means of atonement.[3] Among modern scholars who have examined *teshuvah* only George Foote Moore mentions charity, and even then only in a passing allusion to a Palestinian amoraic tradition.[4] This, taken together with the silence about charity of other scholars of rabbinic *teshuvah*, confirms my own observation that tannaitic literature keeps charity and *teshuvah* completely distinct.

Moore and David Lambert call attention to the tannaitic nominalization of "*teshuvah*" as well as to its construction as a religious practice ("doing" *teshuvah*).[5] Apropos, I would point out that tannaitic literature also mentions people described as "*ba'alei teshuvah*" ("masters of repentance"). *Ba'alei teshuvah* are not simply people who have repented for one or even a handful of sins; *ba'alei teshuvah* have completely and piously reoriented their lives. *Yerushalmi Peah* declares: "nothing stands in the way of *ba'alei teshuvah*."[6] *Mishnah Baba Metzia* forbids reminding a *ba'al teshuvah* to "remember your former deeds," while *Tosefta Sukkah*'s *ba'alei teshuvah* say: "Happy are you, my old age! For you have atoned for my youth."[7] The *volte face* of *ba'alei teshuvah*, their pious self-recreation, is seen as a cognizable shared characteristic that warrants a collective identification.[8] Unlike the term "*teshuvah*" the rabbis certainly did not invent "*tzedaqah*" but, as noted in Chapter 1, they likewise refer to "doing" *tzedaqah*. There is, however, no tannaitic "*ba'alei tzedaqah*" equivalent to "*ba'alei teshuvah*." There are two occurrences of the Aramaic equivalent "*marei mitzvata*" ("master of the commandments," referring to *tzedaqah*) in *Leviticus Rabbah*, but in neither case does the term have the unambiguously positive valence of "*ba'alei teshuvah*." *Leviticus Rabbah* sharply criticizes those who rob and obtain property from others by violence in order to thereby do *tzedaqah* and be called "*marei mitzvata*."[9] A group of rabbis hails a reluctant potential donor as a "*marei mitzvata*," seemingly in order to incentivize his giving.[10]

The change of life direction characteristic of *ba'alei teshuvah* is consistent with a defining characteristic of tannaitic (and later, amoraic) *teshuvah*: its *interiority*. David Lambert, who uses the latter term, describes the rabbinic "discourse of inner, individual control" around *teshuvah*, the need for "proper, internal assent." Lambert summarizes the rabbinic emphasis on the need for interiority as follows: "... the defining element of *teshuva* ... is an interior truth ... indicating sincerity, fullness of intent. It is such intent that is the final arbiter of communal and religious status."[11] Although based on amoraic sources, Lambert's summary is equally applicable to tannaitic literature. Such interiority is clearly on display in M. *Ta'anit* 2:1:

> What is the order of the fasts? They bring out the Ark to the town's main street ... and the eldest among them says crushing words to them: "Our brothers, it was not said about the people of Nineveh 'And God saw their sackcloth and fasts,' rather (Jonah 3:10), '*God saw what they did, how they were turning back (shavu) from their evil ways*,' and it says in the tradition (Joel 2:13), '*Rend your hearts rather than your garments*.'"

The *mishnah*'s context is the public fast in a time of drought. The elder's public sermon to his distressed community stresses the need for their interior transformation. God canceled his dire plans for the Ninevites not because they busied themselves with external acts like wearing sackcloth and fasting, but because they engaged in the interior work of heartfelt penance. Joel 2:13 summarizes

God's true desire: *Rend your hearts rather than your garments, and turn back to the Lord your God.*

A comparison of the elder's sermon and King Monbaz's "scattering" of his and his ancestors' patrimony during a time of drought (T. *Peah* 4:18) is instructive. King Monbaz engages exclusively and assiduously in the charitable equivalent of "rending garments": he "scatters" earthly treasure and "accumulates" heavenly treasure, mentioning neither "turning from evil ways" nor "rending" his "heart." Are Monbaz's *tzedaqah* and the drought-stricken community's *teshuvah* equal, or does one rank higher than the other? While these two passages seem to leave us in a stalemate, a plethora of other tannaitic sources points to the conclusion that *teshuvah*'s interiority renders it superior to charity. We begin with *Sifre Numbers* 134.[12] Apropos of Micah 7:18's *Who is a God like You*, the *Sifre* contrasts God and human beings: a human being can nullify a decree issued by his peer, but none can nullify God's decrees, for *He is one; who can dissuade Him? Whatever He desires, He does* (Job 23:13). R. Yehudah ben Baba proposes a parable that softens this harsh portrayal of God: a man who is placed on an Imperial list of malefactors cannot be removed from it even if he pays "much money," but "you (God) say: 'Do *teshuvah* and I will accept it,'" as it says, *I wipe away your sins like a cloud, Your transgressions like mist* (Isaiah 44:22)." "Much money" cannot remove a man from an Imperial list, but God will remove a person from his own "list" through *teshuvah* alone, without any expenditure of money. *Tzedaqah* may be presumed to be the "money" the expenditure of which God will view favorably, but the *Sifre* clearly makes the point that God is moved by *teshuvah*, not money. *Sifre Numbers* 134 thus tacitly suggests that *teshuvah* is *tzedaqah*'s superior as a mode of atonement and hints at the reason: giving charity is a rather mechanical act as compared with *teshuvah*.[13]

While an expenditure of money cannot take the place of a sincere penitential change in life direction it may be a voluntary *consequence* of it. In *Sifre Numbers* 115 a man described as being "punctilious about the *mitzvah* of *tzitzit*" (fringes) sought out a famous prostitute whose fee was the staggering sum of 400 gold pieces.[14] Finding himself unable to complete the illicit sexual act after his fringes slapped him in the face, he withdrew from the mountain of (seven!) mattresses the prostitute had prepared and sat on the ground. The prostitute asked him to explain this astounding turn of events, and he explained to her the significance of the *mitzvah* of *tzitzit*. Of most relevance to our inquiry is the prostitute's behavior after this encounter: she "scattered"[15] all her money, giving one-third to the Empire, one-third to the poor, and taking one-third with her to the study house frequented by her reluctant client. (Ultimately, she also converts and marries the *tzitzit*-wearing man.) We cannot determine whether the prostitute is Jewish, nor is her precise motivation for giving of one-third of her wealth to the poor described. The prostitute's interior transformation, her change of life direction, *precedes* her religious giving, which is not said to result in the forgiveness of her sins or accumulation of heavenly merits. Nor is her religious giving represented as something she *had* to do to atone for her years of sinful living. The prostitute's charitable giving is an interesting footnote to the *Sifre*'s principal interest in her interior transformation and complete reorientation of her life.

Yom HaKippurim *and* teshuvah *(but not* tzedaqah*)*

The tannaitic construction of *Yom HaKippurim* is tightly bound up with *teshuvah*, with *tzedaqah* nowhere to be found.[16] The holy day's very name is built of the trilateral root "*k-p-r*" ("ransom" or "atonement"). This is reminiscent of the *Mekhilta de-Rabbi Ishmael*'s notion that *tzedaqah* is a "ransom" for sin:

> For a human being can acquire himself by money from the hands of heaven, as it says (Exodus 30:12) *When you take a census of the Israelite people according to their enrollment, each shall pay the Lord a ransom (kofer) for himself.*[17]

Not only does *Yom HaKippurim* go unmentioned in the Mekhiltan redemptive almsgiving passage, *tzedaqah* likewise goes unmentioned in passages dealing with *Yom HaKippurim*. According to M. *Yoma* 8:8: "Death and *Yom HaKippurim* atone with *teshuvah*. *Teshuvah* atones for light transgressions, both positive and negative commandments. For serious transgressions it suspends [punishment] until *Yom HaKippurim* comes and atones." M. *Yoma* 8:8 limns a process of atonement that can last for years—at least until the next *Yom HaKippurim* and possibly even until the penitent's death, years during which he might give atoning charity. But the *mishnah* says nothing about such atoning charity. M. *Yoma* 8:9 implies that proper *teshuvah* requires a true inner transformation; the one who repeatedly says, "I will sin and repent, I will sin and repent" will not be afforded the opportunity to do (true) *teshuvah*. It also takes pains to emphasize that *Yom HaKippurim* is what "atones" for sins between "man and God," while interpersonal reconciliation is additionally required to atone for sins between "man and man." R. Aqiva closes M. *Yoma* 8:9 on the note that God "purifies" the people Israel. In sum, *teshuvah* requires inner transformation, *Yom HaKippurim* atones, God "purifies"—but there is no role for *tzedaqah*.

Tosefta Kippurim's closing passages on atonement ("*kapparah*") are also relevant. In T. *Kippurim* 4:6–8 R. Yishmael—the very same R. Yishmael as in the Mekhiltan redemptive almsgiving passage—describes four atonement scenarios.[18] One who repents violations of positive commandments is immediately forgiven. One who repents violations of negative commandments receives a suspension of his punishment but must wait for atonement until *Yom HaKippurim*. One who repents violations of commandments that entail the severe punishments of *karet* ("excision" from the body of the people Israel) or the judicial death penalty will only receive atonement after suffering afflictions (i.e., neither repentance nor *Yom HaKippurim* suffices). Finally, one who deliberately desecrates the Name of Heaven receives atonement in three parts: one-third by means of *teshuvah* and *Yom HaKippurim*, one-third by means of afflictions, and the final third only upon his death. In these passages R. Yishmael describes atonement for some sins as a process, in some cases even a lengthy process that may take years and certainly more than a single *Yom HaKippurim*. There is certainly time during this lengthy process for the penitent to give *tzedaqah* as at least part of his atonement. Yet *tzedaqah* goes unmentioned. Nor is there any mention of charity in T. *Kippurim* 4:9–17, which discusses other aspects of atonement on *Yom HaKippurim* and at other times, including the offering of sin- and guilt-sacrifices, death, and a penitent's verbal confession of sin.[19]

Does teshuvah *ever require charity? Distinguishing redemptive almsgiving from restitution*

This section is a bit digressive, but necessary for conceptual clarity. Redemptive almsgiving is clearly distinct from financial restitution to injured parties, but some restitution cases blur the boundary between *teshuvah* and redemptive almsgiving. *Teshuvah* for some misdeeds may require that the penitent engage in religious giving, which may include (but not necessarily be limited to) giving to the poor.

We begin with basic principles. The penitent thief eager to do *teshuvah* for robbery or theft is required to restore the very property he stole to its rightful owners; if restoring the property is impossible (for example, it is lost or destroyed) the *taqqanat ha-shavim* ("enactment of penitents") allows the thief to pay money to the injured parties in *lieu* of the stolen items.[20] The point of *taqqanat ha-shavim* is to keep open the door to penance; a sincerely penitent thief's inability to return to his victim precisely what he stole is not allowed to stand in the way of his *teshuvah*.

Other penitent thieves may encounter a different obstacle to making restitution. These thieves may wish to repent of financial sins from which they earned ill-gotten gains, and their penance requires financial restitution. But what if they are unable to identify specific injured parties to whom to give those monies? Restitution in such cases takes the form of *religious giving*, either to the Jerusalem Temple or to the poor.[21] T. *Sanhedrin* 5:2 illustrates the latter.[22] The malefactors at issue are "dealers in Sabbatical year produce" who violate Leviticus 25:6 (*But you may eat whatever the land during its sabbath will produce*) by selling produce that grows by itself during the Sabbatical year. The rabbis understand the verse to permit "eating," but not "selling," the untended produce. The *Tosefta* states that the "repentance" (the word used is "*hazarah*," literally, "return") of these merchants is not "complete" until they refrain from such commerce during the next Sabbatical year (seven years' hence!) But the *Tosefta* is silent about what the penitent merchants should do with their previously accumulated ill-gotten gains. R. Nehemiah holds that verbal expressions of remorse ("*hazarat devarim*," a "return" of "words") are insufficient without an accompanying "*hazarat mammon*" (a "return" of "money"). His distinction between "returns" of "words" and "money" perhaps implies a concern that the dealers' verbal expressions of remorse may be insincere, requiring an infusion of credibility via painful financial sacrifice. But it is equally possible (and perhaps more likely) that R. Nehemiah holds that even sincere verbal expressions of remorse must be accompanied by a disgorging of ill-gotten gains. The financial restitution is part and parcel of the penitent's internal process of transformation; both aspects are necessary, neither alone sufficient.

To whom should the restitution be paid? Who precisely was injured by the merchants' violation of Leviticus 25:6? R. Nehemiah's answer is part of his pre-scribed penitential formula: "I gathered these 200 *dinars* from the fruits of trans-gression; *distribute them to the poor.*" Why the poor? "The poor" as a class would undoubtedly be deleteriously affected by a removal from the fields of untended, readily available Sabbatical-year produce by merchants hoarding it for profit. Given as well the likely difficulty of demonstrating that any particular person (materially poor or otherwise) was damaged by any particular transaction in Sabbatical year produce, these ill-gotten gains are logically directed to the poor as a group. [23] But note: the distribution of the ill-gotten gains to the poor is a form of restitution; it is a public demonstration of the merchants' sincere resolve to separate themselves permanently from their financial sin and its profit-able consequences (for them). Although the merchants are made to refer to "the fruits of transgression," the *Tosefta* does not describe their distribution of that money in language redolent of redemptive almsgiving: "ransom," "buying oneself from heaven," "atoning," or the like. *Tosefta Sanhedrin* is not about redemptive almsgiving; it is about a *teshuvah* scenario that requires financial restitution.[24]

In sum, tannaitic literature keeps *tzedaqah* and *teshuvah* separate and unequal, with strong suggestions of *teshuvah*'s superiority as a mode of atonement. We will see that although Palestinian amoraic literature brings the two together in places, it maintains their inequality, exhibiting and even amplifying a marked preference for *teshuvah.*

Tzedaqah **and** *teshuvah* **in Palestinian amoraic literature**

A twice-told tale in the *Yerushalmi* tells of a Torah student who is baffled and saddened by the community's ignoring the death of his scholarly companion but burying with great honor a tax collector's son who coincidentally died the same day.[25] The surviving student learns that the tax collector's son had one "merit" ("*z'chu*") to his credit: he had assisted the poor—either by giving them a feast he had prepared for no-show town councilors, or by not embarrassing a poor man who picked up a fig-cake that he'd accidentally dropped. His deceased scholarly companion had one demerit ("*hovah*"): he had once put on his head-phylactery prior to his hand-phylactery. The Torah student also observed the pair's differing postmortem fates: his scholarly companion relaxing in paradise by gardens and streams of water, the tax collector's son suffering fiery torment and unable to reach soothing water. The Torah student obviously learns the lesson that the tax collector's son received on earth the (miniscule) divine reward to which he was entitled, and likewise, his scholarly companion received on earth the (miniscule) divine punishment he deserved. The tax collector's son's charity was a shining exception to an otherwise sinful life, and the obverse was true of the scholarly companion.[26] But for our purposes another point stands out: redemptive almsgiving is missing from the story. The tax collector's son's generosity to the poor did not atone for his sins *tout court*, nor did he thereby accumulate merits in heaven. Heaven gave him on earth the paltry reward to which he was entitled; there is also no indication that his generosity saved him from death. One suspects there must be something that atones for sin more comprehensively than charity, and indeed there is: *teshuvah*.

Teshuvah *without* tzedaqah

There are other places in Palestinian amoraic literature in which redemptive almsgiving is conspicuous by its absence. Palestinian amoraic literature identifies the days between *Rosh Hashanah* and *Yom HaKippurim* as the "ten days of repentance between *Rosh Hashanah* and *Yom HaKippurim*."[27] God is said to have "suspended" judgment of the biblical villain Nabal (I Samuel 25:38) in a manner "like [the] ten days," implying that these days are a period in which God watches and waits to see how a wayward person will reform.[28] Given the assumption that these "ten days of repentance" are intended as a period of *teshuvah* leading up to *Yom HaKippurim*, one might expect to find admonitions to give atoning *tzedaqah* during these days—but there are none. There is the barest whiff in *Yerushalmi Peah* of a relationship between *tzedaqah* and those days: R. Hiyyah bar Adda reports on "elders" who would accept *tzedaqah* only during those days and at no other time.[29] But the *Yerushalmi* is silent as to who was providing that *tzedaqah*, whether it was collected during those ten days or previously, and, most tellingly, the *Yerushalmi* does not *prescribe* giving during the penitential period, or even merely recommend it as a worthy practice.

Yerushalmi Yoma—the tractate principally devoted to *Yom HaKippurim*—even takes pains to begin on the note that "just as *Yom HaKippurim* atones for Israel, so do the deaths of the righteous atone for Israel."[30] That is, "*Yom HaKippurim*" atones, the "deaths of the righteous" atone, but *tzedaqah* is nowhere to be found—despite the redemptive proclamation "*zekhun imi*" we find in Palestinian amoraic literature ("acquire merit for yourselves through me"). Looking beyond *Yerushalmi Yoma*, all four extensive treatments of *teshuvah* in the *Yerushalmi* are characterized by the absence of *tzedaqah*.[31] *Pesiqta deRav Kahana* 24:7 deserves a close look:[32]

> *Good and upright is the Lord; therefore He*
> *shows sinners the way* (Psalm 25:8). They asked
> Wisdom: "What is the sinner's punishment?" She
> said to them: "*Misfortune pursues sinners* (Proverbs 13:21)."
> They asked Prophecy: "What is the sinner's punishment?"
> She said to them: "*The person who sins, only he shall die* (Ezekiel 18:4)."
> They asked the Torah: "What is the sinner's punishment?" She said to them:
> "Let him bring a guilt-offering and it will atone for him." They asked the

Holy One, Blessed be He: "What is the sinner's punishment?" He said to them: "Let him do *teshuvah* and it will atone for him." This is what is written: *Good and upright is the Lord; therefore He shows sinners the way.*

David Lambert insightfully suggests that this passage demonstrates rabbinic awareness that *teshuvah* "is not a known component of Scripture but a hidden doctrine of God himself," and the "precariousness of the claims for 'repentance' as a naturalized concept."[33] This is so because God himself teaches *teshuvah* on his own authority, without scriptural support. I note as well that neither the Torah nor God teaches the atoning efficacy of *tzedaqah*. Had the homilist wished to add a reference to *tzedaqah*, the tannaitic anthologies of redemptive almsgiving verses in *Mekhilta de-Rabbi Ishmael* and *Tosefta Peah* were at his disposal. *Tzedaqah* is simply not here.

The interiority of teshuvah *in Palestinian amoraic literature*

In Palestinian amoraic literature, like tannaitic literature, *teshuvah* requires interiority. This arguably renders *teshuvah* superior to a mechanical act of giving. *Yerushalmi Sanhedrin*'s description of the wicked biblical King Manasseh's repentance is a particularly vivid portrayal of the interiority of *teshuvah*:[34]

1   R. Levi said: "They made a copper pot for him, put him in it and lit a fire underneath. When he saw ... he did not fail to call upon every alien god in the world. When he saw this did not help him at all, he said: 'I remember that my father used to read me this verse in the synagogue: (Deuteronomy 4:30–31): *But if you search ... when you are in distress because all these things have befallen you and, in the end, return to the Lord your God and obey Him. For the Lord your God is a compassionate God: He will not fail you nor will He let you perish; He will not forget the covenant which he made on oath with your fathers.* Behold, I [Manasseh] will recite it. If he answers me, all is well; and if not, the sides are even (i.e., it doesn't matter).'

2   And the ministering angels closed the windows so that Manasseh's prayer would not ascend to the Holy One, Blessed be He. And the ministering angels said to the Holy One, Blessed be He: 'Master of the world! Will you accept in *teshuvah* a man who worshiped idolatry and set up an image in the Temple?!' He said to them: 'If I don't accept him in *teshuvah* I will be locking the door in the face of all *ba'alei teshuvah*.' What did the Holy One, Blessed be He, do for him? He drilled a hole beneath His Throne of Glory and heard his [Manasseh's] plea ..."

Manasseh's *teshuvah* is represented as heartfelt, and God as willing, indeed, *required*, to accept it. God's dismissal of the angels' protestations about the depth of Manasseh's sinfulness echoes R. Yehoshua ben Levi's claim that God judges a person—whatever his personal history—on the basis of his sincerity at the particular moment he calls on God.[35]

Genesis Rabbah even hints at an amoraic concern that sinners might perform righteous acts that do not require interiority only to make a show of piety and thereby avoid their deserved punishment. The existence of such a possibility heightens the importance of *teshuvah*; only sincere *teshuvah*, a true inner transformation of a sinful spirit, is guaranteed to be genuine. R. Yonatan muses that death should have been decreed only for evildoers, not the righteous. But had that been the divine will evildoers would try to avoid their fate by mechanically imitating the behavior of the righteous: doing "*mitzvoth*" and "*ma'asim tovim*" ("good acts"). *Genesis Rabbah* observes that evildoers' mechanical performance of those inherently righteous acts would not be "*lishmah*" ("for its own sake"); it would be insincere, a "*teshuvah* of charlatanry."[36] David Lambert describes such a deceptive "*teshuvah*" as "lack[ing] the proper internal assent, even as it *simulates adherence to communal norms*" (emphasis added).[37] Acts without "the proper internal assent" are simply not proper *teshuvah*.

Two other sources illustrate a similar point about the religious worthlessness of mechanically giving *tzedaqah*, specifically. R. Pinchas interprets Proverbs 11:21 (*hand to hand will not cleanse evil*)[38] as a reference to one who "does *tzedaqah* and wishes to take its reward immediately ("*m'yad*)." "*M'yad*" ("immediately") literally means "from hand." R. Pinchas means that one who gives *tzedaqah* "*hand to hand*" and wishes to receive its reward immediately ("from hand") should be admonished that this sort of automatic giving "*will not cleanse evil*."[39] The mere mechanical act of giving charity is not enough to "cleanse evil." *Leviticus Rabbah* 3:1 is also instructive. One who works and "does *tzedaqah* from his own [property]" is judged superior to one who "robs, does violence, and does *tzedaqah* from [the property of] others." The latter only "wishes to be called a '*marei mitzvata*' ("master of the *mitzvoth*," of *tzedaqah*)."[40] Again, the mere mechanical act of giving—in this case, giving by any means necessary—is of no religious value. Charity's mechanical nature, the potential for its being done insincerely and for the wrong reasons, implicitly renders it inferior to *teshuvah*.[41]

The Palestinian amoraic linkage of tefillah, tzedaqah, teshuvah

Palestinian *amoraim* are the first rabbis to link "*tefillah*," "*tzedaqah*," and "*teshuvah*" into a formulaic triad of pious activities: "*tefillah, tzedaqah, teshuvah*." David Levine finds the earliest attestation of a related devotional triad "charity, fasting, prayer" in the apocryphal book Tobit and also observes that the Hebrew Bible links at least two of the three even earlier, one telling example being Isaiah 58's linkage of fasting and care for the poor.[42] David Downs follows the thread of the devotional triad into the New Testament, pointing out Matthew 6:1–18's linkage of "fasting, prayer, and almsgiving."[43] Downs and Levine both trace the apocryphal triad "charity, fasting, prayer" into the writings of Church Fathers, and Levine calls attention as well to the Palestinian rabbinic triad "*tefillah, tzedaqah, teshuvah*."[44]

Not all late antique Christian writers saw the three elements of the triad as equivalent. Helen Rhee quotes *2 Clement*'s (second century) explicit privileging of almsgiving over fasting and prayer: "almsgiving is good, as is repentance from sin. Fasting is better than prayer, while *almsgiving is better than both*…"[45] (emphasis added). Downs hypothesizes that *2 Clement*'s is a polemical emphasis meant to "counter[] the rejection of almsgiving among some Christian groups." The *Gospel of Thomas* presents a striking example of such rejection: "and if you give alms, you will do harm to your spirits."[46] Downs sees *2 Clement*'s privileging of charity as countering such rejection "not merely by advocating … but also by insisting that almsgiving is better…"[47] Downs also observes that *2 Clement* sees charity as superior to fasting and prayer because "care for the needy clearly demonstrates repentance."[48] *2 Clement*'s privileging of charity, and Downs's hypothesis that intra-Christian polemics about charity play a role in it, are useful points to bear in mind as we undertake an examination of the Palestinian amoraic triad "*tefillah, tzedaqah, teshuvah.*"

Y. *Ta'anit* 2:1, 65b is one of four places in Palestinian amoraic literature in which the triad is found.[49] R. Lazar (= Eleazar) teaches that "three things nullify the harsh decree: *tefillah, tzedaqah, teshuvah.*" The sage goes onto point out that all three are found in II Chronicles 7:14: *when My people, who bear My name, humble themselves, pray, and seek My favor and turn from their evil ways, I will hear … and forgive their sins and heal their land.* The scriptural phrase "*humble themselves, pray*" signifies *tefillah.* "*And seek My favor*" (lit.: "face") signifies *tzedaqah* in conjunction with Psalm 17:15: *Then I, justified ("b'tzedeq") will behold Your face.* Finally, the phrase "*and turn from their evil ways*" points to *teshuvah.*

Yerushalmi Sanhedrin's context for the triad "*tefillah, tzedaqah, teshuvah*" is a discussion of the wicked biblical King Manasseh, who has no portion in the World to Come (M. *Sanhedrin* 10:2). The pertinent portion of the long Manasseh passage begins before his birth, with a rabbinic elaboration of the near-fatal illness of his father King Hezekiah and the prophet Isaiah's visit to the stricken king (II Kings 20:1). The *Yerushalmi* constructs a colorful dialogue between king and prophet that supplies a dramatic transition between II Kings 20:1 and 20:2. The *Yerushalmi*'s Isaiah informs the sick Hezekiah that the reason he neither will survive his illness nor have a portion in the world to come is because he refrained from procreating. After an exchange about this, the king says that he will ignore the prophet's proffered advice and rely on the teaching of his ancestor: "If you see bad dreams or visions, jump to three things and you will be saved: these are *tefillah, tzedaqah, teshuvah.*" The Yerushalmi immediately appends the same scriptural derivations of the three as we find in *Yerushalmi Ta'anit.*[50]

At this point the *Yerushalmi* recounts that Hezekiah *turned his face to the wall and prayed* (II Kings 20:2), offering four traditions about the content of his prayer. *Tzedaqah* does not feature in any of the suggestions. According to R. Shimon ben Yohai, Hezekiah calls God's attention to his ancestors' successful amassing of converts as the reason that "you should give me [back] my life."

To Shmuel bar Nahman and R. Hinena bar Papa (each in a distinct way), Hezekiah's ancestors' building of God's Temple is the reason his life should be spared. For "the rabbis," Hezekiah's merit is that none of his 248 limbs ever did anything to anger God. Whatever the content of Hezekiah's prayer, God's response is: *I have heard your prayer.... I will add fifteen years to your life* (II Kings 20:5–6). The *Yerushalmi*'s emphasis on the efficacy of Hezekiah's *tefillah* is undoubtedly compelled by the Hebrew Bible's description of him as praying. But the *Yerushalmi* gives itself considerable latitude in suggesting different sorts of merit that Hezekiah called to God's attention in his *tefillah* and *tzedaqah* is not one of them—despite Hezekiah's own reference to the triad *"tefillah, tzedaqah, teshuvah."*

Genesis Rabbah 44:15 and *Pesiqta deRav Kahana* 28:3 anthologize various other acts—not all of them religious acts—that "nullify the decree" in addition to *tefillah, tzedaqah, teshuvah.*[51]

1   R. Yudan in the name of R. Lazar: "Three things
     nullify the decree: *tefillah, tzedaqah, teshuvah.*
     And all three of them are in one verse (II Chronicles 7:14):
2   *When my people, who bear my name, humble
     themselves, pray*—this is *tefillah.*
3   *And seek My favor*—this is *tzedaqah,* as you say,
     I, with tzedeq, *will see your face* (Psalm 17:15).[52]
4   *And turn from their evil ways*—this is
     teshuvah. And after that: *I will forgive their sins.*"
5   Rav Huna in the name of Rav Yosef: "Even a name change and good
     actions [nullify the decree. We learn about name change] from
     Abraham and Sarah, and [about] good actions from the people of
     Nineveh, as it is said: *God saw what they did, how they were turning
     back, etc.* (Jonah 3:10)."
6   And there is one who says: "Even a change of place [nullifies the
     decree], as it says, *The Lord said to Abram, 'Go forth'* (Genesis 12:1)."
7   R. Mana said: "Even fasting [nullifies the decree], as it says, *May the
     Lord answer you in time of trouble* (Psalm 20:2)."

By their additions to the triad of "name change," "good actions," "change of place," and/or "fasting," *Genesis Rabbah* and *Pesiqta deRav Kahana* somewhat diminish the significance of *"tefillah, tzedaqah, teshuvah"* as a unit and, certainly, the importance of *tzedaqah* alone as a way to "nullify the decree."

We see, then, that none of the four Palestinian amoraic passages in which *"tefillah, tzedaqah, teshuvah"* appears privileges *tzedaqah.* At a minimum, Palestinian *amoraim* do not adopt an attitude like that of *2 Clement,* which privileges charity over prayer and fasting, the other two elements of its own triad. *Yerushalmi Ta'anit* does not indicate which, if any, of the three elements is most important. *Yerushalmi Sanhedrin* privileges *tefillah* over *tzedaqah* due to the biblical context but foregoes an opportunity to incorporate *tzedaqah* into

Hezekiah's prayer as one of the merits entitling him to rescue from death. *Genesis Rabbah* and *Pesiqta deRav Kahana* lessen the importance of the triad overall by adding other elements that also "nullify the decree." We should also point out that none of the four explicitly connects "*tefillah, tzedaqah, teshuvah*" to *Yom HaKippurim* or to the "ten days of repentance."[53]

Separate mentions *of* tefillah, tzedaqah, teshuvah

"*Tefillah,*" "*tzedaqah,*" and "*teshuvah*" are also mentioned separately (or at least not as a fixed triad) in Palestinian amoraic literature, and a survey of those mentions confirms the conclusion that *tzedaqah* is not *primus inter pares*. *Pesiqta deRav Kahana* 24:2 brings together *teshuvah* and *tefillah* without *tzedaqah*; R. Shmuel bar Nahman favorably compares *teshuvah* to *tefillah* in that *teshuvah* is always available, although the gates of *tefillah* might at times be closed.[54] *Pesiqta deRav Kahana* 24:11 presents a long list of individuals and collectivities the *teshuvah* of which God accepted: notable examples include the wicked biblical King Ahab, the people of Nineveh, and the evil biblical King Manasseh.[55] *Tzedaqah* is unmentioned, although "affliction" (which may refer to fasting) is mentioned in connection with Ahab. Moreover, R. Abba son of R. Papi is quoted as saying that "great is the power of *teshuvah*, which nullifies the oath and nullifies the [evil] decree."[56] The "power" to "nullify" oaths and (evil) decrees is attributed to *teshuvah alone*, not to the triad "*tefillah, tzedaqah, teshuvah*" and clearly not to *tzedaqah* alone.

Genesis Rabbah, on the other hand, mentions *tzedaqah* in the context of a public fast for rain without the accompaniment of either *tefillah* or *teshuvah*. This example illustrates how and in what circumstances *tzedaqah* alone can be effective: it must be properly motivated, a concrete manifestation of the giver's internal resolve to demonstrate righteousness before God. After a three-day fast failed to produce rain, R. Tanchumah delivered a public homily in which he entreated his community to "be filled with mercy one for the other, and the Holy Blessed One will be filled with mercy for you." The community then distributed *tzedaqah*, although ultimately the rains came not necessarily on account of that so much as because of one particular man's heightened generosity in giving charity to his economically distressed ex-wife.[57] At first glance, this passage appears to support the notion that *tzedaqah* alone can bring rain. But note *Genesis Rabbah*'s emphasis on interiority in the context of this *tzedaqah*. The rains come ultimately because R. Tanchumah urges that the people be filled with mercy toward one another, and in the same passage R. Abba explains God will be moved to show mercy (and provide rain) when he sees human beings showing mercy to each other. The *tzedaqah* that suffices to bring rain is thus no mere mechanical act of giving; it must be an act of giving that concretizes the giver's interior sense of mercy toward the other. The passage demonstrates this point even more clearly in the example of the man who took all this very much to heart in giving *tzedaqah* to his ex-wife. The *midrash* notes explicitly that "she had no [entitlement to] food from him," that is, she had no legal claim on him.

By giving to her, therefore, the man clearly demonstrated his righteousness before God as we saw this defined in Chapter 1: giving *tzedaqah* to someone lacking a claim on him, notably in this case a legal claim. This is the specific *tzedaqah* example that R. Tanchumah calls to God's attention, with success.

Teshuvah and *tzedaqah* in the Talmud *Bavli*

Interiority over mechanical acts

We begin with five *Bavli* sources that, taken together, illustrate its preference for the interiority of *teshuvah* to atonement through the mere mechanical perform-ance of an act. Three of these sources are narratives in which *tzedaqah* is conspicuously absent as a way for the penitent protagonist to atone for her (or his) sins.

R. Eleazar teaches that in Temple times a person could atone for sin by paying his *sheqel* to the Temple, but in a world without the Temple, "if they do *tzedaqah*, it is well."[58] *Tzedaqah* atones in place of the *sheqel*-tax. One may assume that according to R. Eleazar it is the mechanical act of *tzedaqah* that atones, by analogy to what was presumably the mechanical act of paying the *sheqel*-tax. The position the *Bavli* attributes to the Palestinian *amora* R. Eleazar contrasts with that of Rava. Rava says that the "burnt offering" is a "gift" (*doron*) to God. The *Bavli* narrator supplies the reasoning underlying Rava's position: if the sinner sacrifices the burnt offering without doing *teshuvah*, the sacrifice is that of *the wicked man* and hence an *abomination* (Proverbs 21:27). But should the sinner sacrifice the burnt offering *after* doing *teshuvah*, it is unnecessary because "[the penitent] doesn't move [from where he is standing] until he is forgiven." This being so, the burnt offering is not necessary for atone-ment; it is (merely) a *doron* to God.[59] Rava is obviously not talking about *tzedaqah* but his larger point is relevant to it (indeed, "*doron*" refers to *tzedaqah* on B. *Baba Batra* 10a). Just as sacrifice without *teshuvah* is an "abomination" and *teshuvah* always and completely atones without it, so (we might add): *tzedaqah* without *teshuvah* is of no religious value, and *teshuvah* atones effect-ively without it.[60]

The following three sources are all narratives. B. *Menachot* 44a is the *Bavli*'s re-presentation of *Sifre Numbers*'s story of the prostitute and the fringes-wearing sage. As in *Sifre Numbers*, the *Bavli*'s prostitute distributes one-third of her ill-gotten gains to the poor. And, like *Sifre Numbers*, the prostitute's distribution of possessions follows upon and illustrates her change of heart; the distribution only happens because of that change of heart. Interiority *preceded* the financial distribution; the distribution is not said to have *resulted* in forgiveness of the prostitute's sins.

Apropos, the well-known narrative about [R.] Eleazar ben Dordya recounts that he visited every prostitute in the world.[61] Upon hearing of a far-away prostitute who had not yet merited his attention, he equipped himself with a pouch of *dinars* and set out on a very long journey to meet her. The prostitute broke wind during an awkward moment during their encounter and observed that just as the broken wind could never return, "so they will not accept Eleazar ben Dordya in *teshuvah*." The prostitute's observation precipitates Eleazar ben Dordya's religious crisis; he seeks the intervention first of the mountains, then heaven and earth, and finally the sun and the moon—all in a vain effort to win acceptance of his *teshuvah*. Finally, he realizes that "the matter depends only on me" and places his head between his knees while weeping mightily. He expires, prompting a heavenly voice to "invite [him] to the life of the world to come." Rabbi observes in relevant part that Eleazar ben Dordya is one of the category "*ba'alei teshuvah*" ("masters of repentance"), even called "Rabbi."

By contrast, Elisha ben Abuyah ("Aher") does not "return"; he even hears a heavenly voice that proclaims: "*Turn back, O rebellious children* (Jeremiah 3:22)—except for Aher."[62] "Turn back" is of the trilateral root "*sh-'-v*," also the root of "*teshuvah*." Elisha understands the heavenly voice to mean that he will not be accepted in *teshuvah*, and he consequently puts forth no effort to that end. Two details of the Elisha narrative are relevant to our inquiry. First, Elisha repeats to R. Meir (in R. Aqiva's name) an interpretation of Ecclesiastes 7:14: *The one no less than the other was God's doing.* According to R. Aqiva the verse means that God created both Eden and *Gehinnom* and gave everyone shares in both. Should the righteous man (*tzaddiq*) acquire "merit" (*z-k-'*) he will receive both his own and a wicked man's portion in Eden; should a wicked man be condemned, he will take both his and a righteous man's portion in *Gehinnom*. The "merit" that entitles the righteous to two portions in Eden is not limited to the merit of charity—or any other particular act—but refers to the cumulative effect of various acts of righteousness. Charity is not privileged; it is not even mentioned. The second point is that upon Elisha's death, heaven is in a quandary: "Let him not be judged"—because he engaged in Torah; "let him not enter the world to come"—because he sinned ("*hata*"). Elisha's "sin" (*heit*) appears impossible to expiate, (even) despite his merit in Torah. Although M. *Sheqalim* 5:6 teaches that *yir'ei heit* (fearers of sin) would deposit funds anonymously into the Temple's "hall of secrets" (presumably) to alleviate their burden of sin, note that the option of expiating sin through charity is not mentioned for Elisha ben Abuyah.[63] Indeed, the *Bavli* here expresses its characteristic preference for Torah study (see Chapter 4).

Teshuvah *without* tzedaqah

Bavli Yoma 8, especially its concluding folios B. *Yoma* 85b–88a, includes a lengthy treatment of *teshuvah*. The *mishnah* pericopes under discussion are M. *Yoma* 8:7–10, which emphasize the atoning power of *Yom HaKippurim*, death, and *teshuvah*, and close with R. Aqiva's scriptural derivation of how God himself "cleanses" Israel. Charity as a means of atonement is not at all present on B. *Yoma* 85b–88a. Not only that, the *Bavli*'s construction of *teshuvah* in *Yoma* exhibits a focus on interiority that militates implicitly against atonement by what could be the mechanical means of giving money.

We will illustrate this with a sampling of some of the most relevant passages ranging from B. *Yoma* 86a through 87b. R. Eleazar comments on Exodus 34:7 (*yet He does not remit all punishment*). The Hebrew reads *v'nakeh lo y'nakeh*"; literally, "and he does remit, he does not remit." R. Eleazar points out the impossibility of the verse's saying *"v'nakeh"* (he does remit) because of *"lo y'nakeh"* (he does not remit), as well as the reverse. Rather, says R. Eleazar, the verse means that God "remits" (*v'nakeh*) those "who repent" (*shavin*), and "does not remit" (*lo y'nakeh*) those who do not.[64] God's remission of sin is therefore dependent upon *teshuvah*; and not, I would note, anything else.

The *Bavli* goes on to extol the "greatness" of *teshuvah* in a series of seven traditions each opening with "great is *teshuvah*..." We will focus on two, which most clearly emphasize the interior religious experience of *teshuvah*. R. Hama b. R. Hanina contrasts two clauses of Jeremiah 3:22: *Turn back, O rebellious children* and *I will heal your rebelliousness!*[65] The first clause is said to refer to *teshuvah* done "out of love" and the second to *teshuvah* done "out of fear." R. Hama b. R. Hanina seems to mean that *teshuvah* done out of love, in response to divine invitation (*Turn back*), is superior in that the penitents are called God's *children*. *Teshuvah* done out of fear results in God's healing the penitents' "rebelliousness," but they are not called God's *children*.[66] What is key for our purposes is the preference for *teshuvah* done out of love.[67] The second is Rav Yehudah's contrast of Jeremiah 3:22 and Jeremiah 3:14 (*Turn back, rebellious children ... Since I have mastered you, I will take you, one from a town and two from a clan*).[68] To Rav Yehudah, *teshuvah* done out of "love or fear" results in the penitents' being labeled God's *children*; *teshuvah* done as a result of divinely imposed afflictions renders the penitents like slaves, whom God has "mastered." The inferiority of *teshuvah* done as a response to divinely imposed "afflictions" is presumably because such so-called *"teshuvah"* is a reflexive, defensive response to physical punishment, lacking the interiority and pious resolve to return to God characteristic of true, authentic *teshuvah*.

R. Yitzhaq quotes a tradition from "the West" about the difference between a human being and God: one who offends another person cannot be certain if that person can be appeased at all, or by means of words. By contrast, God is appeased by the words of one who transgresses in secret; moreover, God even ascribes goodness to that person and considers him as one who sacrificed bullocks. This is all offered as an interpretation of Hosea 14:3: *Take words with you and return to the Lord. Say to Him, "Forgive all guilt and accept what is good; instead of bulls we will pay [the offering of] our lips ...*[69] Note: God is "appeased" by "words" of authentic *teshuvah*; there is no mention of *tzedaqah*. *Tzedaqah*'s absence is also keenly felt in light of the immediately preceding tradition, attributed to R. Shmuel bar Nahmani in the name of R. Yonatan: "Great is *teshuvah*, which extends a person's years." *Tzedaqah*, the power of which to rescue from death and extend life we have examined at length in Chapters 3 and 4, goes unmentioned.

The *Bavli* narrator asks: "What is a *ba'al teshuvah*?" Its answer is unsurprising in light of the preceding sources: a *ba'al teshuvah* is characterized by behavior that indicates a successful, sincere, and authentic inner transformation. Rav Yehudah responds that the successful *ba'al teshuvah* avoids the repetition of the atoned-for sin on two later occasions in which the circumstances of temptation are identical.[70] Note: the doing of *tzedaqah* is not identified as part of what makes a penitent a *bona fide ba'al teshuvah*.

The *Bavli*'s emphasis on the importance of the interior experience of *teshuvah* also appears in its extended treatment of the *Yom HaKippurim viddui* (verbal confession of sins) on B. *Yoma* 87b. In response to the anonymous question "what does he say?" the *Bavli* offers the "confession" of Rav Hamnuna Zuta (among others):

> My God, before I was created I was unworthy; now that I have been created it is as if I had not been. I am dust in life, all the more so, in death. Behold, I am before you like a vessel filled with shame and reproach. May it be Your will that I no longer sin (*h-t-'*), and efface the sins I have already committed in Your mercy—but not through afflictions.

This short confession beautifully summarizes the inner transformation the *Bavli* sees as characteristic of authentic *teshuvah.*

Tzedaqah, *the "ten days," and* Yom HaKippurim

The *Bavli* adopts the Palestinian amoraic position that a person's yearly sustenance is set "from" *Rosh Hashanah* "to" *Yom HaKippurim*, with the exception of what he spends during the year on Sabbaths, festivals, and his children's education; should he spend more on those religious priorities he is given more, should he spend less, he will be given less.[71] Significantly, *tzedaqah* expenditures are missing from this list.[72]

The *Bavli* also adopts the Palestinian amoraic development that the ten days between *Rosh Hashanah* and *Yom HaKippurim* are religiously significant. Unlike Palestinian amoraic literature, however, the *Bavli* refers to these days simply as the "ten days between *Rosh Hashanah* and Yom *HaKippurim*," with no mention of *teshuvah*.[73] One hint of this period's special status is found in R. Ami's advice that one who wishes to know whether he will live out the year should light a candle in an airless room during the ten days; if the light goes out, he will not.[74] The *Bavli* nowhere mandates or even recommends the giving of *tzedaqah* during these ten days, although doing so would seem to be a seasonally appropriate, atoning activity.

Nevertheless, four *Bavli* narratives are set during these ten days; one at the time of *Rosh Hashanah* and three "on the eve of the Day of Atonement." A narrative in *Bavli Berachot* about an unnamed *hasid* suggests that *tzedaqah* spending around the time of *Rosh Hashanah* will be repaid by the bountiful replenishment of the funds later.[75] The *hasid* angered his wife by giving a *dinar* to a poor person on *Rosh Hashanah* eve in a year of drought—when presumably she felt that they could have used the *dinar* themselves. After taking his scolding from her, the *hasid* spent the night in a cemetery, where he overheard a conversation among the dead about the appropriate time to plant; heeding what he heard yielded him a handsome profit, and he spent the very same night the following year in the cemetery, with the same result. The narrative makes a point of the *hasid*'s giving the *dinar* to the poor person on *Rosh Hashanah* eve, which indicates something special about the overlap of *tzedaqah* and *Rosh Hashanah*.

The *Bavli* introduces "the eve of the Day of Atonement" into its reworking of *Leviticus Rabbah*'s story of R. Shimon ben Yohai and his nephews. R. Shimon ben Yohai dreams about his nephews' pending financial calamity on the eve of *Rosh Hashanah*; while the *Bavli* leaves the timing of Rabban Yohanan ben Zakkai's dream obscure, it does provide the detail that his nephews succeeded in spending all but seventeen of their ill-fated 700 *dinars* by "the eve of *Yom HaKippurim*."[76] Mar Uqba is described as giving 400 *zuz* annually on the eve of the Day of Atonement to a poor man in his neighborhood;[77] Plimo was humiliated by the outrageous misbehavior of a "poor man" (the *satan* in disguise) who he brought into his home and fed on the eve of the Day of Atonement.[78] Although none of these narratives makes a particular point of highlighting the atoning significance of the time of year, we may assume that their contemporary audience was meant to see a connection between the protagonists' giving *tzedaqah* at that time and the penitential, atoning nature of the "ten days between *Rosh Hashanah* and *Yom HaKippurim*." But again, the *Bavli* does not explicitly prescribe or recommend the giving of *tzedaqah* during the ten days even in these narratives.

Tefillah, tzedaqah, teshuvah *in the* Bavli

The triad components separated (and the importance of fasting)

Like Palestinian amoraic and contemporaneous Christian literature, the *Bavli* links "*tefillah*" with "*tzedaqah*" and the latter also with "fasting."[79] As to "*tefillah*" and "*tzedaqah*," recall that R. Eleazar is said to have given a *perutah* (small coin) to a poor person before praying, basing himself on Psalm 17:15 (*Then I, justified [b'tzedeq] will behold Your face*).[80]

The *Bavli*'s linkage of "fasting" and "*tzedaqah*" is better attested. Rav Huna imposed *tzedaqah* in the context of a public fast.[81] Apropos, R. Eleazar teaches in the name of R. Yitzhaq that any fast day on which *tzedaqah* is delayed is like (a day of) shedding of blood (relying on Isaiah 1:21).[82] Mar Zutra pithily teaches "*agra d'ta'anita tzidqata*," the reward of a fast day lies in the *tzedaqah* (distributed on that day).[83] The *Bavli* also evinces a perception that fasting is even superior to *tzedaqah*. R. Eleazar claims this is so because fasting is done with the body, and *tzedaqah* (only) with one's money.[84] R. Eleazar's contrast of "body" and "money" in the *Bavli* echoes the Palestinian idea attested in the *Yerushalmi* that *gemilut hasadim* is superior to *tzedaqah* because the former is performed with the body and the latter only with money.[85] Rav Sheshet is said to have prayed the following additional prayer on days that he fasted:

> Master of the worlds! It is revealed before You that at the time the
> Temple stood a man would sin and offer a sacrifice. [The priests] would
> only offer its fat and blood and this would atone for him. And now I have
> sat in fasting and my fat and blood have diminished. May it be Your will
> that my diminished fat and blood be as if I have offered it before You and
> may You find it acceptable.[86]

Rav Sheshet offers his own diminution of body mass through fasting as an
atoning substitute for the lost sacrificial offerings of animal fat and blood. He
makes no mention of atoning *tzedaqah* even as an accompaniment to the fast (let
alone as a substitute for it).

The Bavli *'s revision of the triad* "tefillah, tzedaqah, teshuvah"

The *Bavli*'s revision of the triad *tefillah, tzedaqah, teshuvah* brings these devotional activities explicitly and directly into connection with the penitential period
that begins with *Rosh Hashanah*. One change it makes is to place *tzedaqah* first.
But overall, we will see that the impact of the *Bavli*'s revision is to diminish the
status of the triad, thereby also tacitly reaffirming *tzedaqah*'s lack of a special or
higher status than the other linked elements. The pertinent passage is on B. *Rosh
Hashanah* 16b:

1   And R. Yitzhaq said: "Four things tear up a person's
    verdict: *tzedaqah*, crying out (*tz'aqah)*, change of name,
    and change of deeds.

2   *Tzedaqah*: as it is written, *and tzedaqah saves from
    death* (Proverbs 10:2/11:4).

3   Crying out: as it is written, *In their adversity they cried to
    the Lord, and He rescued them from their troubles* (Psalm 107:13).

4   Change of name: as it is written, *As for your wife Sarai, you shall not
    call her Sarai, but her name shall be Sarah.... I will give you a son by
    her* (Genesis 17:15–16).

5   Change of deeds: as it is written, *God saw what they did*, and it is
    written, *And God renounced the punishment He had planned to bring
    upon them, and did not carry it out* (Jonah 3:10)."

6   And there are those who say, "even a change of
    place: as it is written, *The Lord said to
    Abram, 'Go forth from your native land*,' and then, *I
    will make of you a great nation ...* (Genesis 12:1–2)."

This *Bavli* passage is closer to *Genesis Rabbah* 44:12 and its *Pesiqta deRav
Kahana* 28:3 parallel than to *Yerushalmi Ta'anit* and *Yerushalmi Sanhedrin*. The
Bavli's attribution of the passage to the Palestinian *amora* R. Yitzhaq appropri-
ately reflects the Palestinian origin of the tradition about what "tears up the

verdict" (i.e., "nullifies the decree"); the specific choice of R. Yitzhaq as the tradent may be due to this being one of a series of traditions attributed to him on B. *Rosh Hashanah* 16a–16b.

Bavli Rosh Hashanah's reworking of the Palestinian material is striking. *Genesis Rabbah* and *Pesiqta deRav Kahana* are an amalgam of four distinct traditions: (1) the triad *tefillah, tzedaqah, teshuvah* (R. Yudan in the name of R. Lazar); (2) the efficacy of "change of name" and "good actions" (Rav Huna in the name of Rav Yosef); (3) the efficacy of "change of place" (attributed to "one who says"); and (4) the efficacy of fasting (R. Mana). These four distinct traditions yield a total of seven acts that "nullify the decree." *Bavli Rosh Hashanah* condenses most of this material into a tetrad that it attributes in its entirety to R. Yitzhaq. R. Yitzhaq's tetrad is structured for ease of oral recall: the aurally similar "*tzedaqah*" and "*tz'aqah*" (crying out), followed by the paired "change of name" (*shinu'i ha-shem*) and "change of deeds" (*shinu'i ma'aseh*). The *Bavli* condenses seven acts into four by omitting "fasting" and combining *Genesis Rabbah*'s seemingly redundant "*teshuvah*" and "good actions" (*ma'aseh tov*") into the one "change of deeds" (*shinu'i ma'aseh*). "Change of place" (now attributed to "those who say" rather than "one who says") is also retained but left outside the tetrad. "*Tzedaqah*" and "change of name" are clearly the same in both *Genesis Rabbah* and the *Bavli*, but the former's "*tefillah*" becomes the *Bavli*'s "crying out."[87]

At the very least, the *Bavli*'s creation of a tetrad undermines the significance of the older Palestinian triad *tefillah, tzedaqah, teshuvah qua* triad. These three rhyming devotional activities no longer stand out as a unit. The *Bavli* also notably puts *tzedaqah* first and replaces the widely transmitted Palestinian scriptural proofs for its redemptive benefit (II Chronicles 7:14 and Psalm 17:15) with *tzedaqah saves from death* (Proverbs 10:2/11:4). This scriptural substitution is telling. To the best of my knowledge the *Bavli* never quotes II Chronicles 7:14 in relation to *tzedaqah*. It quotes Psalm 17:15 in relation to *tzedaqah* twice— both times on B. *Baba Batra* 10a, once as a demonstration of how giving a coin will allow the giver to see the Divine Presence, and again as the basis for R. Eleazar's practice of giving a small coin to the poor before prayer. The *Bavli* quotes Proverbs 10:2/11:2 five times, this being one of them.[88] Although the *Bavli* obviously does not quote any of these verses with great frequency (at least vis-à-vis *tzedaqah*), it features Proverbs 10:2/11:4 more prominently than the others. The introduction to the new tetrad of *tzedaqah saves from death* raises possibilities about how *tzedaqah* contributes to the "tearing up" of a person's "verdict" that may differ from those of *Genesis Rabbah* and *Pesiqta deRav Kahana*: given the *Bavli*'s multiple understandings of the verse the person may be saved from death itself, from an "unusual" death, or from *dinah shel Gehinnom*.

The *Bavli*'s placing *tzedaqah* at the head of its new tetrad does not imply that it is the superior of the four. Indeed, an examination of the tetrad together with the distinct addition of "change of place" yields evidence of a progression of religious acts from the (relatively) easier to the more difficult, from the more superficial to the more life-altering. *Tzedaqah*, rooted in Proverbs 10:2/11:4 and pertinent *Bavli* intertexts, is about giving, a fairly mechanical act. "Crying out" requires more interiority. "Change of name" and "change of deeds" involve a person's complete reorientation and altered sense of self; "change of deeds" notably includes *teshuvah* (as indicated by the quotation of Jonah 3:10), with all the interiority that itself implies. "Change of place," exile, is an extreme manifestation of a personal reorientation and altered sense of self, as one leaves the familiar and, with authentic faith, embarks for the unknown (as indicated by the quotation of Genesis 12:1–2). On this reading *tzedaqah* is not first because it is *primus inter pares*; it is first because it is the easiest, most mechanical, of the activities to perform, the one that least requires interiority. Or, viewed from another angle, *tzedaqah* is first because its effectiveness for the penitent requires the performance of other acts—such as those found further down on the list—that demand greater interiority.

In sum, this chapter has described an implicit tension in late antique rabbinic literature between the two "magisteria" *tzedaqah* and *teshuvah*. While both are represented as atoning for sin, only *teshuvah* is described as atoning for sin *tout court*; moreover, the rabbis' overall portrayals of both modes of atonement appear to privilege *teshuvah* over *tzedaqah*. This chapter's closing emphasis on a progressively more demanding, internally focused and personally transformative list of acts that will "tear up" a person's "decree" is a good segue to the next. Picking up a thread from Chapter 4, Chapter 6 will explore how some of the *Bavli*'s ideas about charity reflect its broader theological tendency to place limits on the divine while accentuating human agency and responsibility.

Notes

1 See Stephen Jay Gould, *Rocks of Ages: Science and Religion in the Fullness of Life* (repr.; New York: Ballantine Books, 2002). I have enclosed "religion" and "science" in quotation marks in recognition of their being complex, constructed fields of knowledge.

2 On the appropriateness of rendering "*teshuvah*" as "repentance," see most recently David A. Lambert, *How Repentance Became Biblical: Judaism, Christianity, & the Interpretation of Scripture* (New York: Oxford University Press, 2016), 174.

3 *Teshuvah* as a rabbinic religious institution has been frequently explored in modern scholarship. The principal scholars on whom I rely for the discussions of *teshuvah* in this chapter are George Foote Moore, *Judaism in the First Centuries of the Christian Era: The Age of the Tannaim*, 3 vols. (Cambridge: Harvard University Press, 1927), 1:507–534; Solomon Schechter, *Aspects of Rabbinic Theology* (repr.: Woodstock: Jewish Lights, 1993), 313–343; Ephraim E. Urbach, *The Sages*, 1:462–471; and David Lambert, *How Repentance Became Biblical.* I have also consulted the brief, suggestive essay by Jakob Petuchowski, "The Concept of *Teshubhah* in the Bible and the Talmud," in ibid., *Studies in Modern Theology and Prayer* (ed. Elizabeth R. Petuchowski and Aaron M. Petuchowski; Philadelphia: Jewish Publication Society, 1998), 13–25. The studies of *teshuvah* by George Foote Moore, Solomon Schechter, and Ephraim E. Urbach share the methodological approach characteristic of much early- to mid-twentieth century rabbinics scholarship, freely synthesizing sources from rabbinic compilations of various periods and places (Moore and

Schechter even refer to Maimonides). David Lambert is appropriately sensitive to the need to distinguish carefully between tannaitic and amoraic, and between Palestinian and Babylonian, sources.

4   We shall see that in the case of a wrong done to a fellow man ... reparation is the indispensable condition of the divine forgiveness; and that for offenses against God, good works, especially charity ... is one of the things that cause the revocation of the divine decree.

George Foote Moore, *Judaism in the First Centuries of the Christian Era*, 1:514. See also ibid., 1:174.

5   See George Foote Moore, *Judaism in the First Centuries of the Christian Era*, 1:507–508; David Lambert, *How Repentance Became Biblical*, 171, 174; see also Jakob Petuchowski, "The Concept of *Teshubhah*," 13. For an example of "doing" *teshuvah* see, e.g., T. *Qiddushin* 1:16 (ed. Lieberman, 281).

6   Y. *Peah* 1:1, 16b (ed. Academy, 84).

7   See, e.g., M. *Baba Metzia* 4:10; T. *Sukkah* 4:2 (ed. Lieberman, 272).

8   Whether and to what extent this designation had any real-world social consequences requires investigation. The relationship or similarity (if any) between "*ba'alei teshuvah*" and other named groups such as the "*yir'ei heit*" of *Mishnah* and *Tosefta Sheqalim* also merits additional research.

9   *Leviticus Rabbah* 3:1 (ed. Margulies, 56).

10 See *Leviticus Rabbah* 37:2 (ed. Margulies, 857). "*Ba'alei tzedaqah*" appears neither in Palestinian amoraic literature nor in the *Bavli*. It is, however, attested in the early medieval *midrash* compilation *Midrash Proverbs* 21 (ed. Buber).

11 David A. Lambert, *How Repentance Became Biblical*, 177.

12 *Sifre Numbers* 134 (ed. Horovitz, 180).

13 Although we are getting a bit ahead of ourselves, I would point out that this conclusion is consistent with David Levine's comparison of the Christian conjunction of "almsgiving, fasting, and prayer" with the Palestinian rabbinic "*tefillah, tzedaqah, teshuvah.*" Levine concludes that the Christian emphasis is on *acts* while the rabbinic emphasis is on *interiority*. In his words "the goal of the Talmudic homilist is to emphasize the place of *teshuvah.*" Levine understands this goal to be a major part of the theme of the public fast day for rain: "the message [is] that the internal aspect of the day is to be given priority over its ritualistic element." See David Levine, *Communal Fasts and Rabbinic Sermons—Theory and Practice in the Talmudic Period* (Tel Aviv: Hakibbutz Ha-me'uchad, 2001) (in Hebrew), 208–210. We will have much more to say about this below.

14 *Sifre Numbers* 115 (ed. Horovitz, 128–129).

15 The word used is "*bizbeza*," the same verb root used to describe Monbaz in T. *Peah* 4:18.

16 In my discussion of the rabbinic constructions of *Yom HaKippurim* in this chapter, I rely in part upon the discussion in Joseph Tabory, *Jewish Festivals in the Time of the Mishnah and Talmud* (Jerusalem: Magnes Press, 1995), 259–303 and *passim* (in Hebrew).

17 See *Mekhilta de-Rabbi Ishmael* (*Mishpatim*; *Neziqin* 10) (ed. Horovitz-Rabin, 285–286) and the discussion of this passage in Chapter 3.

18 T. *Kippurim* 4:6–8 (ed. Lieberman, 251–252). See also the parallel in *Mekhilta de-Rabbi Ishmael* (Yitro; BaHodesh 7) (ed. Horovitz-Rabin, 228).

19 T. *Kippurim* 4:9–17 (ed. Lieberman, 252–255).

20 See, e.g., T. *Baba Qama* 10:5 (ed. Lieberman, 51), 10:39 (ed. Lieberman, 58); M. *Eduyyot* 7:9. See also Solomon Schechter, *Aspects of Rabbinic Theology*, 320; Jakob Petuchowski, "The Concept of *Teshubhah*," 19–20.

21 M. *Baba Qama* 9:11 exemplifies the former. Should a convert die after the one who has robbed him swears falsely to him that he did not, the robber pays the principal

amount plus an additional fifth to the Temple priests and brings a guilt-offering (cf. Numbers 5:8). The *Mishnah*'s tannaitic intertext is *Sifre Numbers* 4 (ed. Horovitz, 7). Cf. T. *Menachot* 13:17 (ed. Zuckermandel, 533): "as to the robbery of the convert— he [the robber] gives to any priest he wishes." The convert's biological relatives from before his conversion are not considered his "heirs" for purposes of Torah inheritance law. The restitution due him is instead redirected to the priests as religious giving.

22 T. *Sanhedrin* 5:2 (ed. Zuckermandel, 423).

23 Apropos, T. *Baba Metzia* 8:26 (ed. Lieberman, 108) similarly and ambiguously notes that the "*teshuvah*" of tax-collectors is "difficult"; they "return" ("*mahzirin*," also of the root "*h-z-r*") improperly collected monies to those they have actually injured, but as to the rest of the money, "they make use of them for 'public needs.'" cf. T. *Baba Qama* 10:14's ruling that one who steals from the "public" (*rabim*) must return the money to the "public" (ed. Lieberman, 53).

24 Cf. the parallels at Y. *Rosh Hashanah* 1:9, 57c (ed. Academy, 667–668); and Y. *Sanhedrin* 3:3, 21a (ed. Academy, 1281) (with minor variations). Note that M. *Baba Qama* 9:11's priests and T. *Sanhedrin* 5:2's poor play the same role: they are the recipients of restitution that cannot be paid to anyone else, either because the injured party is deceased and has no legal heirs, or because there simply is no identifiable injured party at all.

25 Y. *Sanhedrin* 6:4, 23c (ed. Academy, 1293) (= Y. *Hagigah* 2:2, 7d [ed. Academy, 787]).

26 This narrative is consistent with R. Yohanan's representation that "[if one has] mostly merits and a few transgressions," the latter will be expiated "in this world" in order that he might have "a complete reward" in the "coming future." The inverse is true of one with mostly transgressions and few merits: he will receive the paltry reward to which he is entitled in this world so that God might punish him fully later. See Y. *Peah* 1:1, 16b (ed. Academy, 84). The fate of the tax collector's son resembles that of the rich man in Jesus' parable of Lazarus and the rich man in Luke 16:19–31. The intertextual echoes of the two stories deserve a closer examination.

27 For the "ten days of repentance," see, e.g., *Leviticus Rabbah* 30:2 (ed. Margulies, 694); Y. *Rosh Hashanah* 1:3, 57a (ed. Academy, 665). For a very useful overview of these "ten days" in late antique rabbinic literature, see Joseph Tabory, *Jewish Festivals*, 215–223. Interestingly, Tabory does not at all mention *tzedaqah* in his learned overview of these holidays and the intervening ten days.

28 Y. *Bikkurim* 2:1, 64d (ed. Academy, 354–355).

29 Y. *Peah* 8:9, 21b (ed. Academy, 113) (= Y. *Sheqalim* 5:6, 49b) (ed. Academy, 622).

30 Y. *Yoma* 1:1, 38b (ed. Academy, 559–560). The *Yerushalmi* adds "just as the ashes of the red heifer atone for Israel, so do the deaths of the righteous atone for Israel."

31 These are Y. *Yoma* 8:8, 45b–45c (ed. Academy, 599–600); Y. *Rosh Hashanah* 1:2, 57a–57b (ed. Academy, 665); Y. *Sanhedrin* 10:2, 28c (ed. Academy, 1319–1321); Y. *Shevuot* 1:6, 33b–33c (ed. Academy, 1343–1344).

32 *Pesiqta deRav Kahana* 24:7 (ed. Mandelbaum, 355); see also Y. *Makkot* 2:5, 31d (ed. Academy, 1337).

33 David A. Lambert, *How Repentance Became Biblical*, 173–174.

34 Y. *Sanhedrin* 10:2, 28c (ed. Academy, 1321). See also David A. Lambert, *How Repentance Became Biblical*, 172.

35 Y. *Rosh Hashanah* 1:2, 57a (ed. Academy, 665).

36 *Genesis Rabbah* 9:5 (ed. Theodor-Albeck, 70–71).

37 David A. Lambert, *How Repentance Became Biblical*, 177.

38 The translation of the verse is my own.

39 Y. *Sanhedrin* 10:1, 27d (ed. Academy, 1316).

40 *Leviticus Rabbah* 3:1 (ed. Margulies, 56).

41 Ephraim E. Urbach similarly observes that "acts of charity do not always atone for iniquities or deliver a man from punishment for his transgressions..." He points out

that "'one who says I shall transgress and repent' does not attain to true penitence," from which he concludes "it is obvious that if a man gives liberally to charity, but at the same time sins, he is not to be designated a *saddiq*." See Ephraim E. Urbach, *The Sages*, 1:484–485.

42 See David Levine, *Communal Fasts and Rabbinic Sermons*, 204 and n. 36.

43 See David J. Downs, *Alms*, 222.

44 David Levine, *Communal Fasts and Rabbinic Sermons*, 76–77, 205–210. Cf. Peter Brown's quote of Augustine's linkage of almsgiving and prayer in his *The Ransom of the Soul*, 100: "And we should not only pray, but also give alms ... Those who work ... do so ... with their voices and working with their hands..."

45 See Helen Rhee, *Loving the Poor, Saving the Rich*, 62. On *2 Clement*'s privileging of charity over the other two elements of the triad, see also David J. Downs, *Alms*, 221–224. Downs also points out the linkage of these three elements in the *Gospel of Thomas*.

46 David J. Downs, *Alms*, 206–211.

47 Ibid., 222. See also Downs' more extensive analysis of second-century Christian views on the lack of religious merit in doing charity in his "Almsgiving and Competing Soteriologies in Second-Century Christianity," *Religions* 2018 (doi: 10.3390/rel9070201) (last accessed December 2, 2018).

48 David J. Downs, *Alms*, 222.

49 Y. *Ta'anit* 2:1, 65b (ed. Academy, 712). The others are Y. *Sanhedrin* 10:2, 28c (ed. Academy, 1319–1320); *Genesis Rabbah* 44:15 (ed. Theodor-Albeck, 434–435), and *Pesiqta deRav Kahana* 28:3 (ed. Mandelbaum, 425).

50 Hezekiah is implicitly identified in *Yerushalmi Sanhedrin* as the tradent of both the triad "*tefillah, tzedaqah, teshuvah*" and their scriptural derivations. Two differences between *Yerushalmi Sanhedrin* and the otherwise similar Y. *Ta'anit* 2:1, 65b are that R. Eleazar is identified explicitly as the tradent in *Yerushalmi Ta'anit* (as he is in *Genesis Rabbah* 44:12 and *Pesiqta deRav Kahana* 28:3) and that *teshuvah, tzedaqah, tefillah* are said in *Yerushalmi Ta'anit* to "nullify the harsh decree" rather than "save" from "bad dreams and visions."

51 The translated text is that of *Genesis Rabbah* 44:15.

52 The translation of the verse is my own.

53 All this acknowledged, we must point out the slight hint in *Pesiqta deRav Kahana* of a link between "*tefillah, tzedaqah, teshuvah*" and the penitential period of *Rosh Hashanah* and *Yom Kippur*. *Pesiqta deRav Kahana* 28:2 (*Shmini Atzeret*) implicitly compares *Shmini Atzeret* (the "eighth day of assembly"; cf. Leviticus 23:36) to *Rosh Hashanah* and the "great fast" (*Yom HaKippurim*). The immediately succeeding section, 28:3, is where we find *Pesiqta deRav Kahana*'s reference to "*tefillah, tzedaqah, teshuvah*." See *Pesiqta deRav Kahana* 28:2–3 (ed. Mandelbaum, 424–425).

54 *Pesiqta deRav Kahana* 24:2 (ed. Mandelbaum, 349). *Teshuvah* and *tefillah* (without *tzedaqah*) are also juxtaposed in two succeeding sections of the same passage. See *Pesiqta deRav Kahana* 24:3–4 (ed. Mandelbaum, 351–352).

55 *Pesiqta deRav Kahana* 24:11 (ed. Mandelbaum, 358–368).

56 *Pesiqta deRav Kahana* 24:11 (ed. Mandelbaum, 367).

57 *Genesis Rabbah* 33:3 (ed. Theodor-Albeck, 304–305). There is a parallel to this story in *Leviticus Rabbah* 34:14 (ed. Margulies, 806–809).

58 B. *Baba Batra* 9a.

59 B. *Zebachim* 7b.

60 Rava's view elsewhere that a Torah scholar does not require sacrificial atonement at all is consistent with this (B. *Menachot* 110a). Rava's contrast is between interiority and mechanical acts (like sacrifice); not between *teshuvah* and all other religious acts.

61 B. *Avodah Zarah* 17a. I have put "R." in square brackets because Rabbi Yehudah HaNasi appears to grant him the title in a coda to the narrative.

62 The *Bavli*'s Elisha ben Abuyah narrative is found on B. *Hagigah* 15a–15b. For a very detailed analysis of this story, see Alon Goshen-Gottstein, *The Sinner and the Amnesiac: The Rabbinic Invention of Elisha Ben Abuya and Eleazar Ben Arach* (Stanford: Stanford University Press, 2000).
63 On this passage see also David A. Lambert, *How Repentance Became Biblical*, 177.
64 B. *Yoma* 86a.
65 I have replaced the JPS translation's "*afflictions*" in the latter part of the verse with the more literal "rebelliousness" to highlight the parallelism.
66 B. *Yoma* 86a.
67 On this passage see David A. Lambert, *How Repentance Became Biblical*, 176.
68 B. *Yoma* 86a. I have replaced the JPS translation's "*espoused*" (Jeremiah 3:14) with the more literal "mastery" in the interests of the analysis. See also *Rashi* to B. *Yoma* 86a, s.v. "*u-ketiv ki anokhi ba'alti etchem.*"
69 B. *Yoma* 86b.
70 Ibid.
71 B. *Betzah* 15b–16a (= *Leviticus Rabbah* 30:1 [ed. Margulies, 688]).
72 R. Yitzhaq teaches on B. *Baba Batra* 9b that *tzedaqah* spending is rewarded with more funds to spend on *tzedaqah*, but this reward is not limited to spending between *Rosh Hashanah* and *Yom HaKippurim*.
73 For the *Bavli* locution, see, e.g., B. *Rosh Hashanah* 18a.
74 B. *Keritot* 5b.
75 B. *Berachot* 18b. On this narrative see Aryeh Cohen, "'Do the Dead Know'? On the Representation of Death in the Bavli," *Association for Jewish Studies Review* 24:1 (1999): 45–71.
76 B. *Baba Batra* 10a; cf. *Leviticus Rabbah* 34:13 (ed. Margulies, 796–799).
77 B. *Ketubot* 67b.
78 B. *Qiddushin* 81a–81b.
79 See David Levine, *Communal Fasts and Rabbinic Sermons*, 204 and n. 36 and the pertinent discussion in Chapter 3.
80 B. *Baba Batra* 10a. See the pertinent discussion in Chapter 4.
81 B. *Megillah* 27a–27b. See the discussion of this passage in Chapter 4.
82 B. *Sanhedrin* 35a. Isaiah 1:21 reads: *The faithful city … where righteousness* [*tzedeq*] *dwelt—but now murderers.* "Dwelt" is of the trilateral root "*l-'-n*," which can also mean to "linger," or "delay." So the "delay" of "*tzedeq*" (= *tzedaqah*) results in the townspeople's being labeled "murderers."
83 B. *Berachot* 6b.
84 B. *Berachot* 32b.
85 B. *Sukkah* 49b (= Y. *Peah* 1:1, 15c [ed. Academy, 79]).
86 B. *Berachot* 17a.
87 It should be noted that the *Bavli* does link "fasting" and "crying out," see, e.g., B. *Ta'anit* 15a.
88 B. *Baba Batra* 10a (twice); B. *Shabbat* 156b (twice); and, of course, B. *Rosh Hashanah* 16b.

Bibliography

Primary sources and critical editions

Albeck, Chanoch. 1978. *Shishah Sidre Mishnah: With New Commentary, Introductions, Additions, and Completions.* Tel-Aviv: Dvir

Babylonian Talmud. 1975 (repr.). Vilna-Romm edition with standard commentaries. Jerusalem: n.p.

Buber, Solomon. 1892. *Midrash Proverbs.* Vilna: Romm

Horovitz, H.S. 1966. *Siphre D'be Rab.* Jerusalem: Wahrmann Books

Horovitz, H.S. and I.A. Rabin. 1970. *Mechilta D'Rabbi Ismael.* Jerusalem: Wahrmann Books

Lieberman, Saul. 1955. *The Tosefta: According to Codex Vienna, with Variants from Codex Erfurt, Genizah Mss. And Editio Princeps (Venice 1521). The Order of Zera'im.* New York: The Jewish Theological Seminary of America

Lieberman, Saul. 1962. *The Tosefta: According to Codex Vienna, with Variants from Codex Erfurt, Genizah Mss. And Editio Princeps (Venice 1521). The Order of Mo'ed.* New York: The Jewish Theological Seminary of America

Lieberman, Saul. 1973. *The Tosefta: According to Codex Vienna, with Variants from Codices Erfurt, Genizah Mss. And Editio Princeps (Venice 1521).* New York: The Jewish Theological Seminary of America

Lieberman, Saul. 1988. *The Tosefta: According to Codex Vienna, with Variants from Codex Erfurt, Ms. Schocken and Editio Princeps (Venice 1521). The Order of Nezikin.* New York: The Jewish Theological Seminary of America

Mandelbaum, Bernard. 1962. *Pesikta de Rav Kahana: According to an Oxford Manuscript; With Variants.* New York: The Jewish Theological Seminary of America

Margulies, Mordecai. 1993. *Midrash Wayyikra Rabbah: A Critical Edition Based on Manuscripts and Genizah Fragments with Variants and Notes.* New York and Jerusalem: The Jewish Theological Seminary of America

Talmud Yerushalmi: According to Ms. Or. 4720 (Scal. 3) of the Leiden University Library with Restorations and Corrections. 2005. Introduction by Yaacov Sussman. Jerusalem: The Academy of the Hebrew Language

Theodor, Judah and Chanoch Albeck. 1996 (repr.). *Midrash Bereschit Rabbah.* Berlin and Jerusalem: Akademie für die Wissenschaft des Judentums

Zuckermandel, M.S. 1970. *Tosephta: Based on the Erfurt and Vienna Codices.* Jerusalem: Wahrmann Books

Scholarly studies

Brown, Peter. 2015. *The Ransom of the Soul: Afterlife and Wealth in Early Western Christianity.* Cambridge and London: Harvard University Press

Cohen, Aryeh. 1999. "'Do the Dead Know'? On the Representation of Death in the Bavli." *Association for Jewish Studies Review* 24:45–71

Downs, David J. 2016. *Alms: Charity, Reward, and Atonement in Early Christianity.* Waco: Baylor University Press

Downs, David J. 2018. "Almsgiving and Competing Soteriologies in Second-Century Christianity." *Religions* 2018. Available at: doi: 10.3390/rel9070201

Goshen-Gottstein, Alon. 2000. *The Sinner and the Amnesiac: The Rabbinic Invention of Elisha Ben Abuya and Eleazar Ben Arach.* Stanford: Stanford University Press

Gould, Stephen Jay. 2002 (repr.). *Rocks of Ages: Science and Religion in the Fullness of Life.* New York: Ballantine Books

Lambert, David A. 2016. *How Repentance Became Biblical: Judaism, Christianity, & the Interpretation of Scripture.* New York: Oxford University Press

Levine, David. 2001. *Communal Fasts and Rabbinic Sermons—Theory and Practice in the Talmudic Period.* Tel Aviv: Hakibbutz Ha-me'uchad (in Hebrew)

Moore, George Foote. 1927. *Judaism in the First Centuries of the Christian Era: The Age of the Tannaim,* 3 vols. Cambridge: Harvard University Press

Petuchowski, Jakob. 1998. "The Concept of *Teshubhah* in the Bible and the Talmud." In: Jakob Petuchowski; Elizabeth R. Petuchowski and Aaron M. Petuchowski, eds. *Studies in Modern Theology and Prayer*. Philadelphia: Jewish Publication Society

Rhee, Helen. 2012. *Loving the Poor, Saving the Rich: Wealth, Poverty, and Early Christian Formation*. Grand Rapids: Baker Academic

Schechter, Solomon. 1993 (repr.). *Aspects of Rabbinic Theology*. Woodstock: Jewish Lights

Tabory, Joseph. 1995. *Jewish Festivals in the Time of the Mishnah and Talmud*. Jerusalem: Magnes Press (in Hebrew)

Urbach, Ephraim E. 1979. *The Sages: Their Concepts and Beliefs*, 2nd enlarged ed. Jerusalem: Magnes Press

6 Charity and beyond

The Talmud *Bavli*'s limitations on a divine role in human affairs

The goal of this chapter is to connect the Talmud *Bavli*'s demonstrable limitations on a divine role in charity and concomitant heightened emphasis on charity's human dimensions to its limitations on the divine across a range of other texts and topics. The *Bavli* is certainly not the first rabbinic compilation to emphasize the human dimensions of charity. The Talmud *Yerushalmi*'s innovative imposition of a maximum on individual charitable giving to the poor vividly illustrates an amoraic turn toward a greater focus on charity's potential this-worldly consequences for a donor.[1] *Yerushalmi Peah* describes the Ushan sages' revival of Rabban Gamliel's forgotten 20 percent annual maximum on giving, which the *Yerushalmi* goes on to define more precisely as 20 percent of a person's annual increase in wealth.[2] *Yerushalmi Peah*'s imposition of a maximum is a shift from tannaitic precedent. *Sifre Deuteronomy*'s well-known account of Hillel's lavish provision for a formerly wealthy poor man and its tannaitic parallel are notoriously distinguished by a conspicuous lack of any sense of limitation.[3] King Monbaz "scatters" his and his ancestors' treasures, heedlessly, without limit, and to their unconcealed dismay.[4] An implicit message of *Yerushalmi Peah*'s maximum on charitable giving is that a donor should not be single-mindedly focused on giving to the exclusion of concern about the possible detriment to himself that can result from *profligate* giving. Apropos, *Yerushalmi Peah*'s imposition of a maximum shows that charity is a rabbinic legal institution and set of practices like any other; it is not (solely) a supernal matter immune to rabbinic legislative intervention. And rabbinic charity legislation on earth can, in turn, affect how charity structures the relationship between God and donors.

The *Bavli*'s heightened focus on the this-worldly, human element in charity and concomitant diminution of the divine role and element arguably go far beyond what we see in Palestinian amoraic literature. We saw in Chapter 2 that the *Bavli* explicitly severs the link between "*tzedaqah*" and "*heqdesh*" and that no figure in the *Bavli* is described as "vowing" or "stipulating" (of the trilateral root *p-s-q*) *tzedaqah*.[5] We learned in Chapter 4 that the *Bavli* is openly ambivalent about redemptive almsgiving.[6] Only two Babylonian *amoraim* arguably teach anything resembling redemptive almsgiving, and in neither case does either sage straightforwardly support the proposition that *tzedaqah* for the poor atones for sin.[7] Unlike Palestinian amoraic literature, no non-rabbi in the *Bavli* invites donors to "acquire merit" through him by giving him charity. The *Bavli* is unique among the rabbinic corpora in even de-emphasizing reward entirely through its innovation of doing *tzedaqah* "*lishmah*."[8] The *Bavli* is also distinguished by its negative valuation of accept-ing charity, its negative portrayals of the poor who do so, and its positive por-trayals of the laboring poor.[9] The *Bavli* uniquely emphasizes that only giving to "worthy" recipients will be rewarded,[10] and it valorizes compelling *tzedaqah*.[11] Naturally the *Bavli* adopts and adapts *Yerushalmi Peah*'s charit-able maximum, explicitly justifying the limitation with the realistic concern that an overly generous donor may come to "have need of other created beings (i.e., people)," a concern that dovetails with its demonstrated distaste for accepting charity.[12]

In this chapter we will examine the *Bavli*'s limitation on the divine role in charity in relation to two other broad categories of material: (1) Yaakov Elman's findings about Rava's and the *Bavli* narrator's limitations on divine providence in other areas; and (2) the *Bavli*'s diminution of the divine role and heightening of the human role in the revelation, transmission, creation, and preservation of Torah. We will confine our examination of the second category to three topics: (1) the *Bavli*'s limitations on the divine and accentuation of the human role in the acceptance of Torah at Sinai and its continuing study; (2) the *Bavli*'s elimination of a *Yerushalmi* hint of continuing divine oversight of rabbinic legal innovation; and (3) the *Bavli*'s elimination of a *Yerushalmi* hint of divine involvement in the restoration of forgotten rabbinic laws.

Rava, the *Bavli* narrator, and limitations on the divine

Rava and limitations on the divine in the context of charity

The *amora* Rava is associated with positions on charity that are consistent with the *Bavli* developments just summarized. Rava insists that unlike other vows to dedicate property for sacred purposes, *tzedaqah* vows must be fulfilled immedi-ately because of the presence of the poor.[13] This insistence drives a wedge between "*tzedaqah*" and other "*heqdesh*"; Rava therefore does not entirely view *tzedaqah* as a gift to God and it naturally follows that he does not entirely view it as a gift to the poor *from* God. Unsurprisingly, then, Rava compels R. Natan bar Ami to give *tzedaqah*[14] (which is consequently, then, not the latter's own self-motivated demonstration of righteousness before God) and challenges a for-merly wealthy poor man: "And aren't you concerned about the burden on the community?"[15] Rava obviously does not see that man as a conduit for the trans-mission of redemptive benefits to donors and notably, Rava is nowhere associ-ated with redemptive almsgiving in any form, whether it be charity's atoning for sin or its power to save from death and extend life in this world or the next. Apropos, Rava's ambivalent (at the least) attitude toward the poor is likewise exemplified by his rooting the popular adage "poverty follows the poor" in Leviticus 13:45's mandate that a leper (!) announce himself by calling out: "Unclean! Unclean!"[16]

Rava and limitations on divine providence in other contexts

Rava's limitation on a divine role in charity and heightened attention to the human is consistent with Yaakov Elman's finding that "Rava's name recurs over and over in *sugyot* which tend to limit the operation of Divine Providence."[17] In one case Rava attributes a *baraita* about the reward for performing commandments to R. Ya'aqov, who holds "there is no reward for [performing] a *mitzvah* in this world."[18] Elman goes on to show how Rava's attribution of the *baraita* is related to the *sugya*'s conclusion, which tempers R. Eleazar's optimistic view that "messengers on a *mitzvah* errand will not be harmed" with the frank recognition that this may not be true should the messengers encounter a dangerous situation on their journey. To Elman, Rava's alignment with R. Ya'aqov is the seed of a skepticism about the workings of divine providence that emerges full-blown in the *Bavli* narrator's conclusion that messengers on a *mitzvah* errand might *not* in fact be assured Divine protection from dangers they might encounter while fulfilling their missions.

Elman points out in turn that this blunt realism is linked to Rava's position elsewhere that "one does not rely on a miracle."[19] Unlike Abaye, who holds that Temple pilgrims would not be crushed because the Temple gates would close "miraculously at the proper moment," Rava holds that human guards would close the gates, thus not entirely foreclosing the possibility of disaster.[20] As Elman points out, "[a]ccording to Rava ... one may not rely on miracles even in regard to the Temple service, where, it should be noted, miracles were to be expected."[21] Further, B. *Sotah* 21a shows that "Rava clearly does allow for some reward [for the doing of *mitzvoth*—AG] in this world, though he limits it," and "[B. *Baba Qama* 60a–60b] contains advice, attributed to Rava, to close one's windows in time of plague—not bad advice at all, but not quite in the same category as fasting, prayer, donating charity, etc."[22] Rava also holds that one's length of life, children, and sustenance are determined by astrology, not merit.[23]

Elman also demonstrates how the *Bavli* narrator takes up Rava's consistent association with limits on divine providence.[24] We have also already pointed out in this chapter the consistency of Rava's positions on charity with those of the *Bavli* narrator. One key example that will serve as a capstone illustration is the consistency of Rava's total silence about redemptive almsgiving and the *Bavli* narrator's trumpeted skepticism about it. This display of skepticism culminates in "R. Aqiva"'s insistence that Isaiah 58:7 mandates succoring the poor "today," presumably even without a guarantee of a divinely bestowed redemptive benefit.[25] We now turn to the *Bavli*'s limitation of the divine and accentuation of the human role in the revelation and continuing transmission and study of Torah.

Limitations on the divine role in the revelation, transmission, creation, and preservation of Torah[26]

The acceptance and study of Torah

We begin with B. *Shabbat* 88a:[27]

1   *And they took their places at the foot of the mountain* (Exodus 19:17).
2   Rav Avdimi bar Hama[28] said: "This teaches that the Holy One, blessed be He held the mountain [Sinai] over them like an inverted barrel and said to them, 'If you accept the Torah—good, and if not, there will be your grave.'"
3   Rav Aha bar Ya'aqov said: "This is a *muda'a rabbah* to the Torah."[29]
4   Rava said: "Nevertheless, they accepted it again in the days of Ahasuerus, as it is written, *The Jews fulfilled and accepted upon themselves*[30] (Esther 9:27)—they '*fulfilled*' what they had already '*accepted upon themselves*.'"

This passage consists of three amoraic teachings appended to Exodus 19:17: Rav Avdimi bar Hama presents the tradition under discussion, Rav Aha bar Ya'aqov points out its problematic theological implication, and Rava resolves the problem. Rav Avdimi bar Hama responds to a grammatical oddity in the verse, which reads that Israel was camped "*b'tachtit ha-har*" ("at the foot," or "base," of the mountain) rather than the more straightforward "*tachat ha-har*" ("under the mountain"). This grammatical oddity is the catalyst for the idea that God compelled Israel to accept the Torah by force, an idea found earlier in *Song of Songs Rabbah* 8:2, where God states: "If you receive my Torah upon yourselves, good; and if not, I will crush you with this mountain and kill you."

Neither *Song of Songs Rabbah* nor Rav Avdimi bar Hama does anything more than report the tradition, but the following two *amoraim* problematize it. Rav Aha bar Ya'aqov observes that God's compelling Israel to accept the Torah on pain of annihilation is a "*muda'a rabbah*." In the *Bavli* a *muda'a* is a legal document signed by witnesses, by means of which a party to a commercial transaction affirms that he was coerced into participating in that transaction. The *muda'a* can be used to nullify the transaction.[31] Rav Aha bar Ya'aqov is cleverly using a legal institution current in his time and place as a theological metaphor: Rav Avdimi bar Hama's account of God's compulsion of Israel is itself a *muda'a*, even a "great" (*rabbah*) *muda'a*, attested evidence of Israel's coerced acceptance of Torah at Sinai. It is therefore implied that this *muda'a* can even *nullify* Israel's acceptance of the Torah; the divine display of might and power at Sinai was so overwhelming that Israel literally had no choice but to accept. Implicit in Rav Aha bar Ya'aqov's observation is that Israel's continued adherence to Torah is somehow its own choice: Israel has a foolproof legal means by which to unburden itself of the Torah should it so wish.

Rava affirms the theological problem and offers a way to overcome it. He implicitly accepts Rav Aha bar Ya'aqov's point that the Sinai experience was not a valid acceptance of Torah and that Israel's continued adherence to it is self-motivated. Rava points to Esther 9:27 (*The Jews fulfilled and accepted*) as proof that Israel accepted the Torah again, *after* Sinai, during the Second Temple period in Persia. As he reads the verse, the Jews "*fulfilled*" (in Ahasuerus's Persia) what they had already "*accepted*" (at Sinai). To Rava, only this later, entirely human, acceptance of Torah is valid. Rava's use of Esther 9:27 is particularly poignant because not only does the Persian setting of the Esther scroll echo his own contemporary context, but God is famously entirely absent from that book. Rava's bold point is that the only valid and binding acceptance of Torah by Israel is one that is entirely the result of human initiative, in a time and place in which the divine role in human history is imperceptible and obscure, and human initiative predominant.

The attribution of this remarkable idea to Rava is entirely consistent with the evidence of his charity traditions as well as that developed by Yaakov Elman. The same Rava who is skeptical about the idea of charity as a gift to God and urges consideration of the community's burden, who separates *tzedaqah* from other vows and from *heqdesh*, who insists that the presence of needy people requires immediate fulfillment of charity vows (unlike other vows), and who limits the scope of divine providence outside the charity realm (Yaakov Elman)—this very same Rava holds that Israel's valid acceptance of Torah is recounted not in Exodus 19 but in Esther 9:27, at the end of a book from which God is absent and in which human initiative drives the story toward its triumphal fulfillment.

Once accepted, the Torah is to be studied and transmitted. The rabbis of both rabbinic centers valorize Torah study; for the *Bavli* Torah study is of primary religious, intellectual, and ideological importance.[32] The *Bavli*'s God does not insist upon imposing his view upon human sages via revelation; he allows—indeed, participates and even revels in—the human role in interpreting and expanding Torah. The reader may already be thinking of the much-discussed "Oven of Akhnai" story.[33] As is well known, R. Eliezer seeks to derive support for the oven's purity from a carob tree (which dutifully uproots itself and moves in support of his opinion), a stream of water (which also dutifully flows in reverse), and finally, the very walls of the *bet midrash* (which lean in support of his view). Yet his colleagues refuse at each step to accept these miraculous "proofs." Key for our purpose is God's response; Elijah the prophet tells R. Natan that God laughed and proclaimed: "My children have defeated me; my children have defeated me." God allows that only the human determination of the law will be allowed to stand as *the* determination of the law.

God himself participates in *bet midrash*-style deliberations.[34] R. Evyatar and R. Yonatan dispute the interpretation of the biblical narrative of the concubine at Gibeah (Judges 19). R. Evyatar encounters Elijah the prophet, who tells him that God was also studying that narrative, repeating aloud to himself that "My son

Evyatar says this and my son Yonatan says that." R. Evyatar is amazed to hear that God was repeating the human sages' views to himself, which implies divine uncertainty about the narrative's proper interpretation. Elijah responds, "these and these are the words of the living God"; as Daniel Boyarin points out, God is able to repeat the different sages' views, but not to resolve them. The "parameters of indeterminacy," as Boyarin describes them, are set not by God, but by the two sages.[35] B. *Baba Metzia* 86a presents God as engaged in an active dispute with the entire "heavenly study house," putting himself in the minority by ruling "pure" in the case at issue. The heavenly study house being locked in a stalemate, a messenger (the Angel of Death) is sent to summon Rabbah bar Nahmani, the living human expert on the recondite subject matter. The Angel of Death's access to the sage is obstructed by the latter's uninterrupted Torah study. A fortuitous (for the Angel of Death) wind in the trees disturbs Rabbah bar Nahmani, who dies calling out "pure, pure." A note fell from the heavenly study house to the scholars of Pumbedita, informing them of the "summons" to Rabbah bar Nahmani. Note that God and the heavenly study house *require* the involvement of the human sage Rabbah bar Nahmani; God *needs* the human expert's support to vindicate his legal view as against his interlocutors. Even God and the entire heavenly study house must play by the human rules of the earthly study house.

Making new law

God plays a supporting more than a leading role in this instructive example. The *Yerushalmi* ascribes greater agency to the divine in the establishment of the Purim holiday than does the *Bavli*; the *Bavli* occludes that agency, stressing instead the holiday's entirely human founding. We begin with a tradition the *Bavli* attributes to the transitional tannaitic/amoraic sage R. Yehoshua ben Levi: the "earthly *bet din*" took three legal actions with which the "heavenly *bet din*" agreed after the fact. These were: (1) establishing the reading of the Esther scroll on Purim, (2) greeting people using God's name, and (3) the centralized collection of agricultural tithes.[36] Note how in these three cases heaven follows the lead of human initiative, not vice versa.

We begin our closer examination of the case of the Esther scroll with relevant passages, the first from *Yerushalmi Megillah* (paragraphs 1–3) and the second from *Bavli Megillah* (paragraphs A-F):[37]

1   R. Shmuel bar Nahman in the name of R. Yonatan: "Eighty-five elders, among whom were a number of prophets, were pained about this thing [establishing the reading of the Esther scroll as a fixed commandment]. They said: 'It is written: *These are the commandments that the Lord gave Moses* (Leviticus 27:34)—these are the commandments that we were commanded from Moses's mouth. Thus did Moses say, 'another prophet is not permitted in future to innovate something for you after this.' And Mordecai and Esther seek to innovate something for us?'

2   They did not move from there, and deliberated until God lit up their eyes and they found it written in the Torah, and in the Prophets, and in the Writings..."

* * *

3   Rav, R. Haninah, R. Yonatan, Bar Qappara and R. Yehoshua ben Levi said: "This scroll was uttered to Moses at Sinai, but there is no chronological priority in the Torah."

A   Rav Shmuel bar Yehudah said: "Esther sent [a message] to the sages: 'Establish me [i.e., my story] for [all] generations.'

B   They sent to her: 'You will arouse envy against us among the nations.'

C   She sent to them: 'I [i.e., my story] am already written in the chronicles of the kings of Medea and Persia.' "

* * *

D   Esther sent to the sages: "Write me [i.e., my story] for all generations."

E   They sent to her: "(Proverbs 22:20) *Indeed, I wrote down for you a threefold lore*—threefold and not fourfold."[38]

F   [They searched] until they found a verse written in the Torah (Exodus 17:14): *Inscribe this in a document as a reminder. Inscribe this*—what is written here and in Deuteronomy. *As a reminder*—what is written in the Prophets (I Samuel). *In a document*—what is written in the [Esther] scroll."

The *Yerushalmi*'s R. Yonatan represents that "eighty-five elders," a group including "a number of prophets," held religious authority in the time of Mordecai and Esther. The pair precipitated a religious crisis by seeking to introduce the new commandment to read the Esther scroll annually despite the Torah's express prohibition of introducing new commandments by way of prophetic revelation after Moses. With prophetic authority foreclosed, the elders had to seek a scriptural path to justification: they are ultimately able to find one because God "lit up their eyes," enabling them properly to read and interpret the scriptures they already possessed. The *Yerushalmi* ascribes a role to God, however indirect.

In the *Bavli* there are no "prophets," only "sages." The *Bavli*'s "sages" initially demur as the *Yerushalmi*'s "elders" did, but on an entirely different ground: "You will arouse envy against us among the nations." The *Bavli*'s "sages" are not initially portrayed as worried at all about their (or Esther's) religious authority to institute the annual reading of the Esther scroll, and Esther dismisses their prudential, political concern by pointing out that her story is already recorded for posterity and therefore potentially (if not actually) widely known. Only when their concern about "envy" is dismissed do the *Bavli*'s "sages" raise the issue of a lack of scriptural support. In this retelling the sages once again find scriptural support, but with the crucial difference that there is no mention of God's "lighting up their eyes," indeed, God goes entirely unmentioned. The *Bavli* presents the establishment of the commandment to read the Esther scroll annually as an entirely human project and accomplishment.

The forgetting and restoration of law: the Yerushalmi *leaves room for a divine role in the rabbinic enterprise and the* Bavli *does not*

Yerushalmi Megillah's quotation of Leviticus 27:34 connects the previous section's example to this one, a remarkable example of the *Bavli*'s depriving God of a role in post-Sinaitic Torah study and law-making.[39]

1   Rav Yehudah reported in the name of Shmuel: "Three thousand laws were forgotten during the period of mourning for Moses. They said to Joshua: 'Ask [God].' He replied: '*It is not in the heavens* (Deuteronomy 30:12).' They [the Israelites] said to Samuel: 'Ask [God].' He replied: [Scripture says:] '*These are the commandments* (Leviticus 27:34)[since the revelation of these commandments] no prophet is permitted to innovate anything [i.e., a new commandment].'"

2   R. Yitzhaq Napcha said: "Also the law relating to a sin-offering whose owners have died was forgotten during the period of mourning for Moses. They [the Israelites] said to Phinehas: 'Ask [God].' He said to [them]: '*It is not in the heavens*.' They said to Eleazar: 'Ask [God].' He said to them: '*These are the commandments* [since the revelation of these commandments] no prophet is permitted to innovate anything [i.e., a new commandment].'"

3   Rav Yehudah said in the name of Rav: "When Moses was taking leave [of this world] for the Garden of Eden he said to Joshua: 'Ask me about all your doubts [about the revealed laws].' He said to him: 'My Master, have I ever left you [even] for one hour to go somewhere else? Didn't you write about me in the Torah' (Exodus 33:11): *but his attendant, Joshua son of Nun, a youth, would not stir out of the Tent*? Immediately Joshua's strength weakened, and he forgot three hundred laws, seven hundred doubts [about the revealed laws] emerged [in his mind], and all of Israel stood up to kill him. The Holy One, blessed be He, said to him [Joshua]: 'It is not possible [for me] to tell you [all the forgotten laws and resolve all your doubts.] Go and busy [the people] with war,' as it is said (Joshua 1:1): *After the death of Moses the servant of the Lord, the Lord said to Joshua, son of Nun* and it is said (Joshua 1:11): *Get provisions ready, for in three days' time you are to cross the Jordan, in order to enter and possess the land ...*"

4   It was taught: "1,700 inferences from minor to major (*qal v'homer*) and laws derived by linguistic equivalence between scriptural verses (*gezerah shavah*) and precise, fine points of the Scribes (*diqduqei soferim*) were forgotten during Moses's mourning period." R. Abbahu

said: "Nevertheless, Othniel ben Kenaz restored them through his dialectical abilities, as it is said (Joshua 15:17): *His kinsman Othniel the Kenizzite captured it; and Caleb gave him his daughter Achsah in marriage.*" And why was her name "Achsah"? R. Yohanan said: "Because whoever saw her would be angry at his wife."

Paragraph 1 describes a crisis: a significant portion of the Sinaitic revelation—3,000 *halakhot*—was lost during the period of mourning for Moses. The people initially (and naturally) turn to Moses's successor Joshua and ask that he request God to restore the missing laws. Joshua uses Moses's own Torah to reject their request; the Torah describes itself as no longer resident in heaven and God consequently can no longer reveal any part of it. Paragraph 1 implies that the people live without the missing laws for a lengthy spell, corresponding to the period covered by the biblical books of Joshua and Judges. They eventually approach the prophet Samuel with the same request, but Samuel demurs because of Leviticus 27:34—the very same verse *Yerushalmi Megillah*'s "elders" quote to Esther. Samuel, who is himself a prophet, uses Leviticus 27:34 to stress the limitations of his prophetic role: he is forbidden to innovate after the revelation to Moses.

Prophetic leadership has therefore failed to restore the missing laws (paragraph 1). Paragraph 2 describes the people's turn from prophetic to priestly leadership, but the latter are also unable to restore the forgotten laws: the priests are limited by the same scriptural verses that tied the hands of the prophets Joshua and Samuel. Neither prophetic nor priestly leadership can restore the lost laws.

Paragraph 3 is a closer examination of Joshua, who is described as responding arrogantly to Moses's urging that he seize whatever opportunity he has left to ask the dying prophet about his lingering legal doubts and remaining questions. Joshua assumes—wrongly, as it turns out—that his constant attendance upon Moses guarantees that his knowledge and perfect understanding of the Sinaitic revelation is and will remain intact. In an ironic turn, Joshua's constant attendance upon Moses proves detrimental; Moses is dying, and Joshua's memory also quickly begins to fail. God flatly refuses to supply Joshua with the missing laws and advises that he turn the people's aggression toward him outwards, in military pursuits. Paragraph 3's introduction of God as a character in the narrative raises the legal and theological stakes: whereas paragraphs 1 and 2 describe human prophets and priests confessing their inability to supply the missing laws, paragraph 3 describes God's own refusal to do so. *The divine imposes limitations on itself.* At this point in the passage there seems to be no resolution in sight: if neither prophet, nor priest, nor even God can or will restore the missing laws, what is to become of them? Is the Sinaitic revelation to remain forever incomplete and partial after Moses's death?

Paragraph 4's answer is clearly "No." The hero who restores the lost laws is neither priest nor prophet, and certainly not God; he is a minor biblical character named Othniel the Kenizzite, said to have restored the lost laws through his sharp dialectical skills, of which the rabbis find a hint in his "conquest" of Qiryat-Sefer, literally, the "town of the book" (Joshua 15:16). The *Bavli*'s attribution to Othniel of dialectical skill makes of him a quasi-rabbinic character, and his relative obscurity is thematically significant: this minor biblical figure accomplishes with his unaided human intellect what the prominent biblical heroes Joshua, Eleazar, Phinehas, and Samuel are unable to do through their prophetic or priestly offices. The *Bavli*'s message could not be clearer: the dialectical skills of the rabbis are the ultimate response to the crisis of forgotten law; unaided human intellect is both necessary and sufficient to ensure the restoration and transmission of an intact Sinaitic revelation. God plays no role in this, and *even imposes limits on himself.*

This rich narrative about the crisis of forgotten law is but one of a number of sources about the forgetting and restoration of law in both Talmuds.[40] The *Yerushalmi* sees the forgetting and later restoration of forgotten law as a hint of continuing divine oversight of the rabbinic enterprise; the *Bavli*, by contrast, tends to substitute intentional human legislative action for the "forgetting-restoration" motif, thereby also eliminating any hint of continuing divine oversight. To the *Bavli*, humans and humans alone bear and discharge the responsibility of ensuring the proper state of the law and its observance. We will continue our examination of this theme with a closer examination of *Yerushalmi Peah*'s imposition of a 20 percent maximum on annual charitable giving.[41]

1   And this is like what R. Shimon ben Laqish said in the name of R. Yehudah ben Hanina: "They voted in Usha that a man should separate a fifth of his possessions for *mitzvoth.*"

* * *

2   R. Gamliel ben Ininya asked R. Mana: "Is it one-fifth each year? Then in five years he will lose everything!"
3   [R. Mana] said to him: "In the first [year], it's one-fifth of the principal. From then on, one-fifth of the [annual] appreciation [in income]."

* * *

4   It once happened that R. Yeshebab stood up and distributed all his possessions to the poor. Rabban Gamliel sent to him: "Didn't they say, 'one-fifth of his possessions for *mitzvoth*'?"
5   And wasn't Rabban Gamliel prior to Usha?
6   R. Yose b. R. Bun said in the name of R. Levi: "Such was the law in their hands and they forgot it. And 'the two' stood up and agreed upon what the intention of the early ones had been. This is to teach you that every matter as to which the *bet din* gives their lives will in the end be upheld as if it was said to Moses at Sinai. And this is like what R. Mana said (Deuteronomy 32:47): '*For this is not a trifling thing for you: it is your very life.* And if it is *a trifling thing for you*, why is that? Because you do not wear yourselves out over it. When is it *your very life*? At a time when you do wear yourselves out over it.'"

As was pointed out at the beginning of this chapter, the *Yerushalmi* represents that the Ushan sages legislated a 20 percent maximum on charitable giving. But there is a chronological difficulty: Rabban Gamliel of Yavneh is said to have rebuked R. Yeshebab for giving all his possessions away to charity and violating the 20 percent maximum. How could the Ushan sages have enacted a law that Rabban Gamliel had already enforced years earlier? The late Palestinian *amora* R. Yose b. R. Bun resolves the chronological puzzlement: the 20 percent maximum was indeed the law at the time of Rabban Gamliel, but it was subsequently forgotten. "The two" (a minimum plural, presumably a shorthand reference to the Ushan sages) later enacted into law the very 20 percent charity maximum originally in force in Rabban Gamliel's day. R. Yose b. R. Bun adds: "This is to teach you that every matter as to which the *bet din* gives their lives will in the end be upheld as if it was said to Moses at Sinai."[42] Either R. Yose b. R. Bun or the anonymous *Yerushalmi* goes on to point out that this is consistent with R. Mana's interpretation of Deuteronomy 32:47: the Torah is a "trifling thing for you" when its adherents do not wear themselves out over it, but it is "your life" when they do. The Ushan court's extreme diligence ("giving their lives" for Torah) was rewarded with their recovery of the old law concerning the 20 percent charitable maximum, and this extreme diligence also results in this law's establishment "just like what was said to Moses at Sinai."

Christine Hayes rightly points out that the *Yerushalmi*'s claim is not that laws like this Ushan enactment are *actually* "laws given to Moses at Sinai," but that the expression is used metaphorically, to illustrate the preciousness of a law that was temporarily (and only temporarily) forgotten.[43] The *Yerushalmi*'s metaphor is key to its perspective on the role of divine oversight in the rabbinic legal process. R. Yose b. R. Bun seems to be saying that a *bet din*'s "giving of its life" for a law (through its extreme dedication to Torah) will ensure the law's being established with the same certainty and stability of a law Moses received directly from God. *Yerushalmi Peah* goes on to adduce the examples of the biblical characters Bezalel (the architect of the wilderness tabernacle) and Joshua, both of whom were said to have independently intuited the instructions God gave to Moses at Sinai about their tasks. By juxtaposing these biblical examples to that of the Ushan court, the *Yerushalmi* is making a strong point: a *bet din*'s (i.e., the Ushan court) willingness to "give its life" for a certain law (the 20 percent charitable maximum) will not only result in that law's being established with the certainty of a law given to Moses by God; the Ushan court's restoration of that law makes them like Bezalel and Joshua, who independently and accurately intuited exactly what God had revealed to Moses about them. Thus the same divine providence that made for legal certainty in the long-ago cases of Moses, Bezalel, and Joshua also operates to maintain the accuracy, certainty, and stability of law in the present, specifically, in the case of the Ushan court and the 20 percent charitable maximum. The *Yerushalmi* concludes as follows:

7 R. Yohanan in the name of Benaiah; Rav Huna in the name of Rabbi (Malachi 2:6): "*Proper rulings were in his mouth*—this refers to things

he heard from his teacher; *and nothing perverse was on his lips*—[this refers] even to things that he did *not* hear from his teacher."

8   And the Rabbis say (Proverbs 3:26): "*For the Lord will be your trust* [of the root *k-s-l*]; *He will keep your feet from being caught*—even things as to which you are a fool (*kesil*), *he will keep your feet from being caught.*"

9   R. Dosa said: "[God will protect you from making errors] in legal rulings."

10   And the Rabbis say: "[God will protect you] from sin."

11   R. Levi said: "[God will protect you] from demons."

R. Yohanan's interpretation of Malachi 2:6 is that if "proper rulings were in his mouth" as to things one heard from one's teacher, then "nothing perverse" will be on his lips as to other matters. Accurate preservation of one's teacher's legacy of learning will ensure one's own accurate transmission and teaching. R. Dosa relies on Proverbs 3:26 to make an even sharper point: God protects those who trust in him from making errors in legal rulings. In other words, to the extent rabbis trust in him, God responds by exercising oversight of the rabbinic legal process. Taken all together, the *Yerushalmi*'s juxtaposition of the Ushan court's recovery of the 20 percent charitable maximum, the notion that a *bet din*'s diligence in Torah will be rewarded with legal certainty akin to certainty of revelation, and the notion that trust in God will trigger divine prevention of human legal errors, shows its view that one way or the other, God has continuing providential oversight over the rabbinic legal enterprise. Now let us turn to the *Bavli*'s re-presentation of the origins of the 20 percent charitable maximum.[44]

1   R. Il'a said: "In Usha they instituted that the one who scatters [his wealth] should not scatter more than one-fifth."

2   It was also taught thus [in a *baraita*]: "The one who scatters [his wealth] should not scatter more than one-fifth, lest he the need the help of other created beings."[45]

3   And it once happened that one sought to spend [more than one-fifth] and his companion did not allow him.[46] And who was it? R. Yeshebab. And some say:[47] It was R. Yeshebab [who wished to spend more than one-fifth] and his companion did not allow him. And who was that? R. Aqiva.

The *Bavli* parallel is much terser than the *Yerushalmi* passage; significantly it eliminates the earlier Talmud's emphasis on the forgetting and restoration of law. The *Bavli* does not understand the law concerning the 20 percent charitable maximum to have been forgotten and serendipitously recovered (with tacit divine oversight); rather, R. Il'a teaches that the 20 percent maximum was a straightforward act of Ushan legislation. The recollection that someone— whether it was R. Yeshebab as in *Yerushalmi Peah* or someone else—tried unsuccessfully to give away more than one-fifth of his possessions is placed in the text *after* the description of the Ushan legislation; the passage as composed implies that this unsuccessful attempt occurred after the Ushan court enacted the charitable maximum. The *Bavli*'s elimination of the *Yerushalmi*'s lengthy treatment of the forgetting and recovery of the law is thematically and culturally significant: the *Bavli* thereby also eliminates the *Yerushalmi*'s understanding that the serendipitous restoration of forgotten law is a mark of divine oversight of the rabbinic legal process. The *Bavli* sees the rabbinic legal process as entirely a human enterprise.[48]

In sum, the following are all aspects of the same religious and cultural tendency: the *Bavli*'s limitations on the divine and emphasis on the human dimensions of charity, its limitations on the manifestations of divine providence as discerned by Yaakov Elman, and its diminution or outright elimination of the divine role and concomitant elevation of the human role in the revelation and study of Torah, the making of new rabbinic law, and the forgetting and recovery of laws. The *Bavli* deemphasizes divine initiative; it delimits the divine and broadens the range and importance of human effort and initiative.

Notes

1   I stress "to the poor" because some Palestinian amoraic narratives about giving to rabbis (particularly in *Leviticus Rabbah*) seem somewhat heedless of limits. See Chapter 3.
2   Y. *Peah* 1:1, 15b (ed. Academy, 78). There is a partial parallel on Y. *Ketubot* 4:6, 28d (ed. Academy, 977).
3   *Sifre Deuteronomy* 116 (ed. Finkelstein, 175). See the parallel on T. *Peah* 4:10 (ed. Lieberman, 58) and the pertinent discussion in my "The Formerly-Wealthy Poor." M. *Peah* 8:7 (and its parallel in T. *Peah* 4:8 [ed. Lieberman, 57]) does impose quantification, prescribing the *minimal* amount the *community* is to provide to a *traveling* poor person. There is no tannaitic maximum on *individual* charity.
4   T. *Peah* 4:18 (ed. Lieberman, 60).
5   B. *Arachin* 6a; see also Rav Yosef's countermanding of a man's attempt to revoke his verbal grant to the poor of a money verdict due him on B. *Baba Qama* 36b. The man's verbal grant is not described with a verb having a votive connotation.
6   B. *Baba Batra* 10a.
7   B. *Sanhedrin* 102b; B. *Rosh Hashanah* 18a. See also the pertinent discussion at the beginning of Chapter 4.
8   B. *Baba Batra* 10a.
9   See the relevant discussions in Chapter 4.
10 B. *Baba Batra* 9b; B. *Baba Qama* 16b.
11 See, e.g., B. *Baba Batra* 8a, 8b, 9a, 10a; B. *Megillah* 27a–27b and the discussion of compulsion in Chapter 4.
12 B. *Ketubot* 50a. The parallel on B. *Arachin* 28a interestingly omits "lest he have need of other created beings (= people)."
13 B. *Rosh Hashanah* 6a.
14 B. *Baba Batra* 8b.
15 B. *Ketubot* 67b.
16 B. *Baba Qama* 92a–92b.
17 Yaakov Elman, "Righteousness as its Own Reward": 54. Elman sees Rava as a linchpin in the evolution of Babylonian rabbinic ideas about Divine Providence: Rava builds on earlier teachings of Rav Yosef and Rabbah and, in turn, the *Bavli* narrator

builds on Rava. Elman of course refers to the *Bavli* "*stam*," not the "*Bavli* narrator." He defines "*stam*" as "the final redactional layer of each *sugya*, whatever its date; this layer will often reflect earlier stages in the *sugya*'s history." Elman, ibid., 38–39. Elman is careful to posit that the "*stam*" reflects the final layer of each *sugya*, and not necessarily that it reflects a late (i.e., post-amoraic) stage in the development of either a particular tractate or the *Bavli* overall.

18 B. *Qiddushin* 39b–40a.

19 Yaakov Elman, "Righteousness as its Own Reward": 53; see B. *Pesachim* 64b.

20 Yaakov Elman, "Righteousness as its Own Reward": 53.

21 Ibid.: 54.

22 Ibid.: 54–56, 58. Rava also appears to allow for reward in this world on B. *Horayot* 10b.

23 Yaakov Elman, "Righteousness as its Own Reward": 62; see B. *Moed Qatan* 28a.

24 This demonstration is part of Elman's analysis of B. *Qiddushin* 39b–40a.

25 See B. *Baba Batra* 10a and the discussion of this dialogue in Chapter 4.

26 The goal of this section is not to examine this topic in depth—a project that deserves its own book—but to illustrate the *Bavli*'s thematic consistency. The principal scholars and works that have explored the Bavli's emphasis on the human role in the study of Torah, with all that this implies—its emphasis on debate, multiple interpretations, and the use of human reason to develop the law—include David Kraemer, *The Mind of the Talmud: An Intellectual History of the Bavli* (New York and Oxford: Oxford University Press, 1990); Menachem Fisch, *Rational Rabbis: Science and Talmudic Culture* (Bloomington, Indiana University Press, 1997); Daniel Boyarin, *Borderlines: The Partition of Judaeo-Christianity* (Philadelphia: University of Pennsylvania Press, 2004), especially 151–201; Steven D. Fraade, "Rabbinic Polysemy and Pluralism Revisited"; Azzan Yadin-Israel, "Rabbinic Polysemy: A Response to Steven Fraade," *Association for Jewish Studies Review* 38:1 (2014): 129–141; Richard Hidary, *Dispute for the Sake of Heaven: Legal Pluralism in the Talmud* (Providence: Brown Judaic Studies, 2010); and Christine Hayes, "Theoretical Pluralism in the Talmud: A Response to Richard Hidary," *Dine Israel* 26–27 (2009–2010): 257–307. For a recent take on this issue through literary, philosophical, and psychoanalytic lenses, see William Kolbrener, *The Last Rabbi: Joseph Soloveitchik and Talmudic Tradition* (Bloomington and Indianapolis: Indiana University Press, 2016), 36–63 and *passim*.

27 The translation is my own, although I also consulted H. Freedman, *The Babylonian Talmud: Shabbath; Translated into English with Notes, Glossary and Indices* (London: The Soncino Press, 1938).

28 The printed edition reads "Rav Avdimi bar Hama bar Hasa," which is an error, likely a dittography due to the similarity in the manuscripts between the letters "*mem*" and "*samekh*." The additional "bar Hasa" is found in Ms. Oxford Opp. Add. Fol. 23 and in the early modern Soncino Print. It is missing from Mss. Munich 95 and Paris Heb. 310/136–139.

29 I have left the phrase untranslated in the interest of the unfolding analysis.

30 The translation of this verse is my own.

31 See B. *Baba Batra* 40a–40b; B. *Yebamot* 52a; B. *Ketubot* 19b, 109b; B. *Arachin* 21b; B. *Qiddushin* 12b.

32 See n. 23 in Chapter 4 and the related discussion.

33 B. *Baba Metzia* 59b. The bibliography on this story is vast. For a sampling of the scholarship, see, e.g., Jeffrey L. Rubenstein, *Talmudic Stories: Narrative Art, Composition, and Culture* (Baltimore: Johns Hopkins University Press, 1999), 34–63; Daniel Boyarin, *Borderlines*, 170, 173–174, 181–182; Holger M. Zellentin, *Rabbinic Parodies of Jewish and Christian Literature* (Tübingen: Mohr Siebeck, 2011), 216–220. Rubenstein himself provides a bibliography on the story current up through 1999; see ibid., *Talmudic Stories*, 314 n. 1. Steven Fraade labels this story and a few others generally discussed together with it as "poster children of the Babylonian Talmud," see ibid., "Rabbinic Polysemy and Pluralism Revisited": 37–38.

34 B. *Gittin* 6b; on this text see Daniel Boyarin, *Borderlines*, 174–176.

35 Daniel Boyarin, *Borderlines*, 176. "These and these are the words of the living God" is also found on B. *Erubin* 13b. As with the "Oven of Akhnai," the scholarship on this apothegm is vast. For a philosophical and jurisprudential analysis of the principle in Talmudic and post-Talmudic literature, see, e.g., Avi Sagi, *The Open Canon: On the Meaning of Halakhic Discourse* (trans. Batya Stein; London: Continuum, 2007).

36 B. *Makkot* 23a.

37 Y. *Megillah* 1:4, 70d (ed. Academy, 745); B. *Megillah* 7a.

38 *Rashi* (s.v. *shelishim*) explains that "threefold" refers to mandatory mentions of Israel's eternal enmity against Amalek: in the Pentateuchal books of Exodus and Deuteronomy and in I Samuel.

39 B. *Temurah* 16a. The translation of this narrative is my own. On this narrative see William Kolbrener, *The Last Rabbi*, 22–35; ibid., "Death of Moses Revisited: Repetition and Creative Memory in Freud and the Rabbis," *American Imago* 67:2 (2010): 245–264.

40 On the topic of the forgetting and restoration of law in rabbinic literature see Christine Hayes, "*Halakhah le-Moshe mi-Sinai* in Rabbinic Sources: A Methodological Case Study," in Shaye J.D. Cohen, editor, *The Synoptic Problem in Rabbinic Literature* (Providence: Brown Judaic Studies, 2000), 61–117, especially 102–108. Hayes's short discussion of this topic in the context of her larger study of "*halakhah le-Moshe mi-Sinai*" is rich; this acknowledged, there are many more examples of the phenomenon in rabbinic compilations and further inquiry is warranted in another venue. I plan to return to this issue.

41 Y. *Peah* 1:1, 15a (ed. Academy, 78).

42 For an argument that the *Yerushalmi*'s "gives their lives" is meant metaphorically rather than literally (as martyrdom), see my "A Contribution to the Study of Martyrdom and Identity in the Palestinian Talmud," *Journal of Jewish Studies* 54:2 (Autumn 2003): 261–262.

43 See Christine Hayes, "*Halakhah le-Moshe mi-Sinai*," 103.

44 B. *Ketubot* 50a. See the partial parallels on B. *Ketubot* 67b; B. *Arachin* 28a.

45 This latter clause "lest he need the help…" is missing from Ms. Vatican, Bibliotheca Apostolica, Ebr. 113.

46 Ms. Vatican, Bibliotheca Apostolica, Ebr. 487.11 adds "his companion did not allow him, because he was poor." The phrase I have idiomatically rendered as "because he was poor" is "because the hour was needy for him (*mipnei she-ha-sha'ah tzerikhah lo*)." This addition confirms the *baraita*'s point in paragraph 2: the point of not exceeding the 20 percent charitable maximum is in order that one not become needy oneself. Ms. Vatican also confirms a point made in Chapter 4: the *Bavli* tends to avoid describing sages literally as "poor" (using some version of the root *a-n-'*).

47 Ms. Vatican, Bibliotheca, Apostolica Ebr. 130 reads "*ikka d'amrei*" ("there are those who say") instead of "*v'amrei lah*" ("there are those who express it").

48 Ariel Picard makes a similar observation about the *Yerushalmi* and *Bavli* in *Seeing the Voices: Tradition, Creativity and the Freedom of Interpretation in Judaism* (Tel-Aviv: Yedioth Ahronoth Books and Chemed Books, 2016), 60–62 (in Hebrew).

Bibliography

Primary sources, critical editions, manuscript databases, and dictionaries

Babylonian Talmud. 1975 (repr.). Vilna-Romm edition with standard commentaries. Jerusalem: n.p.

Finkelstein, Louis. 1969. *Sifre on Deuteronomy*. New York: The Jewish Theological Seminary of America

Freedman, H. 1938. *The Babylonian Talmud: Shabbath; Translated into English with Notes, Glossary and Indices.* London: The Soncino Press

Lieberman, Saul. 1955. *The Tosefta: According to Codex Vienna, with Variants from Codex Erfurt, Genizah Mss. And Editio Princeps (Venice 1521). The Order of Zera'im.* New York: The Jewish Theological Seminary of America

Margulies, Mordecai. 1993. *Midrash Wayyikra Rabbah: A Critical Edition Based on Manuscripts and Genizah Fragments with Variants and Notes.* New York and Jerusalem: The Jewish Theological Seminary of America

Saul and Evelyn Henkind Talmud Text Databank. Saul Lieberman Institute of Talmudic Research. The Jewish Theological Seminary of America

Talmud Yerushalmi: According to Ms. Or. 4720 (Scal. 3) of the Leiden University Library with Restorations and Corrections. 2005. Introduction by Yaacov Sussman. Jerusalem: The Academy of the Hebrew Language

Tanakh: *A New Translation of the Holy Scriptures According to the Traditional Hebrew Text.* 1985. Philadelphia, New York, Jerusalem. The Jewish Publication Society

Scholarly studies

Boyarin, Daniel. 2004. *Borderlines: The Partition of Judaeo-Christianity.* Philadelphia: University of Pennsylvania Press

Elman, Yaakov. 1990/1991. "Righteousness as its Own Reward: An Inquiry into the Theologies of the Stam." *Proceedings of the American Academy for Jewish Research* 57:35–67

Fisch, Menachem. 1997. *Rational Rabbis: Science and Talmudic Culture.* Bloomington, Indiana University Press

Fraade, Steven D. 2007. "Rabbinic Polysemy and Pluralism Revisited: Between Praxis and Thematization." *Association for Jewish Studies Review* 31:1–40

Gray, Alyssa M. 2003. "A Contribution to the Study of Martyrdom and Identity in the Palestinian Talmud." *Journal of Jewish Studies* 54:242–272

Gray, Alyssa M. 2009. "The Formerly-Wealthy Poor: From Empathy to Ambivalence in Rabbinic Literature of Late Antiquity." *Association for Jewish Studies Review* 33:101–133

Hayes, Christine. 2000. "*Halakhah le-Moshe mi-Sinai* in Rabbinic Sources: A Methodological Case Study." In: Shaye J.D. Cohen, ed. *The Synoptic Problem in Rabbinic Literature.* Providence: Brown Judaic Studies, pp. 61–117

Hayes, Christine. 2009–2010. "Theoretical Pluralism in the Talmud: A Response to Richard Hidary." *Dine Israel* 26–27:257–307

Hidary, Richard. 2010. *Dispute for the Sake of Heaven: Legal Pluralism in the Talmud.* Providence: Brown Judaic Studies

Kolbrener, William. 2010. "Death of Moses Revisited: Repetition and Creative Memory in Freud and the Rabbis." *American Imago* 67:245–264

Kolbrener, William. 2016. *The Last Rabbi: Joseph Soloveitchik and Talmudic Tradition.* Bloomington and Indianapolis: Indiana University Press

Kraemer, David. 1990. *The Mind of the Talmud: An Intellectual History of the Bavli.* New York and Oxford: Oxford University Press

Picard, Ariel. 2016. *Seeing the Voices: Tradition, Creativity and the Freedom of Interpretation in Judaism.* Tel-Aviv: Yedioth Ahronoth Books and Chemed Books (in Hebrew)

Rubenstein, Jeffrey L. 1999. *Talmudic Stories: Narrative Art, Composition, and Culture.* Baltimore: Johns Hopkins University Press

Sagi, Avi. 2007. *The Open Canon: On the Meaning of Halakhic Discourse.* Translated by
   Batya Stein. London: Continuum

Yadin-Israel, Azzan. 2014. "Rabbinic Polysemy: A Response to Steven Fraade." *Association for Jewish Studies Review* 38:129–141

Zellentin, Holger M. 2011. *Rabbinic Parodies of Jewish and Christian Literature.*
   Tübingen: Mohr Siebeck

7 Select post-Talmudic developments

The first word of this chapter's title is deliberately chosen. A full exploration of all the post-Talmudic developments of the ideas we have examined in Chapters 1–6 cannot fit between the covers of this book. Most of the post-Talmudic developments selected for this survey fall into two broad categories: (1) illustrations of the perdurance of the perception that charity is a gift to God, redemptive almsgiving, and the poor's role as the channel through which donors receive charity's redemptive benefits; and (2) post-Talmudic developments that either entirely lack late antique precedent, or which exemplify novel applications of late antique ideas. Category (1)'s examples illustrate a post-*Bavli* Jewish cultural tendency to adopt robust literary and even behavioral manifestations of ideas about which the *Bavli* and at times even Palestinian amoraic literature was ambivalent or ambiguous. This chapter will also devote a section to Maimonides (1138–1204). It will be argued that Maimonides is a uniquely perceptive and holistic reader and codifier of the *Bavli*'s ambivalence about charity as a gift to God, redemptive almsgiving, and related ideas. He understands charity as essentially a this-worldly set of practices with the this-worldly goal of improving the poor's lot in life; in this sense he can be seen as a medieval forerunner of those who see "*tzedaqah*" not (only) as charity, but also as a signifier of a just social order.

Robust post-Talmudic assertions of charity as a gift to God, redemptive almsgiving, and a mediating role for the poor

God as the true recipient of tzedaqah

Midrash Zuta to Song of Songs 1:15[1] attributes to God the notion that "when you support the poor, it is, as it were, as if you are supporting me," and "even though you are giving to people, I consider you like children supporting their father."[2] Later Jewish religious writers in Spain perpetuate this idea in other ways. Commenting on Deuteronomy 26:1–2, the exegete Bahya ben Asher (*c.*1255–1340) observes "the one who gives *tzedaqah* to a poor person is giving it to the Holy One, blessed is He." Isaac Aboab points out the equivalence of charity and the Temple cult in his fourteenth-century work of religious edification *Menorat Ha-Ma'or*:

Just as in the time when the Temple was standing the Holy One, blessed is He would accept a flour offering as [He would accept] cattle, so in this day, in which the Temple has been destroyed on account of our sins, He accepts the offering of a small coin for one who cannot afford [more], as [He accepts] the one hundred *manehs* of the rich … and by means of a small gift, one may merit receiving the divine presence …[3]

The idea that God is the true recipient of charity also had practical legal consequences in Christian Spain and Ashkenaz. One of these is the thirteenth–fourteenth century identification in Spain of charitable foundations as "*heqdesh*," or "Temple treasury" trusts.[4] The ideational overlap between the Temple and charitable giving took a different form in Ashkenaz: the practice of "*matnat yad*" (the "hand's giving"), evidence of which first appears in Mainz and Worms at the end of the eleventh or beginning of the twelfth century.[5] *Matnat yad* was the pledging of *tzedaqah* after the Torah lection on *Shmini Atzeret* (the "eighth day of assembly") at the end of the *Sukkot* festival week, as well as on the last day of Passover and the second day of the *Shavuot* festival. "*Matnat yad*" derives from Deuteronomy 16:16–17:

> Three times a year—on the Feast of Unleavened
> Bread, on the Feast of Weeks, and on the Feast of Booths—
> all your males shall appear before the Lord your God in the
> place that He will choose. They shall not appear before the
> Lord empty-handed, but each with his own gift (Heb.: matnat yad), accord-
> ing to the blessing that the Lord your God has bestowed upon you.

Deuteronomy refers here to Israelite males' required pilgrimages to the central sanctuary on the "pilgrimage" festivals, and their obligation not to "*appear before the Lord empty-handed*." The Tosafist Eliezer of Metz (*c.*1115–1198) understands "*not appear … empty-handed*" to mean not "empty-handed of *tzedaqah*." This *tzedaqah* has no "fixed measure," just like its sacrificial analogue, the "pilgrimage offerings" (M. *Peah* 1:1).[6] As Judah Galinsky observes, "we may assume that for the learned in the community, the charitable giving was in place of the offering of the festival sacrifice on the [pilgrimage] festivals." In other words, festival *tzedaqah* was not simply a money gift for the benefit of the poor or other communal needs, but also a *sacrificial* offering, reminiscent of those offered in the Temple of old.[7]

God as the donor's "debtor"

A version of *Midrash Proverbs* 19 reaches back over the *Bavli* to resurrect *Leviticus Rabbah* 34:2's radical metaphor of God as the debtor of a donor to the poor (God's "creditor").[8] Quoting Proverbs 19:17 (*He who is generous to the poor makes a loan to the Lord; He will repay him his due*), *Midrash Proverbs* declares: "God considers as *tzedaqah* done with him the *tzedaqah* they, with integrity, do with the poor."[9] Writing in fourteenth-century Spain, Israel ibn al-Nakawa likewise adopts *Leviticus Rabbah*'s radical metaphor, bringing Proverbs 22:7 (*And the borrower is a slave to the lender*) together with Proverbs 19:17 to make the point that God is the debtor of one who succors the poor.[10] The early modern scholar Judah Loewe of Prague (1520–1609) reiterates this point several times. In Chapter 4 of *Netiv Gemilut Hasadim* he notes explicitly that a loan made to the poor "is considered ... to be to God," upon whom it is incumbent to make the person whole."[11] Loewe twice observes in Chapter 4 of *Netiv Ha-tzedaqah*: "one *who is generous to the poor* is God's creditor," even ending the chapter on the note that "what he gives to the poor is considered to be his soul's atonement, for it is considered as if he gave to God."[12]

Redemptive almsgiving

Midrash Tanchuma (*Ki Tissa*) 16 revives the notion that *tzedaqah* earns its givers real treasures in heaven, which flies in the face of the *Bavli*'s neutralization of this notion.[13] The relevant passage is part of an exposition of Moses's vision of God in Exodus 33:18–19 (*He said, "Oh, let me behold your Presence!" ... "I will proclaim before you the name Lord ... "*):

> At that moment the Holy One, blessed is He showed [Moses]
> all the treasuries of rewards established for the righteous. He
> said before Him: "Master of the world! Whose treasury is this?" He
> said to him: "[The treasury] of the doers of *tzedaqah*." "This one is
> whose?" "[The treasury] of those who support orphans." And similarly with
> each and every treasury ...

In Spain, Israel ibn al-Nakawa and Isaac Aboab both re-present the *Bavli*'s fictitious dialogue between Tineius Rufus and R. Aqiva (B. *Baba Batra* 10a) with nary a hint of the *Bavli*'s ambivalence. Addressing R. Aqiva's metaphor of the poor person as the "king's son," ibn al-Nakawa writes:

> What does the poor person resemble? [His situation resembles that
> of] a king who was angry with his son and commanded that he not
> enter his feast. And the king knows that his son is hungry and thirsty
> and he is filled with mercy toward him. And he says to his friend: "Happy is
> he who brings my son into his house and gives him food and drink. I will
> repay him twice, for all I have is of my son's. And not only that, but I will
> consider it as a *tzedaqah* for him." R. Asi said: "Were the scriptural verse
> not written, it would be impossible to say: as it were, *And the borrower is a
> slave to the lender* (Proverbs 22:7)."[14]

Ibn al-Nakawa entirely alters the meaning of B. *Baba Batra* 10a through his selective adaptation and addition to it of the theologically provocative Proverbs 22:7. He sees R. Aqiva's father–son metaphor as key to the passage's message overall, and stresses *tzedaqah*'s redemptive qualities: the king is debtor to the generous friend and the friend's provision of food and drink to the son is considered a *tzedaqah* ("merit") for him. Isaac Aboab later reproduces the entire Tineius Rufus/R. Aqiva dialogue as it appears in the *Bavli*, introducing it as a straightforward illustration of redemptive almsgiving: "Anyone with an intellect would give all he has to save his body from human punishment. And the *tzedaqah* that a person gives to the poor saves him from the judgment of *Gehinnom*."[15] Apropos, Eitan P. Fishbane has very recently noted redemptive almsgiving's presence in the Zohar (thirteenth century), pointing out that a particular homily "continues to emphasize ... that the performance of charity serves to protect the giver from the severity of divine judgment—a clear reflection of ... classical rabbinic thought."[16] Fishbane rightly and tellingly cites the *Yerushalmi*—not the *Bavli*—to support this point.

Ibn al-Nakawa also gives us a glimpse of a real-world practice based on redemptive almsgiving. He writes that he heard that:

> The great ones of northern France and the communal leaders, masters of hospitality ... practice a very honorable custom that has spread among them from the earliest days. They would fashion the table at which they would feed the poor into ... a coffin to be buried in. And all this was to awaken and fix in their hearts that if a person attains the height of wealth, he shouldn't carry with him a tiny bit of his effort ... except for the good he did and the *tzedaqah* with which he would show mercy to the poor. As it is written: "*Your Vindicator (tzidqecha) shall march before you*" (Isaiah 58:8).[17]

The quotation of Isaiah 58:8, capstone to the King Monbaz narrative in *Tosefta Peah* and the *Bavli*, marks this northern French practice as a performance of redemptive almsgiving.

Judah Loewe of Prague later unequivocally affirms redemptive almsgiving in his *Netiv Ha-tzedaqah*: "*tzedaqah* atones; a person's money is his atonement because the money is considered to be like his own body."[18] Nor is Loewe the last to affirm atoning *tzedaqah*; the modern scholar Sholom Noach Berezovsky (1911–2000) affirms the religious merit of giving *tzedaqah* even without regard to the legal limit (20 percent) on such giving; the giver's doing so "in order to cleanse his soul from sins" is superior to his restricting himself to the legal limit absent that intention. Berezovsky even quotes Daniel 4:24.[19]

Warm portrayals of the poor who receive tzedaqah

Apropos, positive images of the poor, and portrayals of the poor praying on behalf of their donors, recur in medieval compilations. Paragraphs 356 and 357 of *Sefer Hasidim* direct that recipients of charity given on behalf of the dead should be informed of the identities of the deceased so that they can pray for them. Within the first year of the honoree's death, charity recipients are to recite a set prayer text that asks that "his sin be atoned" and that "his soul rest in goodness" as a reward for the charity given to the living on his behalf.[20]

Israel ibn al-Nakawa devotes a good deal of space to the image of the poor in his *Menorat Ha-Ma'or*, in which he revives a warm, positive, image of the poor rooted in and reminiscent of Palestinian amoraic literature. God is "with" and "sticks" to the poor person,[21] and poverty is declared to be the fate than which there is none harsher.[22] Ibn al-Nakawa points out "one who does *tzedaqah* with the poor should not imagine that he benefits the poor person; rather, the poor person benefits him," a notion he recognizes is found in *Leviticus Rabbah* 34:8.[23] But ibn al-Nakawa neither deprives the poor of religious agency nor sees them as presumptively above reproach. Ibn al-Nakawa writes of a "test" that the poor "pass" by not rebelling against God: should they "pass," their reward will be double what they would otherwise have received.[24] Inevitably, of course, some will "fail."

Judah Loewe of Prague also later harkens back to *Leviticus Rabbah*, expressing the poor's supernatural role in even stronger terms: "the poor is the one who causes God to make [benefits] flow and give [them to the donor]." This "charity" the poor "gives" to the donor is said to be even greater than what the generous householder does for the poor.[25]

New post-Talmudic developments

Tzedaqah *on behalf of the dead*

Giving *tzedaqah* on behalf of the dead emerges as a novel feature of medieval Jewish piety, related to redemptive almsgiving, but with only the barest link to any of the late antique compilations.[26] There are, however, late antique traces of the idea that the living may take actions that affect the dead's postmortem existence.[27] Israel Lévi provides examples of the living's offering prayers on behalf of, or reciting rabbinic traditions in the name of, the deceased.[28] One of these is found in the *Yerushalmi*; two others are sources the *Bavli* identifies as Palestinian. Given the Palestinian provenance (or at least attribution) of Lévi's examples, the absence from Palestinian rabbinic sources of charity on behalf of the dead is especially curious. Palestinian rabbis lived in chronological and geographical proximity to Eastern Christians who preached and practiced it: the *Apostolic Constitutions* (close in time and place to the redaction of the *Yerushalmi*) lists the fixed days after a person's death on which charity and prayers are to be offered to obtain forgiveness for his sins, and John Chrysostom similarly preached in Antioch (fourth century CE) that God would hear the prayers of charity recipients on behalf of the deceased in whose name they received it.[29] Yet the rabbis represent neither themselves nor other Jews as preaching or practicing likewise.

The plot thickens when we examine *Sifre Deuteronomy* 210 and what may be a bit of its *Bavli* afterlife. This passage and its *Bavli* intertext bring us closer to the idea that the dead require the sacrificial atonement of the living, but does not clearly support that proposition; moreover, *tzedaqah* as the means of atoning for the dead goes entirely unmentioned. Interpreting Deuteronomy 21:8 (*Absolve, O Lord, Your people Israel whom You redeemed ...*), the *Sifre* states:

When it says: "*whom You redeemed*" this teaches that this atonement atones for those who left Egypt. *Absolve ... Your people*—these are the living. *Whom You redeemed*—these are the dead. This shows that the dead require atonement.[30]

I have bolded the language that Louis Finkelstein considered to be an authentic (i.e., tannaitic) part of *Sifre Deuteronomy*.[31] Looking at the entire passage—bolded and unbolded language alike—its representation that the dead require atonement through the agency of the living is consistent with the late antique examples collected by Israel Lévi. If we read only the bolded, "authentic" tannaitic *Sifre Deuteronomy*, we see that it refers only to atonement for the dead (and the living) *who had left Egypt*. The unbolded language arguably can refer additionally to any and all deceased persons of whatever time. And, whether we read the passage in its entirety or only its "authentic" portion, *tzedaqah* is not mentioned as a means of atonement.

B. *Horayot* 6a quotes a truncated version of this *midrash* (attributed to the Babylonian *amora* Rav Papa) as part of its extensive discussion of whether sacrificial atonement may be offered for the dead. B. *Horayot* 6a's overall source-critical complexity is work for another venue, but we may make a few pertinent observations. The *Bavli* quickly settles there on precisely the same understanding of Deuteronomy 21:8 presented by *Sifre Deuteronomy*'s bolded, "authentic" language: it refers to the Israelites that left Egypt—both those still alive at the time of Moses's preaching of Deuteronomy and those who had already died. *Tzedaqah* also goes unmentioned on B. *Horayot* 6a, although the ideational imbrication of *tzedaqah* and sacrifice suggests that should there be sacrificial atonement for the dead, they might also be atoned for through *tzedaqah*. Ephraim E. Urbach and Zvi Aryeh Steinfeld—B. *Horayot* 6a's two contemporary closest readers—agree (albeit on different grounds) that the passage in its entirety does *not* support the idea that there is sacrificial atonement for the dead.[32] If they are correct, then there is absolutely no basis on which to see the passage as even hinting that *tzedaqah* atones for the dead.

Our very brief survey of *Sifre Deuteronomy* 210 and B. *Horayot* 6a does not *prove* that giving charity to atone for the dead was unknown to the redactors of either compilation. All that can be said with certainty is that such a practice leaves no unimpeachable literary trace in those or other late antique rabbinic compilations. Following this thread a bit further, we might identify the literary emergence of this idea in the standard printed edition of the eighth- or ninth century *Midrash Tanchuma* (*Ha'azinu*) 1, which reads:

"*Absolve Your people Israel*"—these are living;
"*whom You redeemed*"—these are dead. From here
[we learn] that the living redeem the dead. Consequently
we are accustomed to mention the dead on *Yom HaKippurim*
and [to] stipulate *tzedaqah* for them, for as we learn in
Torat Kohanim:[33] "is it possible that *tzedaqah* will not benefit

them when they are dead? Scripture states: '*whom You redeemed.*' From here [we learn] that when we stipulate
tzedaqah for them we remove them [from *Gehinnom*] and bring them out [from there] like an arrow from a bow ..."[34]

Ephraim E. Urbach also points to a likely medieval interpolation into the *Sifre Deuteronomy* according to which "*whom You redeemed*" is said explicitly to refer "to those who are atoned for *by the alms of the living*" (emphasis added).[35] In sum, then, whether or not the late antique rabbis were aware of the idea that the living may give *tzedaqah* to atone for the dead, the literary manifestations of that notion likely post-date the *Bavli.*

We are on more solid ground in observing that pre-thirteenth century Ashkenazic Jews recited prayers and gave charity on behalf of and for the sake of the dead.[36] Elisheva Baumgarten has carefully and extensively analyzed this "practice of piety" as part of her study of the Nürnberg Memorbuch, a liturgy for honoring the dead along with many lists of deceased members of the community and the donations pledged by them for their souls' sakes.[37] Yitzhak (Eric) Zimmer and Judah Galinsky both point to a blurring of the liturgical line between *matnat yad* and *hazkarat neshamot* (the "recollection of souls [of the dead]") in some Ashkenazic communities.[38] Galinsky distinguishes heuristically between three forms of *tzedaqah* on behalf of the dead: (1) a donor's own gifts before death in order to gain atonement for himself (accompanied by weekly prayers of remembrance on the Sabbath in the synagogue after the Torah lection); (2) *matnat yad* and the practice of "stipulating *tzedaqah* for the dead" on *Yom HaKippurim*; and (3) the hybrid practice that developed in Regensburg (eastern Germany) from a blending of *matnat yad* and *hazkarat neshamot*, resulting in the recitation of a *hazkarat neshamot* liturgy on each of the three pilgrimage festivals (not only *Yom HaKippurim*).[39] This hybrid practice is reminiscent of the *yizkor* (memorial) prayer liturgy as it appears in the prayer books of most movements of Judaism to this day.

Revisiting the partially overlapping magisteria: tzedaqah *and* teshuvah

Medieval *midrash* compilations openly acknowledge a tension between *tzedaqah* and *teshuvah* and present different views as to which is superior. We begin with two passages from *Midrash Proverbs*:[40]

1 R. Aqiva's students asked him, "Master, which is greater, *teshuvah* or *tzedaqah*?"[41]
2 He said to them, "*Teshuvah.* Because sometimes one gives *tzedaqah* to an unworthy person, but he [the penitent] does *teshuvah* by himself."
3 They said to him, "Rabbi, haven't we already found *tzedaqah* is greater than *teshuvah*? [The Torah says] about Abraham ... *He reckoned it to his merit* [*tzedaqah*] (Genesis 15:6), and it says in another place, *It will*

be therefore to our merit [*tzedaqah*] (Deuteronomy 6:25). Moreover, David came and explained ... *Your beneficence* [*tzedaqah*] *is like the high mountains* ... (Psalm 36:7)."

R. Aqiva's students bluntly ask: which is greater, *teshuvah* or *tzedaqah*? R. Aqiva implicitly draws in his response on the *Bavli*'s innovative notion that donors are only entitled to divine reward if they give *tzedaqah* to "worthy" recipients. *Tzedaqah*'s religious efficacy for the donor is therefore contingent upon another person and hence inferior to *teshuvah*, which depends solely on the penitent. The students reject R. Aqiva's response. Their extensive quotation of scripture indicates that the major sticking point for them is R. Aqiva's lack of scriptural support for the superiority of *teshuvah* and scripture's clear advocacy of *tzedaqah*. Moreover, the students appear subtly to take a jab at R. Aqiva's (and hence the *Bavli*'s) focus on an "unworthy person"; the *tzedaqah* verses the students quote make no reference to worthiness.

But *Midrash Proverbs* 11 is, in a sense, "R. Aqiva's revenge," taking direct aim at the notion that giving *tzedaqah* alone effectively atones for sin. Interpreting Proverbs 11:21 (*Assuredly, the evil man will not escape*), the homilist teaches "Come and see: a man has two hands; if he steals with one and gives charity with the other [thinking that the latter will atone for the former], he *will not escape*."[42] In the same passage, we read:

> R. Yohanan said: "This is a parable. [This matter may be compared] to one who went and sinned and paid the prostitute her fee. No sooner had he exited the door of her house than he met a poor person, who said, 'Give me *tzedaqah*.' He gave to him and the poor person went on his way. The man then said [to himself], 'Had God not wanted me to atone for my sins, he would not have sent that poor person so that I could give him *tzedaqah* and earn atonement for what I had done.' God says him, 'Evil one! Don't think that way. Rather, go and learn from Solomon's wisdom, who states clearly ... *the evil man will not escape!*'"

Midrash Proverbs 11 squarely confronts the religious problem with atoning *tzedaqah*. Redemptive almsgiving can be seen as an "atonement ATM"— "money in, atonement out." "Money in, atonement out" does not at all de-incentivize sin; one may repeatedly sin and atone through charity in an endless cycle. To return to the language of Chapter 5: "money in, atonement out" lacks *interiority*, the inner work and resolve to reform that is the core of true *teshuvah*.

A passage in a version of *Midrash Psalms* 17 makes the case against *tzedaqah* alone as efficacious atonement, and in favor of interiority:

> David said to [God]: "Master of the world, you have written in your Torah, *Do not take bribes* (Exodus 23:8) ... but it is Your wish to take a bribe ... and from where do we know that the Holy One, blessed is He, takes a bribe? As it is said, *The wicked man draws a bribe out of his bosom* (Proverbs

17:23). And what is the bribe that [God] takes from the evildoers in this world? *Teshuvah, tefillah*, and *tzedaqah*."[43]

Here, the "bribe" God takes from "*the wicked man*" is (not only) *tzedaqah*, but also *teshuvah* and *tefillah*. *Tzedaqah* alone, therefore, is presumptively insufficient to "bribe" God, although it is a component of the "bribe." Toward the end of its treatment of Psalm 17, the homilist asks why David explicated "the merit of *tzedaqah* alone" in verse 15 (*Then I, justified* [*b'tzedeq*] *will behold Your face*). The question implies that stressing the merits of *tzedaqah* in isolation is odd; the oddity may well be that *tzedaqah* without *teshuvah* and/or *tefillah* is somehow deficient.

Midrash Psalms 17's version of the Palestinian amoraic triad (*teshuvah, tefillah, tzedaqah*) is noticeably the same as that found in the stirring liturgical poem *Unetaneh Tokef*, part of the Ashkenazic (northern European) and Italian prayer rites for the Days of Awe.[44] *Midrash Tanchuma* (*Noah*) 8's version (in the Warsaw edition) is also like that of *Midrash Psalms* and *Unetaneh Tokef*, and it demonstrates awareness of elements of B. *Rosh Hashanah* 16b as well:[45]

> And what is the remedy for the evil inclination? *Teshuvah*,
> as R. Yehudah b. R. Shalom said in the name of R. Eliezer: "Three things
> nullify the harsh decree and these are: *teshuvah*, and *tefillah*, and *tzedaqah*."
> R. Yose said: "Even a change of name and good acts." Therefore, the Holy
> One, blessed is He hoped that the Flood generation would do *teshuvah*.
> Once they did not do *teshuvah*.... [He destroyed them and left only Noah
> and his family alive].

Where, when, (and perhaps why) did "*tefillah, tzedaqah, teshuvah*" become "*teshuvah, tefillah, tzedaqah*"? The land of Israel is likely the "where." Scholars concur that *Unetaneh Tokef* is of Palestinian provenance, largely because of its inclusion of the triad *tefillah, tzedaqah, teshuvah* (albeit in the newer order) and apparent ignorance of the *Bavli*'s reworking of the triad into a tetrad. Most recently, John H. Planer has revived Naphtali Wieder's decades-old suggestion that *Unetaneh Tokef* is datable to the third or fourth centuries.[46] The difficulty with Planer's suggestion is that Palestinian amoraic compilations entirely lack any reference to the reformulated atoning triad *teshuvah, tefillah, tzedaqah*. It is difficult to imagine that this reformulation would have left no trace in the *Yerushalmi* or Palestinian *midrash* compilations. This silence suggests that *Unetaneh Tokef* may date from no earlier than the fifth century, contemporaneous with or shortly after the gelling of the Palestinian amoraic collections into distinct compilations. It is also possible that *Unetaneh Tokef*'s Palestinian composer was aware of and chose to neglect the *Bavli*'s reformulated tetrad; this choice may have been a deliberate, if tacit, polemic against the *Bavli*. If so, then *Unetaneh Tokef*'s date might have to be pushed back to the seventh century or even a bit later.

Why the change in order? What does it mean? The German scholar Jacob Moellin (*c*.1365–*c*.1427) was troubled by the change in order, but even more by the suggestion of some of his contemporaries that *Unetaneh Tokef* be emended to restore the older Palestinian amoraic triad. Moellin strenuously defended the by-then traditional *Unetaneh Tokef* text against this proposed (and by some, practiced) change; his defense brings us back to the tension between *teshuvah* and *tzedaqah* as modes of atonement.[47] Moses Mat (sixteenth century) quotes Moellin as arguing that *teshuvah* must precede *tefillah* because if a person is not willing to turn from his evil ways, he has no business "crying out" (in prayer) before God. Also, as one of the "seven things created before the creation of the world," *teshuvah* must take precedence over the others.[48] Moellin finds what he describes as a "hint" of *Unetaneh Tokef*'s order in Deuteronomy 30:14 (*No, the thing is very close to you, in your mouth and in your heart, to observe it*). "*In your mouth*" refers to "*teshuvah*" (verbal confession), "*in your heart*" to "*tefillah*" (prayer being the "service of the heart"),[49] and "*to observe it*" to "*tzedaqah.*" "*To observe it*" is of the same trilateral Hebrew root (*a-s-'*) as Isaiah 32:17's *for the work* (Heb.: *ma'aseh*) *of righteousness shall be peace*; "*righteousness*," of course, is the translation of "*tzedaqah.*"

Whether or not Moellin accurately divines the "original intent" of *Unetaneh Tokef*'s composer is impossible to ascertain. But Moellin clearly believes that as components of a penitential process, *teshuvah* and *tefillah* (must) precede *tzedaqah*. *Tzedaqah* is a *consequence* of a penitent and prayerful heart; *tzedaqah*'s power to effect atonement, and, in *Unetaneh Tokef*'s terms, to "cause the evil decree to pass away," is *contingent* upon *teshuvah* and *tefillah*. At best the three are coequal, but Moellin seems to understand *Unetaneh Tokef* as implying they are not.[50]

But Moellin's late medieval assertion of the superiority of a religious practice characterized by greater interiority over one requiring only a mechanical act is not the last word on the subject. The contemporary scholar Sholom Noach Berezovsky upends the notion that *tzedaqah*'s lack of interiority renders it inferior to religious practices requiring interiority. Berezovsky notes that while the spiritual efficacy of religious acts that require interiority can be undermined by intrusive "alien thoughts," an act of kindness ("*hesed*") is complete even if the doer had "alien thoughts" while engaged in it.[51] Berezovsky's is a psychologically astute acknowledgment that whole-hearted inner spiritual elevation is a very difficult state for most people to achieve most of the time; most people at most times are, however, capable of successfully accomplishing religious acts that only require "doing"—like *hesed* (including *tzedaqah*).

Maimonides: centering the human and marginalizing the divine in *tzedaqah*

The towering jurist and philosopher Maimonides stands out among medieval Jewish writers in his holistic absorption and literary expression of the *Bavli*'s ambivalence about the intersection of charity and the divine. Building this case will not only require that we survey his ideas on charity, atonement, and rewards, but that we also examine elements of his codification of the laws of charity. That

codification arguably demonstrates a this-worldly social vision—one encom-
passing both the present and the Messianic future—that may be seen as an early
forerunner of an ideational transition from *tzedaqah* as "charity" to "*tzedaqah*"
as an ingredient in the making of a "just" society.

Maimonides does not define "*tzedaqah*" in his law code *Mishneh Torah*, notwithstanding the term's ubiquity. The reader of Laws of Gifts to the Poor is
starkly confronted with the absence of a definition as she turns from Chapter 6 to
Chapter 7. Chapters 1 through 6 of those Laws deal with the different categories
of agricultural gifts to the poor, including but not limited to "corners of the field"
(*peah*), gleanings (*leqet*), and forgotten sheaf *(shich'chah)*. Laws of Gifts to the
Poor 7:1 abruptly shifts from agricultural gifts to *tzedaqah* with its opening declaration "it is a positive commandment to give *tzedaqah* to the poor," but
"*tzedaqah*" is left undefined. Writing later in Chapter 53 of section III of his
Guide of the Perplexed, Maimonides explains that "*tzedaqah*" is derived from
"*tzedeq*," which he defines using the Arabic *'adl* and the related *'adāla*. As a
noun *'adl* can be rendered as "justice"; adjectivally, it refers to balance, as exemplified by the evenness of various sides of a geometric figure. *'Adāla* can be rendered as "state of moral and religious perfection"; it "describes the state of a
person who in general obeys the moral and religious law."[52] The *Guide*'s modern
English translator Shlomo Pines renders *tzedeq* and *'adl* as "justice"; the medieval Hebrew translator Samuel ibn Tibbon, perhaps mindful of *'adala*, renders
these terms as "*yosher*" ("uprightness").[53]

Maimonides initially explains in the *Guide* that "*tzedaqah*" means "granting
to everyone who has a right to something, that which he has a right to and giving
to every being that which corresponds to his merits." He immediately qualifies
this definition by pointing out that paying workers their duly earned wages (for
example) is not "*tzedaqah*." Rather, "the fulfilling of duties with regard to others
imposed upon you on account of moral virtue … is called *sedaqah*."[54] Hence the
qualification: paying workers their duly earned wages is not an obligation
imposed "on account of moral virtue," it is an obligation imposed on an
employer *qua* employer. Maimonides illustrates his definition of "*tzedaqah*" by
means of Deuteronomy 24:13, which we have extensively examined earlier in
this book (*you must return the pledge to him at sundown, that he may sleep in
his cloth and bless you; and it will be to your merit* [*tzedaqah*] *before the Lord
your God*). To Maimonides Deuteronomy 24:13's "*tzedaqah*" means: "when you
walk in the way of the moral virtues, *you do justice unto your rational soul,
giving her the due that is her right*" (emphasis added).[55] Significantly,
Maimonides elides the late antique rabbinic interpretation of Deuteronomy
24:13's "*tzedaqah*" as an accumulation of heavenly merit.

What might this mean for Maimonides' view of redemptive almsgiving? In
Laws of Murder and of the Preservation of Life 12:15 Maimonides takes direct
aim at Daniel 4:24 (*Redeem your sins by beneficence and your iniquities by
generosity to the poor*). The paragraph begins with the ruling that giving good
advice to a Gentile is forbidden. Such "good advice" includes counseling a
Gentile who lives and intends to continue living an "evil" life to do a *mitzvah.*

Maimonides illustrates his ruling with the example of Daniel, who "was only subjected to a trial because he gave Nebuchadnezzar advice to give *tzedaqah*" (citing Daniel 4:24). Terse though it is, this passage illustrates three ways in which Maimonides marginalizes redemptive almsgiving. First, Maimonides codifies this interpretation of Daniel 4:24 in a rather obscure place (from the perspective of redemptive almsgiving)—not Laws of Repentance or Laws of Gifts to the Poor, but in Laws of Murder and of the Preservation of Life. Second, Maimonides' interpretation of Daniel 4:24 is clearly drawn from B. *Baba Batra* 4a, which attributes Daniel's punishment (however understood) to his advice to Nebuchadnezzar. Maimonides thus codifies this example of the *Bavli*'s ambivalence about Daniel 4:24 and redemptive almsgiving as law. Third, and apropos, Maimonides implicitly understands Daniel 4:24 and its redemptive almsgiving lesson as applicable only to Gentiles.

Maimonides' marginalization of redemptive almsgiving in Laws of Murder and of the Preservation of Life helps make sense of how he contextualizes *tzedaqah* in Laws of Repentance. Laws of Repentance 1:3 states that *teshuvah* "atones for all transgressions," and that "there is only *teshuvah*" in the absence of the Temple and its "altar of atonement." One who "repents of his evil and dies is a *ba'al teshuvah*, one of the sons of the world to come" (Laws of Repentance 3:14). A person "should endeavor to do *teshuvah* and to shake his hands of his sins in order that he die a *ba'al teshuvah* and merit the life of the world to come" (Laws of Repentance 7:1). Maimonides does not refer here to *tzedaqah* as a means of expiating sin or even as a necessary adjunct to *teshuvah*.

Laws of Repentance 2:2–4 describes the "mechanics" of *teshuvah*. *Teshuvah* is the sinner's abandonment of his sin, removal of it from his mind, and inner resolve never to repeat it (2:2). Verbal confession is necessary but insufficient without that inner resolve (2:3). Maimonides adapts B. *Rosh Hashanah* 16b in ruling that changes of name, actions, and even location may be aspects of *teshuvah* (2:4), along with "crying out always before God with tears and supplication," "doing *tzedaqah* as one is able," and "distancing oneself exceedingly from the matter as to which he sinned." Note the role Maimonides assigns *tzedaqah*: a penitent's *tzedaqah* is an act that, along with other acts, illustrates the genuineness of a penitent's *teshuvah*. By implication, *tzedaqah alone* does not atone for sin *tout court.*

Maimonides famously describes the sounding of the *shofar* as a wake-up call and urges people to see themselves throughout the year—not just during the Days of Awe—as balanced precariously between righteousness and wickedness, one deed away from being classified as the one or the other (Laws of Repentance 3:4). Because one's deeds will be tallied and judgment as "righteous" or "wicked" rendered during the Days of Awe "all of Israel is accustomed to multiply *tzedaqah* and good deeds and to engage in the commandments from *Rosh Hashanah* until *Yom HaKippurim*, more so than other days of the year..." *Tzedaqah* is indeed singled out here, but its role in ensuring a favorable heavenly verdict is no different or superior to the other meritorious acts Maimonides lists: "good deeds" and engagement in the "commandments." Doing more *tzedaqah* during this critical time of year is, then—along with good deeds and engagement in the commandments—an excellent *sign* that one is on the right path. Other such signs include "rising at night ... praying in the synagogues with words of entreaty and humility until the day dawns." Indeed, Maimonides himself explicitly calls *tzedaqah* a "sign" in Laws of Gifts to the Poor 10:1: "for *tzedaqah* is a sign (*siman*) of a righteous person, the seed of Abraham our father..." Laws of Gifts to the Poor 10:1 states explicitly that which is implicit in the Laws of Repentance: doing *tzedaqah* is a "sign" that demonstrates something (quite positive) about the giver, but Maimonides says nothing that would support the idea that *tzedaqah* atones for sin *tout court.* And again, Maimonides says nothing about *tzedaqah* as the stockpiling of heavenly merits.

Maimonides also implicitly adopts and expands upon R. Yitzhaq's understanding (B. *Baba Batra* 9b) that the purpose of rewarding *tzedaqah* with the preservation or augmentation of wealth is not simply to provide the giver of *tzedaqah* with a windfall of riches, but to guarantee him the means by which to continue giving. Laws of Gifts to the Poor 10:2 states "a person will never be impoverished through *tzedaqah*, nor will any bad thing or damage come about on account of *tzedaqah*..." Maimonides here promises the *tzedaqah* giver preservation of wealth, but not necessarily its augmentation. In Laws of Repentance 9:1 he states that the reward for keeping the commandments is that

> [God] will remove from us all the things that prevent us from doing [the Torah] ... and will shower on us all the good things that strengthen our hands in doing the Torah, such as plenty, peace, and the multiplication of silver and gold ... thus does he say in the Torah after promising us all the good things of this world, *It will be therefore to our merit* (*tzedaqah*) (Deuteronomy 6:25).

Maimonides does not see Deuteronomy 6:25's "*tzedaqah*" as an otherworldly, redemptive benefit, but as the "merit" of earning *in this world* the means to be able to continue observing the Torah *in this world.* As one of the "commandments" *tzedaqah* therefore may well entail a this-worldly reward of augmented wealth ("the multiplication of silver and gold"), but Maimonides leaves that implicit, in contrast to his explicit stress in Laws of Gifts to the Poor 10:2 on how it (only) *preserves* wealth. Whatever *tzedaqah*'s this-worldly reward is, Maimonides' position in these two passages is clear: doing *tzedaqah* is rewarded in the here and now, and the point of its this-worldly rewards (like those for keeping all the other commandments) is that God will perpetuate the conditions and grant the means to continue keeping the commandments, including, of course, doing *tzedaqah.*

Maimonides recognizes the ideational link between charity and sacrifice but here too, he reproduces the idea with a distinctly humanistic, this-worldly application.[56] Laws of Things Forbidden for the Altar 7:11 is an example:

> Behold, it is said in the Torah: *and Abel, for his part, brought the choicest of the firstlings of his flock. The Lord paid heed to Abel and his offering...*

(Genesis 4:4). And this is the law as to each thing that is [brought] in the name of the good God—it must be of the nicest and best. If one builds a house of prayer, it should be nicer than his dwelling. If one feeds the hungry, one should feed him from the best and sweetest of his table. If one clothes the naked, he should clothe [him] from the nicest of his garments. If one dedicates an item, he should dedicate from among the finest of his possessions. And thus does [scripture] say: *all fat is the Lord's* (Leviticus 3:16).[57]

Maimonides here clearly equates Temple offerings/dedications and charity (the feeding of the hungry and clothing of the naked); charity is a species of the genus "gifts to God." But Maimonides uses this equivalence to make an ethical point: one must always dedicate to God the best one has, be it a dedication to *heqdesh* ("If one dedicates an item"), building a synagogue, or feeding and clothing the needy. To Maimonides the significance of the equation of charity and gifts to God is not only that both partake in the votive institution of vows, but that doers of charity can learn real-world ethical lessons from donors to *heqdesh*.[58]

With all this as prologue we should not be surprised that Maimonides sees the underlying purpose of charity to be this-worldly and human-centered: its bedrock purpose is to provide a needy person with what he needs to take his place as a dignified member of Jewish society. To Maimonides, Deuteronomy 15:8 (*Rather, you must open your hand and lend him sufficient for whatever he needs*) is *the* pivotal charity verse. In his list of the 613 commandments, Maimonides describes "positive commandment #195" in pertinent part as follows: "Commandment #195 is that we are commanded to do *tzedaqah*, and to strengthen ... the weak ... this command appears in various forms ... we should help and strengthen them *sufficient for their sustenance* (*dei sippukam*)..." I have italicized Maimonides' original formulation "*dei sippukam*" ("sufficient for their sustenance"), which is a paraphrase of Deuteronomy 15:8's *sufficient for whatever he needs*. Maimonides indicates here that the point of *tzedaqah*, whatever the commandment's various manifestations, is to supply the needy with what they lack in order to enable them to live dignified lives.

Laws of Gifts to the Poor 7:1 states that there is a biblical commandment to give *tzedaqah* "according to what is necessary for the poor if the donor can afford it." Paragraph 3 (based on Deuteronomy 15:8) expressly directs that the poor person be given "what [he] lacks"; Maimonides itemizes the examples of clothing, household utensils, a spouse, and a horse (for a previously wealthy poor person accustomed to having one). Paragraph 5 provides that if a donor cannot afford to provide a poor person *sufficient for whatever he needs* after being asked to do so, the donor must give whatever he can: 20 percent "of his possessions" is ideal, 10 percent average, and less than that "stingy."[59] Beggars are entitled to "small," not "large," gifts (Laws of Gifts to the Poor 7:7). A synthesis of these various passages reveals how Maimonides understands the biblical command that the poor be provided *sufficient for whatever he needs*. An individual donor must give the poor *sufficient for whatever he needs* should three conditions be met: (1) the poor person asks the donor to provide him with what would be *sufficient for whatever he needs*; (2) the poor person is not a beggar; and (3) the individual donor can afford to give the poor person what is *sufficient for whatever he needs*. If these conditions are not met the individual donor is obligated to give *tzedaqah* as he can afford: 20 percent of his possessions being the ideal amount and 10 percent being an average gift.

There is also a communal element to *sufficient for whatever he needs*. In Laws of Gifts to the Poor 9:3 Maimonides declares that he never heard of a Jewish community without a communal charity fund, which is a not-quite-subtle way of making the point that every Jewish community should have one. The importance to Maimonides of the scriptural *sufficient for whatever he needs* is also apparent in Maimonides' addition of the phrase to his codification of two Talmudic passages from which it is absent. B. *Baba Batra* 8b rules that two people collect for and three distribute to the poor from the communal charity fund. Distributions require three people because decisions about charitable distribution are matters of judgment, and three judges are required to adjudicate monetary cases.[60] Maimonides glosses the Talmudic language with an addition not found in any extant manuscripts or printed editions: "for they (the charity collectors) give to each and every one *sufficient for whatever he needs* for the week" (Laws of Gifts to the Poor 9:5).[61] Similarly, Laws of Gifts to the Poor 9:18 provides that should monies collected for a particular poor person happen to exceed that person's "*needs*," he can keep the extra money. M. *Sheqalim* 2:5, the source for this rule, does not mention "*needs*," nor do its extant manuscripts.[62]

Maimonides thus sees both the individual (under certain circumstances) and the community as legally obligated to provide the poor with *sufficient for whatever he needs*. The individual's obligation to do so dovetails with Maimonides' emphasis in Laws of Gifts to the Poor 10:2 on compassion for the poor as a key element in an individual Jew's character. The communal obligation dovetails with Maimonides' ideological emphasis in Laws of Gifts to the Poor 9:3 on the Jewish community's obligation to maintain a communal charity fund. To Maimonides Deuteronomy 15:8's *sufficient for whatever he needs* is the foundational principle of rabbinic charity and a matter of individual and communal *Bildung*.

Charity as *Bildung* appears as well in Laws of Character Traits. Maimonides states: "one should not scatter all his money, rather, he should give *tzedaqah* as he can afford and lend as appropriate to one who is in need" (Laws of Character Traits 1:4). Maimonides also stresses in several places the importance of extending a sympathetic hand to the poor generally and to widows and orphans specifically, whether or not they are materially poor. This is because "their spirit is downcast, even if they are very wealthy" (Laws of Character Traits 6:10). Similarly, giving more "gifts to the poor" on the Purim holiday is superior to making a magnificent holiday feast or giving many gifts to one's friends because "there is no greater or more glorious joy than to gladden the hearts of the poor, orphans, widows, and strangers. And the one who gladdens the hearts of these unfortunates resembles the divine presence..." (Laws of Megillah and Hanukkah 2:17).[63] Maimonides reminds his readers that "God is close to the poor's cry"

(Laws of Gifts to the Poor 10:3), and points out that "everyone who feeds and gives the poor and orphans to drink at his table will be answered when he calls on God" (Laws of Gifts to the Poor 10:16). At bottom, then, Maimonides links charitable giving to the cultivation of the positive personal trait of sympathy for the downtrodden, a sympathy that should encompass all the socially vulnerable, whether or not they are also economically vulnerable. But Maimonides does not idealize the poor; there is an element of charity as *Bildung* that applies uniquely to them. In Laws of Character Traits 5:11 he points out that "fools" marry before ensuring that they are materially prepared to support a family, with the inevitable result that they must "be supported through *tzedaqah*."[64] Famously, his highest degree of *tzedaqah* is providing economic opportunity so that a poor person will not need *tzedaqah* (Laws of Gifts to the Poor 10:7). And tellingly, he closes the Laws of Gifts to the Poor with the promise that a needy person who deprives himself and does his best to live without communal *tzedaqah* "so as not to impose a burden on the community" will not die before being in a position to support others (10:19). Maimonides' reference in the latter paragraph to not imposing a burden on the community precisely echoes Rava's concern about the communal burden imposed by his demanding interlocutor (B. *Ketubot* 67b). In these various rulings Maimonides follows the *Bavli* in seeing *tzedaqah* as a less-than-best option for the needy, whose character and sense of self are better served by cultivating self-reliance and independence.

Laws of Gifts to the Poor 10:1 points toward *tzedaqah*'s role in a future-oriented Maimonidean social vision. The message of Isaiah 54:14 (*You shall be established through righteousness* [*tzedaqah*]) is that the "throne of Israel" and the "true religion" ("*dat ha-emet*") only endure through *tzedaqah*.[65] The rare Maimonidean phrase "true religion" ("*dat ha-emet*") only appears in two other places in the *Mishneh Torah*. In Laws of the Festival Offering 3:6 Maimonides describes the Israelite king's septennial public reading of the Torah scroll at the end of the Sabbatical year as necessary in order to "strengthen the true religion (*dat ha-emet*)." In Laws of Kings and Their Wars 4:10 Maimonides notes that a Jewish king's entire agenda and all his thoughts should be devoted to "elevating the true religion (*dat ha-emet*)." Laws of Gifts to the Poor 10:1's reference to "*tzedaqah*," then, is not only a charity reference: "*tzedaqah*" is also a communal, public practice of "righteousness" that demonstrates the truth of the "true religion," presumably by modeling a just social order based on divine law. Apropos, Maimonides points out "Israel will only be redeemed through *tzedaqah*" (quoting Isaiah 1:27).[66] Maimonides' source for this seems to be B. *Baba Batra* 10a, where a similar point about redemption is made by way of Isaiah 56:1 (*Thus said the Lord: Observe what is right and do what is just; For soon My salvation shall come, and my deliverance be revealed*). The difference between the two Isaianic contexts is key to Maimonides' switch of verses. Isaiah 56:1 is followed by verses about keeping the Sabbath, holding fast to God's covenant, prayer, and offering sacrifice—ritual performances. In Isaiah 1 the prophet excoriates his contemporaries for their cheating, thievery, greed, and murder; he decries *the faithful city that was filled with justice* but which *has become a harlot* and is filled with murderers—social injustice and societal breakdown. For Maimonides, then, Isaiah 1:27 is preferable to Isaiah 56:1 as the scriptural source for the notion that *tzedaqah* will lead to a redemption of Israel exemplified by the establishment and endurance of a just and humane Jewish social order, in which everyone has *sufficient for whatever he needs.*[67]

Notes

1 The medieval *midrash* compilations' traditions and (at times) unique perspectives on charity are as yet understudied. "Medieval *midrash* compilations" is an admittedly imprecise designation for a set of *midrash* compilations that, although difficult to date, are generally accepted as having gelled as literary compilations after the redaction of the *Bavli*. The four principal compilations appearing in this chapter are *Midrash Zuta* to Song of Songs (specifically, the extended charity passage it presents in 1:15) (of indefinite date, possibly tenth century), *Midrash Psalms* (of indefinite date, *terminus a quo* is possibly the Geonic period), *Midrash Proverbs* (ninth century), and *Midrash Tanchuma* (eighth or ninth centuries). On these works, see, e.g., Strack and Stemberger, *Introduction to the Talmud and Midrash*, 302–306, 319–320, 322–324, 340–342; Anat Reizel, *Introduction to the Midrashic Literature* (Hotza'at Tevunot, Miklelet Herzog: Alon Shevut, 2011), 164–165 and *passim* (*Midrash Zuta* to Song of Songs), 234–244 (*Midrash Tanchuma*), 281–301 (*Midrash Psalms* and *Midrash Proverbs*) (in Hebrew). On the post-Talmudic origins of the charity homily in *Midrash Zuta* to Song of Songs, see Marc Hirshman, *A Rivalry of Genius: Jewish and Christian Biblical Interpretation in Late Antiquity* (Albany: State University of New York Press, 1996), 148 n. 13.
2 *Midrash Zuta* to Song of Songs 1:15 (ed. Buber, 23).
3 Isaac Aboab, *Menorat Ha-Ma'or* (ed. Yehudah Paris Horev; Jerusalem: Mossad HaRav Kook, 1961), 397.
4 On these trusts see Judah D. Galinsky, " 'And it is for the Glory of the Great that their Name be Remembered' "; ibid., "Commemoration and Heqdesh in the Jewish Communities of Germany and Spain during the 13th Century"; and ibid., "Jewish Charitable Bequests and the Hekdesh Trust in 13th Century Spain." Madeline Kochen has explored the phenomenon of the medieval charitable *heqdesh* from the perspective of the development of legal doctrine; see her " 'It Was Not for Naught That They Called It *Hekdesh*' and ibid., *Organ Donation and the Divine Lien*, 122–146.
5 On the practice of *matnat yad*, see Israel J. Yuval, "Donations from Nürnberg to Jerusalem (1375–1392)," *Zion* 46 (1981): 182–197 (in Hebrew); Yitzhak (Eric) Zimmer, "Minhag 'Matnat Yad' V'Hazkarat Neshamot," in Joseph Hacker and Yaron Harel, editors, *"Lo Yasur Shevet M'Yehudah": Hanhagah, Rabbanut U-Kehillah B'Toldot Yisrael; Mehkarim Mugashim L'Professor Shimon Schwartzfuchs* (Jerusalem: Mossad Bialik, 2011), 71–87; Judah D. Galinsky, "Charity and Prayer in the Ashkenazi Synagogue," in Itamar Dagan, editor, *"Ve-Hinneh Rivka Yotzet"*: *Essays in Jewish Studies in Honor of Rivka Dagan* (Israel: Tzur-ot, 2017), 163–174 (in Hebrew).
6 Eliezer of Metz, *Sefer Yere'im* 425 (ed. Avraham A. Schiff; Vilna, 1892; repr.: Israel: n.p., n.d.), 247. For more on Eliezer of Metz and *tzedaqah*, see my "R. Eliezer of Metz's Twelfth-Century Exclusion from Charity of the Jewish *'Avaryan B'mezid'* (Deliberate Transgressor)," in Sharon Farmer, editor, *Approaches to Poverty in Medieval Europe: Complexities, Contradictions, Transformations, c. 1100–1500* (Turnhout: Brepols, 2016), 67–92.
7 Judah Galinsky, "Charity and Prayer," 171.
8 See the discussion in Chapter 2 about how the *Bavli* neutralizes this notion on B. *Baba Batra* 10a.

9 *Midrash Proverbs* 19 (ed. Buber, 85).

10 Israel ibn al-Nakawa, *Menorat Ha-Ma'or* (ed. H.G. Enelow; New York: Bloch, 1929), 60.

11 Judah Loewe, *Netivot Olam* (*Netiv Gemilut Hasadim*) (2 vols.; ed. Harav Hayyim Pardes; Tel Aviv: Yad Mordecai, 1981), 1:390.

12 Judah Loewe, *Netivot Olam* (*Netiv Ha-tzedaqah*) (ed. Pardes; 1:426, 427) (two mentions that God is the donor's debtor); 1:430 (the giver of *tzedaqah* gives to God).

13 *Midrash Tanchuma* (ed. Buber, 116). For the *Bavli*'s discussion of this notion, see Chapter 4.

14 Israel ibn al-Nakawa, *Menorat Ha-Ma'or* (ed. Enelow, 60). Enelow adds a reference to Proverbs 19:17 in his notes to the passage.

15 Isaac Aboab, *Menorat Ha-Ma'or* (ed. Horev, 407).

16 See Eitan P. Fishbane, *The Art of Mystical Narrative: A Poetics of the Zohar* (New York: Oxford University Press, 2018), 308. Fishbane's extended treatment of charity in the Zohar is on pp. 296–314.

17 Israel ibn al-Nakawa, *Menorat Ha-Ma'or* (ed. Enelow, 35).

18 Judah Loewe, *Netivot Olam* (*Netiv Ha-tzedaqah*) (ed. Pardes; 1:430).

19 See Sholom Noach Berezovsky, *Sefer Netivot Shalom*, 2 vols. (Jerusalem: Yeshivat Beit Avraham Slonim, n.d.), 1:225.

20 *Sefer Hasidim* paragraphs 356, 357 (ed. Wistinetzki, 108).

21 Israel ibn al-Nakawa, *Menorat Ha-Ma'or* (ed. Enelow, 61).

22 Ibid., 62. See also Isaac Aboab, *Menorat Ha-Ma'or* (ed. Horev, 398).

23 Israel ibn al-Nakawa, *Menorat Ha-Ma'or* (ed. Enelow, 33); cf. *Leviticus Rabbah* 34:8 (ed. Margulies, 791).

24 Israel ibn al-Nakawa, *Menorat Ha-Ma'or* (ed. Enelow, 31–32).

25 Judah Loewe, *Netivot Olam* (*Netiv Ha-tzedaqah*) (ed. Pardes; 1:432).

26 A reference to the practice appears in the pre-rabbinic work 2 Maccabees 12:39, 42–45 (second century BCE). See Daniel Schwartz's introductory comments to 2 Maccabees in Michael D. Coogan, editor, *The New Oxford Annotated Apocrypha: New Revised Standard Version* (4th ed.; New York and Oxford: Oxford University Press, 2010), 241–242. This practice must be distinguished from giving charitable gifts or making bequests *in anticipation* of one's (or another's) approaching death. For the latter, see the *Bavli*'s account of Mar Uqba's deathbed conduct (B. *Ketubot* 67b). An echo of Mar Uqba appears much later, in the "*heqdesh*" trusts of thirteenth- and fourteenth-century Christian Spain. Judah Galinsky has shown that donors would establish *heqdesh* trusts for their own sakes while they were alive, and he has specifically called attention to the redemptive motivations underlying their establishment as he finds them in both responsa and Latinate wills: "for the benefit of my soul," "for the sake of my soul," "as ransom (or atonement) for my soul." See Judah Galinsky, "Commemoration and Heqdesh," 194. He points out that another motivation is the natural human desire to be remembered, as the trusts were structured so as to provide for continual reinvestment of the monies and hence perpetual endurance. See Judah Galinsky, "'And it is for the Glory of the Great'"; ibid., "Jewish Charitable Bequests."

27 See Israel Lévi, "La Commemoration des Ames Dans Le Judaisme," *Revue des Études Juives* 29 (1894): 49–50.

28 Lévi points (ibid., p. 51 and nn. 1–2) to examples like Y. *Sanhedrin* 10:5, 29c (ed. Academy, 1326) (either Moses or Hannah improved the postmortem lot of the rebellious Korahides through prayer), B. *Sotah* 10b (David's prayers raised his rebellious son Absalom up through the seven layers of *Gehinnom*), and B. *Qiddushin* 31b (a *baraita* states that one reciting a tradition in the name of his dead father within the first year of his death should refer to himself as his father's "atonement").

29 See Richard Finn, *Almsgiving in the Later Roman Empire*, 106.

30 *Sifre Deuteronomy* 210 (ed. Finkelstein, 244).

31 Louis Finkelstein points out that the unbolded language is missing from two manuscripts and found in a different place in a third. See *Sifre Deuteronomy* 210 (ed. Finkelstein, 244), notes to lines 4–5.

32 See Ephraim E. Urbach, *The Sages*, 1:509; Urbach's complete discussion of atonement for the dead in classical rabbinic literature is on 1:509–510. See also Zvi Arie Steinfeld, "Kapparah L'Meitim," *Sidra* 17 (1962): 217–228; repr.; ibid., *Tractate Horayot: Studies in the Mishna and Talmud* (Ramat-Gan: Bar-Ilan University Press, 2016), 254–266.

33 The reference is to *Sifre Deuteronomy*.

34 *Midrash Tanchuma* (*Ha'azinu* 1). This passage is not found in *Midrash Tanchuma* (ed. Buber). This is not the place to explore more fully the textual relationship between the different editions of *Midrash Tanchuma* and the interpolations into the *Sifre Deuteronomy*.

35 Ephraim E. Urbach, *The Sages*, 1:510 and 2:916 n. 13.

36 See Judah Galinsky, "'And it is for the Glory of the Great'"; ibid., "Charity and Prayer"; Yitzhak (Eric) Zimmer, "Minhag 'Matnat Yad'"; Elisheva Baumgarten, *Practicing Piety*.

37 On the Nürnberg Memorbuch see, e.g., Elisheva Baumgarten, *Practicing Piety*, 104–107; see also 107–115. The Memorbuch was created by one Isaac ben Samuel Meiningen in 1296.

38 See Yitzhak (Eric) Zimmer, "Minhag 'Matnat Yad,'" 75, 80, 81; Judah Galinsky, "Charity and Prayer," 172.

39 Judah Galinsky, "Charity and Prayer."

40 This passage is from *Midrash Proverbs* 6 (ed. Buber, 54). Some comparisons to Burton L. Visotzky, *The Midrash on Proverbs: Translated from the Hebrew with an Introduction and Annotations* (New Haven and London: Yale University Press, 1992), will be made in the succeeding notes ("trans. Visotzky").

41 *Midrash Proverbs* (trans. Visotzky, 37–38) reads "R. Joshua" in accordance with Ms. Vatican 44, 11.

42 *Midrash Proverbs* 11 (ed. Buber, 69).

43 *Midrash Psalms* (ed. Buber, 127). The version of the triad found in the Venice printing of *Midrash Psalms* (1546) is different in another way: "*teshuvah, ma'asim tovim, tefillah.*"

44 On the adoption of *Unetaneh Tokef*, first in Germany, then in northern France, see, e.g., Avraham Frankel, "Demuto Ha-historit Shel R' Amnon M'Magenza V-gulgulav Shel Ha-piyyut 'Unetaneh Tokef' B'Italiah, B'Ashkenaz, U-b'Tzarfat," *Zion* 67:1 (2002): 125–138. Frankel hypothesizes that the liturgical poem came to Germany by way of Italy by the beginning of the eleventh century, and to northern France at some point thereafter. Much scholarship has been devoted to investigating Isaac b. R. Moses of Vienna's (*c.*1200–1270) alleged recollection that he "found" Ephraim ben Jacob of Bonn's written account that *Unetaneh Tokef* was composed by a dying medieval German martyr named R. Amnon of Mainz. See Isaac ben Moses of Vienna, *Or Zaru'a* (Laws of *Rosh Hashanah*) 2:276. Thanks to Isaac ben Moses, the story of R. Amnon of Mainz's choice of martyrdom over apostasy has become a well-known part of Jewish cultural lore; however, the historical existence of this martyr figure is unlikely. See Eli Yassif, "Legend and History: Historians Read Hebrew Legends of the Middle Ages," *Zion* 64:2 (1999): 187–219 (in Hebrew); Ivan (Israel) Marcus, "Kiddush Hashem B'Ashkenaz V'sippur Rabbi Amnon M'Magenza," in Yeshayahu Gafni and Aviezer Ravitzky, editors, *Kedushat Hahayyim V'heruf Ha-nefesh: Kovetz Ma'amarim L'Zikhro Shel Amir Yekutiel* (Jerusalem: Merkaz Zalman Shazar, 1993), 140 (the story of R. Amnon "tells of a 'historical' figure that never lived"). The suggestion that "R. Amnon" is a literary creation derives indirect support from the fact that Isaac ben Moses's account is thickly threaded through with biblical allusions to the stories of Joseph and Potiphar's wife, Esther, and aspects of the life of the

patriarch Jacob. On these allusions, see Ivan (Israel) Marcus, "Kiddush Hashem B'Ashkenaz V'sippur Rabbi Amnon M'Magenza," 142, 143; Jonathan Breuer, "Sippur Rabbi Amnon M'Magenza U-makbilotav Ba-Mikra," in Amnon Bazak, editor, *U-Ve-Yom Tzom Kippur Yehatemun: Studies on Yom HaKippurim* (Alon Shevut: Tevunot, 2005), 301–309. Avraham Frankel is less willing than Marcus to deny R. Amnon's historicity, although he does acknowledge that the name "Amnon" was common in Italy and would likely not have been a name borne by a native German scholar. See Avraham Frankel, "Demuto Ha-historit Shel R' Amnon M'Magenza," 132–133.

45 *Midrash Tanchuma* (*Noah*) 8 (ed. Warsaw; repr.: Jerusalem, 1962), 14; B. *Rosh Hashanah* 16b. See Menahem Schmelzer, "Penitence, Prayer and (Charity?)," in Marc Brettler and Michael Fishbane, editors, *Minhah le-Nahum: Biblical and Other Studies Presented to Nahum M. Sarna in Honour Of His 70th Birthday* (Journal for the Study of the Old Testament; Supplement Series 154; Sheffield: Sheffield Academic Press, 1993), 291–299. Schmelzer rather unpersuasively relies on his observation about the triad's presence in this order in *Midrash Tanchuma* to argue that *Unetaneh Tokef*'s composer relied on *Midrash Tanchuma*. See Menahem Schmelzer, ibid., 294. Yaakov Spiegel takes issue with Schmelzer's conclusion in his "Berur B'divrei Hapayyetan 'U-teshuvah u-tefillah u-tzedakah Ma'avirin Et Ro'a Ha-gezerah' V'al Kefifut Ha-payyetanim L'halakhah," *Netuim* 8 (2001): 23–42, see especially 29 n. 25. For a very recent analysis of the Talmudic origin of *Unetaneh Tokef*'s triad, see Judith Hauptman, "A Talmudic Reading of the High Holiday Prayer *Un'taneh Tokef*," *Zeramim: An Online Journal of Applied Jewish Studies* 2:3 (Spring 2018/5778).

46 See Yaakov Spiegel, "Berur B'divrei Hapayyetan 'U-teshuvah u-tefillah u-tzedakah Ma'avirin Et Ro'a Ha-gezerah' " (The sixth-century liturgical poet Yannai composed *Unetaneh Tokef*). Joseph Yahalom has also taken this position; see his journalistic article "Who Shall be the Author, and Who Shall Not," *Haaretz* (September, 6, 2002) (accessed May 21, 2018 at www.haaretz.com/1.5136767). See also John H. Planer, "The Provenance, Dating, Allusions, and Variants of *U-n'taneh tokef* and Its Relationship to Romanos's *Kontakion*," *Journal of Synagogue Music* 38 (Fall 2013): 166–192, especially 173, 191. The reference is to Naphtali Wieder's "A Controversial Mishnaic and Liturgical Expression," *Journal of Jewish Studies* 18 (1967): 1–7.

47 See the discussions in Menaham Schmelzer, "Penitence, Prayer and (Charity?)," 294–296; Yaakov Spiegel, Berur B'divrei Hapayyetan 'U-teshuvah u-tefillah u-tzedakah Ma'avirin Et Ro'a Ha-gezerah," 29–32; Elie Munk, *The World of Prayer* (2 vols.; New York: Philipp Feldheim, 1963), 2:209–210. Schmelzer points to (294 n. 2) manuscript evidence of how Hebrew letters were used to mark the "real" (i.e., Palestinian amoraic) order of the triad as opposed to its liturgical order: "*teshuvah*" was marked with the letter *gimmel* (signifying it is really third in sequence), then "*tefillah*" with an *alef*, and "*tzedaqah*" with a "*bet*."

48 B. *Nedarim* 39b.

49 B. *Ta'anit* 2a.

50 Menahem Schmelzer arrives at a similar conclusion through his reading of Solomon ibn Gabirol's poem *Keter Malkhut*; see Menahem Schmelzer, "Penitence, Prayer and (Charity?)," 297–299.

51 See Sholom Noach Berezovsky, *Sefer Netivot Shalom*, 1:137.

52 *The Encyclopaedia of Islam: New Edition* (Leiden: E.J. Brill, 1960), vol. 1 ('*Adl*), 209–210.

53 See Moses Maimonides, *The Guide of the Perplexed: Volume Two: Translated and with an Introduction and Notes by Shlomo Pines* (Chicago and London: University of Chicago Press, 1963), 631; *Sefer Moreh Nevuchim L'Harambam* (repr.: Jerusalem: n.p., 1960), 3:69.

54 Moses Maimonides, *The Guide of the Perplexed* (ed. Pines, 631).

55 Ibid.

56 Madeline Kochen correctly points out that Maimonides codifies the applicability of the votive institution of "vows" to both charity and Temple sacrifices. See Madeline Kochen, " 'It Was Not for Naught That They Called it *Hekdesh*' ": 139 and nn. 27–28; ibid., *Organ Donation and the Divine Lien*, 140–141 and nn. 59–60.

57 The trilateral root "*h-le-v*" ("fat") of Leviticus 3:16 is found also in the description of Abel's offering in Genesis 4:4, where the verse, says, in literal terms, that Abel brought "the choicest of his sheep" and "their fat." Maimonides takes the meaning of Genesis 4:4 to be that Abel brought the "fattest," hence, "the best," which he then also roots in Leviticus 3:16.

58 This passage's import was not lost on Joseph Caro, one of Maimonides' most perceptive pre-modern readers, who quotes it in full in *Bet Yosef* to *Tur Yoreh De'ah* 248, n. 8; and in an abbreviated version in *Shulhan Arukh Yoreh De'ah* 248:8.

59 It was pointed out at the beginning of Chapter 6 that Y. *Peah* 1:1, 15b (ed. Academy, 78) prescribes that one is not to spend more than one-fifth (20 percent) of one's *annual increase in wealth* on charity. The parallels on B. *Ketubot* 50a and B. *Arachin* 28a refer simply to "one-fifth" (20 percent); Maimonides adopts the *Bavli's* formulation.

60 B. *Baba Batra* 8b.

61 B. *Baba Batra* 8b and mss. Munich 95; Escorial G-I-3; Hamburg 165; Florence II-1–9; Paris 1337; Vatican 115; and the Pesaro Print (1511).

62 M. *Sheqalim* 2:5 and mss. Kaufmann and Parma.

63 On this ruling see Isadore Twersky, "On Law and Ethics in the *Mishneh Torah*: A Case Study of *Hilkhot Megillah* II:17," *Tradition* 24:2 (1989): 138–149.

64 Note that Maimonides reserves these harsh words for the thoughtless *adult, male* poor, reserving softer tones for widows and orphans.

65 On Maimonides' rationalist vision of the Messianic era, see, e.g., Joel L. Kraemer, "On Maimonides' Messianic Posture," in Isadore Twersky, editor, *Studies in Medieval Jewish History and Literature II* (Cambridge: Harvard University Press, 1984), 109–142.

66 The translation of the verse is my own.

67 By contrast, Maimonides points out in Laws of Repentance 7:5 that "Israel will only be redeemed through *teshuvah*," quoting at length from Deuteronomy 30:1–4. Deuteronomy's context is that Israel's exile was due to their abandonment of the covenant, notably through idolatry. Maimonides thus subtly makes *tzedaqah* and *teshuvah* equal partners in securing Israel's redemption, much as they (together with *tefillah*) are equal partners in an individual Jew's atonement.

Bibliography

Primary sources, critical editions, and translations

Aboab, Isaac. *Menorat Ha-Ma'or*. 1961. Yehudah Paris Horev, ed. Jerusalem: Mossad HaRav Kook

Babylonian Talmud. 1975 (repr.). Vilna-Romm edition with standard commentaries. Jerusalem: n.p.

Buber, Solomon. 1892. *Midrash Proverbs*. Vilna: Romm

Buber, Solomon. 1894. *Midrasch Suta: Schir ha-Schirim, Ruth, Echah und Koheleth*. Berlin: Itzkowski

Buber, Solomon. 1913. *Midrash Tanchuma*. Vilna: Romm

Buber, Solomon. 1966 (repr.). *Midrash Psalms*. Jerusalem, n.p.

Coogan, Michael D, ed. 2010. *The New Oxford Annotated Apocrypha: New Revised Standard Version*, 4th ed. New York and Oxford: Oxford University Press

Eliezer of Metz. 1892. n.d. (repr.). *Sefer Yere'im.* Avraham A. Schiff, ed. Israel, n.p.

Finkelstein, Louis. 1969. *Sifre on Deuteronomy.* New York: The Jewish Theological Seminary of America

Isaac ben Moses of Vienna. 2010. *Or Zaru'a.* Jerusalem: Machon Yerushalayim

Israel ibn al-Nakawa. 1929. *Menorat Ha-Ma'or.* H.G. Enelow, ed. New York: Bloch

Judah Loewe. 1981. *Netivot Olam*, 2 vols. Harav Hayyim Pardes, ed. Tel Aviv: Yad Mordecai

Margulies, Mordecai. 1993. *Midrash Wayyikra Rabbah: A Critical Edition Based on Manuscripts and Genizah Fragments with Variants and Notes.* New York and Jerusalem: The Jewish Theological Seminary of America

Moses Maimonides. 1960 (repr.). *Sefer Moreh Nevuchim L'Harambam.* Jerusalem: n.p.

Moses Maimonides. 1963. *The Guide of the Perplexed.* Translated and with an Introduction and Notes by Shlomo Pines. Chicago and London: University of Chicago Press

Moses Maimonides. 1975. *Mishneh Torah.* Book of Zmanim. Hotzaat Shabse Frankel

Moses Maimonides. 1990. *Mishneh Torah.* B'nei Brak: Meshor

Moses Maimonides. 1998. *Mishneh Torah.* Book of Shoftim. Hotzaat Shabse Frankel

Moses Maimonides. 2001. *Mishneh Torah.* Book of Hamada. Hotzaat Shabse Frankel

Saul and Evelyn Henkind Talmud Text Databank. Saul Lieberman Institute of Talmudic Research. The Jewish Theological Seminary of America

Visotzky, Burton L. 1992. *The Midrash on Proverbs: Translated from the Hebrew with an Introduction and Annotations.* New Haven and London: Yale University Press

Wistinetzki, Jehuda. 1924. *Sefer Hasidim.* Frankfurt a.M.: M.A. Wahrmann Verlag

Scholarly studies and other contemporary works

Baumgarten, Elisheva. 2014. *Practicing Piety in Medieval Ashkenaz: Men, Women, and Everyday Religious Observance.* Philadelphia: University of Pennsylvania Press

Berezovsky, Sholom Noach. n.d. *Sefer Netivot Shalom*, 2 vols. Jerusalem: Yeshivat Beit Avraham Slonim

Breuer, Jonathan. 2005. "Sippur Rabbi Amnon M'Magenza U-makbilotav Ba-Mikra." In: Amnon Bazak, ed. *U-Ve-Yom Tzom Kippur Yehatemun: Studies on Yom HaKippurim.* Alon Shevut: Tevunot, pp. 301–309

The Encyclopaedia of Islam: New Edition. 1960. Leiden: E.J. Brill

Finn, Richard. 2006. *Almsgiving in the Later Roman Empire: Christian Promotion and Practice; 313–450.* Oxford: Oxford University Press

Fishbane, Eitan P. 2018. *The Art of Mystical Narrative: A Poetics of the Zohar.* New York: Oxford University Press

Frankel, Avraham. 2002. "Demuto Ha-historit Shel R' Amnon M'Magenza V-gulgulav Shel Ha-piyyut 'Unetaneh Tokef' B'Italiah, B'Ashkenaz, U-b'Tzarfat." *Zion* 67:125–138

Galinsky, Judah. 2004. " 'And It Is for the Glory of the Great That Their Name Be Remembered': Commemorating the Dead and the Practice of Establishing a *Hekdesh* in Christian Spain." *Masechet* 2:113–131 (in Hebrew)

Galinsky, Judah. 2004. "Jewish Charitable Trusts and the Hekdesh Trust in Thirteenth-Century Spain." *Journal of Interdisciplinary History* 33:423–440

Galinsky, Judah. 2005. "Commemoration and Heqdesh in the Jewish Communities of Germany and Spain in the 13th Century." In: Michael Borgolte, ed. *Stiftungen in Christentum, Judentum und Islam vor der Moderne.* Berlin: Akademie, pp. 191–204

Galinsky, Judah D. 2017. "Charity and Prayer in the Ashkenazi Synagogue." In: Itamar Dagan, ed. *"Ve-Hinneh Rivka Yotzet"*: *Essays in Jewish Studies in Honor of Rivka Dagan.* Israel: Tzur-ot, pp. 163–174 (in Hebrew)

Gray, Alyssa M. 2016. "R. Eliezer of Metz's Twelfth-Century Exclusion from Charity of the Jewish *'Avaryan B'mezid'* (Deliberate Transgressor)." In: Sharon Farmer, ed. *Approaches to Poverty in Medieval Europe: Complexities, Contradictions, Transformations, c. 1100–1500.* Turnhout: Brepols, pp. 67–92

Hauptman, Judith. 2018. "A Talmudic Reading of the High Holiday Prayer *Un'taneh Tokef.*" *Zeramim: An Online Journal of Applied Jewish Studies* 2. Available at: https://zeramim.org/past-issues/volume-ii-issue-3-spring-2018-5778/

Hirshman, Marc. 1996. *A Rivalry of Genius: Jewish and Christian Biblical Interpretation in Late Antiquity.* Albany: State University of New York Press

Kochen, Madeline. 2008. " 'It Was Not for Naught that They Called It *Hekdesh*': Divine Ownership and the Medieval Charitable Foundation." In: Joseph Fleishman, ed. *Jewish Law Association Studies* XVIII:131–142

Kochen, Madeline. 2014. *Organ Donation and the Divine Lien in Talmudic Law.* New York: Cambridge University Press

Kraemer, Joel L. 1984. "On Maimonides' Messianic Posture." In: Isadore Twersky, ed. *Studies in Medieval Jewish History and Literature II.* Cambridge: Harvard University Press, pp. 109–142

Lévi, Israel. 1894. "La Commemoration des Ames Dans Le Judaisme." *Revue des Études Juives* 29:43–60

Marcus, Ivan (Israel). 1993. "Kiddush Hashem B'Ashkenaz V'sippur Rabbi Amnon M'Magenza." In: Yeshayahu Gafni and Aviezer Ravitzky, eds. *Kedushat Hahayyim V'heruf Ha-nefesh: Kovetz Ma'amarim L'Zikhro Shel Amir Yekutiel.* Jerusalem: Merkaz Zalman Shazar, pp. 131–147

Munk, Elie. 1963. *The World of Prayer*, 2 vols. New York: Philipp Feldheim

Planer, John H. 2013. "The Provenance, Dating, Allusions, and Variants of *U-n'taneh tokef* and Its Relationship to Romanos's *Kontakion.*" *Journal of Synagogue Music* 38:166–192

Reizel, Anat. 2011. *Introduction to the Midrashic Literature.* Hotza'at Tevunot, Miklelet Herzog: Alon Shevut (in Hebrew)

Schmelzer, Menahem. 1993. "Penitence, Prayer and (Charity?)." In: Marc Brettler and Michael Fishbane, eds. *Minhah le-Nahum: Biblical and Other Studies Presented to Nahum M. Sarna in Honour of His 70th Birthday.* Journal for the Study of the Old Testament; Supplement Series 154. Sheffield: Sheffield Academic Press, pp. 291–299

Spiegel, Yaakov. 2001. "Berur B'divrei Hapayyetan 'U-teshuvah u-tefillah u-tzedaqah Ma'avirin Et Ro'a Ha-gezerah' V'al Kefifut Ha-payyetanim L'halakhah." *Netuim* 8:23–42

Steinfeld, Zvi Arie. 1962, "Kapparah L'Meitim." *Sidra* 17:217–228. 2016 (repr.). *Tractate Horayot: Studies in the Mishna and Talmud.* Ramat-Gan: Bar-Ilan University Press, pp. 254–266

Strack, H.L. and Günter Stemberger. 1996. *Introduction to the Talmud and Midrash.* Minneapolis: Fortress

Twersky, Isadore. 1989. "On Law and Ethics in the *Mishneh Torah*: A Case Study of *Hilkhot Megillah* II:17." *Tradition* 24:138–149

Urbach, Ephraim E. 1979. *The Sages: Their Concepts and Beliefs*, 2nd enlarged ed. Jerusalem: Magnes Press

Wieder, Naphtali. 1967. "A Controversial Mishnaic and Liturgical Expression." *Journal of Jewish Studies* 18:1–7

Yahalom, Joseph. 2002. "Who Shall be the Author, and Who Shall Not." *Haaretz*. Available at: www.haaretz.com/1.5136767

Yassif, Eli. 1999. "Legend and History: Historians Read Hebrew Legends of the Middle Ages." *Zion* 64:187–219 (in Hebrew)

Yuval, Israel J. 1981. "Donations from Nürnberg to Jerusalem (1375–1392)." *Zion* 46:182–197 (in Hebrew)

Zimmer, Yitzhak (Eric). 2011. "Minhag 'Matnat Yad' V'Hazkarat Neshamot." In: Joseph Hacker and Yaron Harel, eds. *"Lo Yasur Shevet M'Yehudah": Hanhagah, Rabbanut U-Kehillah B'Toldot Yisrael; Mehkarim Mugashim L'Professor Shimon Schwartzfuchs.* Jerusalem: Mossad Bialik, pp. 71–87

8 Conclusion

Righteous before God

Two metaphors have reverberated throughout this book: that of multiple voices and that of the many and variously colored threads that wind their way through successive rabbinic compilations from late antiquity (even) into modernity. At times some voices are heard above others; some threads break off or only seem to, perhaps reappearing later as part of newer and different patterns. Whatever the metaphor, the lesson learned in each chapter is that the multiplicity of ideas about charity, atonement, and rewards is real and must be allowed expression; forcing diverse, even contradictory ideas into a methodological Procrustean bed of any sort—too rigid a positing of distinctions between the land of Israel and Babylonia, too precise a description of historical development, too fine a parsing of literary layers, as in the Talmud *Bavli*—can impede rather than enhance understanding. The problem is, of course, the "too," not the methodological approaches themselves.

In the hands of Palestinian rabbis "*tzedaqah*" carries the broad meaning of demonstrating righteousness; the ubiquitous expression "doing *tzedaqah*" epitomizes its dynamic character. One demonstrates righteousness either by giving something to someone to which the latter has no moral (or legal) entitlement or, if one is a judge, by—among other ways—compelling a liable party to demonstrate its righteousness by conveying money or property to the deserving party. Babylonian rabbis alter *tzedaqah*'s meaning of "demonstrating righteousness" somewhat by introducing the idea that *tzedaqah* can be compelled and that *tzedaqah* done under duress is religiously valid *tzedaqah*.

Palestinian rabbinic compilations and sources the *Bavli* attributes to Palestinian sages include many expressions of the idea that *tzedaqah* is a gift to God. Palestinian rabbinic literature does not at all speak with one voice on this issue. *Sifre Deuteronomy* lists "*tzedaqah*" alongside other sacra without distinction; by contrast, the *Tosefta* distinguishes *tzedaqah* from other sacra by allowing the *tzedaqah* votary to change its purpose until it has come into the hands of the "*parnasin.*" The *Yerushalmi* follows suit in its portrayal of a rabbi's acting on his own authority to distribute *tzedaqah* monies to rabbis rather than the widows and orphans the donors intended. Another aspect of the idea that *tzedaqah* is a gift to God is tannaitic literature's threatening dire consequences for those who "stipulate" *tzedaqah* but fail to fulfill those pledges; Palestinian amoraic literature limits the dire consequences to those who fail to make good on their *public* stipulations. "Stipulating" (*p-s-q*) *tzedaqah* is known from extra-rabbinic sources to have a votive connotation; both *tannaim* and *amoraim* therefore recognize the votive nature of these undertakings but also recognize that many people did not take those stipulations seriously as vows. Palestinian *amoraim* cope with this lack of seriousness by limiting dire consequences only to those who fail to fulfill "public" stipulations and by their tacit refusal to stigmatize such persons as vow-breakers. The *Bavli* in turn describes no one as "stipulating" *tzedaqah*, and explicitly affirms that *tzedaqah* is not *heqdesh*. The *Bavli* consequently does not recognize a tolerable period of delay in the fulfillment of *tzedaqah* vows (which makes those unlike other vows to dedicate *sacra*), averring instead that the immediate presence of the poor requires that a *tzedaqah* vow be fulfilled immediately. The *Bavli* also questions *Leviticus Rabbah*'s understanding that Proverbs 19:17 binds God in obligation to the charitable donor, and Rava bluntly challenges (although he ultimately submits to) a poor man's implicit assumption that the support he receives from the community comes directly from God.

Redemptive almsgiving is its own case study in the existence and perdurance of a multiplicity of voices in the rabbinic compilations. *Tannaim* represent that charity atones for sin and accrues a heavenly treasury of merits for the giver. Palestinian amoraic literature perpetuates these ideas, adding a new emphasis on charity's power to rescue the donor from death. The *Yerushalmi* bridges the tannaitic focus on "heaven" and the amoraic focus on "rescue from death" with its unique understanding that Proverbs 10:2/11:4 means that charity saves from death "in the coming future." Babylonian *amoraim* do not teach that charity atones for sin, and there is a discernible *Bavli* tendency to privilege Torah study over charity; moreover, the *Bavli* tends to offer Babylonian-attributed Torah study interpretations of verses interpreted by Palestinian sages as referring to redemptive almsgiving. The *Bavli* is bluntly skeptical about redemptive almsgiving, is unique among the rabbinic compilations in urging that *tzedaqah* be done "*lishmah*," uncouples "real" heavenly treasure from charity, and stresses charity's power to rescue from death and extend life in this world. The *Bavli* does, however, also preserve the notion that charity may be a factor in a person's having a portion in the "world to come" and in his rescue from "*dinah shel Gehinnom*." Both rabbinic centers' demonstrable (albeit at times tacit) preference for *teshuvah* over *tzedaqah* as a way to atone for sin is another voice—a powerful dissenting voice—raised alongside the redemptive almsgiving "chorus."

This brief survey of the multiplicity of voices about the definition of *tzedaqah*, *tzedaqah* as a gift to God, and redemptive almsgiving also demonstrates a constant movement back and forth between heaven and earth in the literatures of both rabbinic centers. *Tzedaqah* is a factor in the vertical relationship between God above and the donor below, but it also has a profound horizontal dimension, constructing certain roles and relationships between human beings on this earth: donors, the poor, and (also) rabbis. Unlike *tannaim*, both Palestinian and Babylonian *amoraim* portray themselves as mediators between donors and the poor, in addition to whatever heavenly consequences are at stake. The *Bavli* in particular (although not exclusively) tends to focus on *tzedaqah*'s horizontal dimension: it is unique in introducing the idea that only *tzedaqah* to "worthy" recipients will be rewarded, and it contains the starkest expressions of distinction between *tzedaqah* and (other) *heqdesh* and of skepticism about redemptive almsgiving. The *Bavli* delimits the divine role in *tzedaqah* and heightens the role of human effort and initiative in a way that we demonstrated to be consistent with its limitations on divine providence in other areas. The rabbinic compilations' constant movement between heaven and earth epitomizes an important element of their worldview as it relates to *tzedaqah*: *tzedaqah* does not fit exclusively into one or the other realm but resides in both simultaneously. A person does *tzedaqah* on earth with one hand and in heaven with the other; what the giver accomplishes with her *tzedaqah* on earth has some effect—however understood—in heaven. Not heaven *or* earth, but *both.*

These reflections on multiple voices and threads, and two-way traffic between heaven and earth, is a reminder that no one voice, thread, or locus can be identified as "*the*" dominant one. We may turn to Steve Moyise for assistance in assessing the significance of this observation. Toward the end of his intertextual study of the Hebrew Bible's book of Ezekiel and the New Testament book of Revelation, Moyise reflects on "how one group of scholars have a book full of violent imagery" that they try to insist is used "in a non-militaristic sense" (emphasis removed), while "another group have an exceptionally passive text and try to persuade us that it is really about resisting empire." He proposes: "[w]ould it not be more true to say that there are multiple voices in both books which *could* lead to the views just discussed if readers *choose* to amplify one of the voices."[1]

Moyise's proposal makes good sense of some of the changes and adaptations of ideas we see in the late antique compilations. For example, Palestinian *amoraim* retain elements of the tannaitic focus on charity's impact on a donor's postmortem fate but choose to amplify the scriptural voices pointing toward charity's redemptive power to rescue from death on earth. Tannaitic literature emphasizes one voice, Palestinian amoraic literature, another. In turn the *Bavli*, a "reader" of the Palestinian rabbinic corpus, chooses to "amplify" the amoraic focus on redemptive almsgiving as rescue from death and longer life (whether in this world or the next), and to deemphasize and even tacitly criticize the tannaitic representation of charity as atoning for sin. The key question is not: how might one precisely mark the stages of linear development from one idea to another? Rather: which voices are being amplified in which compilation, which not, and what does that say about the rabbinic culture that produced the compilation?

Thinking in terms of "readers" who "choose to amplify" one of "multiple voices" in the rabbinic canon also helps make sense of some of the post-Talmudic developments. The examples of some of the early medieval *midrash* compilations and medieval and later Jewish religious writers show readers choosing to amplify some of the vertical, heaven-centered aspects of the rabbinic charity legacy, notably charity as a gift to God and as atoning for sin. Other medieval readers choose to amplify the late antique preference for *teshuvah* over *tzedaqah*. *Midrash Proverbs* starkly manifests the perduring cultural tension about the relationship of *teshuvah* and *tzedaqah* by privileging the former in one passage and displaying a contradictory preference for *tzedaqah* in another. Maimonides is a parade example of a reader who chooses to amplify the *Bavli*'s tendency to delimit the divine and emphasize the human role and element in *tzedaqah*. Naturally, by choosing to amplify this characteristic *Bavli* tendency he concomitantly chooses to deemphasize and marginalize other, mostly Palestinian, elements that pertain more to *tzedaqah*'s vertical aspect, notably redemptive almsgiving.

Maimonides' choice to amplify the *Bavli*'s horizontal, human *tzedaqah* focus suggests his being a medieval forerunner of understanding "*tzedaqah*" as a signifier of a just, humane, social order. The contemporary focus on "*tzedaqah*" as "social justice"—although this phrase itself requires precise definition—is also no more and no less a choice to amplify particular voices in the rabbinic (and later) *tzedaqah* canon. Following Maimonides (and earlier rabbinic and biblical precedents), it may indeed be justifiably asserted that *tzedaqah* refers to a just social order—but that is not its only meaning in the rabbinic *tzedaqah* canon. Whatever metaphor one chooses—multiple voices, multiple threads—the rabbinic *tzedaqah* legacy is variegated enough that one may choose to focus on its horizontal, social dimension, or on its vertical, heavenly dimension. The voices of the canon all continue to speak; one reader's choice to amplify one is not more "authentic" or "right" than is another's choice to amplify a different one.

Earlier in this book we noted a contemporary scholar's observation about the absence of charity's vertical dimension from some relevant Jewish writing.[2] We will use this observation as a springboard from which to reflect briefly on two (perhaps surprising) examples of lesser-known, or at least less prominent, contemporary choices to amplify the vertical, heavenly focused voice: (1) retellings of the tale of R. Moses Hagiz's *converso*; and (2) the bereaved relative's pledge to give *tzedaqah* on behalf of the deceased in the "*yizkor*" memorial prayer services of the major streams of Judaism.

We observed at the beginning of Chapter 2 that the story of R. Moses Hagiz's *converso* is predicated on the ancient and medieval notion that *tzedaqah* is a gift to God. That colorful story continues to circulate in versions that may heuristically be grouped under two thematic headings.[3] Following Lawrence Kushner and others we might call one "God's Hands," and the other "making the world better." At the end of *In God's Hands* the rabbi asks both men to realize:

> Now that you know that God does not eat challah and God does not bake challah, you will have to do something even harder, you will have to go on baking the bread anyway. David, you will have to go on eating the bread also. Now you understand that your hands are God's hands.[4]

God is silent in Kushner's version of the story, the point of which is that both the donor's and recipient's hands are *God's* hands. Both are made to realize that God is not directly involved in either the giving or receiving of the bread. God desires *tzedaqah*, but he is not a necessary or vital part of the *tzedaqah* transaction, a point the rabbi acknowledges may be difficult for the men to accept.[5] The rabbi gently moves the men away from gross anthropomorphism (the possibility that God eats, or at least bakes, *challah*) to what is portrayed as a more mature understanding: their hands are "God's hands." The "God's Hands" theme has been taken up by religious communities and leaders as diverse as the Indianola Presbyterian Church[6] and the cantor of a Conservative Jewish synagogue, who draws the following conclusion:

> God was in both the giving and the taking ... the men's hands were the hands of God. [R. Isaac Luria] encourages them to keep up the practice of giving and receiving challot, only to do so in person: one does not have to put challah in the ark or receive challah from the ark for God to be a participant in tzedakah.[7]

Here, God is "a participant in tzedakah," a contemporary revision in a passive register—whether knowingly or not—of the late antique and medieval notion that God is its "recipient." In all these retellings of the "God's Hands" variety the Ark melts away: it functions as a representation of an invisible, silent God and, once God's role in the story—and in encouraging charity—is understood by the protagonists, God himself is unnecessary.

Stories that fall under the heading "making the world better" distance God even farther from the charitable transaction, rooting charity entirely in this world almost as a species of the genus "social justice." One pair of contemporary rabbi/ storytellers has framed their version of the story this way:

> *Tzedakah* is a way of responding to the seemingly arbitrary and unequal way wealth is distributed ... heroes ... are those who make the world better by giving of their funds and of themselves to
> others ...
>
> We give to others as an expression of thanksgiving to God for what we have ... as an acknowledgment that we are bringing the holiness of God's loving generosity to our shattered ... world.
>
> Seen in this way, *tzedakah* is a way of participating in *tikkun olam*, repairing what is broken.[8]

The audience of stories of the "making the world better" variety is schooled that God's "loving generosity" is an inspiration to repair the world (*tikkun olam*) by giving *tzedaqah*. It again goes without saying that God is not constructed as the recipient of *tzedaqah* in the late antique and medieval sense. That late antique/ medieval voice echoes in the background, or, to return to the thread metaphor: this faded, frayed thematic thread of *tzedaqah* as a gift to God is now being taken up and woven into a new and contemporary pattern of charity ideas together with the thread "social justice."

The same is true of *yizkor*. There is a fixed text by which a bereaved relative undertakes a solemn obligation to give *tzedaqah* on behalf of a deceased loved one in the traditional "*yizkor*" memorial prayers recited on Yom Kippur and the three pilgrimage festivals. I take the core text from R. Philip Birnbaum's *High Holyday Prayer Book* (American Orthodox): "May God remember the soul ... I pledge charity (*noder tzedaqah*) in ... behalf [of the deceased]."[9] The purpose of this *tzedaqah* is to atone for the deceased, to improve in some way on their postmortem fate (see Chapter 7). The history of this text, and especially its career in non-Orthodox prayer books in the Anglophone Jewish world, is a scholarly desideratum that certainly will not be satisfied here. My point is—very selectively—to illustrate and reflect on the revival of this text and the practice it reflects in the twentieth- and twenty-first centuries. It should be noted that not all Birnbaum's traditionally minded contemporaries brought *tzedaqah* together with *yizkor*. R. Morris Silverman's *High Holiday Prayer Book*—also published in 1951—omits it, as does the 1948 *Sabbath and Festival Prayer Book* (American Conservative).[10] *Tzedaqah* is likewise omitted from the 1963 reprint of the 1948 British *Authorised Daily Prayer Book*, issued by authority of the Chief Rabbi.[11] We can only speculate that the omission reflects these liturgists' sense that the pledging of *tzedaqah* in remembrance of the dead was somehow incompatible with the religious sensibilities of their mid-twentieth century co-religionists.

But change was afoot in American Conservative Judaism. The revised *The New Maḥzor* of 1977–1978 introduces charity into the English text: "In tribute ... I pledge to perform acts of charity and goodness," but maintains its omission from the Hebrew.[12] There is a restored Hebrew reference to "*noder(et) tzedaqah*," rendered as "pledge charity" in the 1985 *Siddur Sim Shalom*, which is altered in the 2016 *Siddur Lev Shalem* to "*nodev/et tzedaqah*," rendered (partially) into English as "pledge *tzedakah*"; the shift from "charity" to "*tzedaqah*" is itself a culturally telling change, the examination of which is work for another day.[13] Note also the 2016 alteration of "*noder(et)*" to "*nodev*," which denotes a "*nedavah*," a freewill gift rather than a "vow," and which, like "*noder(et)*," also echoes the ancient sacrificial service and terminology.[14]

Changes in the stated purpose of this *tzedaqah* are also of great interest. In *The New Maḥzor* the purpose is—along with other deeds—"to keep [the] soul bound up in the bond of life as an enduring source of blessing."[15] In *Siddur Sim Shalom* (1985) it is "to help perpetuate ideals important to [the deceased]. Through such deeds ... are their souls bound up in the bond of life."[16] Similarly, in *Siddur Lev Shalem* (2016) the purpose is "to help perpetuate ideals important to [the deceased]. Through such deeds ... may [the deceased's] soul be bound up in the bond of life."[17] All three refer to the soul's being bound up in the bond of life,[18] and the latter two add the this-worldly aspect that the *tzedaqah* is also intended to "help perpetuate ideals" of importance to the deceased. The point is not, as in the Middle Ages, the improvement of the deceased's postmortem "life" by means of the charity of the living; it is now the this-worldly perpetuation and continued life of *ideals* the deceased held dear.

Change was also afoot in American Reform Judaism, whose various prayer books had omitted *tzedaqah* from *yizkor* for decades. In *Mishkan Hanefesh* (2015), a new pair of prayer books for *Rosh Hashanah* and *Yom Kippur*, the latter volume includes a reference to the worshipper's being "*nodev/et tzedaqah*" in memory of a deceased loved one, which is translated/explained as "For the sake of *tikkun olam*, I freely give *tzedakah* in [the deceased's] memory." The worshipper also expresses the hope that her various devotional acts will "bind [the deceased] to the bond of life."[19]

In none of these formulations is the purpose of the *tzedaqah* to atone for the deceased in the medieval sense. The *tzedaqah* is intended either to perpetuate the deceased's cherished ideals, or, in the Reform addition, "*tikkun olam*." Taken together, the "*challahs* in the Ark" and *yizkor* examples show that the vertical, heavenly dimensions of *tzedaqah* are not muted voices, faded, broken thematic threads, or neglected heirlooms in the attic. Medieval *tzedaqah* ideas that seemed neglected even in some traditional twentieth-century Anglophone Jewish circles have been newly reclaimed—even in some twenty-first century liberal Jewish circles. Not just newly reclaimed, but also adapted and revised to reflect fresh theological interpretations of the interplay of *tzedaqah*'s heavenly and earthly dimensions.

In sum, both *tzedaqah*'s heavenly and earthly dimensions were and remain inextricably intertwined in rabbinic literature, its successor literatures, and even lived Jewish practice. A reader who chooses to amplify certain voices of the rabbinic *tzedaqah* canon will produce a reading of the canon different from that of the reader who makes a different choice. Neither dimension, neither set of choices, nor either resulting reading is inherently more "the right one" than the other. This is as true for scholars making interpretive choices in the course of academic research as it is for religious practitioners making devotional and behavioral choices. The rabbinic *tzedaqah* canon shows the many ways in which the rabbis and their heirs understood *tzedaqah* to bind together God, the living, and the dead, past and present, heaven and earth; how *tzedaqah* is a way to demonstrate one's righteousness before God.

Notes

1 Steve Moyise, "Dialogical Intertextuality," in B.J. Oropeza and Steve Moyise, editors, *Exploring Intertextuality: Diverse Strategies for New Testament Interpretations of Texts* (Eugene: Cascade Books, 2016), 14.

2 See, e.g., Peter Brown, *Ransom of the Soul*, 28–29.

3 For example, Daniel Barash has identified this story as part of the inspiration for his "Challah-it-Forward" initiative (www.challahitforward.com). "Challah-it-Forward" is a delightful play on the contemporary expression "pay it forward." Barash coined the expression "challah it forward" to describe his take on the old story related by Moses Hagiz, which he has written as lyrics to a song he performs. See www. challahitforward.com/the-folktale/.

4 See Lawrence Kushner, *The Book of Miracles: A Young Person's Guide to Jewish Spiritual Awareness* (Woodstock: Jewish Lights, 1997), 67–71. He credits Rabbi Zalman Schachter-Shalomi with the story. See also ibid., *In God's Hands*

(Woodstock: Jewish Lights, 2005). As part of the "God's Hands" thematic thread, see also Dr. Ron Wolfson, *God's To-Do List: 103 Ways to Be an Angel and Do God's Work on Earth* (Woodstock: Jewish Lights, 2007), 89–93; Seymour Rossel, *God, Torah, Israel & Faith: The Essential Jewish Stories* (Jersey City: Ktav, 2011), 359–360. The version of the story related by Rossel ends with Isaac Luria saying: "it is God who bakes and God who eats and God is no less present among you than before."

5 Howard Schwartz published a version of the story in 1983 that ends with R. Isaac Luria's saying "I want you to believe with perfect faith that if you bring the *challahs* directly to the *shames*, God will be pleased no less"—again, God is not an indispensable participant in this charitable transaction. For Schwartz, the essential point of the story is the human responsibility to care for the needy. See Howard Schwartz, *Gates to the New City: A Treasury of Modern Jewish Tales* (New York: Avon, 1983), 540–543. Like Kushner, Schwartz credits his version to "Zalman Schachter."

6 "God's Hands." www.indianolapres.org/joomla/content/view/716/38/. Last accessed January 17, 2019.

7 Hazzan Joanna Dulkin, "HazzanNotes," in the bulletin of The Jewish Center (Princeton; December, 2014). See www.thejewishcenter.org/getattachment/ed732757-f1d0-4f36-9c27-e45096c64490/December-2014.

8 See Rabbi Kerry M. Olitzky and Rabbi Rachel T. Sabath, *Striving Toward Virtue: A Contemporary Guide for Jewish Ethical Behavior* (Hoboken: Ktav, 1996), 104–109. The quote is from p. 105. In this version a synagogue worshipper incompletely hears the rabbi talk about the Temple showbread through the haze of a doze; the following Friday morning he places a dozen Sabbath loaves in the Ark, from which they are retrieved by a hungry, prayerful synagogue beadle who prays that God should provide him food. This went on for a while; the rabbi became aware and thought at first that he would interfere, but then decided that God was at work in this double-blind bread transaction.

9 *High Holyday Prayer Book: Translated and Annotated with an Introduction by Philip Birnbaum* (New York: Hebrew Publishing Company, 1951), 730. Birnbaum translates the Hebrew *"noder"* as "pledge" rather than the literal "vow"; one may speculate that this rendering is meant to elide the worshipper's entanglement in the complex Jewish laws of vows.

10 *Sabbath and Festival Prayer Book: With a New Translation, Supplementary Readings and Notes* (New York: The Rabbinical Assembly of America and The United Synagogue of America, 1948), 225–226; *High Holiday Prayer Book: Rosh Hashanah—New Year's Day; Yom Kippur—Day of Atonement; With a New Translation and Explanatory Notes, together with Supplementary Prayers, Meditations, and Readings in Prose and Verse; Compiled and arranged by Rabbi Morris Silverman* (New York: The United Synagogue of America, 1951), 325–326.

11 The *Authorised Daily Prayer Book: Revised Edition; Hebrew Text, English Translation with Commentary and Notes; by Dr. Joseph H. Hertz; the Late Chief Rabbi of the British Empire* (repr.; New York: Bloch Publishing Company, 1963), 1106–1108.

12 *The New Mazor for Rosh Hashanah and Yom Kippur; Revised and Expanded Version.* Compiled and edited by Rabbi Sidney Greenberg and Rabbi Jonathan D. Levine (Bridgeport: The Prayer Book Press, 1977, 1978), 573–575.

13 *Siddur Sim Shalom: A Prayerbook for Shabbat, Festivals, and Weekdays; Edited, with translations, by Rabbi Jules Harlow* (New York: The Rabbinical Assembly; The United Synagogue of America, 1985), 518–521; *Siddur Lev Shalem for Shabbat & Festivals* (New York: The Rabbinical Assembly, 2016), 335.

14 This change, like Birnbaum's earlier translation "pledge" for *"noder,"* is also likely a strategy to elide the law of vows.

15 *The New Mahzor*, 573.

16 *Siddur Sim Shalom*, 521.

17 *Siddur Lev Shalem*, 335.
18 The Conservative and Reform references to the "bond of life" reflect what is likely a studied ambiguity; a contemporary Orthodox rendering of the Hebrew source as "the bond of everlasting life" reveals that what is at stake is extended life beyond death. See *The Koren Siddur: With Introduction, Translation and Commentary by Chief Rabbi Lord Jonathan Sacks* (Jerusalem: Koren Publishers, 2013), 798.
19 *Mishkan Hanefesh: Machzor for the Days of Awe; Yom Kippur* (New York: CCAR Press, 2015), 570–571.

Bibliography

Scholarly studies and other contemporary works

The Authorised Daily Prayer Book: Revised Edition; Hebrew Text, English Translation with Commentary and Notes; by Dr. Joseph H. Hertz; the Late Chief Rabbi of the British Empire. 1963 (repr.). New York: Bloch Publishing Company

Brown, Peter. 2015. *The Ransom of the Soul: Afterlife and Wealth in Early Western Christianity.* Cambridge and London: Harvard University Press

"Challah It Forward." Available at: www.challahitforward.com

Dulkin, Joanna. 2014. "HazzanNotes." Available at: www.thejewishcenter.org/getattachment/ed732757-f1d0-4f36-9c27-e45096c64490/December-2014

"God's Hands." Available at: www.indianolapres.org/joomla/content/view/716/38/

High Holiday Prayer Book: Rosh Hashanah—New Year's Day; Yom Kippur—Day of Atonement; With a New Translation and Explanatory Notes, Together with Supplementary Prayers, Meditations, and Readings in Prose and Verse. 1951. Compiled and arranged by Rabbi Morris Silverman. New York: The United Synagogue of America

High Holyday Prayer Book. Translated and Annotated with an Introduction by Philip Birnbaum. 1951. New York: Hebrew Publishing Company

The Koren Siddur: With Introduction, Translation and Commentary by Chief Rabbi Lord Jonathan Sacks. 2013. Jerusalem: Koren Publishers

Kushner, Lawrence. 1997. *The Book of Miracles: A Young Person's Guide to Jewish Spiritual Awareness.* Woodstock: Jewish Lights

Kushner, Lawrence. 2005. *In God's Hands.* Woodstock: Jewish Lights

Mishkan Hanefesh: Machzor for the Days of Awe; Yom Kippur. 2015. New York: CCAR Press

Moyise, Steve. 2016. "Dialogical Intertextuality." In: B.J. Oropeza and Steve Moyise, eds. *Exploring Intertextuality: Diverse Strategies for New Testament Interpretations of Texts.* Eugene: Cascade Books, pp. 3–15

The New Mahzor for Rosh Hashanah and Yom Kippur; Revised and Expanded Version. 1977, 1978. Compiled and edited by Rabbi Sidney Greenberg and Rabbi Jonathan D. Levine. Bridgeport: The Prayer Book Press

Olitzky, Kerry M., Rabbi and Rabbi Rachel T. Sabath. 1996. *Striving Toward Virtue: A Contemporary Guide for Jewish Ethical Behavior.* Hoboken: Ktav

Rossel, Seymour. 2011. *God, Torah, Israel & Faith: The Essential Jewish Stories.* Jersey City: Ktav

Sabbath and Festival Prayer Book: With A New Translation, Supplementary Readings and Notes. 1948. New York: The Rabbinical Assembly of America and The United Synagogue of America

Schwartz, Howard. 1983. *Gates to the New City: A Treasury of Modern Jewish Tales.* New York: Avon

Siddur Lev Shalem for Shabbat & Festivals. 2016. New York: The Rabbinical Assembly

Siddur Sim Shalom: A Prayerbook for Shabbat, Festivals, and Weekdays. Edited, with Translations, by Rabbi Jules Harlow. 1985. New York: The Rabbinical Assembly; The United Synagogue of America

Wolfson, Ron. 2007. *God's To-Do List: 103 Ways to Be an Angel and Do God's Work on Earth.* Woodstock: Jewish Lights

Index

Made in the USA
Coppell, TX
24 September 2021

62852460R00125